At a time of severe partisanship that has infected many accounts of our nation's past, this brilliant new history, *Land of Hope*, written in lucid and often lyrical prose, is much needed. It is accurate, honest, and free of the unhistorical condescension so often paid to the people of America's past. This generous but not uncritical story of our nation's history ought to be read by every American. It explains and justifies the right kind of patriotism.

GORDON S. WOOD
author of *Friends Divided: John Adams and Thomas Jefferson*

Those who are acquainted with Wilfred McClay's writing will not be surprised that *Land of Hope*, his latest book, is a lucid and engaging account of the "great American story." McClay is a charming storyteller – and a first-rate scholar and appreciator of America's political and cultural development.

MICHAEL BARONE
resident fellow at the American Enterprise Institute,
senior political analyst at the Washington Examiner,
and coauthor of *The Almanac of American Politics*

We've long needed a readable text that truly tells the American story, neither hiding the serious injustices in our history nor soft-pedaling our nation's extraordinary achievements. Such a text cannot be a mere compilation of facts, and it certainly could not be written by someone lacking a deep understanding and appreciation of America's constitutional ideals and institutions. Bringing his impressive skills as a political theorist, historian, and writer to bear, Wilfred McClay has supplied the need.

ROBERT P. GEORGE
McCormick Professor of Jurisprudence
Princeton University

In a time when America seems pulled in opposite directions, Wilfred McClay has written a necessary book – the most balanced, nuanced history of the United States I have read in the past fifty years.

DANIEL HENNINGER
deputy editor, editorial page, *The Wall Street Journal*

Wilfred McClay has written more than a textbook. His affirmative, even-handed review of American history, institutions, and character is refreshing, and comes none too soon, when so many accounts are merely trying to settle scores. Beautifully written and fair minded, *Land of Hope* ranks among the finest surveys of the nation's past.

GILBERT T. SEWALL
Director, American Textbook Council

No one has told the story of America with greater balance or better prose than Wilfred McClay. *Land of Hope* is a history book that you will not be able to put down. From the moment that "natives" first crossed here over the Bering Strait, to the founding of America's great experiment in republican government, to the horror and triumph of the Civil War, and to the stirring election of Barack Obama, McClay's account will capture your attention while offering an unforgettable education.

JAMES W. CEASER
Professor of Politics, University of Virginia

I wish *Land of Hope* had been there when I was teaching U.S. history. It is history as literature – broad, detailed, compassionate – and it can help anyone who wants to know where we came from and how we got here. Professor McClay has made a welcome gift to the history of our country.

WILL FITZHUGH
Founder, *The Concord Review*

This is the most cheerful and inspiring history of America written so far this century. Where most historians emphasize fragmentation and oppression, McClay makes the case for a unified national story characterized by optimism and achievement. Without downplaying dismaying episodes, past and present, he shows how they have been offset by the American pursuit of reform, revival, and improvement. Old heroes like George Washington are restored to their rightful place. America is far from perfect, McClay admits, but it is genuinely dedicated to the ideals of equality and democracy, and there is much to be proud of. I can imagine schools and colleges assigning this book with a sense of gratitude and confidence.

PATRICK ALLITT
Cahoon Family Professor of American History,
Emory University

In *Land of Hope*, Bill McClay succeeds at multitasking. He has written not only a learned and readable history of the United States, from Columbus to Trump, with balance and integrity but has provided an insightful primer on the meaning of citizenship itself. McClay reminds us that although history holds no easy lessons, its honest practice proves indispensable in preventing the future from proceeding in darkness. Those entrusted with teaching young minds about the discipline of history as well as history will find in this volume much to fortify them.

ROBERT PAQUETTE
Professor of History and President,
The Alexander Hamilton Institute

Land of Hope is in every way a remarkable piece of work, clearly written and as balanced and fair-minded as any American history you will ever read. *Land of Hope* operates on the assumption that the past remains a necessary part of us, something we must both understand and learn from. It refuses the all-too-common view that we today are simply superior to our own history, a history that amounts to little more than a grab bag of chicanery, venality, and self-interest. Instead, it is an attempt to lay out the political history of our nation, the dilemmas we faced, the choices we made, and the ideas that shaped and reshaped our American creed.

JOHN AGRESTO
Professor of Political Science, former President of St. John's College,
and author of *Rediscovering America*

Land of Hope seems written for such a time as this, when ideology, combined with a profound historical ignorance, has left several generations belonging to no internalized story larger than their own experiences. Here we encounter a habitable story that comes complete with the principles, obligations, and privileges of citizenship.

TED MCALLISTER
Law & Liberty

To hear many historians today tell it, the American past offers a choice: you can love your country or you can learn its history – but not both. McClay rejects this dichotomy. *Land of Hope* proves that patriotism is not only compatible with a clear view of America's past – it should proceed from it as well.

TIM RICE
City Journal

The antidote to the damage caused by Howard Zinn's wretched *A People's History of the United States*. Give it to every millennial on your Christmas list.

GEORGE WEIGEL
First Things

Written most immediately for high school students taking Advanced Placement courses, the book looks and feels the part of a history textbook. But unlike most of those dreary tomes, it reads like a bestselling thriller. In finely wrought yet readable prose, history comes alive in McClay's expansive and thoughtful appraisal of the American story.

MIKE SABO
Intercollegiate Studies Institute

Professors and teachers across America should cancel their fall book orders and replace their current textbooks with Wilfred McClay's *Land of Hope*. McClay, the G. T. and Libby Blankenship Chair in the History of Liberty at the University of Oklahoma, satisfies the promise made in the title of his latest work. In it, he invites everyone to learn how ideals drove America's creation and success.

STEPHEN TOOTLE
National Review

Wilfred McClay's new book *Land of Hope* is a gift for Americans aiming to revive a more unifying approach to national history and civics. McClay is clear from the start: He aspires to tell America's story in a way that is both accurate and inspiring. This book is not an academic screed, but a compelling narrative spun across centuries. Key moments are smoothly tied together so students can see history's progression from the Boston Tea Party to the Louisiana Purchase to the closing of the frontier, and so on.

ANDY SMARICK
Philanthropy Magazine

McClay's book does not whitewash our history, but presents an honest and fair accounting that recognizes the astonishing success of the American experiment. If any U.S. history survey in recent memory has a chance to unseat Zinn in the classroom, it just might be McClay's delightfully written tome.

THE EDITORS
Real Clear Books

A Teacher's Guide to

LAND OF HOPE

AN INVITATION TO
THE GREAT AMERICAN STORY

WILFRED M. MCCLAY
and JOHN MCBRIDE

A Teacher's Guide to

LAND OF HOPE

An Invitation to the Great American Story

Encounter
BOOKS

New York · London

First American edition published in 2020 by Encounter Books,
an activity of Encounter for Culture and Education, Inc.,
a nonprofit, tax exempt corporation.
Encounter Books website address: www.encounterbooks.com

Manufactured in the United States and printed on
acid-free paper. The paper used in this publication meets
the minimum requirements of ANSI/NISO Z39.48 – 1992
(R 1997) (*Permanence of Paper*).

FIRST AMERICAN EDITION

To our fellow teachers, and our fellow students

CONTENTS

A TEACHER'S GUIDE TO THE *TEACHER'S GUIDE*

WELCOME TO THIS *Teacher's Guide*, which has been designed as a resource for educators who are making use of Wilfred McClay's book *Land of Hope* in their classrooms.

Individual teachers will of course use these materials as they think best, taking full account of the varying circumstances of their particular courses and sections and the varying institutions in which they find themselves teaching. What follow are some general suggestions as to what may work well for them in various situations. But the individual teacher is always the best judge of that.

1.   The first question to be asked is, how much time is available? U.S. history survey courses have typically been two semesters, or a full year, in length, but single-semester courses are, sadly, increasingly common. Even in the longer courses, the question has always been what to leave out, and if the teacher has only a single term, what will have to be omitted is quite a lot. The good news is that while *Land of Hope* is a relatively compressed book that did indeed have to cut a lot of details, what remains is still (we hope) a well-written and coherent narrative – and the larger themes and trends, the changing shapes of the forest, are more visible without a thicket of trees, without an inundation of names and dates that can impede students' understanding. The difficult but necessary choice that was made in writing *Land of Hope* was that when in doubt, coherence and clarity were to be preferred over comprehensiveness, with the clear understanding that the book's priorities made it impossible to render every important detail or every subtlety of historical interpretation. The book is called an "invitation" for a reason – it's meant to be inviting.

If teachers are offering a single-semester course, then they should find that *Land of Hope*, and this *Guide*, will provide them with all or most of what is required. If fifteen weeks are available, then thirty pages of reading per week will complete the text. Three chapters every two weeks is about right, and teachers can focus on "teaching the book" with the help of this *Guide*. In the happy event that two semesters are available, one chapter a week provides a solid foundation and leaves ample time for other materials and activities to widen knowledge and deepen understanding.

2. The *Guide* includes five different kinds of resources for each chapter. First, it provides a short summary of the contents of each chapter, followed by questions and answers for each chapter, objective questions for each chapter, one or more primary source documents (with questions) that relate to the chapter's themes and time period, and questions and answers for each document.

The questions and answers most commonly follow the contents of the book fairly closely, often with both questions and answers taken directly from the book. In some cases, they may draw on additional insights or information *not* taken from the book. Such questions will generally begin with a phrase like "Teachers may …"

Here is an example from chapter 1:

> 15. What technological innovations aided in overcoming the barriers mentioned above? (p. 9)
>
>> New ship designs (ships that could sail against the wind by tacking) and improved navigation through things such as compasses and map design.
>>
>> Teachers may need to explain how sailing ships can make progress even sailing against the wind by angling their sails and "tacking" from side to side. Ships relying on human muscles for power (rowers) might work in confined areas, such as the Mediterranean, but harnessing a natural force (the wind) increased the available power many times over.

Another category of "question" is a quotation from the book with key words or phrases in **boldface** type:

> 11. America would be "an unusual kind of offshoot": **unpredictable, unplanned, unanticipated.** (p. 7)

The purpose of these fill-in-the-blanks is to call attention to key ideas, often expressed in provocative language. Students ought to be able, after class discussion, to restate these ideas in their own words. Chapter tests may well include one or more of these direct quotes, requiring students to explain the quote in their own words and then give examples from the text.

Occasionally, a question asks for an opinion – but needless to say, it must be an informed one! Here's an example:

> 15. Be able to contrast the motives and experiences and principles of Virginia and New England. (*For thought:* Which do you think has shaped America more? Be prepared to defend your answer in class or in writing.)

Whether these opinions are gathered from students in a group discussion or from individual essays depends on the teacher's needs and preferences. The example given here, from chapter 2, would be a good question to include on a semester or final exam, as students will by then have been exposed to many examples, good and bad, of the long-term influences of Virginia and New England.

3. The *Guide* also includes four Special Units, for teaching the Declaration of Independence, the Constitution, the Bill of Rights, and the two-party system. These materials can be integrated with or incorporated into the regular chapter units or used independently of them, providing instructors with the flexibility to do a more in-depth study of the particular documents or institutions at hand.

4. The questions and answers in this *Guide* are primarily for use by and with students. But teachers are cautioned against providing students with the full set of questions to answer as homework. The questions do indeed serve as something of an outline of the chapters, and may satisfy the need of many students to assure themselves that they are "studying the right stuff," but the danger is that students will skim the text looking for the answers and so not actually read the narrative for understanding. They will then emerge with a list of isolated and hard-to-remember factoids lacking context. Teachers should instead insist that their students learn the story, that they master the narrative by adding it to their memory – not just until the next test but permanently. It is recommended that the questions be used primarily as a basis for class discussion after students have first tried to read the chapter on their own, and then secondarily for review. But of course, the ultimate judgment is to be made by individual teachers themselves, and we regard the freedom of the teacher in his or her classroom as a sacrosanct element of good pedagogy.

5. Following each of the chapter questions and answers, we have provided some objective questions. These are mostly put-in-order exercises with some matching

exercises as well. The items to be put in proper time sequence are either quite far apart in time or have an important cause-and-effect relationship:

Put in order:

_____ Alien and Sedition Acts   (2)
_____ Virginia and Kentucky Resolutions   (3)
_____ XYZ Affair   (1)

The XYZ Affair led directly to the Alien and Sedition Acts, which in turn led to the Virginia and Kentucky Resolutions. A good use for these objective questions might be in quizzes, as part of a final exam, or as review for a final exam.

6. Each chapter includes, immediately after the objective questions, a primary source document, one or two per chapter. The readings have in some instances been pared back from the originals to save space in the printed text. We have provided some study questions with these readings. These are designed to help guide students' reading comprehension but can also be drawn upon and tailored to the needs of individual classrooms – and needless to say, they can be refined and expanded and otherwise improved upon.

Finally, and in that spirit of improvement, we have one request to make of you, the reader and user of this *Teacher's Guide*. Because we want the *Guide* to be as useful as possible, we ask that you please feel free to be in touch with us regarding any and all manner of suggestions, including errors or misleading or otherwise unhelpful entries. No observation is too trivial or too sweeping. We want (and need) to hear from you. We want to do steadily better and better, and the principal way of doing that will be through the feedback that we get from you, the teacher on the front lines. Moreover, please be aware that this print edition of the *Guide* is just a first installment of a more extensive digital resource that we will be creating, and any advice, requests, criticisms, suggestions, and the like that you may have will help us better shape that resource. In any event, whatever you have to say will be attended to by all of us. Please feel free to write us at this address:

Land of Hope Teacher's Guide
Center for the History of Liberty
Carnegie Building, Room 309
University of Oklahoma
Norman, OK 73026
wmcclay@ou.edu or amurray@ou.edu

ONE LONG STORY

Summary

THE EPIGRAPH AND INTRODUCTION to *Land of Hope* are reflections on the meaning and value of history, including some initial thoughts about what it means to be a "land of hope." We urge teachers to devote some time to a consideration of these matters in their classrooms. *Land of Hope* is built around the idea that history is not just an inert rendering of indisputable facts; instead, it is a reflective task whose meaning reaches the depths of our humanity. We should try to model that fact in the way we teach.

For that reason, we encourage you to give some attention to the epigraph, a quotation from the novelist John Dos Passos. Such quotations are often seen as merely decorative in character, but in this particular book, the epigraph is key to the meaning of all that follows. It appears in *Land of Hope* immediately after the dedication page and before the table of contents, but here it is in its entirety, for your convenience:

> *Every generation rewrites the past. In easy times history is more or less of an ornamental art, but in times of danger we are driven to the written record by a pressing need to find answers to the riddles of today. We need to know what kind of firm ground other men, belonging to generations before us, have found to stand on. In spite of changing conditions of life they were not very different from ourselves, their thoughts were the grandfathers of our thoughts, they managed to meet situations as difficult as those we have to face, to meet them sometimes lightheartedly, and in some measure to make their hopes prevail. We need to know how they did it.*

In times of change and danger when there is a quicksand of fear under men's reasoning, a sense of continuity with generations gone before can stretch like a lifeline across the scary present and get us past that idiot delusion of the exceptional Now that blocks good thinking. That is why, in times like ours, when old institutions are caving in and being replaced by new institutions not necessarily in accord with most men's preconceived hopes, political thought has to look backwards as well as forwards.

JOHN DOS PASSOS

"The Use of the Past," from *The Ground We Stand On: Some Examples from the History of a Political Creed* (1941)

Epigraph Questions and Answers

1. When do we need history? Why?

   We need history in times of danger, to discover what kind of firm ground other generations have found.

2. What do you think Dos Passos means by "the idiot delusion of the exceptional Now"?

   With that pungent phrase, Dos Passos is pushing back against the wrongheaded idea that the present age is so unique, so unprecedented, so radical a break with all previous human experience that the past has nothing to teach us.

3. Do the conditions Dos Passos is describing apply today? That is, are old institutions caving in and being replaced by new institutions? Give some examples.

   Some examples are the changes and disruptions caused by the internet, porous national borders, global labor markets, and the free movement of capital across the globe. Ask students to provide other examples.

4. Dos Passos wrote this in 1941. Are our problems today greater or more frightening than then? Do we suffer from the same "idiot delusion" as did previous times and peoples?

   The times are perhaps *as* frightening, but not more so. Anyway, without a knowledge of history, we would have no basis for a comparison. Hence the necessity of this course of study!

Introduction Questions and Answers

1. What does this book seek to accomplish? What are its guiding intentions? (p. xi)

   It seeks to deepen our sense of our country and make us more capable of responsible citizenship.

2. What does the author mean by "citizenship"? (p. xi)

   He means the sense of membership in society.

3. "We are, at our core, **remembering** and **story-making** creatures, and **stories** are one of the chief ways we find meaning in the flow of events." (pp. xi–xii)

4. "**Historical consciousness** is to civilized society what **memory** is to individual identity." (p. xii)

5. "A culture without **memory** will necessarily be barbarous and easily tyrannized, even if it is technologically advanced." (p. xii)

6. Where do we most reliably find our lives' meaning? (p. xii)

   We find it, at least in large part, in the stories we learn and tell.

7. What aspect of American history does the author emphasize, treating it as "the skeleton of the story"? (pp. xii–xiii)

   He emphasizes political history.

8. "History is the study of **change** through **time,** … but it must be **selective** if it is to be intelligible." (p. xiii)

9. History means "**asking questions**" again and again. "The past does not speak for itself, and it cannot speak to us directly. We must first ask." (pp. xiii–xiv)

10. "Hope has both **theological** and **secular** meanings, **spiritual** ones as well as **material** ones." (p. xiv)

    Make sure students know what *theological* and *secular* mean.

11. What is the danger of having high ideals? (p. xiv)

    High ideals make you vulnerable to criticism when you fail.

12. "All human beings are **flawed,** as are all human enterprises. To believe otherwise is to be **naive,** and much of what passes for cynicism in our time is little more than naiveté in deep disguise." (p. xiv)

13. "The history of the United States, and of the West more generally, includes the activity of **searching** self-**criticism** as part of its foundational makeup." (p. xiv)

14. "One of the worst sins of the present ... is its tendency to **condescend** toward the past." (p. xiv)

    Consider the derisive term *old-fashioned*.

15. *For Thought:* What is history? Is it a science, or a branch of literature? What is the difference between good history and bad history?

> A good working definition: *History is what the present finds useful to remember about the past.* The past does not change, nor does human nature, but the present changes constantly, as does usefulness. And memory is necessarily selective and only partly under our control. Complete objectivity is impossible when human beings are studying human beings, so history is best understood as a branch of literature. History strives to tell the truth but can only approximate it, at best. Any account of the past that is factually in error is bad history, but the same set of facts may support different interpretations, narratives, or stories. People are complex, especially in their motivations, and there is rarely a single or simple cause for important events. The reality of the past was almost always more complicated than the historian says it is. Nevertheless, we need a knowledge of the past to have something against which to measure the present – which we also do not fully comprehend.

CHAPTER ONE

BEGINNINGS

Settlement and Unsettlement

Summary

The settlement of America had its origins in the unsettlement of Europe.
LEWIS MUMFORD

FROM THE TIME of the ancient Greeks, there has been a mystique about the West as a site of renewal, a mystique that would help fuel the European fascination with America. In fact, it is impossible to understand the history of America apart from the history of Europe; America was an offshoot of Europe that grew up during a time when Europe was undergoing large economic, social, religious, technological, and cultural changes. America would prove to be a new land where laws and customs and ideas from Europe would have freedom to develop and flourish.

Initially, though, the European discovery of America was the result of Europe's growing commercial interest in the East. By the Late Middle Ages (1300–1500), Europe was undergoing continent-wide transformation into a modern age of innovation, exploration, trade, and expansion of its global power. By the late 1400s, France, England, Spain, and Portugal had emerged as wealthy nations with motivation to explore water routes to the Far East ("the Indies") to expand trade routes and commerce.

The Italian explorer Christopher Columbus became convinced that sailing west would be a faster and more direct way to reach the East, and he persuaded the Spanish monarchs Ferdinand and Isabella to support him in that endeavor. Columbus began his exploratory voyage westward on August 3, 1492, and on October 12, his party spotted one of the islands of the Bahamas, which Columbus named "San Salvador," meaning "Holy Savior." Columbus would go on to command four round-trip voyages between Spain and the Americas between 1492 and 1503, establishing contact between the Old World and the New World, which would eventually give rise to the establishment and settlement of America. Yet ironically, he never quite understood what it was that he had found. America was hard to see.

Questions and Answers

1. You should assume that the author chose the title and subtitle of the chapter as indicative of its major themes. Look at and read through the portraits and pictures following p. 224 and select the three you believe best embody or exemplify these themes. Consider all the images from the beginning to the present day: which individuals and which pictures most suggest "beginnings" and "settlement" and "unsettlement"? Be prepared to defend your choices in class or in writing.

> There are many good choices, such as several self-made men like Lincoln and Douglas. Walking on the moon is a beginning, and unsettling. The ruins of 9/11, immigrants and tenements, African Americans voting for first time – all may suggest "beginnings" and/or "unsettlement."

2. There are fewer than twenty named individuals in this chapter, of whom two are worldwide religious figures (Christ and Mohammed) and two are modern writers (Mumford and Frost). Excluding those four, which THREE of the remainder seem to you most significant in the story of what will become the United States of America? Be prepared to defend your answers in class or in writing.

> Columbus is plainly the most important. There are no clear best choices for the other two.

3. As Question 2 suggests, the most important content of this chapter comprises not particular people nor dates but *ideas*. Students should be able to explain each in their own words. The relevant pages for each idea are given.

4. "History always begins in **the middle of things.**" (p. 3)

5. "What we call history is a **selection,** organized wisely and **truthfully.**" (p. 4)

6. "The goal [of the book], in short, is to 'be full members of a society of which we are already a part.'" (p. 4)

7. Who "can truly be called 'native' to America"? (p. 4) Why?

> Nobody can; even the "Indians" migrated here from Asia.

8. "The lost civilizations of **the first Americans,** and the explorations of the **Norse** and **Vikings** do not play an important role in this book, simply because they had no direct connection with the establishment of the United States." (pp. 5–6)

9. Yet the two answers above who do *not* play an important role in the book nevertheless "point to the presence of America in the world's imagination as a land of **hope** and **refuge**." (pp 6–7)

10. "We will start our history of America in the **middle** of Europe's history." (p. 7)

11. America would be "an unusual kind of offshoot": **unpredictable, unplanned, unanticipated.** (p. 7)

12. "The settlement of America had its origins in the **unsettlement** of Europe." (pp. 7–8) What did Mumford mean by this?

> Europe was rapidly changing, and while many of the new political institutions and economic practices it was generating were disruptive to Europe, they found a home in the newness of America.

13. "A great upsurge in fresh energies and disruptions, converging from many different directions at once, was unsettling a great deal of what had become familiar in the older world." What were these fresh energies and disruptions, which were economic, social, religious, technological, and cultural? (pp. 8–10)

> They were the Age of Discovery; the rise of a commercial middle class, nation-states, and monarchies; the scientific revolution; religious upheavals, including the Reformation; and new technologies like gunpowder and the printing press, all happening more or less together and impacting each other.

14. How did the Crusades indirectly create economic wants among Europeans? What were the barriers to satisfying these wants? (pp. 8–9)

> They brought Europeans into contact with riches from the East; the barriers were distance and the hostile cultures that controlled the known overland route (the Old Silk Road) to Asia.

15. What technological innovations aided in overcoming the barriers mentioned above? (p. 9)

> New ship designs (ships that could sail against the wind) and improved navigation through things such as compasses and map design.
>
> Teachers may need to explain how sailing ships can make progress even sailing against the wind by angling their sails and "tacking" from side to side. Ships relying on human muscles for power (rowers) might work in confined areas, such as the Mediterranean, but harnessing a natural force (the wind) increased the power available many times over.

16. Trade and exploration empowered but were also enabled by the rise of two new socioeconomic and political groups: a merchant class, who might become merchant-princes, and national monarchies, of which the first four to emerge were in **France, England, Spain, and Portugal.** (pp. 9–10)

17. **Portugal** took the lead under the guidance of **Prince Henry the Navigator.** What was the goal of this national effort? How, when, and by whom was it achieved? (p. 10)

> The goal was to reach Asia by sailing around Africa, if they could. Bartolomeu Dias discovered the Cape of Good Hope (the southern tip), and Vasco da Gama took a fleet all the way to India and began establishing a Portuguese trading empire there.
>
> Teachers may point out that until Dias's voyage, the Portuguese did not even know whether Africa had a southern end that could be sailed around.

18. Why did the success of the Portuguese make them *less* interested in Columbus's project but the Spanish *more* interested? (pp. 10–11)

> The Portuguese had the route to the East, around Africa, and held it as a fiercely guarded secret. The Spanish were playing catch-up; Columbus offered an alternate route that avoided Portuguese territory.

19. Examine the Martellus map carefully (p. 2). Is the world depicted as mostly land or mostly water? What was Columbus right about? What was Columbus wrong about? (pp. 11–12)

> The earth is depicted as mostly land (it is in fact three-fourths water). Columbus believed the world's amplitude is much smaller than it is in fact.
>
> Teachers may explain that educated people have known that the earth is round for thousands of years; an ancient Greek (Eratosthenes) even estimated *how* big around it is. Columbus's theory was that the

round earth was much smaller than believed, and he was mistaken. If there had not been an unknown continent for him to run into, he and his men would have died halfway across an enormous single ocean. None of these considerations, though, should be taken to minimize Columbus's remarkable gifts of seamanship and navigational skill.

20. Why is Columbus an example of what Frost means, that America is hard to see? (p. 13)

Columbus was unable to see that he had found a new continent. That was finally confirmed when Balboa crossed Panama and saw the "Sea of the South" (the Pacific Ocean).

21. "What we **find** is not always what we were **looking for,** and what we **accomplish** is not always what we **set out to do.**" (p. 13)

This precisely described Columbus's predicament – and those of most historical actors.

Objective Questions

Answers are in parentheses.

Put in order:

_____ Balboa discovers the Pacific Ocean	(3)
_____ Columbus discovers America	(2)
_____ Dias discovers the Cape of Good Hope	(1)

Match the individual with his nation: (*answers may be used more than once or not at all*)

_____ Bartolomeu Dias	(C)	A. England
_____ Columbus	(D)	B. France
_____ Prince Henry the Navigator	(C)	C. Portugal
_____ Vasco da Gama	(C)	D. Spain

Document

COLUMBUS'S LOG OF HIS FIRST VOYAGE, 1492

NOTE: *Columbus was interested in everything. In the interest of brevity, what follows has been edited to remove most of the geographic and botanical information. The entire log is much longer.*

Thursday, 11 October. At two o'clock in the morning the land was discovered, at two leagues' distance; they took in sail and remained under the square-sail lying to till day, which was Friday, when they found themselves near a small island, called in the Indian language Guanahani. Presently they descried people, naked, and the Admiral landed in the boat, which was armed, along with Martin Alonzo Pinzon, and Vincent Yanez his brother, captain of the Nina. The Admiral bore the royal standard; this contained the initials of the names of the King and Queen each side of the cross, and a crown over each letter Arrived on shore, they saw trees very green many streams of water, and diverse sorts of fruits. The Admiral called upon the two Captains to bear witness that he took possession of that island for the King and Queen his sovereigns, making the requisite declarations.

Numbers of the people of the island straightway collected together. Here follow the precise words of the Admiral: "As I saw that they were very friendly to us, and perceived that they could be much more easily converted to our holy faith by gentle means than by force, I presented them with some red caps, and strings of beads to wear upon the neck, and many other trifles of small value, wherewith they were much delighted, and became wonderfully attached to us. Afterwards they came swimming to the boats, bringing parrots, balls of cotton thread, javelins, and many other things which they exchanged for articles we gave them, such as glass beads, and hawk's bells; which trade was carried on with the utmost good will.

But they seemed on the whole to me, to be a very poor people. They all go completely naked, even the women, though I saw but one girl. All whom I saw were young, not above thirty years of age, well made, with fine shapes and faces; their hair short, and coarse like that of a horse's tail, combed toward the forehead, except a small portion which they suffer to hang down behind, and never cut. Some paint the face, and some the whole body; others only the eyes, and others the nose. Weapons they have none, nor are acquainted with them, for I showed them swords which they grasped by the blades, and cut themselves through ignorance. They have no iron, their javelins being without it, and nothing more than sticks, though some have fish-bones or other things at the ends. They are all of a good size and stature, and handsomely formed.

I saw some with scars of wounds upon their bodies, and demanded by signs the origin of them; they answered me in the same way, that there came people from the other islands in the neighborhood who endeavored to make prisoners of them, and they defended themselves. I thought then, and still believe, that these were from the continent.

It appears to me, that the people are ingenious, and would be good servants and I am of opinion that they would very readily become Christians, as they appear to have no religion. They very quickly learn such words as are spoken to them. If it please our Lord, I intend at my return to carry home six of them to your Highnesses, that they may learn our language. I saw no beasts in the island, nor any sort of animals except parrots." These are the words of the Admiral.

Saturday, 13 October. At daybreak great multitudes of men came to the shore, all young and of fine shapes, very handsome; their hair not curled but straight and coarse like horse-hair, and all with foreheads and heads much broader than any people I had hitherto seen; their eyes were large and very beautiful; they were not black, but the color of the inhabitants of the Canaries, which is a very natural circumstance, they being in the same latitude with the island of Ferro in the Canaries. They were straight-limbed without exception, and not with prominent bellies but handsomely shaped. They came to the ship in canoes, made of a single trunk of a tree, wrought in a wonderful manner considering the country; some of them large enough to contain forty or forty-five men, others of different sizes down to those fitted to hold but a single person. They rowed with an oar like a baker's peel, and wonderfully swift. If they happen to upset, they all jump into the sea, and swim till they have righted their canoe and emptied it with the calabashes they carry with them. They came loaded with balls of cotton, parrots, javelins, and other things too numerous to mention; these they exchanged for whatever we chose to give them.

I was very attentive to them, and strove to learn if they had any gold. Seeing some of them with little bits of this metal hanging at their noses, I gathered from them by signs that by going southward or steering round the island in that direction, there would be found a king who possessed large vessels of gold, and in great quantities. I endeavored to procure them to lead the way thither, but found they were unacquainted with the route. I determined to stay here till the evening of the next day, and then sail for the southwest; for according to what I could learn from them, there was land at the south as well as at the southwest and northwest and those from the northwest came many times and fought with them and proceeded on to the southwest in search of gold and precious stones.

The natives are an inoffensive people, and so desirous to possess any thing they saw with us, that they kept swimming off to the ships with whatever they could find, and readily bartered for any article we saw fit to give them in return, even such as broken platters and fragments of glass. I saw in this manner sixteen balls of cotton thread which weighed above twenty-five pounds, given for three Portuguese ceutis. This traffic I forbade, and suffered no one to take their cotton from them, unless I should order it to be procured for your Highnesses, if proper quantities could be met with. It grows in this island, but from my short stay here I could not satisfy myself fully concerning it; the gold, also, which they wear in their noses, is found here, but not to lose time, I am determined to proceed onward and ascertain whether I can reach Cipango. At night they all went on shore with their canoes.

Sunday, 14 October. In the morning, I ordered the boats to be got ready, and coasted along the island toward the north- northeast to examine that part of it, we having landed first at the eastern part. Presently we discovered two or three villages, and the people all came down to the shore, calling out to us, and giving thanks to God. Some brought us water, and others victuals: others seeing that I was not disposed to land, plunged into the sea and swam out to us, and we perceived that they interrogated us if we had come from heaven. An old man came on board my boat; the others, both men and women cried with loud voices – "Come and see the men who have come from heavens. Bring them victuals and drink." There came many of both sexes, every one bringing something, giving thanks to God, prostrating themselves on the earth, and lifting up their hands to heaven.

It was to view these parts that I set out in the morning, for I wished to give a complete relation to your Highnesses, as also to find where a fort might be built. I discovered a tongue of land which appeared like an island though it was not, but might be cut through and made so in two days; it contained six houses. I do not, however, see the necessity of fortifying the place, as the people here are simple in war-like matters, as your Highnesses will see by those seven which I have ordered to be taken and carried to Spain in order to learn our language and return, unless your Highnesses should choose to have them all transported to Castile, or held captive in the island. I could conquer the whole of them with fifty men, and govern them as I pleased. I returned to the ship, and setting sail, discovered such a number of islands that I knew not which first to visit; the natives whom I had taken on board informed me by signs that there were so many of them that they could not be numbered; they repeated the names of more than a hundred. I determined to steer for the largest, which is about five leagues from San Salvador; the others were some at a greater, and some at a less distance from that island. They are all very level, without mountains, exceedingly fertile and populous, the inhabitants living at war with one another, although a simple race, and with delicate bodies.

Monday, 15 October. About sunset we anchored near the cape which terminates the island towards the west to enquire for gold, for the natives we had taken from San Salvador told me that the people here wore golden bracelets upon their arms and legs. I believed pretty confidently that they had invented this story in order to find means to escape from us, still I determined to pass none of these islands without taking possession, because being once taken, it would answer for all times. We anchored and remained till Tuesday, when at daybreak I went ashore with the boats armed. The people we found naked like those of San Salvador, and of the same disposition. They suffered us to traverse the island, and gave us what we asked of them.

The natives we found like those already described, as to personal appearance and manners, and naked like the rest. Whatever they possessed, they bartered for what we chose to give them. I saw a boy of the crew purchasing javelins of them with bits of platters and broken glass. Those who went for water informed me that they had entered their houses and found them very clean and neat, with beds and coverings of cotton nets. Their houses are all built in the shape of tents, with very high chimneys. None of the villages which I saw contained more than twelve or fifteen of them. Here it was remarked that the married women wore cotton breeches, but the younger females were without them, except a few who were as old as eighteen years. Dogs were seen of a large and small size, and one of the men had hanging at his nose a piece of gold half as big as a castellailo, with letters upon it. I endeavored to purchase it of them in order to ascertain what sort of money it was but they refused to part with it.

Source: http://www.christopher-columbus.eu/logs.htm

Document Questions and Answers

1. What was Columbus's first priority? Why?

   He claimed the lands for Spain. He was serving the king and queen who financed his voyage – and whom he hoped would finance more.

2. Assuming that different goals and motives are mentioned in the log more or less in order of importance – is this a reasonable assumption? – what was Columbus's second priority after claiming the territory for Spain?

   The next thing mentioned is conversion to Christianity: "As I saw that they were very friendly to us, and perceived that they could be much more easily converted to our holy faith by gentle means than by force, I presented them …"

3. What two topics does Columbus consider next?

    He considers their lack of wealth and their military weakness: "But they seemed on the whole to me, to be a very poor people. They all go completely naked.… Weapons they have none, nor are acquainted with them, for I showed them swords which they grasped by the blades, and cut themselves through ignorance. They have no iron, their javelins being without it, and nothing more than sticks, though some have fish-bones or other things at the ends."

4. Were the natives ignorant of war?

    No. "I saw some with scars of wounds upon their bodies, and demanded by signs the origin of them; they answered me in the same way, that there came people from the other islands in the neighborhood who endeavored to make prisoners of them, and they defended themselves."

5. Some historians have interpreted the following to mean that Columbus immediately envisioned the natives as slaves: "It appears to me, that the people are ingenious, and would be good servants and I am of opinion that they would very readily become Christians, as they appear to have no religion. They very quickly learn such words as are spoken to them." Ask students how they would interpret these words and, more generally, how they would judge Columbus's attitudes toward the natives.

CHAPTER TWO

THE SHAPING OF BRITISH NORTH AMERICA

Summary

DURING THE HIGH MIDDLE AGES, which culminated around 1300, Roman Catholicism dominated Western Europe. But under the surface, there was a growing tension between the Church and people of all classes. While the great cathedrals marking the landscape testified to the Church's wealth, power, and cultural influence, many of the poor began to grow resentful at the great divide between the opulence of the Church and the poverty of their own circumstances. The middle class, too, came to feel that the Church interfered with economic life, and the increasingly powerful monarchs resented the Church's interference in matters of taxation, property, and legal jurisdiction. On top of that, a growing number of clergy and theologians were troubled by what they saw as doctrinal errors within the Church and sought reforms to correct them.

These and other factors led to the Protestant Reformation, which transformed the European religious landscape. Two theological reformers in particular led the way: Martin Luther, whose Ninety-Five Theses would catalyze the Reformation in Germany in 1517, and John Calvin, a French lawyer who rejected the hierarchical church-governance structure of Catholicism and sought to found the state and community on restored religious principles.

The Reformation's direction in England was unique, however – a fact that would eventually have enormous implications for the shape of religion in the North American colonies. King Henry VIII of England separated the Church of England from the Roman Catholic Church as a result of the pope's refusal to grant him an annulment and solidified the change by directing Parliament to pass the Act of Supremacy. But unlike Luther and Calvin, Henry had little interest in the theological reform of the Church, a fact that made the English Church different from its peers on the European continent. Hence the Church of England found itself steering an uneasy middle course, neither entirely Catholic nor entirely Protestant, and with contending factions on both sides that hoped to push the Church one way or another.

But for most of the century after Columbus's voyages to America, the Catholic Spanish were the dominant force in the New World. It was not until the epochal defeat of the Spanish Armada in 1588 that the way was opened for English dominance in North America, which in turn strongly influenced the institutions, laws, and government structures that would come to prevail in North America.

There were a variety of motives behind English colonization, a variety well illustrated by the contrast between Virginia and New England. Virginia was the first permanent English colony, established in 1607 at Jamestown. Many of the initial 105 inhabitants were men sent by the Virginia Company, a joint-stock company, seeking material wealth. These urban-dwelling gentlemen were peculiarly unsuited for the rigors of colonial life, and the colony would never have survived without the discovery of tobacco, which brought security to the local economy through the revenues from extensive exports to Europe. By 1639, Virginia's tobacco production had exploded to three million pounds per year.

By contrast, the New England colonies were founded by Puritans, men and women with deeply held Calvinist religious conviction and zeal, who believed that the Church of England had not yet done enough to purify itself from the corruptions of Roman Catholicism. These Puritans wanted to restore the purity of apostolic Christianity, to build a New Zion in a new land. In drafting and signing the Mayflower Compact in 1620, the "Pilgrims" of Plymouth Plantation committed themselves to one another, and to the laws and authorities, constituting themselves as a civil society before they even set foot on American soil. Ten years later, at the settlement of the Massachusetts Bay Colony, John Winthrop's "A Modell of Christian Charity" laid out the settlement's mission and guiding purposes, which were profoundly and exclusively religious in character.

That tension between material and spiritual motives would mark much of the American colonial experience.

Questions and Answers

1. Fewer than thirty individuals are named in this chapter, ten of whom are kings or queens of England. Below is the short version of "English history Americans should know":

TUDOR DYNASTY (five rulers in three generations)

Henry VII (r. 1485–1509): took the throne by force

Henry VIII (r. 1509–47): six wives; broke England away from Roman Catholic Church; succeeded by three children

Edward VI (r. 1547–53): Henry VIII's sickly son; Church of England became more Protestant during his reign

Mary I (r. 1553–58): "Bloody Mary"; Henry VIII's eldest daughter; tried to restore the Catholic Church; died after a brief reign

Elizabeth I (r. 1558–1603): "Virgin Queen" under whom expansion to Ireland and America began; stable on the throne once it was established that she would not marry; the Stuart king of Scotland would succeed her

Tudor dynastic instability and weakness prevented English expansion overseas until Elizabeth, but began the establishment of English sea power (defeat of the Spanish Armada in 1588), the English conquest of Ireland, and its attempted colonization of Virginia and set the stage for the English Civil Wars of the mid-1600s.

STUART DYNASTY (six rulers in four generations)

James VI of Scotland/James I of England (r. England 1603–25): king of Scotland who took the English throne by prearrangement when Elizabeth died; this is the "James" of Jamestown and the King James Bible; refused to give the Puritans what they demanded, stating "no bishops, no king," and persecuted them so that many left for New England

Charles I (r. 1625–49): drove many Puritans to Massachusetts Colony; tried to rule without Parliament; executed after losing Civil Wars

Interregnum (1649–60): England ruled by Puritan military dictator Oliver Cromwell; some royalists ("Cavaliers") fled to Virginia

Restoration (1660): King and Parliament restored after Cromwell's death in 1659

Charles II (r. 1660–84): the "merry monarch" under whom was much colonization; New York, New Jersey, Pennsylvania, and the Carolinas ("Restoration colonies") established; was careful not to challenge Parliament's authority

James II (r. 1684–88): brother of Charles II; former naval commander and Duke of York; overthrown by Parliament in Glorious Revolution of 1688 because he was Catholic

Mary II and husband, William of Orange (r. 1689–1702): Mary was the daughter of James II; Protestant rulers of the Netherlands invited by Parliament to succeed James II – note that Parliament is hiring and firing kings

Anne (r. 1702–14): sister of Mary; also Protestant; ruled until she died childless; succeeded by the Hanover Dynasty

Twelve of the thirteen colonies were settled under Stuart rule. Circumstances in England led directly to various groups wanting or needing to go to America.

HANOVER DYNASTY

Protestant kings of Hanover in Germany; became rulers of England beginning in 1714 until the present day

George I spoke no English, George II only poor English

George III (king in 1776) was the first fully English monarch from the family, which changed its name from Hanover to Windsor during World War I (because Hanover was part of Germany and on the other side)

Colony of Georgia established in 1732 under George II (last of thirteen, and only one established after 1700)

Teachers should stress that "separation of church and state" is a modern idea; during the 1600s and later, most Churches agreed that the correct number of Churches was *one*: theirs. Churches were "established," meaning tax supported and basically part of the government. Changing the Church was tantamount to changing the government, which is a revolution.

2. The Reformation was a huge event in world history, breaking down medieval **Roman Catholicism,** reinforcing the rise of the modern nation-state (including national churches like the Church of England), and igniting a century and a half of religious wars, mainly in Europe but also worldwide. But the reformers (collectively

termed Protestants) also divided among themselves: the first, the German monk **Martin Luther,** was followed by the French lawyer **John Calvin.** Lutherans and Calvinists warred against Catholics and against each other, and the Presbyterian Kirk founded by **John Knox** became the national church of Scotland. The English Civil Wars of 1639–49 were three-sided religious as well as political conflicts: King Charles I and his Church of England versus Calvinist Puritans who dominated Parliament versus Scots Presbyterians. All three groups were prominent in certain colonies: the Anglicans (Church of England) in Virginia, the Puritans in New England, and eventually the Presbyterian Scots-Irish in western Pennsylvania. It is important to remember that the peoples of the thirteen colonies that eventually become the *United* States had been at least rivals and often deadly enemies back in Britain.

3. What did Calvinists believe? Why did English Calvinists come to be called Puritans? How did Queen Elizabeth settle the tension between Anglicans and Calvinists? (pp. 17–18)

> The "Elizabethan settlement" left the Church of England Protestant in doctrine but episcopal (ruled by bishops) and retaining Catholic liturgy. This created "Puritans," who wanted to make the Church fully Protestant rather than half and half.
>
> Calvinists reject the episcopal form of church organization (bishops who are appointed by other bishops), preferring either the Presbyterian model (representative government elected by members) or congregationalism (each local church is independent). The Presbyterian Kirk (church) was the national church of Scotland and waged war against both the Church of England (Protestant but not Calvinist) and the English Puritans (Calvinist and Congregationalists) in the three-sided Civil Wars of 1639–49.
>
> Calvinists believe in the absolute sovereignty of God, including "election" (predestination), "providence" (everything happens according to God's plan), and "calling" – God places you where he wants you and expects you to be the very best you can be, whatever that is. Calvinists believe that salvation is by grace alone, that grace is a gift of God, and that authority rests in the Bible alone (*sola scriptura*).
>
> One might think that belief in predestination would lead Calvinists to fatalism ("whatever will be will be"), but in fact Calvinists see themselves as servants of God, basically soldiers in God's army – and God's army will triumph. Any defeat, even death, is insignificant and temporary. Calvinists need only concern themselves with doing their best at whatever God has set them to do and trusting in him for the outcome.

4. Why and how was Spain the dominant power in the western hemisphere (and indeed in the world) from 1500 to, say, 1588? (pp. 20–22)

> Spain's conquest of Mexico and Peru gave it gold literally by the ton, making Spain by far the wealthiest nation. The Spanish army was the best in the world and dominated Europe. The defeat of the Armada by English "sea dogs" in 1588 prevented Spain's achievement of hegemony and began the slow slide of Spain into the second and then third rank of power.

5. What was the single most important factor in the destruction of various indigenous peoples after contact with Europeans? What was the Columbian Exchange? Could the deadly diseases have been avoided? (p. 21)

> The natives of America had no inherited immunity to diseases like small-pox, measles, and mumps. These killed them by the millions – no one knows how many died. The Columbian Exchange also applied to animals like horses and to crops such as maize. No one could have anticipated or prevented the spread of disease; no one even knew how diseases spread or how to cure them.

6. Sea power trumps land power. The defeat of the Spanish Armada in 1588 changed the course of world history and especially the history of what became the United States. How? (pp. 21–22)

> Sea dogs like Sir Francis Drake were involved in the English expansion into Ireland and then Virginia; in fact, one of the early attempts to plant a colony in Virginia had to be abandoned because the ships had to be redirected to fight the Armada. Had the Spanish been able to invade England, or even had the Spanish fleet been able to dominate the Atlantic, English colonization of America would have been impossible.

7. How were Spanish (and later French) governance and institutions fundamentally different than those of England? (p. 23)

> Spain was Roman Catholic and far more absolutist and domineering of its colonies than Protestant England. Power was centralized, and self-rule was all but absent.

8. English colonization of the New World was not **a centrally directed government project.** (p. 23)

9. What is a joint-stock company? Why is this form of business organization best for financing risky endeavors? (pp. 23–24)

> Joint-stock companies are the predecessors of modern corporations.

Stock owners elect directors (one vote per share). Investors can limit risk, as many people pool their funds to finance a venture.

10. Why did Jamestown nearly perish? Why did it finally survive? ("Pioneering is the process of discovering new ways to get killed.")

They were in an unhealthy swamp and wasted time looking for nonexistent gold. Powhatan's Indians were a formidable enemy. The food ran out. The all-cause death rate approached 90 percent. What saved them was a steady reinforcement from England and the discovery of tobacco as a cash crop.

11. Who was Nathaniel Bacon? (p. 25)

He led "the less advantaged people of the colony" against the wealthiest planters (of whom he was one) over an "anti-expansionist Indian policy that thwarted access to land on the frontier."

Teachers may add that Bacon's Rebellion of 1676 is complex in origin and susceptible to conflicting interpretations; it is not clear who were the "good guys." But it did mark the point at which Virginia began to move away from the system of white indentured servanthood and toward black chattel slavery. They needed the whites to be armed because of the Indians, and it is difficult to keep armed men subservient.

12. What is the (only real) difference between the Pilgrims and the Puritans? (pp. 25–26)

Both were Calvinists and Congregationalists. The Pilgrims were Separatists who had given up on reforming corrupt England, while the Puritans saw Massachusetts as a means of demonstrating the practical value of their beliefs in order to persuade old England to adopt them. Once England became a Puritan dictatorship under Oliver Cromwell (1650–59), this goal became moot, and Plymouth Plantation was easily absorbed into the large Massachusetts Colony.

13. What is the "social contract"? (We will see this idea again in the Declaration of Independence and the Constitution.) (p. 27)

It is the agreement by which a people create for themselves a government to serve their needs.

14. What was John Winthrop's vision for Puritan Massachusetts? (pp. 26–28)

Winthrop saw the colony as a model society, "a city on a hill," to be a "light unto the nations."

15. Be able to contrast the motives and experiences and principles of Virginia and New England. Which do you think has shaped America more? Be prepared to defend your answer in class or in writing.

> Virginia was founded primarily for economic reasons and retained much of the social structure of the mother country, with a planter aristocracy, some middle-class whites, and black slaves. Its economy was focused on staple crop agriculture, and its society was paternalistic and deferential.
>
> New England was founded primarily for religious reasons, though its inhabitants were not indifferent to material prosperity. The economy was based on the sea: on fishing and, especially, shipping. Merchants were often wealthy but typically lived modest lives not much different from the lives of the large middle class. Towns were governed democratically, with most men able to vote. Slavery was legal until independence but not very widespread.

16. How did dissidence among the Massachusetts Puritans lead (in two opposite directions) to two new colonies? (p. 28)

> More extreme Puritans left to found Connecticut, and dissident Puritans were driven out to found Rhode Island.

17. How did Pennsylvania come to be? (p. 29)

> King Charles II owed William Penn a lot of money and paid him with land, to create a haven for Quakers.

18. Which was the last colony to be founded? When and why? (p. 29)

> Georgia was founded in 1732 as a planned refuge for debtors and to provide silk for the mother country. It was also a buffer to protect the Carolinas against the Spanish in Florida. The plan was unrealistic and failed, although General Oglethorpe did defeat the Spanish.

19. To what extent were colonies founded in pursuit of high ideals, and to what extent by practical desires like wealth? (p. 30)

> About half and half, but the high ideals were hard to sustain in the face of harsh realities.

20. "Being a land of **hope** also means, at times, being a land of **disappointment.**" (p. 30)

21. "Colonial life was **experimental,** and even when **experiments** fail, something important is learned from them." (p. 30)

> Historian Daniel Boorstin described the colonies as "a disproving ground for utopias" (p. 30). Yet the colonies did develop a tradition of self-rule, based on English laws and customs, being too distant (and also too fractious and well armed) to be ruled from across the ocean.

Objective Questions

Answers are in parentheses.

Put in order:

____	Elizabeth I	(3)
____	Henry VIII	(1)
____	Mary I	(2)

Match the individual with the colony: (*some answers may not be used*)

____	John Winthrop	(B)	A.	Georgia
____	James Oglethorpe	(A)	B.	Massachusetts
____	Roger Williams	(D)	C.	Pennsylvania
____	John Smith	(F)	D.	Rhode Island
____	William Penn	(C)	E.	South Carolina
			F.	Virginia

Document 1

THE MAYFLOWER COMPACT (AGREEMENT BETWEEN THE SETTLERS AT NEW PLYMOUTH), 1620

IN THE NAME OF GOD, AMEN. We, whose names are underwritten, the Loyal Subjects of our dread Sovereign Lord King James, by the Grace of God, of Great Britain, France, and Ireland, King, Defender of the Faith, &c. Having undertaken for the Glory of God, and Advancement of the Christian Faith, and the Honour of our King and Country, a Voyage to plant the first Colony in the northern Parts of Virginia; Do by these Presents, solemnly and mutually, in the Presence of God and one another, covenant and combine ourselves together into a civil Body Politick, for our better Ordering and Preservation, and Furtherance of the Ends aforesaid: And by Virtue hereof do enact, constitute, and frame, such just and equal Laws, Ordinances, Acts, Constitutions, and Officers, from time to time, as shall be thought most meet and convenient for the general Good of the Colony; unto which we promise all due Submission and Obedience. IN WITNESS whereof we have hereunto subscribed our names at Cape-Cod the eleventh of November, in the Reign of our Sovereign Lord King James, of England, France, and Ireland, the eighteenth, and of Scotland the fifty-fourth, Anno Domini; 1620.

Source: https://avalon.law.yale.edu/17th_century/mayflower.asp

Document 1 Questions and Answers

1. What, in this context, is meant by a covenant or compact?

> It is an agreement to which God is considered to be a party or witness, of greater weight and permanence than a normal human-only contract.

2. What is the purpose of the establishment of the Plymouth Colony?

> "The Glory of God, and Advancement of the Christian Faith, and the Honour of our King and Country." Explain if the order of these four listed purposes is deliberate.

3. The Pilgrims secured a land patent from the Virginia Company, permitting them to establish an English colony where they could practice their faith freely. Yet they made landfall in 1620 at what is today Cape Cod, which created a problem for the group. What was the problem?

> Cape Cod was outside of the Virginia Company's jurisdiction and, indeed, outside the jurisdiction of any known government. The leaders of the group were worried that the colony might not be able to hold together as a law-abiding entity in the absence of any larger controlling authority.

4. What did the Mayflower Compact do?

> It solved their problem. "We … Do by these Presents, solemnly and mutually, in the Presence of God and one another, covenant and combine ourselves together into a civil Body Politick."
>
> Some sixty years later, the English philosopher John Locke would systematically lay out the idea of the "social contract," by which people agree to act as one civil body, and to create a government to serve their

needs and purposes. The Pilgrims had been and remained subjects of King James, and while aboard ship, they were under the authority of its captain; but upon landing, they would need a civil authority, a government.

5. What did they believe to be the function of government?

    "For our better Ordering and Preservation, and Furtherance of the Ends aforesaid: And by Virtue hereof do enact, constitute, and frame, such just and equal Laws, Ordinances, Acts, Constitutions, and Officers, from time to time, as shall be thought most meet and convenient for the general Good of the Colony; unto which we promise all due Submission and Obedience."

6. The men who signed the Compact obviously were bound by it. Who *else* was bound by it?

    Their families and their descendants, and anyone choosing to enter and live within the boundaries of this "civil Body politick," were bound by it. A social contract is permanent, to be changed only under extraordinary circumstances.

Document 2

JOHN WINTHROP, "A MODELL OF CHRISTIAN CHARITY," 1630 (EXCERPTS)

The end [of our actions] is to improve our lives to do more service to the Lord; the comfort and increase of the body of Christ, whereof we are members; that ourselves and posterity may be the better preserved from the common corruptions of this evil world, to serve the Lord and work out our Salvation under the power and purity of his holy ordinances.

For the means whereby this must be effected: they are twofold, a conformity with the work and end we aim at. These we see are extraordinary, therefore we must not content ourselves with usual ordinary means. Whatsoever we did, or ought to have, done, when we lived in England, the same must we do, and more also, where we go. That which the most in their churches maintain as truth in profession only, we must bring into familiar and constant practice; as in this duty of love, we must love brotherly without dissimulation, we must love one another with a pure heart fervently. We must bear one another's burdens. We must not look only on our own things, but also on the things of our brethren. Neither must we think that the Lord will bear with such failings at our hands as he do the from those among whom we have lived.…

Thus stands the cause between God and us. We are entered into covenant with Him for this work. We have taken out a commission. The Lord hath given us leave to draw our own articles. We have professed to enterprise these and those accounts, upon these and those ends. We have hereupon besought Him of favor and blessing. Now if the Lord shall please to hear us, and bring us in peace to the place we desire, then hath he ratified this covenant and sealed our Commission, and will expect a strict performance of the articles contained in it; but if we shall neglect the observation of these articles which are the ends we have propounded, and, dissembling with our God, shall fall to embrace this present world and prosecute our carnal intentions, seeking great things for ourselves and our posterity, the Lord will surely break out in wrath against us; be revenged of such a [sinful] people and make us know the price of the breaches of such a covenant.

Now the only way to avoid this shipwreck, and to provide for our posterity, is to follow the counsel of Micah, to do justly, to love mercy, to walk humbly with our God. For this end, we must be knit together, in this work, as one man. We must entertain each other in brotherly affection. We must be willing to abridge ourselves of our superfluities, for the supply of other's necessities. We must uphold a familiar commerce together in all meekness, gentleness, patience and liberality. We must delight in each other; make other's conditions our own; rejoice together, mourn together, labor and suffer together, always having before our eyes our commission and community in the work, as members of the same body. So shall we keep the unity of the spirit in the bond of peace. The Lord will be our God, and delight to dwell among us, as his own people, and will command a blessing upon us in all our ways. So that we shall see much more of his wisdom, power, goodness and truth, than formerly we have been acquainted with. We shall find that the God of Israel is among us, when ten of us shall be able to resist a thousand of our enemies; when he shall make us a praise and glory that men shall say of succeeding plantations, "the Lord make it like that of New England." For we must consider that we shall be as a city upon a hill. The eyes of all people are upon us. So that if we shall deal falsely with our God in this work we have undertaken, and so cause him to withdraw his present help from us, we shall be made a story and a by-word through the world. We shall open the mouths of enemies to speak evil of the ways of God, and all professors for God's sake. We shall shame the faces of many of God's worthy servants, and cause their prayers to be turned into curses upon us till wee be consumed out of the good land whither we are a going.

I shall shut up this discourse with that exhortation of Moses, that faithful servant of the Lord, in his last farewell to Israel, Deut. 30: Beloved there is now set before us life and good, Death and evil, in that we are commanded this day to love the Lord our God, and to love one another, to walk in his ways and to keep his Commandments and his Ordinance and his laws, and the articles of our Covenant with him, that we may live and be multiplied, and that the Lord our God may blesse us in the land whither we go to possess it. But if our hearts shall turn away, so that we will not obey, but shall be seduced, and worship and serve other Gods, our pleasure and profits, and serve them; it is propounded unto us this day, we shall surely perish out of the good land whither we pass over this vast sea to possess it;

Therefore let us choose life – that we, and our seed may live, by obeying His voice and cleaving to Him, for He is our life and our prosperity.

Source: From John Winthrop, "A Model of Christian Charity," Collections of the Massachusetts Historical Society (Boston, 1838), 3rd series 7:31–48. https://teachingamericanhistory.org/library/document/a-model-of-christian-charity/

Document 2 Questions and Answers

1. Winthrop lists four "ends" (purposes) of actions. Which comes first, and which comes last? What might that order tell us about the character of the colony Winthrop was founding?

> "Service to the Lord" and to the community comes first, while personal salvation is fourth. The emphasis is on the creation of a vibrant *community* of believers who "bear one another's burdens."

2. What is the difference between the churches in England and those in Massachusetts?

> "That which they maintain as truth in profession only, we must bring into familiar and constant practice."

3. What will happen if Massachusetts fails to live up to its "commission" or covenant with God?

> "The Lord will surely break out in wrath against us; be revenged of such a [sinful] people and make us know the price of the breaches of such a covenant."

4. What are the obligations of one to another within the community or body?

> "We must delight in each other; make other's conditions our own; rejoice together, mourn together, labor and suffer together."

5. What powerful scriptural image (later picked up by Ronald Reagan) does Winthrop employ?

> "a city upon a hill"

6. How will Massachusetts know whether it is doing God's will?

> Life and prosperity will result, or else "we shall surely perish out of the good land whither we pass over this vast sea to possess it."

CHAPTER THREE

THE REVOLUTION OF SELF-RULE

Summary

SELF-GOVERNMENT and economic growth flourish in settings where people are free from top-down governance, where they are free to govern themselves. And it was self-rule that served as the ultimate philosophy of the American Revolution and the birth of the new nation in 1776.

The Great Awakening and the Enlightenment were both movements that flourished in Colonial America. The Great Awakening was the name given to a wave of religious and spiritual revival led by great preachers such as George Whitfield and Jonathan Edwards, whose rhetoric encouraged a great revitalization of individual piety among ordinary folk. The Enlightenment brought a revolution of thought in a nation where the idea was taking hold that every individual possessed natural rights – derived from nature and God rather than from the monarch or government. The Great Awakening and the Enlightenment were not fundamentally in conflict with one another in the American experience, because they had important things in common: both empowered individualism, and both supported skepticism about received or traditional institutions and encouraged individuals to withhold their deference to established forms of authority.

It was the outbreak of the French and Indian War (1754–63), however, and the decisive British defeat of the French that would change the map of North America and pave the way for the American Revolution. The war's conclusion with the signing of the Treaty of Paris in 1763 placed North America under near-complete British domination. But the conduct of the war had planted unexpected seeds, stirring up national sentiment among the colonials and leading to the convening of the Albany Congress in 1754 and the exploration of an initial Plan of Union. The colonials were beginning to think of themselves as Americans.

The French and Indian War was extremely costly to Great Britain, and there was growing British sentiment that the colonies needed to pay their fair share of the expense, since the war had been fought largely for their sake. But to do so would entail levying taxes, something that had not been done before, and that would involve restructuring the colonies' loose relationship with the mother country and challenging elements of self-rule to which colonists had become accustomed.

What followed was a series of attempted taxes on the colonies, which produced little or no revenue while provoking great and growing resistance. As Great Britain began to institute laws and acts in conflict with the constitution and overextending authority, a shift began to occur in the hearts and minds of colonists who were used to self-rule and self-governance and cherished the sacredness of their rights as Englishmen. When, in spring 1775, the royal governor of Massachusetts, Thomas Gage, received orders to aggressively stop the rebellion, he marched seven hundred red-coated British troops to Concord to seize a military supply depot established by Patriot forces. Shots were fired in Lexington, and the troops' advance on Concord turned into a rout. The American Revolution was all but under way.

But there needed to be a strong rationale for the drastic act of separation. Some of that rationale was supplied by the 1776 publication of Thomas Paine's wildly popular pamphlet *Common Sense*, which argued powerfully for the "necessity" of independence. The Continental Congress followed suit. On June 7, Richard Henry Lee of Virginia introduced a motion "that these United Colonies are, and of right ought to be, free and independent states" (p. 48). The resolution passed on July 2, and on July 4, the Congress adopted the Declaration of Independence, penned by Thomas Jefferson.

Questions and Answers

1. Why were the colonies mostly left to their own devices? Why was this a good thing? (p. 31)

> Britain was distracted by revolution and civil war during much of the seventeenth century, when the colonies were being founded, and some colonies were used as havens for the oppressed or the losers in the wars: Puritans in New England, Catholics briefly in Maryland, Cavaliers in Virginia, Quakers in Pennsylvania. The ocean itself is a significant barrier; to send a letter across the Atlantic and then get a reply took three to six

months. Close supervision at such a distance was simply not feasible. And the earliest colonies, like Virginia and Massachusetts, had no western boundary specified because no one knew what was out there. There was no master plan.

This was a good thing, because local conditions often required adjustments. The planned colony of Georgia failed at first precisely because it had a plan made in London that did not fit the American reality. "Self-government and economic growth are more likely to flourish in circumstances in which people are free of remote external government and ambitious entrepreneurs are allowed to operate freely, without the constraints imposed by the stifling hand of centralized government direction."

2. What difference did it make that the British Empire came to dominate North America as opposed to the Spanish and French Empires? (pp. 31–35)

England's system of constitutional government was established gradually, in large part as a result of the upheavals of the seventeenth century. It was not typical of European nations, most of which had highly centralized governments, under absolute rulers like Louis XIV of France. It is a crucial fact of world history that the British Empire, with its tradition of limited government and the idea that individuals have rights that governments are obliged to respect, came to dominate North America rather than the authoritarian Spanish or French Empire, which might well have done so.

Teachers may note that politicians (like the rest of us) are good at making up idealistic rationalizations justifying things they are already doing for practical and sometimes reprehensible reasons. The British Empire ignored the colonies because it was distracted and indifferent. But by the 1720s, the British government had declared that in fact it did have a colonial policy: a "wise and salutary neglect." Yes, we are ignoring you, but we are doing it on purpose and for your own good.

3. Who could participate in government? (p. 34)

Only free white men could participate, and in many cases only if they owned land or paid taxes. "Such equality as we insist on today did not then exist any place in the world."

4. "The French and Indian War was enormously consequential." Why? (pp. 35–37)

The period between 1690 and 1815 saw Britain and France at war more than 50 years out of 125. These were world wars, as both nations struggled not only in Europe but also for colonies and territory in North

America, the Caribbean, the Mediterranean, and India. The French and Indian War of 1754–63 (with most fighting ending in 1759) was the fourth of a series of North American conflicts and produced a decisive British victory, as General James Wolfe captured Quebec and, with it, control of Canada and the Ohio Valley.

Yet the British victory over the French led rather directly to the outbreak of revolution against Britain by the colonies only a dozen years later. For one thing, the threat from Canada (Indian raiders supported by the French) had kept the colonies dependent on British protection; that threat was now removed. Instead, it was Britain herself, in the aftermath of Pontiac's rebellion (p. 42), blocking the colonists from moving into Ohio, as the Royal Proclamation of 1763 (see the map on p. 36) tried to prevent future wars between the colonists and the now-British-allied tribes in Ohio.

Even more importantly, the war had left Britain with an enormous debt, plus the need to keep an army stationed in North America permanently (otherwise, the French population of Canada, and the French-allied Indians, would go right back to being part of the French Empire). Britain needed and wanted to raise revenue from the colonies, and this led to an abandonment of "salutary neglect."

5. Fighting the French and Indians had given the colonists some sense of themselves as members of a larger American culture; the first occasion for Franklin's famous *Unite or Die* cartoon (in the gallery following p. 224) was the 1754 Albany conference to develop a joint strategy against the French threat. Were there other important sources of national consciousness?

An equally large unifying force was religion, specifically the wave of revival between the 1730s and the 1750s called the (First) Great Awakening. Itinerant preachers like George Whitefield traveled the colonies, and stationary preachers like Jonathan Edwards (portrait following p. 224) published widely read books of sermons, emphasizing a faith based on personal conversion (available to anyone) and not dependent on any established church's discipline or authority nor requiring sophisticated education. Americans from New England to Georgia had heard Whitefield preach, sharing a profound experience not based on their status as English colonists.

6. What was the Enlightenment? How did it affect America? How did it coexist with the Great Awakening? (pp. 39–41)

The Enlightenment was primarily a European intellectual movement, although Americans like Benjamin Franklin and Thomas Jefferson contributed to it. It was the philosophical exploration of the implications of Isaac Newton's discovery of mathematically expressed universal laws of motion. The Enlightenment emphasized the use of reason to discover natural laws – not just in physics but ultimately in politics and religion. It was an enormously optimistic philosophy: "Nature, and nature's laws, lay hid in night; God said, 'Let Newton be' and all was light." The religious expression of the Enlightenment was Deism, a belief in a logically necessary First Cause who was not, however, a personal god who intervened miraculously in nature. Many Americans professed Deism.

The idea of natural rights was first developed by English Enlightenment philosopher John Locke to justify the Glorious Revolution of 1688 and was then used by Jefferson in the Declaration of Independence to justify the American Revolution.

Although the rationalism of the Enlightenment was in many respects the opposite of the fervor of the Great Awakening, both believed "in some version of the Biblical God" and in "an ordered and knowable universe." Both shared a skepticism about received or traditional institutions and a lack of deference to established forms of authority; both understood themselves as an expression of the spirit of liberty. Franklin, a Deist, heard Whitefield preach and admired him very much. Jonathan Edwards and Franklin "could be taken as contrasting symbols" of these two intellectual currents, but they were not as contrasting as they might seem. (p. 41)

7. How did Britain first attempt to raise revenue in America? What resulted? (pp. 42–45)

The Sugar Act and the Currency Act (1764) taxed imports and prevented the colonies from printing their own paper money. (Under the system of mercantilism, colonies were permanently in debt to their mother country, and any gold and silver would have to be sent there, so other forms of currency were needed in the colonies but unwelcome by the mother country.)

The Stamp Act (1765) required a revenue stamp on all sorts of legal and commercial documents and on newspapers; it was bitterly resisted in the colonies. (Contemplate the folly of Parliament passing a tax that fell most heavily on merchants, lawyers, and printers, the three professions best able to organize a protest movement.)

Colonists wrote letters to British friends and business partners arguing that the Stamp Act was counterproductive, as it would reduce the lucrative and heavily taxed British trade with the colonies. This pressure eventually led Parliament to repeal the act in 1766. But the colonists also organized the Sons of Liberty, who used mob tactics (tarring and feathering and similar acts of intimidation) to prevent the law from being enforced. The impression in the colonies was that Parliament had done something, the colonies had reacted violently, and Parliament had changed their mind and repealed it. But Parliament repealed the Stamp Act not because of the rioting but in spite of it, declaring that Parliament had the right to legislate for the colonies "in all cases whatsoever." This dangerous misunderstanding guaranteed that future conflicts over taxes would be increasingly bitter and violent, and ultimately either the representative assemblies would be supreme within each colony or Parliament's authority would prevail throughout the empire.

8. The second attempt to tax the colonies was the Townshend Acts (1767, repealed 1770), taxing imports of tea, glass, lead, paint, and paper. How did the colonies respond? What resulted? (p. 45)

Because these taxes were collected at the docks, it was difficult for mobs to interfere. Instead, colonists organized to boycott British goods. This was difficult, as boycotts are only effective if everyone – every merchant in every port in every colony – participates, which is difficult to coordinate when news travels slowly. And if every other merchant is boycotting, one who does import can make lots of money. So the job of the Sons of Liberty was to enforce nonimportation (and, later, nonconsumption) agreements through intimidation of colonists.

These efforts were only partially effective in preventing the British from collecting revenue – but they did provide Americans with a lot of experience working together toward a common goal. After the Boston Massacre (1770), the British finally repealed the Townshend Acts, except for the tax on tea, which was no longer enforced.

9. The third attempt to tax the colonies was the Tea Act, and the issue by now had shifted from revenue to authority. Parliament provided a subsidy to the East India Tea Company (which was the largest corporation in the world) so that the company could sell taxed tea at an irresistibly lower price to the colonists – establishing the principle that the colonies would pay a tax, and also perhaps giving the company a monopoly on tea in America – which prospect terrified American merchants. How did the colonists respond? (p. 45)

The tea had to be prevented from going on sale. In most colonies, the ships were forced to return to England without being unloaded, or the tea was allowed to rot under guard on the docks. But in Boston, the tea was destroyed in the famous Tea Party by Sons of Liberty disguised as Indians (fooling nobody).

The Tea Party was a risk for the American radicals (led by Sam Adams) who carried it out, because many Americans hated the idea of a mob destroying private property – not to mention challenging the world's strongest empire. If Parliament had not reacted so strongly, things might have gone differently. But the Coercive Acts, called by Americans the Intolerable Acts, punished Boston but also dismantled the Massachusetts government, implying a British threat to self-government in any and all the colonies – which rallied around Boston and called the first Continental Congress. (pp. 45–46)

10. How did the Continental Congress respond to the Coercive Acts? (p. 46)

They issued a Declaration of American Rights, endorsed the boycotts, and began to prepare for armed resistance. Since the royal government controlled at least part of the old militia organization, new militia units called Minutemen were formed. Americans were determined to resist the Intolerable Acts, and Britain was determined to enforce them – an armed clash was inevitable. It finally occurred at Lexington and Concord, outside Boston, in April 1775.

11. Was war inevitable? Was independence? (p. 47)

The war had already begun when the Second Continental Congress assembled in Philadelphia in May. John Dickinson of Pennsylvania attempted an Olive Branch Petition, which King George III refused even to look at.

Independence was a different matter and was not declared until July 1776, a full fourteen months after the fighting started. Tom Paine's pamphlet *Common Sense* helped change a lot of minds with his argument that not only was George III a "royal brute" but that the whole idea of monarchy ill suited a free people. A practical concern was the hope of aid from France; that kingdom might help the rebellious colonies in order to hurt Britain, but only if the colonies severed all ties to their mother country.

12. The argument in Jefferson's Declaration of Independence is derived from what? (p. 49)

Jefferson drew on John Locke's *Second Treatise of Civil Government* and justified in universal terms the right of a people to overthrow any government destructive of their natural rights – but only if the oppressive government is engaged in a "long train of abuses" showing its intent to enslave. Most of the Declaration is therefore a list of British actions considered to be such abuses.

13. Why are governments instituted? (p. 49)

They are instituted to protect people in the enjoyment of natural rights that exist before government is even organized. This is the social contract.

Teachers may clarify that some rights are indeed created by government, such as the right to vote, as without government, there would be no elections to vote in. These government-made rights are called "civil rights." But the rights, for example, of freedom of thought and expression and of self-defense are natural rights that do not come from government, though government is obligated to respect and protect them.

14. What does it mean to say that "all men are created equal"? (p. 50)

This is one of the greatest questions in American history – and even today, when nearly all Americans readily assent to the "self-evident truth" of this proposition, they are often at a loss to say what they think it means. It certainly meant, in the immediate context of its historical moment, that an American citizen was fully the equal of a British citizen. But if that were all that Jefferson meant by it, the phrase would have faded away in importance, rather than growing in scope and influence since the day he first uttered it. And its meaning is by now not restricted only to what he may have meant by it. It has never been solely his private possession. It is by now the possession of the American people, and the world. American history has, in part, been a process of exploring the meaning of those five words. We are still sorting it all out.

So what *do* they mean? Clearly they do *not* mean that all of us are created equal in ability, skill, intellect, beauty, and a dozen other attributes. Nor can they refer only to a civic equality, an equality of all citizens before the law, since such a description would exclude the young, the disabled, and others who are unable to participate in public life. But these words surely do at least mean that the natural rights of life, liberty, and the pursuit of happiness belong to all men and women and come to them as a gift of the Creator, a gift not subject to review by any earthly authority. This suggests that the source of our equality is something very deep in us, some inherent dignity in our possession of a human nature, something akin to the biblical idea that man is made in the image of God.

Teachers may wish to explore with their classes whether a philosophy of natural rights necessarily entails a religious or theological grounding or can be established on strictly secular terms.

Objective Questions

Answers are in parentheses.

Put in order:

_____	Declaratory Act	(2)
_____	Stamp Act	(1)
_____	Townsend Acts	(3)

Put in order:

_____	Boston Massacre	(1)
_____	Intolerable Acts	(3)
_____	Tea Party	(2)

Matching:

_____	Ben Franklin	(A)	A.	Enlightenment
_____	George Whitefield	(B)	B.	Great Awakening
_____	Isaac Newton	(A)	C.	Middle Ages
_____	Jonathan Edwards	(B)		

Document

THOMAS PAINE, *COMMON SENSE* (EXCERPTS), 1775–76

Volumes have been written on the subject of the struggle between England and America. Men of all ranks have embarked in the controversy, from different motives, and with various designs; but all have been ineffectual, and the period of debate is closed. Arms, as the last resource, decide this contest; the appeal was the choice of the king, and the continent hath accepted the challenge....

The sun never shined on a cause of greater worth. 'Tis not the affair of a city, a county, a province, or a kingdom, but of a continent – of at least one eighth part of the habitable globe. 'Tis not the concern of a day, a year, or an age; posterity are virtually involved in the contest, and will be more or less affected, even to the end of time, by the proceedings now. Now is the seed-time of continental union, faith and honour. The least fracture now will be like a name engraved with the point of a pin on the tender rind of a young oak; the wound will enlarge with the tree, and posterity read it in full grown characters.

By referring the matter from argument to arms, a new era for politics is struck; a new method of thinking hath arisen. All plans, proposals, &c. prior to the nineteenth of April, i.e. to the commencement of hostilities, are like the almanacs of the last year; which, though proper then are superseded and use-less now. Whatever was advanced by the advocates on either side of the ques-tion then, terminated in one and the same point. viz. a union with Great-Britain: the only difference between the parties was the method of effecting it; the one proposing force, the other friendship; but it hath so far happened that the first hath failed, and the second hath withdrawn her influence.

As much hath been said of the advantages of reconciliation which, like an agreeable dream, hath passed away and left us as we were, it is but right, that we should examine the contrary side of the argument, and inquire into some of the many material injuries which these colonies sustain, and always will sustain, by being connected with, and dependent on Great Britain: To examine that con-nection and dependence, on the principles of nature and common sense, to see what we have to trust to, if separated, and what we are to expect, if dependant.

I have heard it asserted by some, that as America hath flourished under her former connection with Great Britain that the same connection is necessary towards her future happiness, and will always have the same effect. Nothing can be more fallacious than this kind of argument. We may as well assert that because a child has thrived upon milk that it is never to have meat, or that the first twenty years of our lives is to become a precedent for the next twenty. But even this is admitting more than is true, for I answer roundly, that America would have flour-ished as much, and probably much more, had no European power had any thing to do with her. The commerce, by which she hath enriched herself, are the neces-saries of life, and will always have a market while eating is the custom of Europe.

But she has protected us, say some. That she has engrossed us is true, and defended the continent at our expense as well as her own is admitted, and she would have defended Turkey from the same motive, viz. the sake of trade and dominion.

Alas, we have been long led away by ancient prejudices, and made large sacrifices to superstition. We have boasted the protection of Great Britain, without considering, that her motive was INTEREST not ATTACHMENT; that she did not protect us from OUR ENEMIES on OUR ACCOUNT, but from HER ENEMIES on HER OWN ACCOUNT, from those who had no quarrel with us on any OTHER ACCOUNT, and who will always be our enemies on the SAME ACCOUNT. Let Britain wave her pretensions to the continent, or the continent throw off the dependence, and we should be at peace with France and Spain were they at war with Britain. The miseries of Hanover's last war ought to warn us against connections.

It has lately been asserted in parliament, that the colonies have no relation to each other but through the parent country, i. e. that Pennsylvania and the Jerseys, and so on for the rest, are sister colonies by the way of England; this is certainly a very round-about way of proving relationship, but it is the nearest and only true way of proving enemyship, if I may so call it. France and Spain never were, nor perhaps ever will be our enemies as AMERICANS, but as our being the subjects of GREAT BRITAIN.

But Britain is the parent country, say some. Then the more shame upon her conduct. Even brutes do not devour their young, nor savages make war upon their families; wherefore the assertion, if true, turns to her reproach; but it happens not to be true, or only partly so and the phrase PARENT or MOTHER COUNTRY hath been jesuitically adopted by the king and his parasites, with a low papistical design of gaining an unfair bias on the credulous weakness of our minds. Europe, and not England, is the parent country of America. This new world hath been the asylum for the persecuted lovers of civil and religious liberty from EVERY PART of Europe. Hither have they fled, not from the tender embraces of the mother, but from the cruelty of the monster; and it is so far true of England, that the same tyranny which drove the first emigrants from home, pursues their descendants still.

In this extensive quarter of the globe, we forget the narrow limits of three hundred and sixty miles (the extent of England) and carry our friendship on a larger scale; we claim brotherhood with every European Christian, and triumph in the generosity of the sentiment.

It is pleasant to observe by what regular gradations we surmount the force of local prejudice, as we enlarge our acquaintance with the world. A man born in any town in England divided into parishes, will naturally associate most with his fellow-parishioners (because their interests in many cases will be common) and distinguish him by the name of NEIGHBOUR; if he meet him but a few miles from home, he drops the narrow idea of a street, and salutes him by the name of TOWNSMAN; if he travel out of the county, and meet him in any other, he forgets the minor divisions of street and town, and calls him COUNTRYMAN, i. e. COUNTRYMAN; but if in their foreign excursions they should associate in France or any other part of EUROPE, their local remembrance would be enlarged into that of ENGLISHMEN. And by a just parity of reasoning, all Europeans meeting in America, or any other quarter of the globe, are COUNTRYMEN; for England, Holland, Germany, or Sweden, when compared with the whole, stand in the same places on the larger scale, which the divisions of street, town, and county do on the smaller ones; distinctions too limited for continental minds. Not one third of the inhabitants, even of this province, are of English descent. Wherefore I reprobate the phrase of parent or mother country applied to England only, as being false, selfish, narrow and ungenerous.

But admitting, that we were all of English descent, what does it amount to? Nothing. Britain, being now an open enemy, extinguishes every other name and title: And to say that reconciliation is our duty, is truly farcical. The first king of England, of the present line (William the Conqueror) was a Frenchman, and half the Peers of England are descendants from the same country; therefore, by the same method of reasoning, England ought to be governed by France.

Much hath been said of the united strength of Britain and the colonies, that in conjunction they might bid defiance to the world. But this is mere presumption; the fate of war is uncertain, neither do the expressions mean any thing; for this continent would never suffer itself to be drained of inhabitants, to support the British arms in either Asia, Africa, or Europe.

Besides what have we to do with setting the world at defiance? Our plan is commerce, and that, well attended to, will secure us the peace and friendship of all Europe; because, it is the interest of all Europe to have America a FREE PORT. Her trade will always be a protection, and her barrenness of gold and silver secure her from invaders.

I challenge the warmest advocate for reconciliation, to shew, a single advantage that this continent can reap, by being connected with Great Britain. I repeat the challenge, not a single advantage is derived. Our corn will fetch its price in any market in Europe, and our imported goods must be paid for, buy them where we will.

But the injuries and disadvantages we sustain by that connection, are without number; and our duty to mankind at large, as well as to ourselves, instruct us to renounce the alliance: Because, any submission to, or dependence on Great Britain, tends directly to involve this continent in European wars and quarrels; and sets us at variance with nations, who would otherwise seek our friendship, and against whom, we have neither anger nor complaint. As Europe is our market for trade, we ought to form no partial connection with any part of it. It is the true interest of America to steer clear of European contentions, which she never can do, while by her dependence on Britain, she is made the make-weight in the scale of British politics.

Europe is too thickly planted with kingdoms to be long at peace, and whenever a war breaks out between England and any foreign power, the trade of America goes to ruin, BECAUSE OF HER CONNECTION WITH ENGLAND....

No man was a warmer wisher for reconciliation than myself, before the [clashes at Lexington and Concord on the] fatal nineteenth of April 1775, but the moment the event of that day was made known, I rejected the hardened, sullen tempered Pharaoh of England for ever; and disdain the wretch, that with the pretended title of FATHER OF HIS PEOPLE can unfeelingly hear of their slaughter, and composedly sleep with their blood upon his soul....

But where, says some, is the King of America? I'll tell you. Friend, he reigns above, and doth not make havoc of mankind like the Royal Brute of Britain. Yet that we may not appear to be defective even in earthly honors, let a day be solemnly set apart for proclaiming the charter; let it be brought forth placed on the divine law, the word of God; let a crown be placed thereon, by which the world may know, that so far as we approve of monarchy, that in America THE LAW IS KING. For as in absolute governments the King is law, so in free countries the law OUGHT to be King; and there ought to be no other. But lest any ill use should afterwards arise, let the crown at the conclusion of the ceremony, be demolished, and scattered among the people whose right it is.

A government of our own is our natural right: And when a man seriously reflects on the precariousness of human affairs, he will become convinced, that it is infinitely wiser and safer, to form a constitution of our own in a cool deliberate manner, while we have it in our power, than to trust such an interesting event to time and chance. If we omit it now, some Massanello may hereafter arise, who laying hold of popular disquietudes, may collect together the desperate and the discontented, and by assuming to themselves the powers of government, may sweep away the liberties of the continent like a deluge. Should the government of America return again into the hands of Britain, the tottering situation of things will be a temptation for some desperate adventurer to try his fortune; and in such a case, what relief can Britain give? Ere she could hear the news, the fatal business might be done; and ourselves suffering like the wretched Britons under the oppression of the Conqueror. Ye that oppose independence now, ye know not what ye do; ye are opening a door to eternal tyranny, by keeping vacant the seat of government. There are thousands, and tens of thousands, who would think it glorious to expel from the continent that barbarous and hellish power, which hath stirred up the Indians and

Negroes to destroy us; the cruelty hath a double guilt, it is dealing brutally by us, and treacherously by them.

To talk of friendship with those in whom our reason forbids us to have faith, and our affections wounded through a thousand pores instruct us to detest, is madness and folly. Every day wears out the little remains of kindred between us and them, and can there be any reason to hope, that as the relationship expires, the affection will increase, or that we shall agree better, when we have ten times more and greater concerns to quarrel over than ever?

Ye that tell us of harmony and reconciliation, can ye restore to us the time that is past? Can ye give to prostitution its former innocence? Neither can ye reconcile Britain and America. The last cord now is broken, the people of England are presenting addresses against us. There are injuries which nature cannot forgive; she would cease to be nature if she did. As well can the lover forgive the ravisher of his mistress, as the continent forgive the murders of Britain. The Almighty hath implanted in us these unextinguishable feelings for good and wise purposes. They are the guardians of his image in our hearts. They distinguish us from the herd of common animals. The social compact would dissolve, and justice be extirpated from the earth, or have only a casual existence were we callous to the touches of affection. The robber, and the murderer, would often escape unpunished, did not the injuries which our tempers sustain, provoke us into justice.

O ye that love mankind! Ye that dare oppose, not only the tyranny, but the tyrant, stand forth! Every spot of the old world is overrun with oppression. Freedom hath been hunted round the globe. Asia, and Africa, have long expelled her – Europe regards her like a stranger, and England hath given her warning to depart. O! receive the fugitive, and prepare in time an asylum for mankind….

Source: https://teachingamericanhistory.org/library/document/common-sense/

Document Questions and Answers

1. How, in Paine's view, has the debate changed?

The ongoing war means that all the old debates are irrelevant.

2. If reconciliation is now impossible, what is Paine's argument for a war to achieve independence?

That is the rest of the essay!

3. How does Paine refute "England is our mother country"?

> Children grow up, and "not one third" of the colonists are of English descent. Europe, not England, is the parent.

4. Does England protect the colonies in wartime?

> No: being part of the British Empire drags the colonies into wars. "Our plan is commerce, and that, well attended to, will secure us the peace and friendship of all Europe; because, it is the interest of all Europe to have America a FREE PORT. Her trade will always be a protection, and her barrenness of gold and silver secure her from invaders."

5. Who (or what) should be king in America?

> The Law should be.

6. Is Paine familiar with Locke's theory of government?

> Yes: he writes of natural rights and the social compact – and he assumes that his readers are familiar with these concepts.

7. How does Paine criticize the British for attempting to use slaves and Indians against the rebellious colonies? What does he mean when he says "the cruelty hath a double guilt"?

> "That barbarous and hellish power, which hath stirred up the Indians and Negroes to destroy us; the cruelty hath a double guilt, it is dealing brutally by us, and treacherously by them." (Royal governor Dunmore of Virginia recruited and armed hundreds of slaves against the Revolutionaries in 1775.)

8. Can peace and reconciliation restore the old relationship?

> "There are injuries which nature cannot forgive; she would cease to be nature if she did. The robber, and the murderer, would often escape unpunished, did not the injuries which our tempers sustain, provoke us into justice. O ye that love mankind! Ye that dare oppose, not only the tyranny, but the tyrant, stand forth!"

Special Unit

TEACHING THE DECLARATION OF INDEPENDENCE

We recommend that students be assigned to read only the text of the Declaration itself (Section D). Teachers should lead them through the precise language of the opening paragraphs during a class, either in lecture format or (preferably) as a guided discussion (Section C). The material below about Locke (Section A) and Mason's 1776 Virginia Declaration of Rights (Section B) may be used to "thicken" students' background knowledge or may be summarized by the teacher or dropped altogether if time is limited.

The very long quote from Jefferson's "Notes on the State of Virginia" (in Section C) explains the evil of slavery as powerfully, perhaps, as anyone has ever done. It can be incorporated into the course in many places – including, as is done here, as an example of the perplexing contrast between ideals and realities. Some teachers may wish to omit it here and to draw upon it elsewhere during the course.

A. Teachers should point out that most of the Declaration is a long list of grievances against the British King and Parliament. The final paragraph is the actual declaration that "these United Colonies are, and of Right ought to be Free and Independent States." But it is the first two paragraphs, and especially the second, that lay out a philosophy of what government should be and why it exists.

These opening paragraphs are beautifully written and pack an enormous amount into just a few words. Jefferson was able to write with such economy for two reasons. First, he was drawing on the previous work of English philosopher and politician John Locke, in his second of *Two Treatises on Government*, "Of Civil Government." Several phrases in the Declaration ("a long train of abuses," "evinces a design") are taken directly from Locke.

Second, Jefferson was rehearsing an argument with which his American readers – and, he thought, his English readers – were thoroughly familiar. Locke was very popular among Americans, who did not realize that he was mostly forgotten in England. Locke had written to justify an English revolt, the Glorious Revolution of 1688, in which the English people had driven James II out of the kingdom and Parliament had then invited his daughter and her husband, Mary and William, who were the rulers of the Netherlands, to take the English throne as well. Locke wrote, a year later, to justify a revolution that had just occurred. Jefferson saw Locke's argument as applying with equal force to the American situation, while perhaps also speaking to Englishmen in a familiar context.

B. To see how widely accepted in America were the ideas expressed first by Locke and then by Jefferson in the Declaration, teachers may cite the Virginia Declaration of Rights written by George Mason and passed by a Virginia convention on June 12, 1776. Its first three articles are substantially identical to material in the Declaration of Independence, because Mason and Jefferson were both working from Locke. Much of the rest of the Virginia Declaration of Rights anticipates the U.S. Bill of Rights, of which Mason is considered the "father."

VIRGINIA DECLARATION OF RIGHTS

Introduced by George Mason at the Virginia Convention in the Capitol in Williamsburg.

Unanimously adopted June 12, 1776.

A DECLARATION OF RIGHTS made by the representatives of the good people of Virginia, assembled in full and free Convention, which rights do pertain to them, and their posterity, as the basis and foundation of government.

1. THAT all men are by nature equally free and independent, and have certain inherent rights, of which, when they enter into a state of society, they cannot, by any compact, deprive or divest their posterity; namely, the enjoyment of life and liberty, with the means of acquiring and possessing property, and pursuing and obtaining happiness and safety.

2. That all power is vested in, and consequently derived from, the people; that magistrates are their trustees and servants, and at all times amenable to them.

3. That government is, or ought to be, instituted for the common benefit, protection, and security, of the people, nation, or community; of all the various modes and forms of government that is best, which is capable of producing the greatest degree of happiness and safety, and is most effectually secured against the danger of mal-administration; and that whenever any government shall be found inadequate or contrary to these purposes, a majority of the community hath an indubitable, unalienable, and indefeasible right, to reform, alter, or abolish it, in such manner as shall be judged most conducive to the publick weal.

4. That no man, or set of men, are entitled to exclusive or separate emoluments or privileges from the community, but in consideration of publick services; which, not being descendible, neither ought the offices of magistrate, legislator, or judge, to be hereditary.

5. That the legislative and executive powers of the state should be separate and distinct from the judicative; and, that the members of the two first may be restrained from oppression, by feeling and participating the burthens of the people, they should, at fixed periods, be reduced to a private station, return into that body from which they were originally taken, and the vacancies be supplied by frequent, certain, and regular elections, in which all, or any part of the former members, to be again eligible, or ineligible, as the laws shall direct.

6. That elections of members to serve as representatives of the people, in assembly, ought to be free; and that all men, having sufficient evidence of permanent common interest with, and attachment to, the community have the right of suffrage, and cannot be taxed or deprived of their property for publick uses without their own consent, or that of their representatives so elected, nor bound by any law to which they have not, in like manner, assented, for the publick good.

7. That all power of suspending laws, or the execution of laws, by any authority without consent of the representatives of the people, is injurious to their rights, and ought not to be exercised.

8. That in all capital or criminal prosecutions a man hath a right to demand the cause and nature of his accusation, to be confronted with the accusers and witnesses, to call for evidence in his favour, and to a speedy trial by an impartial jury of his vicinage, without whose unanimous consent he cannot be found guilty, nor can he be compelled to give evidence against himself; that no man be deprived of his liberty except by the law of the land, or the judgement of his peers.

9. That excessive bail ought not to be required, nor excessive fines imposed, nor cruel and unusual punishments inflicted.

10. That general warrants, whereby any officer or messenger may be commanded to search suspected places without evidence of a fact committed, or to seize any person or persons not named, or whose offence is not particu-

larly described and supported by evidence, are grievous and oppressive, and ought not to be granted.

11. That in controversies respecting property, and in suits between man and man, the ancient trial by jury is preferable to any other, and ought to be held sacred.

12. That the freedom of the press is one of the greatest bulwarks of liberty, and can never be restrained but by despotick governments.

13. That a well regulated militia, composed of the body of the people, trained to arms, is the proper, natural, and safe defence of a free state; that standing armies, in time of peace, should be avoided, as dangerous to liberty; and that, in all cases, the military should be under strict subordination to, and be governed by, the civil power.

14. That the people have a right to uniform government; and therefore, that no government separate from, or independent of, the government of Virginia, ought to be erected or established within the limits thereof.

15. That no free government, or the blessings of liberty, can be preserved to any people but by a firm adherence to justice, moderation, temperance, frugality, and virtue, and by frequent recurrence to fundamental principles.

16. That religion, or the duty which we owe to our CREATOR and the manner of discharging it, can be directed only by reason and conviction, not by force or violence; and therefore all men are equally entitled to the free exercise of religion, according to the dictates of conscience; and that it is the mutual duty of all to practice Christian forbearance, love, and charity towards each other.

Students will recognize that Articles 1, 2, and 3 are very similar to the second paragraph of the Declaration of Independence. Most of the other articles were incorporated into the U.S. Bill of Rights or into the U.S. Constitution.

Teachers should point out that the men primarily responsible for drafting the various founding documents – Jefferson the Declaration, Madison the Constitution, Mason the Bill of Rights – knew each other well, served together in the Virginia legislature and in Congress, read the same books, and studied the same English history. The ideas contained in the Declaration and Constitution with its Bill of Rights were widely discussed and debated and applied in various ways by the revolutionary generation. (Remind students that each of the thirteen former colonies had to draft a state constitution after independence in 1776; many of these ideas can be found there.)

C. Teachers should guide students through the first part of the Declaration, helping them understand the meanings of key words and phrases and also their implications:

the Laws of Nature and of Nature's God

This is an Enlightenment formulation; God exists, but as a logically necessary First Cause and not as a person (with a personality, with likes and dislikes) who actively and miraculously intervenes in creation. The Christians who composed the majority of the Founders would have accepted this phrase as true but incomplete. (Teachers may remind students that Jefferson produced his own version of the Bible, keeping the ethical teachings but editing out all the miracles.)

We hold these truths to be self-evident

Self-evident truths are obvious truths, truths that are so fundamental that they cannot be effectively questioned. They are, however, confirmed by logic and common experience. They are not just assumptions or "givens"; they are *tested* assumptions.

If students want more about self-evident truths, ask them about mathematical propositions, such as the whole being greater than the part, or if they learned these two from their mothers as young children: first, treat others as you want to be treated; second, if universalizing a behavior creates an undesirable outcome, then it is wrong for an individual to behave that way. "How would you like it if somebody did that to you?" and "What would happen if everyone acted like that?" Is there anything that children learn to do earlier than they learn to say *"that's not fair"*?

that all men are created equal,

"Men" here means all humanity and includes women, slaves, indigenes, and so on. "Created equal" means it is a natural and fundamental equality, however unequal the structures of society may be. Some would contend that it mainly meant, in the immediate context of its historical moment, that an American citizen was fully the equal of a British citizen. But Jefferson meant more than that by it. The use of the verb *created* (and later the use of *Creator*) suggests that the source of our equality is an inherent dignity that is planted in our human nature, something that transcends all of our abilities and inabilities, something that (as we shall see) cannot be taken away from us and that we cannot give away or forfeit.

that they are endowed by their Creator

"Endowed" means "given permanently"; this is a statement of "natural rights."

with certain unalienable Rights

This is a much more powerful statement than most of us realize. To alienate something is to separate it from oneself; to say that a right is un-alienable (or inalienable, the more modern spelling) means it cannot be given up voluntarily or taken away. To have an inalienable right to liberty means that we do not have the right to sell ourselves into slavery, even if we wanted to.

that among these are Life, Liberty and the pursuit of Happiness

"Among these" indicates that there are others beyond the three listed. George Mason included "property" in his list in the Virginia Declaration of Rights.

An "unalienable right" to life does not mean someone cannot die; it means that no one has a right to kill, either himself or another, without good cause. Self-defense or defense of innocents is a good cause.

Again, an "unalienable right" to liberty logically excludes slavery. That Jefferson saw this clearly is evident from the following analysis in his "Notes on the State of Virginia" written in 1782:

There must doubtless be an unhappy influence on the manners of our people produced by the existence of slavery among us. The whole commerce between master and slave is a perpetual exercise of the most boisterous passions, the most unremitting despotism on the one part, and degrading submissions on the other. Our children see this, and learn to imitate it; for man is an imitative animal. This quality is the germ of all education in him. From his cradle to his grave he is learning to do what he sees others do. If a parent could find no motive either in his philanthropy of his self-love, for restraining the intemperance of passion towards his slave, it should always be a sufficient one that his child is present. But generally it is not sufficient. The parent storms, the child looks on, catches the lineaments of wrath, puts on the same airs in the circle of smaller slaves, gives a loose to the worst of his passions, and thus nursed, educated, and daily exercised in tyranny, cannot but be stamped by it with odious particularities.

The man must be a prodigy who can retain his manners and morals unde-praved by such circumstances. And with what execration should the statesman be loaded, who permitting one half the citizens thus to trample on the rights of the other, transforms those into despots, and these into enemies, destroys the morals of the one part, and the amor patri of the other. For if a slave can have a country in this world, it must be any other in preference to that in which he is born to live and labor for another: in which he must lock up the faculties of his nature, contribute as far as depends on his individual endeavours to the evan-ishment of the human race, or entail his own miserable condition on the end-less generations proceeding from him. With the morals of the people, their industry also is destroyed. For in a warm climate, no man will labor for himself who can make another labor for him. This is so true, that of the proprietors of slaves a very small proportion indeed are ever seen to labor. And can the liber-ties of a nation be thought secure when we have removed their only firm basis, a conviction in the minds of the people that these liberties are the gift of God? That they are not to be violated but with his wrath? Indeed, I tremble for my country when I reflect that God is just; that his justice cannot sleep for ever: that considering numbers, nature and natural means only, a revolution of the wheel of fortune, an exchange of situation is among possible events: that it may become probable by supernatural interference!

The Almighty has no attribute which can take side with us in such a con-test. – But it is impossible to be temperate and to pursue this subject through the various considerations of policy, of morals, of history natural and civil. We must be contented to hope they will force their way into every one's mind. I think a change already perceptible, since the origin of the present revolution. The spirit of the master is abating, that of the slave is rising from the dust, his condition mollifying, the way I hope preparing, under the auspices of heaven, for a total emancipation, and that this is disposed, in the order of events, to be with the consent of the masters, rather than by their extirpation.

Jefferson's optimism was misplaced (see Eli Whitney and the cotton gin), and he never freed his many slaves.

That to secure these rights, Governments are instituted among Men

This is the social contract by which government is created out of a "state of nature" in which there is no government. This actually happened, for example, in the Mayflower Compact or when wagon trains crossing the continent would draft rules for the many months that they would be outside the jurisdiction of any existing government.

deriving their just powers

"Just" powers implies the existence of unjust powers.

from the consent of the governed,

What constitutes consent? Voting, of course, but also accepting the benefits of living under the laws of a society. Is it right to accept the privileges without accepting the accompanying obligations and responsibilities?

That whenever any Form of Government becomes destructive of these ends, it is the Right of the People to alter or to abolish it

What is the "end" or purpose of government? It is to "secure" or protect inalienable natural rights. Government is created by the social contract, and if one party fails to abide by its terms, the other party is released from its obligations.

and to institute new Government, laying its foundation on such principles and organizing its powers in such form, as to them shall seem most likely to effect their Safety and Happiness

This is the final natural right: the right of revolution. And then a new government is created by a new social contract.

Prudence, indeed, will dictate that Governments long established should not be changed for light and transient causes; and accordingly all experience hath shewn, that mankind are more disposed to suffer, while evils are sufferable, than to right themselves by abolishing the forms to which they are accustomed.

When is a revolution justified? It is not justified every time the government does something stupid or even corrupt; in that case, there would be a constant revolution! Perfection from government is not humanly possible and is not to be demanded.

But when a long train of abuses and usurpations, pursuing invariably the same Object evinces a design to reduce them under absolute Despotism, it is their right, it is their duty, to throw off such Government, and to provide new Guards for their future security.

However, if the government is doing the same stupid or corrupt things over and over, in such a way as to make it seem that it is doing it on purpose in pursuit of some plan ("evinces a design") to destroy liberty, then the people have not only a right but a duty (to themselves and to future generations and, arguably, to God as the creator of their natural rights) to overthrow that government.

Teachers may illustrate what "evinces a design" means by an example from basketball. "Block or charge" fouls are often close calls, depending on the perception of the referee. Over the course of a game, a number of such problematical calls may be made, and it is reasonable to expect that roughly half will favor each team. But if a dozen close calls are made, and eleven of them favor the home team that provides the officials, visitors may suspect "home cooking" – that the officials are not being objective. Random mistakes should be evenly distributed; if all the mistakes tend in one direction, it "evinces a design."

Most of the rest of the Declaration is a "history of repeated injuries and usurpations, all having in direct object the establishment of an absolute Tyranny over these States." It is this history, this pattern, that "evinces a design" against the liberties that government is created to protect and so justifies and requires a revolution.

Benjamin Franklin is said to have remarked, as the delegates signed a Declaration that would surely be considered treasonable by the strongest empire in the world, that "we must all hang together, or we shall assuredly all hang separately."

D. Now incorporate these insights into students' reading of the full text of the Declaration of Independence.

THE DECLARATION OF INDEPENDENCE

In Congress, July 4, 1776.

The unanimous Declaration of the thirteen united States of America.

When in the Course of human events, it becomes necessary for one people to dissolve the political bands which have connected them with another, and to assume among the powers of the earth, the separate and equal station to which the Laws of Nature and of Nature's God entitle them, a decent respect to the opinions of mankind requires that they should declare the causes which impel them to the separation.

We hold these truths to be self-evident, that all men are created equal, that they are endowed by their Creator with certain unalienable Rights, that among these are Life, Liberty and the pursuit of Happiness. – That to secure these rights, Governments are instituted among Men, deriving their just powers from the consent of the governed, – That whenever any Form of Government becomes destructive of these ends, it is the Right of the People to alter or to abolish it, and to institute new Government, laying its foundation on such principles and organizing its powers in such form, as to them shall seem most likely to effect their Safety and Happiness. Prudence, indeed, will dictate that Governments long established should not be changed for light and transient causes; and accordingly all experience hath shewn, that mankind are more disposed to suffer, while evils are sufferable, than to right themselves by abolishing the forms to which they are accustomed. But when a long train of abuses and usurpations, pursuing invariably the same Object evinces a design to reduce them under absolute Despotism, it is their right, it is their duty, to throw off such Government, and to provide new Guards for their future security. – Such has been the patient sufferance of these Colonies; and such is now the necessity which constrains them to alter their former Systems of Government. The history of the present King of Great Britain is a history of repeated injuries and usurpations, all having in direct object the establishment of an absolute Tyranny over these States. To prove this, let Facts be submitted to a candid world.

He has refused his Assent to Laws, the most wholesome and necessary for the public good.

He has forbidden his Governors to pass Laws of immediate and pressing importance, unless suspended in their operation till his Assent should be obtained; and when so suspended, he has utterly neglected to attend to them.

He has refused to pass other Laws for the accommodation of large districts of people, unless those people would relinquish the right of Representation in the Legislature, a right inestimable to them and formidable to tyrants only.

He has called together legislative bodies at places unusual, uncomfortable, and distant from the depository of their public Records, for the sole purpose of fatiguing them into compliance with his measures.

He has dissolved Representative Houses repeatedly, for opposing with manly firmness his invasions on the rights of the people.

He has refused for a long time, after such dissolutions, to cause others to be elected; whereby the Legislative powers, incapable of Annihilation, have returned to the People at large for their exercise; the State remaining in the mean time exposed to all the dangers of invasion from without, and convulsions within.

He has endeavoured to prevent the population of these States; for that purpose obstructing the Laws for Naturalization of Foreigners; refusing to pass others to encourage their migrations hither, and raising the conditions of new Appropriations of Lands.

He has obstructed the Administration of Justice, by refusing his Assent to Laws for establishing Judiciary powers.

He has made Judges dependent on his Will alone, for the tenure of their offices, and the amount and payment of their salaries.

He has erected a multitude of New Offices, and sent hither swarms of Officers to harass our people, and eat out their substance.

He has kept among us, in times of peace, Standing Armies without the Consent of our legislatures.

He has affected to render the Military independent of and superior to the Civil power.

He has combined with others to subject us to a jurisdiction foreign to our constitution, and unacknowledged by our laws; giving his Assent to their Acts of pretended Legislation:

For Quartering large bodies of armed troops among us:

For protecting them, by a mock Trial, from punishment for any Murders which they should commit on the Inhabitants of these States:

For cutting off our Trade with all parts of the world:

For imposing Taxes on us without our Consent:

For depriving us in many cases, of the benefits of Trial by Jury:

For transporting us beyond Seas to be tried for pretended offences

For abolishing the free System of English Laws in a neighbouring Province, establishing therein an Arbitrary government, and enlarging its Boundaries so as to render it at once an example and fit instrument for introducing the same absolute rule into these Colonies:

For taking away our Charters, abolishing our most valuable Laws, and altering fundamentally the Forms of our Governments:

For suspending our own Legislatures, and declaring themselves invested with power to legislate for us in all cases whatsoever.

He has abdicated Government here, by declaring us out of his Protection and waging War against us.

He has plundered our seas, ravaged our Coasts, burnt our towns, and destroyed the lives of our people.

He is at this time transporting large Armies of foreign Mercenaries to compleat the works of death, desolation and tyranny, already begun with circumstances of Cruelty & perfidy scarcely paralleled in the most barbarous ages, and totally unworthy the Head of a civilized nation.

He has constrained our fellow Citizens taken Captive on the high Seas to bear Arms against their Country, to become the executioners of their friends and Brethren, or to fall themselves by their Hands.

He has excited domestic insurrections amongst us, and has endeavoured to bring on the inhabitants of our frontiers, the merciless Indian Savages, whose known rule of warfare, is an undistinguished destruction of all ages, sexes and conditions.

In every stage of these Oppressions We have Petitioned for Redress in the most humble terms: Our repeated Petitions have been answered only by repeated injury. A Prince whose character is thus marked by every act which may define a Tyrant, is unfit to be the ruler of a free people.

Nor have We been wanting in attentions to our Brittish brethren. We have warned them from time to time of attempts by their legislature to extend an unwarrantable jurisdiction over us. We have reminded them of the circumstances of our emigration and settlement here. We have appealed to their native justice and magnanimity, and we have conjured them by the ties of our common kindred to disavow these usurpations, which, would inevitably interrupt our connections and correspondence. They too have been deaf to the voice of justice and of consanguinity. We must, therefore, acquiesce in the necessity, which denounces our Separation, and hold them, as we hold the rest of mankind, Enemies in War, in Peace Friends.

We, therefore, the Representatives of the united States of America, in General Congress, Assembled, appealing to the Supreme Judge of the world for the rectitude of our intentions, do, in the Name, and by Authority of the good People of these Colonies, solemnly publish and declare, That these United Colonies are, and of Right ought to be Free and Independent States; that they are Absolved from all Allegiance to the British Crown, and that all political connection between them and the State of Great Britain, is and ought to be totally dissolved; and that as Free and Independent States, they have full Power to levy War, conclude Peace, contract Alliances, establish Commerce, and to do all other Acts and Things which Independent States may of right do. And for the support of this Declaration, with a firm reliance on the protection of divine Providence, we mutually pledge to each other our Lives, our Fortunes and our sacred Honor.

Special Unit

TEACHING THE CONSTITUTION

The following three questions make splendid essay topics:

1. The United States is a **federal system** with several levels of government, including a national government and the state (and local) governments. What is the relationship between We the People and our various levels of government?

2. The U.S. government is "**mixed and balanced**." What does that mean?

3. What view of human nature does the Constitution rest upon?

See the discussion of each topic in the following pages.

A. The Nature of the American Federal System

Ask students what *federal* means, and then ask them to look up the term in the dictionary. The most common usage today, as in "the federal government," is almost the opposite of what the term is supposed to mean. Clarity would suggest that the government established by the Constitution, centered in Washington, D.C., should be called the *national government, which is a part of the federal system that also includes the states.* But supporters of a stronger central government, such as Alexander Hamilton, called themselves "Federalists" and called their opponents "Anti-Federalists." This was deliberate obfuscation done for political advantage. Federalism was a popular idea, while a strong central government was not popular; we had just fought a war to get free of a powerful British government. The Federalists were actually nationalists, but they mislabeled themselves to win support. Moreover, the "Anti-Federalists" believed in federalism at least as much as their opponents did; the United States under the Articles of Confederation was a federal system, including a relatively weak central government plus the states. The Constitution that replaced the Articles strengthened the central government and weakened the states but remained a federal system.

Teachers might use this as an example of the importance of names and the framing of issues. If you allow your opponents to name you, and to frame the issue to suit themselves, they are on their way to winning. A contemporary example is the debate about abortion. One side calls itself "pro-choice," and the other calls itself "pro-life," because "choice" and "life" are both seen as good things. Neither side wants to be anti-something. In 1787, the supporters of ratification were well organized and called themselves "Federalists"; their opponents were scattered and unorganized and received the name "Anti-Federalists" from the other side. But in fact, everyone on both sides agreed that the United States should remain a federal system.

Teachers may ask, rhetorically since the answer is obvious, which existed first, the states or the United States? (Actually, the original thirteen existed first, then the United States, then the remaining thirty-seven.) Under the Articles of Confederation, the states created the central government, which was limited to a Congress in which each state had one vote (like the modern United Nations), and there was no national executive or judiciary; laws were enforced at the state level.

The genius of the Constitution was the idea, expressed in the Preamble beginning "We the People," that *all power originates from the people, who can create different governments to serve different purposes*. Teachers can use this analogy: in a wealthy household, one does not ask whether the cook or the gardener is the higher power; they both serve the same employer or master. The cook is the chief servant where food is concerned, and the gardener is the chief servant where the grounds are concerned. If the debate is whether to plant roses or onions, it must be resolved by their common superior.

In the American federal system, some matters (how and by whom children should be educated, for example) are the responsibility of local and state governments – who vary widely on how they perform them. (*States are called the "laboratories of democracy" because different approaches to the same problem can be tried and outcomes compared.*) Other matters, first and foremost defense and foreign policy, must be handled at the national level.

Teachers should call attention to the two lists in Article I: section 8 is *powers granted to Congress*; section 10 is *powers denied to the states*. Students should understand the implication: the states had originally possessed *all* the powers and retained all of those not explicitly denied them in section 10; the U.S. Congress, it could be argued, began with *no* powers (since it did not exist until created by the Constitution) and so had *only* those listed in section 8. (This is a good time to refer to the debate between Jefferson and Hamilton in Washington's first cabinet over the bank bill and the *"necessary and proper" or "elastic" clause* at the end of section 8.)

The federal system is based on "concurrent powers" that are common to all levels of government; the main two are the power to tax and the power to enforce laws. (The root of *enforce* is *force*, which in political terms means "violence or threat of violence.") Americans pay local, state, and national ("federal") taxes, and all three levels of government employ armed officers to see that the laws are obeyed.

The Constitution provides (Article VI, clause 2) that "*This Constitution, and the laws of the United States* that are made in pursuance thereof, and treaties" are "*the supreme law of the land*" and "judges in every state are bound thereby" when they conflict with state laws. This is called the *supremacy clause*. When federal and state laws conflict, the federal law prevails (assuming it is constitutional).

Students should understand the concept of "sovereignty." *A sovereign power is one above which there is no higher power*. Note that "no higher power" is not the same as "the highest power"; there can be multiple equal sovereignties, for example, each independent nation is sovereign within its own borders. *Sovereignty in the American federal system is complex*: ultimately, *the people are sovereign*, and *the supremacy clause* means that national ("federal") law prevails over state law when they conflict. But *the states retain their sovereignty* as well. For example, the Supreme Court (whose responsibilities include resolving questions of conflicting sovereignties) has held that states are immune from the U.S. law requiring employers to enroll their workers into the Social Security system; state governments may choose to do that or may set up their own retirement systems for their employees. The Court has also held that the states are not mere administrative subunits of the U.S. government and may not be obliged to enforce U.S. laws. Congress has mostly relied on federal grants to states to affect their behavior; for example, states set their own speed limits, but a national 55 mph speed limit was enforced by the threat to withhold federal funds for highway construction from states that failed to comply.

Ratification of the Constitution settled some questions but left others open. One was whether states could *secede* – whether they could withdraw from the union once they had joined it. That eventually required a bloody civil war to resolve.

Another question was who was to interpret the Constitution, which is silent on the topic. *Judicial review* (the power to declare legislative acts unconstitutional) is not expressly granted but was assumed by the Supreme Court under John Marshall (*Marbury v. Madison*, 1803) and was both highly controversial and very rarely used. (The second time the Court declared an act of Congress unconstitutional was the disastrous *Dred Scott* decision in 1854. The Court had also overturned a number of state laws by then.)

The argument that states might intervene to block enforcement of federal laws ("nullification") goes back to Jefferson and Madison and the Virginia and Kentucky Resolutions but has never been successfully maintained in the long run, partly because the argument is always made by the party out of power, which promptly forgets it as soon as it wins an election!

Although most of the conflicting interpretations of the federal system were resolved as a result of the Civil War, the controversies over "sanctuary cities" opposing the enforcement of immigration laws or "Second Amendment sanctuary counties" opposing expanded gun control laws show that some ambiguities still remain.

Teachers should explain that *states determine how elections are conducted* even in federal elections. (Various amendments now restrict how states can do this: no poll taxes, no restriction on voting due to sex or color or previous condition of servitude, no restriction on age if at least eighteen.) States determine who votes (convicted felons? sixteen- or seventeen-year-olds?); when, where, and how the votes are recorded; who counts them; and so forth. For many years, some states required that voters be taxpayers or property owners; these requirements mostly disappeared during the Jacksonian era.

As a puzzle, teachers may ask students to find and cite the exact language in the Constitution that determines who can vote in federal elections (for members of Congress originally and now also for senators and presidential electors). The answer is in Article I, section 2: "The House of Representatives shall be composed of members chosen every second year by the people of the several states, and the electors in each state shall have the qualifications requisite for electors of the most numerous branch of the state legislature." What that means in plain English is that if a state has two houses in its legislature (as all but one does), then one of those houses will be more numerous: sixty state representatives, say, and twenty state senators. Anyone who is allowed to vote for a state representative is automatically also eligible to vote for the U.S. House of Representatives.

B. A "Mixed and Balanced" Government

Government must do three things, in this order:
The *legislative function* creates the laws;
the *executive function* enforces the laws;
and the *judicial function* applies general laws to specific cases.

The legislative must come first; otherwise, there would be no laws for the executive to enforce.

The Constitution follows this order: Article I creates the legislature, the Congress; Article II creates the presidency as a unitary executive; and Article III creates the Supreme Court. *These are the three "branches" of government*, and they are *coequal* under the Constitution.

The Founders believed that it was *essential that these three functions be carried out by different people*; the very definition of tyranny or despotism is when one person or group can do all three: can make the law, enforce the law, and apply the law to particular cases. The condemnatory phrase "taking the law into your own hands" is based in part on this idea.

Informed by ancient history, especially the analysis of the government of Republican Rome done by the Greek historian Polybius (ca. 208–ca. 128 B.C.), the Founders wanted *a mixed and balanced government*. It had to be mixed before it could be balanced. Polybius divided governments into how many men ruled:

> *Rule by ONE is monarchy* or its corrupt form, despotism.
> *Rule by a FEW is aristocracy* or its corrupt form, oligarchy.
> *Rule by MANY is democracy* or its corrupt form, mob rule.

Each has its own advantages and disadvantages:

> **Rule by one is decisive;** it can *act* in a crisis. The disadvantage is that if the one is corrupt or a fool, then so is the entire government.

> **Rule by a few is wise;** "two heads are better than one." But aristocracy can be paralyzed by factionalism, and debate takes time not available in an emergency.

> **Rule by the many** is neither decisive nor wise, but it is *stable and strong*. The large Roman middle class, small farmers who were economically independent and who composed the army, were the basis of the government and could not be overthrown.

A mixed government combines elements of monarchy, aristocracy, and democracy. The president represents the monarchical principle; the Senate and the judiciary represent the aristocratic principle; and the House of Representatives embodies the democratic principle.

These three branches can then be *balanced*. This is done by mingling their responsibilities and also by giving each branch various checks upon the other two.

The legislative branch (the two houses of Congress) must make the laws and has two particular powers over the other two: it can *impeach* and remove from office, and it controls the taxing and spending of public revenues, the *power of the purse*. Therefore, in a battle with the other branches, Congress has the final say – provided Congress can manage to act! Congress is not just an enormous committee; it is two committees that must agree. That is, the Constitution gives the greatest power to the branch that is least able to use it efficiently.

The president is the executive branch all by himself (a *unitary* executive) with very extensive powers, some of which can be used to check Congress (the veto) or the courts (the power to pardon). In wartime, the president, as *commander in chief*, is very close to being a dictator, because restrictions on him by

Congress or the courts may be seen as risking defeat and destruction. The pattern (e.g., with Lincoln, with Wilson, and with Franklin Roosevelt) has been great expansion of presidential authority as long as the guns are firing and then a vigorous reclaiming of authority by Congress and the courts as soon as peace is restored. (It helped in the three cases mentioned that the wartime president was either dead or incapacitated after the war.)

The judiciary appears to be the most powerful or influential, since it is frequently tasked with resolving conflicts between the other two branches. However, the courts' authority depends almost entirely on it being accepted by the other two. The courts have no way to compel the other branches to obey. Enforcing court orders is the responsibility of the president, who may decline to enforce them upon himself. In wartime, presidents may ignore courts with impunity, as when they suspend habeas corpus. A president's refusal to obey a court order might be grounds for the House of Representatives to impeach him; that is, in a dispute between two of the branches, the outcome is likely to depend on the third branch. However, a two-thirds vote in the Senate is required for conviction and removal from office by *impeachment*. A president who retains the support of 34 percent of the Senate cannot be removed until his term expires.

Teachers should direct students' attention to Article III and ask what powers Congress has over the federal courts. Point out that Congress determines how many justices serve on the Supreme Court (it was originally five and is now nine; Franklin Roosevelt failed to persuade Congress to increase it to fifteen). Congress also creates all lower federal courts, and anything Congress creates, it can also regulate or even abolish. Congress determines the *jurisdiction* in most cases, even of the Supreme Court. In short, the courts are reluctant to pick fights with Congress, because Congress has many ways of hitting back. (But again, Congress is two giant committees and often has trouble exerting its theoretical powers in practice.)

C. Adding It All Up

Combining A and B, we arrive at a political system in which power is divided both vertically (some at the national level, some at the state and local levels) and also horizontally (legislative, executive, and judicial branches). The result is a system that is anything but efficient, and the Founders considered that a feature, not a problem. As Madison wrote in *Federalist* 51, "in the compound republic of America, the power surrendered by the people is first divided between two distinct governments, and then the portion allotted to each subdivided among distinct and separate departments. Hence a double security arises to the rights of the people. The different governments will control each other, at the same time that each will be controlled by itself."

The American system rests on a skeptical view of human nature: "But the great security against a gradual concentration of the several powers in the same department, consists in giving to those who administer each department the necessary constitutional means and personal motives to resist encroachments of the others. The provision for defense must in this, as in all other cases, be made commensurate to the danger of attack. Ambition must be made to counteract ambition. The interest of the man must be connected with the constitutional rights of the place. It may be a reflection on human nature, that such devices should be necessary to control the abuses of government. But what is government itself, but the greatest of all reflections on human nature? If men were angels, no government would be necessary. If angels were to govern men, neither external nor internal controls on government would be necessary. In framing a government which is to be administered by men over men, the great difficulty lies in this: you must first enable the government to control the governed; and in the next place oblige it to control itself" (Madison, *Federalist* 51).

The United States can act decisively only in circumstances of "clear and present danger," when widespread popular support makes action plainly necessary. Groups such as the Progressives, whose view of human nature is more benign, find this inefficiency frustrating. But the Founders were at least as afraid of what a government might do to them as hopeful about what it might do for them.

CHAPTER FOUR

A WAR, A NATION, AND A WOUND

Summary

The war was not about home rule, but about who would rule at home.

CARL BECKER

DECLARING INDEPENDENCE was the easy part. But the task of delivering independence and unification of the colonies through the American Revolution was immense, with one-third of American colonists remaining loyal to the Crown and opposed to the Revolution. Moreover, the revolutionary leaders were up against the greatest military power and the most powerful empire in the world. Yet the Americans had two great advantages: first, they were playing defense on their home shores, and second, they had an exceptional leader in George Washington, whom the Congress of the Second Continental Convention had named commander in chief of the Continental army in June 1775.

The greatest immediate challenge Washington faced was recruiting, deploying, and maintaining an effective army to sustain the revolutionary cause. The winter of 1776–77 was exceptionally harsh for Washington's military, and the outlook for a Patriot victory seemed bleak. But Washington was able to hold the army together, and after a surprising American victory at Saratoga on October 27, 1777, the outlook brightened, since the French were now willing to support the revolutionary cause against their hated British rivals. It would take another four harrowing years, however, before the decisive victory over British general Cornwallis at Yorktown, Virginia, on October 19, 1781. On September 3,

1783, the Treaty of Paris was signed, and American independence was established.

Now the American people had to establish a government to guide their new nation forward. That would not be easy. Since 1777, the country had lived under the Articles of Confederation, which were sufficient for the war years but deficient as a long-term constitutional instrument. By 1786, there was strong interest in the possibility of reforming or replacing the Articles with a stronger union. On May 25, 1787, fifty-five men gathered in Philadelphia for the Constitutional Convention. They faced two fundamental problems: first, how much power needed to be given to an expanded national government, and second, how to ensure that this empowered national government would itself be fully accountable and not become too powerful.

The key issue was representation, and the delegates came up with two plans for that: the Virginia Plan (which featured representation by population) and the New Jersey Plan (which followed the Articles' pattern of representation by state). The convention finally settled on a compromise between the two in the form of a bicameral (two-chamber) structure: the more populous states were accorded representation by population in the House of Representatives, while the smaller states would retain equal footing in the Senate, where each state would be accorded two representatives irrespective of size or population. Legislation would have to clear both houses and be signed by the president to be enacted into law.

The new nation and the new Constitution were far from perfect, however. Slavery was enmeshed in one segment of the national economy, and the Constitution necessarily reflected this fact, protecting the institution of slavery in some respects while working toward its eventual extirpation in others. Americans would be living inside this moral inconsistency for years to come.

Questions and Answers

1. What were the main problems facing the newly independent United States in winning the war? (p. 52)

> The central authority, the Continental Congress, was very weak, with no effective executive. Moreover, Americans were divided, with a substantial minority, perhaps one-third, remaining loyal to the British Crown.

2. What advantages did the Americans have? (pp. 53–54)

> They were playing defense and had time on their side. They could hope for aid from Britain's enemies, especially France. And they had George

Washington, who attended the Continental Congress wearing his old uniform from the French and Indian War – a political statement that he was willing to use force against the British, and also a reminder that he was one of the few experienced commanders the colonies had.

3. Washington's defense of New York City was probably doomed from the start, and he was fortunate to extract his army from Long Island in the face of British naval superiority. Driven out of New York and across New Jersey in a series of defeats, his army dwindled from twenty-eight thousand in August 1776 to three thousand in December. This was the crisis. What happened to turn things around?

Tom Paine's second pamphlet, *The American Crisis*, rallied the people ("These are the times that try men's souls: the summer soldier and the sunshine patriot"), and Washington brilliantly won two small victories against parts of the British army, at Trenton and then a week later at Princeton. Captured enemy soldiers were paraded through Philadelphia and across New Jersey to prove that the war was still winnable.

4. The British called 1777 "the year of the hangman" when the rebellion would be crushed. What was their plan? What part of it worked, and what part failed? (pp. 55–56)

General Howe and the main British army defeated Washington again and captured Philadelphia. But meanwhile, a smaller British army under Burgoyne pushed down from Canada toward Albany, intending to split New England away from the rest of the states along the Hudson River–Lake Champlain line. (Britain's naval strength gave them control of any navigable waterway.) Burgoyne's Indian allies terrorized the civilian population, and his army drowned in a sea of American militia who turned out to defend their families from this danger. The surrender of Burgoyne at Saratoga did not win the war – his was the smallest of three British armies in America, the other two being at Philadelphia and New York – but it did bring France into the war as an ally. Spain also declared war on Britain. The war was now a worldwide struggle, and Britain's resources had to be split to defend her far-flung empire.

5. What happened at Valley Forge over the winter of 1777–78? (pp. 56–57)

Washington's army nearly perished for lack of food, but the arrival of General von Steuben provided professional training that made the Continentals a far more cohesive force.

6. Who was George Rogers Clark? (p. 57)

> He commanded Virginia's Illinois Regiment and managed to capture key posts in the Ohio Valley, giving the Americans a solid hold on the Northwest.

7. What happened when the British under Lord Cornwallis moved into the South? (p. 57)

> They started well, capturing Savannah and Charleston, but when Cornwallis moved into Virginia, he found himself trapped at Yorktown as Washington brought his army down from the North and the French landed an army to work with the Continentals. A French fleet prevented the British navy from rescuing Cornwallis, and he surrendered on October 19, 1781. The main British army still held New York, but it was clear that the British now had no hope of subduing the states.

8. Was the war a fight for independence or a truly revolutionary struggle? Was it about "home rule" or "who should rule at home"? (pp. 58–59)

> Both, and neither, probably. The Loyalists were often disarmed and stripped of property (and many were settled in the north after the war to found English-speaking Canada), but few were executed. Mostly the war was fought without the sort of political killings that often characterize revolutions. The war was a contest between two elements of the same political system – the colonial assemblies versus the King and Parliament – and local governments at the town and county levels did not change much. That is, the Revolution was conservative rather than radical, aimed at protecting what already existed (self-rule) and not at creating something new.
>
> Except that the Revolutionaries believed they were creating *novus ordo seclorum*, a new order of the ages. Republicanism was a powerful ideology, and many doubted that it could work, except within a small homogeneous city-state. The founding generation thought of themselves as engaged in a grand experiment, and one by no means assured of success.
>
> Teachers may also mention the role of the militia, which was composed of every free adult male. It was the people, under arms. Militias were of uneven effectiveness on the battlefield; Washington did not trust them and hated to rely on them. Too often they ran away from the British bayonets. Yet the militia was the key to the American victory. They controlled every area, except where the British armies were, and that control allowed the Patriots to draw men and supplies from the population and conferred political legitimacy.

And the militia was an engine for political mobilization. Many men would doubtless have preferred to stay home and out of the fighting, and then cheer loudly for whoever eventually won. But when the British army invaded a state, that state's militia would be called out, and every man would be forced to choose: either he turned out to fight the British, and had then joined the Revolution, or he refused to go and was labeled a Loyalist and probably a coward – and punished accordingly. The militia system was one of the keys to winning a revolutionary war between two sides that were both claiming to be the legitimate government of the same set of people.

The British eventually figured this out and tried in the South, in the last years of the war, to organize the Loyalists into their own militia. Patriot and Loyalist militias fought bitterly, neighbor against neighbor, as law and order broke down and old animosities and feuds, and outright banditry, were incorporated into the political struggle. The Carolinas and Georgia during 1782 and 1783 (the period between Cornwallis's surrender and the Peace of Paris) saw as vicious and bloody a civil war as has ever existed. So parts of the war certainly looked like what we think of as a revolutionary struggle.

9. What sort of national government did the Articles of Confederation provide for the United States? Why did it not matter that they were not finally ratified until 1781? (p. 60)

Congress was already operating as the Articles provided, so nothing had to change. There was no national executive or judiciary. Each state had one vote regardless of population, and it took three-fourths (nine out of thirteen) to pass a law and unanimity to amend them. Congress lacked the power to tax or to regulate commerce.

10. What was the "singularly impressive and enduring accomplishment" of Congress under the Articles? (p. 61)

The Northwest Land Ordinances of 1784 and 1787 organized the territories in such a way as to see them admitted as new states equal in status to the original thirteen. This prevented the east–west conflicts that had been a feature of colonial history. The result was a steadily growing nation, not an empire with the eastern states as the mother country and the West as dependent colonies. The Ordinance of 1787 was also notable for its promotion of education in the territories and its prohibition of the introduction of slavery.

Teachers may point to this as one of the Roman elements in the formation of the United States, along with "Senate" and "veto." As the Romans expanded within Italy (among peoples who spoke the same language and worshiped the same gods), they conferred Roman citizenship on conquered foes, with representation in the Roman Senate. (This generosity ended when Rome expanded outside Italy among alien peoples; they were enslaved.)

11. What problems did the United States face after the war? How effective was the Confederation Congress in dealing with them? (p. 62)

The British refused to vacate forts in the Northwest and restricted American imports while flooding American markets with their own cheap goods. There was no good currency, especially as taxes were increased. Farmers might have had wealth in land or cattle, but they had no money to pay the tax collector.

12. How serious a threat was Shay's Rebellion in Massachusetts? (pp. 61–63)

Not very serious in actuality, but the perception – helped along by Henry Knox and others who wanted a stronger government – was that radicals were threatening property and law and order, so that something needed urgently to be done. Washington played a leading role in calling for a constitutional convention.

13. Who was the intellectual leader among the many very talented men at the Philadelphia convention? (p. 64)

James Madison, the principal architect of the Constitution, was the intellectual leader.

Teachers may point out that every one of the thirteen former colonies had to write a new constitution after independence. These state constitutions varied as different ideas were tried. Pennsylvania started with an extremely democratic plan, with annual elections, but switched to a more conservative constitution a few years later. When the states sent delegates to the Philadelphia convention, of course they sent men who had already participated in drafting plans of government at the state level. If the U.S. Constitution was excellent, part of the reason is that the drafters had had practice.

14. What did the Philadelphia convention agree on from the start? (p. 65)

It agreed on a republican government (based on a scheme of representation) and a federal system in which states retained a large measure of autonomy.

15. What was the fundamental problem? (pp. 65–66)

> Recognizing the corrupting effect of power, all agreed that it needed to be distributed, both vertically (between the central government and the states and local governments) and also horizontally (among the legislative, executive, and judicial branches). But what exactly would this look like?

16. Why was there reluctance to create a strong executive? Why did they do so anyway? (p. 66)

> The colonial legislatures had feuded with royal governors for a century, and the revolution was against a king. Yet they realized an executive was necessary, and all assumed that Washington, who had demonstrated his trustworthiness in resisting the temptations of power, would be the first president.

17. What was the great issue regarding representation? How was it resolved? (pp. 67–68)

> Did population matter? Or was each state equal, as had been the case in the Continental and Confederation Congresses? The "Great Compromise" was a bicameral Congress with a lower house based on population and an upper in which each state had two votes. The smaller states would never have approved or joined a union without a way to protect themselves from the large and populous states.

18. What are the three functions of government? How was the system of checks and balances achieved? (p. 68)

> The legislative makes laws, the executive enforces them, and the judiciary interprets and applies the general law to specific cases. But each branch participates in what the other two branches do. The president must get Senate confirmation of appointments and negotiated treaties and can recommend legislation and either signs or vetoes a completed bill – a legislative function; the president can pardon – a judicial function; Congress can impeach and try officials – a judicial function; and so on.

19. "We are forever about the business of making a workable **unity** out of our unworkable **plurality,** and our Constitution accepted the inevitability of our **diversity** in such things, and the inevitability of **conflicts** arising out of our differences." (p. 69)

20. What would counteract the ambitions of powerful men? (p. 69)

> The ambitions of other powerful men. This is the theme of *Federalist* 51.

21. "Unlike the Declaration of Independence, the Constitution's spirit is **undeclared, unspoken;** it would be revealed not through words but through **actions,** through **processes,** and through **events** that would express the unfolding demands of history." (p. 69)

22. What was the main labor system during the seventeenth century? (p. 70)

> Indentured servitude was similar to slavery in that workers were not free, but it was time limited, applying only for a term of years. Perhaps as many as half of white immigrants came as indentured servants.

23. Why did black chattel slavery supplant the indenture system? (pp. 70–71)

> Indentured servants who completed their terms then needed land of their own, and their children were born free. Slaves provided a more permanent (and also movable) labor force. Bacon's rebellion dramatized that the need to arm all whites was inconsistent with a dependent unfree class of white workers.

24. How do we understand the irony and contradictions of the Founders' acceptance of slavery in an otherwise free society? (pp. 71–72)

> Many of them regarded slavery as an evil but also as a necessity and struggled with the implications of that contradiction. Jefferson did not free his slaves but was eager to block the expansion of the system, for example, in the Northwest Land Ordinances. There was widespread and sincere hope among the Founders that slavery would gradually disappear. But all in all, there are no easy or comforting answers to this puzzle.

25. How is slavery recognized, and how not, in the Constitution? (p. 72)

> The Constitution avoided using the words "slave" and "master" but did provide for a fugitive slave law (which also applied to runaway indentured servants). It prohibited abolishing the international slave trade until 1808 and agreed that slaves would count as three-fifths of a free person both for purposes of taxation and representation. (The North wanted them counted 100 percent for taxation and 0 percent for representation; the South wanted the opposite.)

26. How did slavery in the southern states compare with the situation in Latin America? (p. 73)

Latin American society was more accepting of nonwhites (and some of that attitude was visible in Louisiana), but working conditions were dreadful. Death rates were high, and the slave force needed constant replenishment from Africa. In contrast, Virginia ended importation in 1778, under the leadership of Governor Thomas Jefferson, and conditions were healthy enough that the population of slaves increased naturally. "In fact, slaves in the antebellum south would have the highest rate of natural increase of any slave society in history."

27. "We live today on the other side of a great transformation in moral sensibility … that was not yet completed, in the very years that the United States was being formed. Hence it would be profoundly wrong to contend, as some do, that the United States was '**founded on**' slavery. No, it was *founded* on other principles entirely, on principles of **liberty** and **self-rule**, that … would win out in the end, though not without much struggle and striving, and eventual bloodshed." (p. 73)

Objective Questions

Answers are in parentheses.

Put in order:

	Articles of Confederation	(1)
	Philadelphia Convention	(3)
	Shay's Rebellion	(2)

Matching:

	Charles Cornwallis	(B)	A. American
	Comte de Grasse	(C)	B. British
	Friedrich von Steuben	(A) or (D)	C. French
	George Washington	(A)	D. Prussian
	George Rogers Clark	(A)	
	John Burgoyne	(B)	
	Marquis de Lafayette	(A) or (C)	

Document

THE NORTHWEST ORDINANCE, JULY 13, 1787

An Ordinance for the government of the Territory of the United States northwest of the River Ohio.

Sec. 1. Be it ordained by the United States in Congress assembled, that the said territory, for the purposes of temporary government, be one district, subject, however, to be divided into two districts, as future circumstances may, in the opinion of Congress, make it expedient.

Sec. 2. Be it ordained by the authority aforesaid, that the estates, both of resident and nonresident proprietors in the said territory, dying intestate, shall descend to, and be distributed among their children, and the descendants of a deceased child, in equal parts; the descendants of a deceased child or grandchild to take the share of their deceased parent in equal parts among them: And where there shall be no children or descendants, then in equal parts to the next of kin in equal degree; and among collaterals, the children of a deceased brother or sister of the intestate shall have, in equal parts among them, their deceased parents' share; and there shall in no case be a distinction between kindred of the whole and half blood; saving, in all cases, to the widow of the intestate her third part of the real estate for life, and one third part of the personal estate; and this law relative to descents and dower, shall remain in full force until altered by the legislature of the district. And until the Governor and judges shall adopt laws as hereinafter mentioned, estates in the said territory may be devised or bequeathed by wills in writing, signed and sealed by him or her in whom the estate may be (being of full age), and attested by three witnesses; and real estates may be conveyed by lease and release, or bargain and sale, signed, sealed and delivered by the person being of full age, in whom the estate may be, and attested by two witnesses, provided such wills be duly proved, and such conveyances be acknowledged, or the execution thereof duly proved, and be recorded within one year after proper magistrates, courts, and registers shall be appointed for that purpose; and personal property may be transferred by delivery; saving, however to the French and Canadian inhabitants, and other settlers of the Kaskaskies, St. Vincents and the neighboring villages who have heretofore professed themselves citizens of Virginia, their laws and customs now in force among them, relative to the descent and conveyance, of property.

Sec. 3. Be it ordained by the authority aforesaid, that there shall be appointed from time to time by Congress, a Governor, whose commission shall continue in force for the term of three years, unless sooner revoked by Congress; he shall reside in the district, and have a freehold estate therein in 1,000 acres of land, while in the exercise of his office.

Sec. 4. There shall be appointed from time to time by Congress, a secretary, whose commission shall continue in force for four years unless sooner revoked; he shall reside in the district, and have a freehold estate therein in 500 acres of land, while in the exercise of his office. It shall be his duty to keep and preserve the acts and laws passed by the legislature, and the public records of the district, and the proceedings of the Governor in his executive department, and transmit authentic copies of such acts and proceedings, every six months, to the secretary of Congress: There shall also be appointed a court to consist of three judges, any two of whom to form a court, who shall have a common law jurisdiction, and reside in the district, and have each therein a freehold estate in 500 acres of land while in the exercise of their offices; and their commissions shall continue in force during good behavior.

Sec. 5. The Governor and judges, or a majority of them, shall adopt and publish in the district such laws of the original states, criminal and civil, as may be necessary and best suited to the circumstances of the district, and report them to Congress from time to time: which laws shall be in force in the district until the organization of the General Assembly therein, unless disapproved of by Congress; but afterwards the Legislature shall have authority to alter them as they shall think fit.

Sec. 6. The Governor, for the time being, shall be commander in chief of the militia, appoint and commission all officers in the same below the rank of general officers; all general officers shall be appointed and commissioned by Congress.

Sec. 7. Previous to the organization of the General Assembly, the Governor shall appoint such magistrates and other civil officers in each county or township, as he shall find necessary for the preservation of the peace and good order in the same: After the General Assembly shall be organized, the powers and duties of the magistrates and other civil officers shall be regulated and defined by the said assembly; but all magistrates and other civil officers not herein otherwise directed, shall during the continuance of this temporary government, be appointed by the Governor.

Sec. 8. For the prevention of crimes and injuries, the laws to be adopted or made shall have force in all parts of the district, and for the execution of process, criminal and civil, the Governor shall make proper divisions thereof; and he shall proceed from time to time as circumstances may require, to lay out the parts of the district in which the Indian titles shall have been extinguished, into counties and townships, subject, however, to such alterations as may thereafter be made by the legislature.

Sec. 9. So soon as there shall be five thousand free male inhabitants of full age in the district, upon giving proof thereof to the Governor, they shall receive authority, with time and place, to elect a representative from their counties or townships to represent them in the General Assembly: Provided, that, for every five hundred free male inhabitants, there shall be one representative, and so on progressively with the number of free male inhabitants shall the right of representation increase, until the number of representatives shall amount to twenty-five; after which, the number and proportion of representatives shall be regulated by the legislature: Provided, that no person be eligible or qualified to act as a representative unless he shall have been a citizen of one of the United States three years, and be a resident in the district, or unless he shall have resided in the district three years; and, in either case, shall likewise hold in his own right, in fee simple, two hundred acres of land within the same; Provided, also, that a freehold in fifty acres of land in the district, having been a citizen of one of the states, and being resident in the district, or the like freehold and two years residence in the district, shall be necessary to qualify a man as an elector of a representative.

Sec. 10. The representatives thus elected, shall serve for the term of two years; and, in case of the death of a representative, or removal from office, the Governor shall issue a writ to the county or township for which he was a member, to elect another in his stead, to serve for the residue of the term.

Sec. 11. The General Assembly or legislature shall consist of the Governor, Legislative Council, and a House of Representatives. The Legislative Council shall consist of five members, to continue in office five years, unless sooner removed by Congress; any three of whom to be a quorum: and the members of the council shall be nominated and appointed in the following manner, to wit: As soon as representatives shall be elected, the Governor shall appoint a time and place for them to meet together; and, when met, they shall nominate ten persons, residents in the district, and each possessed of a freehold in five hundred acres of land, and return their names to Congress; five of whom Congress shall appoint and commission to serve as aforesaid; and, whenever a vacancy shall happen in the council, by death or removal from office, the house of representatives shall nominate two persons, qualified as aforesaid, for each vacancy, and return their names to Congress; one of whom congress shall appoint and commission for the residue of the term. And every five years, four months at least before the expiration of the time of service of the members of council, the said house shall nominate ten persons, qualified as aforesaid, and return their names to Congress; five of whom Congress shall appoint and commission to serve as members of the council five years, unless sooner removed. And the Governor, legislative council, and house of representatives, shall have authority to make laws in all cases, for the good government of the district, not repugnant to the principles and articles in this ordinance established and declared. And all bills, having passed by a majority in the house, and by a majority in the council, shall be referred to the Governor for his assent; but no bill, or legislative act whatever, shall be of any force without his assent. The Governor shall have power to convene, prorogue, and dissolve the General Assembly, when, in his opinion, it shall be expedient.

Sec. 12. The Governor, judges, legislative council, secretary, and such other officers as Congress shall appoint in the district, shall take an oath or affirmation of fidelity and of office; the Governor before the president of congress, and all other officers before the Governor. As soon as a legislature shall be formed in the district, the council and house assembled in one room, shall have authority, by joint ballot, to elect a delegate to Congress, who shall have a seat in Congress, with a right of debating but not voting during this temporary government.

Sec. 13. And, for extending the fundamental principles of civil and religious liberty, which form the basis whereon these republics, their laws and constitutions are erected; to fix and establish those principles as the basis of all laws, constitutions, and governments, which forever hereafter shall be formed in the said territory: to provide also for the establishment of states, and permanent government therein, and for their admission to a share in the federal councils on an equal footing with the original States, at as early periods as may be consistent with the general interest:

Sec. 14. It is hereby ordained and declared by the authority aforesaid, That the following articles shall be considered as articles of compact between the original States and the people and States in the said territory and forever remain unalterable, unless by common consent, to wit:

Art. 1. No person, demeaning himself in a peaceable and orderly manner, shall ever be molested on account of his mode of worship or religious sentiments, in the said territory.

Art. 2. The inhabitants of the said territory shall always be entitled to the benefits of the writ of habeas corpus, and of the trial by jury; of a proportionate representation of the people in the legislature; and of judicial proceedings according to the course of the common law. All persons shall be bailable, unless for capital offenses, where the proof shall be evident or the presumption great. All fines shall be moderate; and no cruel or unusual punishments shall be inflicted. No man shall be deprived of his liberty or property, but by the judgment of his peers or the law of the land; and, should the public exigencies make it necessary, for the common preservation, to take any person's property, or to demand his particular services, full compensation shall be made for the same. And, in the just preservation of rights and property, it is understood and declared, that no law ought ever to be made, or have force in the said territory, that shall, in any manner whatever, interfere with or affect private contracts or engagements, bona fide, and without fraud, previously formed.

Art. 3. Religion, morality, and knowledge, being necessary to good government and the happiness of mankind, schools and the means of education shall forever be encouraged. The utmost good faith shall always be observed towards the Indians; their lands and property shall never be taken from them without their consent; and, in their property, rights, and liberty, they shall never be invaded or disturbed, unless in just and lawful wars authorized by Congress; but laws founded in justice and humanity, shall from time to time be made for preventing wrongs being done to them, and for preserving peace and friendship with them.

Art. 4. The said territory, and the states which may be formed therein, shall forever remain a part of this Confederacy of the United States of America, subject to the Articles of Confederation, and to such alterations therein as shall be constitutionally made; and to all the acts and ordinances of the United States in Congress assembled, conformable thereto. The inhabitants and settlers in the said territory shall be subject to pay a part of the federal debts contracted or to be contracted, and a proportional part of the expenses of government, to be apportioned on them by Congress according to the same common rule and measure by which apportionments thereof shall be made on the other states; and the taxes for paying their proportion shall be laid and levied by the authority and direction of the legislatures of the district or districts, or new states, as in the original states, within the time agreed upon by the United States in Congress assembled. The legislatures of those districts or new states, shall never interfere with the primary disposal of the soil by the United States in Congress assembled, nor with any regulations Congress may find necessary for securing the title in such soil to the bona fide purchasers. No tax shall be imposed on lands the property of the United States; and, in no case, shall nonresident proprietors be taxed higher than residents. The navigable waters leading into the Mississippi and St. Lawrence, and the carrying places between the same, shall be common highways and forever free, as well to the inhabitants of the said territory as to the citizens of the United States, and those of any other states that may be admitted into the confederacy, without any tax, impost, or duty therefor.

Art. 5. There shall be formed in the said territory, not less than three nor more than five states; and the boundaries of the states, as soon as Virginia shall alter her act of cession, and consent to the same, shall become fixed and established as follows.... And, whenever any of the said states shall have sixty thousand free inhabitants therein, such state shall be admitted, by its delegates, into the Congress of the United States, on an equal footing with the original states in all respects whatever, and shall be at liberty to form a permanent constitution and State government: Provided, the constitution and government so to be formed, shall be republican, and in conformity to the principles contained in these articles; and, so far as it can be consistent with the general interest of the confederacy, such admission shall be allowed at an earlier period, and when there may be a less number of free inhabitants in the state than sixty thousand.

Art. 6. There shall be neither slavery nor involuntary servitude in the said territory, otherwise than in the punishment of crimes whereof the party shall have been duly convicted: Provided, always, that any person escaping into the same, from whom labor or service is lawfully claimed in any one of the original states, such fugitive may be lawfully reclaimed and conveyed to the person claiming his or her labor or service as aforesaid.

Be it ordained by the authority aforesaid, that the resolutions of the 23rd of April, 1784, relative to the subject of this ordinance, be, and the same are hereby repealed and declared null and void.

Done by the United States, in Congress assembled, the 13th day of July, in the year of our Lord 1787, and of their sovereignty and independence the twelfth.

Document Questions

1. What is remarkable about Section 2 of the Ordinance?

    It is the first federal measure to explicitly abolish the practice of primogeniture, as regards the distribution of property in inheritance. In the Old World, primogeniture had meant that the first-born son would inherit all of the father's property. This would not be permitted in the more egalitarian environment of the new American nation.

2. Where do you see Daniel Boorstin's "add a state plan" idea in this document?

    Several of the six articles in Section 14 make it clear that the new states to be formed out of the Territory are to enter the union on an equal footing with the already existing states.

3. What does the Ordinance have to say about slavery?

    Article 6 forbids the introduction of slavery and involuntary servitude in the territory. It does, however, respect the legitimacy of fugitive slave laws.

4. What about education?

    "Schools and the means of education shall forever be encouraged." It is notable that the Ordinance connects schooling with the cultivation of "religion, morality, and knowledge, being necessary to good government and the happiness of mankind."

5. What about the treatment of the native population?

    "The utmost good faith shall always be observed towards the Indians; their lands and property shall never be taken from them without their consent; and, in their property, rights, and liberty, they shall never be invaded or disturbed, unless in just and lawful wars authorized by Congress; but laws founded in justice and humanity, shall from time to time be made for preventing wrongs being done to them, and for preserving peace and friendship with them."

6. And religious liberty?

> The "fundamental principles of civil and religious liberty" are established as "the basis of all laws, constitutions, and governments." Article 1 insists that "no person … shall ever be molested on account of his mode of worship or religious sentiments."

Special Unit

TEACHING THE BILL OF RIGHTS

Teachers may find the following amendment-by-amendment explication and commentary on the Bill of Rights helpful for classroom, study, or testing use.

First Amendment: Congress shall make no law respecting an establishment of religion, or prohibiting the free exercise thereof; or abridging the freedom of speech, or of the press; or the right of the people peaceably to assemble, and to petition the Government for a redress of grievances.

> Begin by calling students' attention to the curious phrasing: "Congress shall make no law …" Congress is forbidden from doing its basic and principal function – legislating, or making laws – with respect to religion, speech, the press, assembly, or petitioning for redress of grievances. Ask students if the First Amendment establishes freedom of speech. If they say yes, ask them to quote the exact wording that does that – which they cannot.
>
> The implication is that these freedoms already exist; Congress is simply prohibited from abridging them. Teachers may explain that the idea of "natural rights" is explicit in both the Declaration of Independence and the First Amendment. That is, freedom of thought and expression is a natural right, derived (in Judeo-Christian terms) from all humans being created in God's image, or (in Enlightenment terms) from all humans possessing the ability to reason. Governments do not create natural rights (which exist before government) but are formed via the social contract to protect them. Governments may be changed or even overthrown if they fail to protect natural rights.
>
> ("Civil rights," such as voting and "due process," are not natural rights but are granted by government; without an existing political system, there would be no elections and so no such thing as voting, and no laws to administer fairly, and so no such thing as "due process.")

The First Amendment begins by prohibiting Congress from legislating about "an establishment of religion." Massachusetts and several other states at that time had established churches. ("Established" means government approved and supported by taxes.) The First Amendment had no effect on these; it only prevented Congress from establishing a national church. Massachusetts did not disestablish the Congregational Church until 1833.

Teachers may ask, when is everyone in favor of minority rights? The answer is, when everyone is in a minority. If everyone is divided into two groups, one will be the majority. But if people are divided among three or more groups, it is likely that each will be a minority. Back in Britain, neither Anglicans (members of the established Church of England) nor Presbyterians nor Congregationalists believed in religious toleration; each wanted to be the only established church, and they fought a very bloody series of three-sided wars between 1639 and 1649 about it. But in America, none of the three was dominant nationally, and other groups, such as the Baptists, were growing. So religious toleration was everyone's fallback position.

The First Amendment now applies to states as well as to Congress, as a result of the "incorporation" of rights by the Fourteenth Amendment, which begins "No state shall make or enforce any law which shall abridge the privileges or immunities of citizens of the United States; nor shall any state deprive any person of life, liberty, or property, without due process of law; nor deny to any person within its jurisdiction the equal protection of the laws."

The second half of the religion clause is that Congress shall make no law "prohibiting the free exercise thereof." Until the Anglican Church was disestablished in Virginia (1783), it controlled who could and could not preach; a Baptist, for example, might be arrested and jailed for preaching without the permission of the local Anglican priest. These issues would be resolved state by state, because Congress was denied any power to legislate on them.

Teachers may ask students whether there is a constitutional right to travel; assure them that there is, and ask them to cite the precise language. It is necessary to travel in order to "assemble." Events such as Martin Luther King Jr.'s March on Washington are explicitly protected, both as peaceable assemblies and as occasions for petitioning for redress of grievances.

Second Amendment: A well regulated Militia, being necessary to the security of a free State, the right of the people to keep and bear Arms, shall not be infringed.

The militia was, and remains today, the body of the people, under arms. Each state had its own militia laws, which varied as to details, but in general, every free adult male was considered part of the militia. In Virginia, the most populous state, the militia was composed of all free men between the ages of sixteen and fifty. Exemptions were granted to a very few categories, such as ministers and millers (upon whose work all depended). Free blacks were included in the militia, but in unarmed roles, such as musicians. The militia was commanded by the county lieutenant (the governor's deputy) and under the authority of the county court martial, comprising the higher-ranking militia officers. Militia companies mustered monthly, typically on a Sunday afternoon after church. Men were required to have a firearm and necessary ammunition and might be ordered to fire a round or two to demonstrate that everything worked. Men without weapons were fined unless they could prove indigence, in which case they might be equipped by the county from funds provided by the fines of others – and would then have to show at each muster that they still had possession of the county's weapon. The militia were not trained, nor were they equipped (e.g., with bayonets) to fight as regular troops in a formal battle, but they were effective in enforcing the laws and protecting against threats like Indian or pirate raids and slave uprisings.

The revolutionary generation was deeply suspicious of standing armies that might be instruments of coercion by a tyrannical king. The militia was weaker militarily but far more trustworthy in a political and social sense. It was also locally controlled. During the Revolutionary War, the militia was often ineffective against professional troops, but it controlled everywhere, except in the immediate vicinity of the British army, allowing the Patriots to draw recruits and supplies and political legitimacy from the population.

Note that the phrase "the right of the people" appears in the First, Second, and Fourth Amendments and presumably carries the same meaning in all three. In the context of the militia, the keeping and bearing of arms was not only a right of the people but an individual duty and legal obligation.

U.S. law today, as defined by the Militia Act of 1903, recognizes two categories of militia: the organized militia consists of state militia forces, notably, the National Guard and Naval Militia; and the unorganized militia consists of every able-bodied man of at least seventeen years and under forty-five years of age who is not a member of the National Guard or Naval Militia.

Third Amendment: No Soldier shall, in time of peace be quartered in any house, without the consent of the Owner, nor in time of war, but in a manner to be prescribed by law.

This was a major grievance among the colonists in places such as Boston, where prominent citizens had been subjected to the indignity of losing the right to control over their own homes and been forced to accept unruly and uncouth British enlisted soldiers in their dwellings.

Fourth Amendment: The right of the people to be secure in their persons, houses, papers, and effects, against unreasonable searches and seizures, shall not be violated, and no Warrants shall issue, but upon probable cause, supported by Oath or affirmation, and particularly describing the place to be searched, and the persons or things to be seized.

British practice was to issue "writs of assistance" requiring all loyal subjects to help a customs inspector search for contraband. No limits were placed on where the search might look. The Fourth Amendment requires a judicial warrant that is specific both as to place and object of the search.

Fifth Amendment: No person shall be held to answer for a capital, or otherwise infamous crime, unless on a presentment or indictment of a Grand Jury, except in cases arising in the land or naval forces, or in the Militia, when in actual service in time of War or public danger; nor shall any person be subject for the same offence to be twice put in jeopardy of life or limb; nor shall be compelled in any criminal case to be a witness against himself, nor be deprived of life, liberty, or property, without due process of law; nor shall private property be taken for public use, without just compensation.

This long amendment prohibits several types of government mischief with which the colonists were familiar. The function of a grand jury is to determine that a crime has in fact been committed, before individual guilt or innocence is determined. Most students will be familiar with "taking the Fifth" and not testifying against oneself. "Due process" covers a number of basic requirements of fairness; for example, governments must notify individuals before, say, seizing their property for nonpayment of taxes. And governments are allowed to take private property under eminent domain (e.g., to build a highway), but the owner must be paid a fair price.

Sixth Amendment: In all criminal prosecutions, the accused shall enjoy the right to a speedy and public trial, by an impartial jury of the State and district wherein the crime shall have been committed, which district shall have been previously ascertained by law, and to be informed of the nature and cause of the accusation; to be confronted with the witnesses against him; to have compulsory process for obtaining witnesses in his favor, and to have the Assistance of Counsel for his defence.

Thanks to television crime and courtroom dramas, most students will be familiar with these rights of the accused. Teachers may note that equally valid and important rights may sometimes come into conflict, for example, the freedom of the press to report on a scandalous crime may impact the right of the accused to a speedy and public trial by an impartial jury of the district in which the crime has been committed. It is the responsibility of the trial judge to balance these conflicting rights.

Seventh Amendment: In Suits at common law, where the value in controversy shall exceed twenty dollars, the right of trial by jury shall be preserved, and no fact tried by a jury, shall be otherwise re-examined in any Court of the United States, than according to the rules of the common law.

The common law is English jury-made law. For example, a common law principle is that one cannot be convicted of a criminal trespass if done to save a life – you can break into a locked building or jump over someone's fence around a pond if someone is in danger of burning to death or drowning. Enough juries refused to convict in such circumstances that it became a generally recognized legal principle. English common law is valid in every state, except Louisiana (which uses the French Code Napoleon), and applies unless there is a statute (a law passed by the legislature) to the contrary.

Juries, typically twelve citizens chosen at random who must all agree on a verdict, embody the sovereign "We the People" in a particular case. The only higher authority above a jury fact-finding is the common law, which is based on the precedents of previous juries. (Judges instruct juries as to the law, but juries can and do, in extraordinary circumstances, refuse to convict despite what the law says; that is where the common law comes from.)

Eighth Amendment: Excessive bail shall not be required, nor excessive fines imposed, nor cruel and unusual punishments inflicted.

It is up to the courts to determine what is excessive, or "cruel and unusual."

Ninth Amendment: The enumeration in the Constitution, of certain rights, shall not be construed to deny or disparage others retained by the people.

When the Anti-Federalists demanded a Bill of Rights, the Federalists quibbled that listing some rights might imply that there were no others. This fixes that.

Tenth Amendment: The powers not delegated to the United States by the Constitution, nor prohibited by it to the States, are reserved to the States respectively, or to the people.

Powers reserved to the states include establishing local governments; issuing licenses (driver, hunting, marriage, etc.); regulating intrastate (within the state) commerce; conducting elections; ratifying amendments to the U.S. Constitution; and maintaining the "police power," which is generally providing for public health and safety.

Note that states conduct all elections, including those for U.S. senators and members of Congress, and the Electoral College that chooses the president. The United States has in effect fifty-one different political systems, as election laws vary from state to state.

The people are the repository of all power, which they grant, in part and on a temporary basis, to various governments through constitutions.

CHAPTER FIVE

THE EXPERIMENT BEGINS

Summary

The preservation of the sacred fire of liberty, and the destiny of the Republican model of Government, are justly considered as deeply, perhaps as finally staked on, the experiment entrusted to the hands of the American people.

GEORGE WASHINGTON

FOR THE NEW U. S. CONSTITUTION to become the supreme law of the land, it would have to be ratified by the states – and the outcome of the ratification process was far from certain. The fierce debates that surrounded the ratification process reflected the different political views and expressions between the Federalists and the Anti-Federalists. The Federalists strongly supported implementation of the new Constitution with a centralized national government. The Anti-Federalists, on the other hand, distrusted the Constitution's concentration of power in a national government (especially the presidency). The Anti-Federalists favored retaining the Articles' loose and decentralized approach to government, in which the states retained most of their sovereignty.

Alexander Hamilton, John Jay, and James Madison wrote eighty-five articles in support of ratification and a centralized government over a ten-month period beginning in October 1787. Published serially in New York newspapers under the collective pen name of Publius, the papers making up *The Federalist* are still regarded as the best account of the Constitution as the Framers intended and understood it.

In the end, the states ratified the U.S. Constitution. But the Anti-Federalists left their mark too. Fearing the possibility of tyranny and the abuse of fundamental rights and liberties that might result from an overly powerful central government, they insisted upon a Bill of Rights being added to the U.S. Constitution during the First Congress, which was adopted by the states in 1791. It is impossible to imagine the Constitution without these amendments, which emerged out of the often fierce debates between Federalists and Anti-Federalists.

George Washington was unanimously elected to serve as the first president on April 6, 1789. In establishing his cabinet, Washington selected Thomas Jefferson as secretary of state, Alexander Hamilton as secretary of the treasury, General Henry Knox as secretary of war, and Edmund Randolph as the first attorney general.

Faced with a fragile economy, the vigorous and inventive Hamilton proposed a three-part plan for bringing America's finances into healthy order and growing its economy. First, the national government would pay off all national debt at face value and would assume all war debts on behalf of the states. Second, high tariffs would be imposed on imported goods, protecting the development of American industries. Third, Congress would create a national bank for storage of government funds and printing of bank notes, providing a basis for a stable U.S. currency.

All initiatives were adopted, though not without controversy, for they opened up the philosophical differences between Hamilton and Jefferson. Jefferson favored a decentralized republican form of government that would oversee a society mainly inhabited by small, self-sufficient farmers. Hamilton, on the other hand, supported urban commercial interests and sought to expand the economy through extensive trade and manufacturing and use of a powerful, active central government.

After two terms, Washington stepped down as president, and when he delivered his Farewell Address on September 17, 1796, the underlying theme was the need for national unity. His vice president, John Adams, won the 1796 election for the presidency but suffered the misfortune of following in George Washington's footsteps and being subject to constant comparison. Adams erred in supporting the Alien and Sedition Acts of 1798, authorizing the president to expel "dangerous" aliens at his pleasure and severely limiting freedom of speech and acts. In response to Adams's actions, Jefferson and Madison drafted the equally rash Kentucky and Virginia Resolutions, proclaiming the right of states to interpose or nullify acts of the federal government. In the midst of all this turmoil came George Washington's death in December 1799, serving as a somber reminder of the heroic role he played in America's fragile beginnings and raising questions about whether those who succeeded him would be up to the challenges of national leadership.

In 1800, Thomas Jefferson won the fiercely contested presidential election, a victory that marked a change in the nation's political direction – the first transfer of power between competing parties in the nation's history. And yet the "Revolution of 1800" proved to be a step toward unification and maturation of the fledgling republic. Indeed, the generous tone of Jefferson's inaugural address delivered in the new capital city of Washington, D.C., was one of humility and conciliation.

Questions and Answers

1. Of the fourteen individuals named in this chapter, seven are pictured or alluded to in the book's inserted picture gallery: Washington, Jefferson, Madison, Hamilton, the Adamses, and L'Enfant's plan for the capital city. Have students study the material there about each of them.

2. Of the remaining eight, one (Flexner) is a modern biographer, and one (Tallyrand) was a foreign diplomat. Which two of the remaining five (Jay, Henry, Knox, Randolph, and Burr) were most important in their impact on the new nation? Be prepared to defend your selections in class or in writing.

> All were roughly of the same importance, secondary to those pictured but still making significant contributions. Knox and Randolph were the other members of Washington's first cabinet, alongside Hamilton and Jefferson, and so would be good choices.

3. Consult a reference source about Aaron Burr and write a paragraph describing his relationships with Thomas Jefferson and with Alexander Hamilton.

> Each of the three hated the other two. Burr betrayed Jefferson in the election of 1800, and Hamilton threw his support to Jefferson on grounds that Burr was a scoundrel but Jefferson was merely a fool and would do less damage. Burr later killed Hamilton in a duel. Jefferson later put Burr on trial for treason and would have hanged him had not Chief Justice John Marshall blocked it.

4. How was the U.S. Constitution ratified? Why was this important? (p. 74)

> It bypassed the state legislatures, which had a vested interest in keeping their autonomy under the Articles, and instead appealed directly to the people, through popularly elected delegates to state ratification conventions.

5. The Federalists of 1787–88 were really nationalists favoring a strong central government, an unpopular idea. So they called themselves Federalists, which *was* a popular idea. (A federal system is one in which power is divided among the central and the various state governments.) Then (it was Hamilton's idea) they brilliantly labeled their opponents *Anti*-Federalists, even though the Articles of Confederation had also created a federal union, though with more power in the states and less at the center than the Constitution. That is, both sides believed in a federal system with a central government and states retaining significant powers; what then was the "persistent tension" that divided the Federalists and Anti-Federalists and that persists to this day? (p. 75)

> *How* powerful is the central authority to be in relation to the states? And in particular, how may states respond when the central government does something unjust?

6. Who wrote *The Federalist* (or *The Federalist Papers*)? Why are they classics? Where were they first published, and what does this suggest about the state of public debate today? (p. 75)

> James Madison, Alexander Hamilton, and John Jay wrote them. All were brilliant men, and their analysis of the new Constitution is masterful. They were published in the New York City newspapers to sway public opinion, demonstrating that voters two hundred years ago were better readers, and much more thoughtful, than they are today.

7. According to *Federalist* 10, what is the cure for the problem of factions? (p. 76)

> Prevent majority factions by making the republic as large and diverse as possible. This reversed the historical understanding that republics were only suitable for small, homogeneous states.

8. According to *Federalist* 51, what protects the rights of the people? (p. 76)

> Checks and balances protect their rights: "ambition must counteract ambition."

9. What view of human nature does the Constitution rest on? (p. 76)

> It rests on the view that human nature is inherently fallible or corrupted; men are not to be trusted, particularly when it comes to the exercise of unchecked power.

10. Why is the writing and ratification of the U.S. Constitution an important event in world history? (pp. 76–77)

It exemplified the idea that governments need not be created accidentally or by the strongest but can be constructed by rational deliberation for the benefit of all.

11. What did the Anti-Federalists contribute to the outcome of this struggle? (p. 77)

They insisted on, and got, the Bill of Rights.

12. Why is the irony of the opponents of the Constitution contributing so greatly to its success "not as ironic as it might seem"? (p. 78)

The Constitution was explicitly designed to harness competing ideas and energies.

13. What remained to be done when Washington was sworn in as the first president? Why did Flexner call him "the indispensable man"? Why did Washington agonize over every decision? (pp. 79–80)

Every sort of procedure had to be worked out, and Washington knew that from that point on, every president would tend automatically to do things the way Washington had done them. Washington was indispensable because he was trusted; he had rejected opportunities to act corruptly, for his own power, so people relied on him to be honorable.

14. What was Washington's attitude toward political parties? Who was in his first cabinet? (p. 80)

He disliked parties, considering them "factions." He deliberately chose two brilliant men who disagreed on almost everything, Hamilton as secretary of the treasury and Jefferson as secretary of state (handling foreign policy). Secretary of war was Knox, and attorney general was Edmund Randolph. (Randolph was an ally of Jefferson and Knox an ally of Hamilton.) Washington wanted both sides well represented as policy was debated and decided.

15. What were the three main elements of Hamilton's financial plan? How well did each succeed?

Hamilton wanted the United States to assume responsibility for state war debts, wanted a revenue tariff, and wanted a national bank. All three were successful.

16. What was the debate over the creation of the national bank? (pp. 81–82)

The Constitution limits the powers of Congress, and chartering a corporation (the bank) is not listed. Hamilton argued that a bank was a "necessary and proper" means of carrying out constitutional duties like borrowing money. Jefferson argued that this "elastic clause" would give the government unlimited power. Washington agreed with Hamilton, and the First Bank of the United States was chartered for twenty years.

17. Be able to write a detailed description of the rival views of Hamilton and Jefferson. Include their visions for what sort of republic the United States should be and how it should be governed. Be sure to include their views on foreign policy and world affairs. (pp. 82–83)

Hamilton admired the British system and wanted to make America as much like it as possible. Jefferson initially admired the French Revolution – though he was repulsed by the Reign of Terror – and viewed Britain as corrupt and not as an example to be followed. Hamilton looked east, across the Atlantic, and aspired to make the United States a powerful member in the world of European states; Jefferson looked west, eschewing large cities and manufacturing in favor of independent, small farmers. Hamilton thought the U.S. government under the Constitution was too weak and worked to strengthen it; Jefferson feared it was too strong and worked to hold it in check (except when he was president!).

18. Teachers should help students understand that the wars of the French Revolution and Napoleon (1791–1815, almost without interruption) meant a worldwide war between the two superpowers, the British and French Empires. The United States was very small and weak in comparison, yet it could not avoid involvement. This conflict dominated both world and U.S. history until Napoleon's final defeat in 1815. Because the French army was dominant on land while the British Royal Navy was dominant at sea, the war was "an elephant against a whale." Neither side could win a decisive victory, and so the war lasted decades. Also, both sides turned to economic warfare, which entailed restricting U.S. shipping.

19. What was Washington's policy regarding the wars in Europe? Why was this both necessary and unpopular, as exemplified in the Jay Treaty? (pp. 83–84)

Washington held to a strict policy of neutrality. The United States had many grievances against the British, still, and technically was still allied to France. But the United States was far too weak to get involved in the wars, and a bad treaty like Jay's was better than risking conflict.

20. How bitter and intense did party conflict become during the 1790s? Why? (pp. 84–85)

> Neither side believed in parties; each viewed itself as representing the people and the rival party as a wicked faction needing to be destroyed. Political passions were intense and bitter, and each side used personal attacks to discredit the other.

21. Why is Washington's Farewell Address an American classic? What rule did it lay down for the United States' relationships with other countries? (p. 85)

> Washington stressed national unity and warned of "entangling alliances."

22. Why was John Adams's presidency so contentious? Who was Adams's vice president? (This is the best evidence that the Philadelphia convention neither wanted nor anticipated political parties.) (p. 86)

> The original Constitution made no allowance for parties; the winner in the Electoral College became president, and the runner-up became vice president. Adams defeated Jefferson in the 1796 election, and Jefferson became vice president. Adams had to deal with the same issues as Washington, without Washington's charisma or prestige, and in the face of bitter opposition from the Jeffersonians. The worst crisis was an undeclared naval war with France.

23. What was the XYZ Affair? How did it lead to the Alien and Sedition Acts? How did those lead to the Virginia and Kentucky Resolutions? (pp. 87–88)

> Adams attempted to negotiate an end to hostilities with France, but the French insulted the U.S. diplomats, demanding bribes for themselves (X, Y, and Z). Adams published the insult, and Congress passed acts restricting immigration and criticism of the government. (Several Jeffersonian newspaper editors were imprisoned under the Sedition Act.) Jefferson and Madison responded with resolutions passed by the Virginia and Kentucky legislatures condemning the acts as unconstitutional and threatening intervention by the states to protect their citizens from tyranny. This is the origin of the idea of nullification.

24. What was the state of the public press (newspapers) in the 1790s? (p. 87)

> Newspapers were "a veritable flood of wild fabrications and misrepresentations" attacking the other party.

25. How did each party portray its opponent during the election of 1800?

> The Federalists painted their opponents as wild-eyed Jacobins, atheists, and bloody-minded radicals; the Jeffersonians portrayed the Federalists as cryptomonarchists and would-be aristocrats – enemies of liberty.

26. How did it happen that Hamilton was responsible for the election of his arch-rival Jefferson? Why was the Twelfth Amendment necessary after 1796 and 1800? (pp. 88–89)

> Jefferson and his running mate, Aaron Burr, won, but they failed to make provision for Burr to get one less vote in the EC. So Jefferson and Burr tied for president, Burr refused to step back, and the election went to the House of Representatives, where each state gets one vote. The Federalists had lost the election but still controlled enough states to decide between Jefferson and Burr. Hamilton used his influence to elect Jefferson on the grounds that he would do less harm than Burr. The Twelfth Amendment provided for the current system, in which electors vote separately for president and vice president; each party nominates both to run together as a pair.

27. What was "revolutionary" about the "Revolution of 1800"? (pp. 89–90)

> Power was transferred peacefully to an opposing party.

28. How did Jefferson address the nation in his First Inaugural? What did Jefferson change, and what did he leave, of Hamilton's plan after he gained power in 1800?

> The winner, Jefferson, went out of his way to be conciliatory; "we are all federalists, we are all republicans." Jefferson had to keep Hamilton's financial plan to pay off the war debts, as it had been in operation more than ten years, and too many people had planned on it. He did reduce spending to try to retire the remaining debt faster.

29. How did L'Enfant's layout of Washington, D.C., shape its development as a city? (pp. 91–92)

> L'Enfant created space for parks and gardens and public buildings, a future focal point for an emerging nationalism.

Answers are in parentheses.

Put in order:

    ____ Hamilton and Jefferson debate the national bank   (3)
    ____ The Constitution is ratified   (1)
    ____ Washington is sworn in as first president   (2)

Put in order:

    ____ Alien and Sedition Acts   (2)
    ____ Virginia and Kentucky Resolutions   (3)
    ____ XYZ Affair   (1)

Matching: (*author to document*)

    ____ Declaration of Independence   (D)   A. Alexander Hamilton
    ____ *Federalist Papers*   (A) and (B)   B. James Madison
    ____ U.S. Constitution   (B)   C. John Adams
                                                     D. Thomas Jefferson

Document 1

JAMES MADISON, *FEDERALIST* 10

Among the numerous advantages promised by a well-constructed union, none deserves to be more accurately developed, than its tendency to break and control the violence of faction. The friend of popular governments, never finds himself so much alarmed for their character and fate, as when he contemplates their propensity to this dangerous vice. He will not fail, therefore, to set a due value on any plan which, without violating the principles to which he is attached, provides a proper cure for it.... Complaints are everywhere heard from our most considerate and virtuous citizens, equally the friends of public and private faith, and of public and personal liberty, that our governments are too unstable; that the public good is disregarded in the conflicts of rival parties; and that measures are too often decided, not according to the rules of justice, and the rights of the minor party, but by the superior force of an interested and overbearing majority. However anxiously we may wish that these complaints had no foundation, the evidence of known facts will not permit us to deny that they are in some degree true....

By a faction, I understand a number of citizens, whether amounting to a majority or minority of the whole, who are united and actuated by some common impulse of passion, or of interest, adverse to the rights of other citizens, or to the permanent and aggregate interests of the community.

There are two methods of curing the mischiefs of faction: The one, by removing its causes; the other, by controlling its effects.

There are again two methods of removing the causes of faction: The one, by destroying the liberty which is essential to its existence; the other, by giving to every citizen the same opinions, the same passions, and the same interests.

It could never be more truly said, than of the first remedy, that it is worse than the disease. Liberty is to faction, what air is to fire, an element, without which it instantly expires. But it could not be a less folly to abolish liberty, which is essential to political life, because it nourishes faction, than it would be to wish the annihilation of air, which is essential to animal life, because it imparts to fire its destructive agency.

The second expedient is as impracticable, as the first would be unwise. As long as the reason of man continues fallible, and he is at liberty to exercise it, different opinions will be formed. As long as the connection subsists between his reason and his self-love, his opinions and his passions will have a reciprocal influence on each other; and the former will be objects to which the latter will attach themselves. The diversity in the faculties of men, from which the rights of property originate, is not less an insuperable obstacle to an uniformity of interests. The protection of these faculties, is the first object of government. From the protection of different and unequal faculties of acquiring property, the possession of different degrees and kinds of property immediately results; and from the influence of these on the sentiments and views of the respective proprietors, ensues a division of the society into different interests and parties.

The latent causes of faction are thus sown in the nature of man; and we see them everywhere brought into different degrees of activity, according to the different circumstances of civil society. A zeal for different opinions concerning religion, concerning government, and many other points, as well of speculation as of practice ... have, in turn, divided mankind into parties, inflamed them with mutual animosity, and rendered them much more disposed to vex and oppress each other, than to co-operate for their common good. So strong is this propensity of mankind, to fall into mutual animosities, that where no substantial occasion presents itself, the most frivolous and fanciful distinctions have been sufficient to kindle their unfriendly passions, and excite their most violent conflicts. But the most common and durable source of factions, has been the various and unequal distribution of property. Those who hold, and those who are without property, have ever formed distinct interests in society.... The regulation of these various and interfering interests, forms the principal task of modern legislation, and involves the spirit of party and faction in the necessary and ordinary operations of government....

It is in vain to say, that enlightened statesmen will be able to adjust these clashing interests, and render them all subservient to the public good. Enlightened statesmen will not always be at the helm: nor, in many cases, can such an adjustment be made at all, without taking into view indirect and remote considerations, which will rarely prevail over the immediate interest which one party may find in disregarding the rights of another, or the good of the whole.

The inference to which we are brought, is, that the causes of faction cannot be removed; and that relief is only to be sought in the means of controlling its effects.

If a faction consists of less than a majority, relief is supplied by the republican principle, which enables the majority to defeat its sinister views, by regular vote. It may clog the administration, it may convulse the society; but it will be unable to execute and mask its violence under the forms of the constitution. When a majority is included in a faction, the form of popular government, on the other hand, enables it to sacrifice to its ruling passion or interest, both the public good and the rights of other citizens. To secure the public good, and private rights, against the danger of such a faction, and at the same time to preserve the spirit and the form of popular government, is then the great object to which our inquiries are directed....

By what means is this object attainable? Evidently by one of two only. Either the existence of the same passion or interest in a majority, at the same time, must be prevented; or the majority, having such co-existent passion or interest, must be rendered, by their number and local situation, unable to concert and carry into effect schemes of oppression. If the impulse and the opportunity be suffered to coincide, we well know, that neither moral nor religious motives can be relied on as an adequate control. They are not found to be such on the injustice and violence of individuals, and lose their efficacy in proportion to the number combined together; that is, in proportion as their efficacy becomes needful....

A republic, by which I mean a government in which the scheme of representation takes place ... promises the cure for which we are seeking. Let us examine the points in which it varies from pure democracy, and we shall comprehend both the nature of the cure and the efficacy which it must derive from the union.

The two great points of difference, between a democracy and a republic, are, first, the delegation of the government, in the latter, to a small number of citizens elected by the rest; secondly, the greater number of citizens, and greater sphere of country, over which the latter may be extended.

The effect of the first difference is, on the one hand, to refine and enlarge the public views, by passing them through the medium of a chosen body of citizens, whose wisdom may best discern the true interest of their country, and whose patriotism and love of justice, will be least likely to sacrifice it to temporary or partial considerations. Under such a regulation, it may well happen, that the public voice, pronounced by the representatives of the people, will be more consonant to the public good, than if pronounced by the people themselves, convened for the purpose. On the other hand, the effect may be inverted. Men of factious tempers, of local prejudices, or of sinister designs, may by intrigue, by corruption, or by other means, first obtain the suffrages, and then betray the interests of the people. The question resulting is, whether small or extensive republics are most favorable to the election of proper guardians of the public weal; and it is clearly decided in favor of the latter by two obvious considerations.

In the first place, it is to be remarked, that however small the republic may be, the representatives must be raised to a certain number, in order to guard against the cabals of a few; and that, however large it may be, they must be limited to a certain number, in order to guard against the confusion of a multitude. Hence, the number of representatives in the two cases not being in proportion to that of the constituents, and being proportionally greatest in the small republic, it follows, that if the proportion of fit characters be not less in the large than in the small republic, the former will present a greater option, and consequently a greater probability of a fit choice.

In the next place, as each representative will be chosen by a greater number of citizens in the large than in the small republic, it will be more difficult for unworthy candidates to practice with success the vicious arts, by which elections are too often carried; and the suffrages of the people being more free, will be more likely to center in men who possess the most attractive merit, and the most diffusive and established characters.

It must be confessed, that in this, as in most other cases, there is a mean, on both sides of which inconveniences will be found to lie. By enlarging too much the number of electors, you render the representative too little acquainted with all their local circumstances and lesser interests; as by reducing it too much, you render him unduly attached to these, and too little fit to comprehend and pursue great and national objects. The federal constitution forms a happy combination in this respect; the great and aggregate interests, being referred to the national, the local and particular to the state legislatures.

The other point of difference is, the greater number of citizens, and extent of territory, which may be brought within the compass of republican, than of democratic government; and it is this circumstance principally which renders factious combinations less to be dreaded in the former, than in the latter. The smaller the society, the fewer probably will be the distinct parties and interests composing it; the fewer the distinct parties and interests, the more frequently will a majority be found of the same party; and the smaller the number of individuals composing a majority, and the smaller the compass within which they are placed, the more easily will they concert and execute their plans of oppression. Extend the sphere, and you take in a greater variety of parties and interests; you make it less probable that a majority of the whole will have a common motive to invade the rights of other citizens; or if such a common motive exists, it will be more difficult for all who feel it to discover their own strength, and to act in unison with each other. Besides other impediments, it may be remarked, that where there is a consciousness of unjust or dishonorable purposes, communication is always checked by distrust, in proportion to the number whose concurrence is necessary.

Hence it clearly appears, that the same advantage, which a republic has over a democracy, in controlling the effects of faction, is enjoyed by a large over a small republic, – is enjoyed by the union over the states composing it.…

In the extent and proper structure of the union, therefore, we behold a republican remedy for the diseases most incident to republican government. And according to the degree of pleasure and pride we feel in being republicans, ought to be our zeal in cherishing the spirit, and supporting the character of federalists.

Source: https://teachingamericanhistory.org/library/document/federalist-no-10/

Document 1 Questions

1. What does Madison mean by a "faction"?

"A number of citizens, whether amounting to a majority or minority of the whole, who are united and actuated by some common impulse of passion, or of interest, adverse to the rights of other citizens, or to the permanent and aggregate interests of the community."

2. What are the two methods of curing faction? Why are they undesirable or impossible?

The two methods are destroying liberty and imposing the same opinions on all people. But "liberty is to faction, what air is to fire," and differences of opinion are an inevitable result of the "diversity in the faculties of men." Neither cure can work without destroying the patient.

3. What then is to be concluded about faction?

> "That the causes of faction cannot be removed; and that relief is only to be sought in the means of controlling its effects."

4. How does Madison distinguish between a republic and a democracy?

> "The two great points of difference, between a democracy and a republic, are, first, the delegation of the government, in the latter, to a small number of citizens elected by the rest; secondly, the greater number of citizens, and greater sphere of country, over which the latter may be extended."

5. Why does "extending the sphere" offer relief from the problem of faction?

> "Extend the sphere, and you take in a greater variety of parties and interests; you make it less probable that a majority of the whole will have a common motive to invade the rights of other citizens; or if such a common motive exists, it will be more difficult for all who feel it to discover their own strength, and to act in unison with each other."

Document 2

ROBERT YATES, *BRUTUS* I

The first question that presents itself on the subject is, whether a confederated government be the best for the United States or not? Or in other words, whether the thirteen United States should be reduced to one great republic, governed by one legislature, and under the direction of one executive and judicial; or whether they should continue thirteen confederated republics, under the direction and control of a supreme federal head for certain defined national purposes only?

This enquiry is important, because, although the government reported by the convention does not go to a perfect and entire consolidation, yet it approaches so near to it, that it must, if executed, certainly and infallibly terminate in it.

This government is to possess absolute and uncontrollable power, legislative, executive and judicial, with respect to every object to which it extends, for by the last clause of section 8th, article Ist, it is declared "that the Congress shall have power to make all laws which shall be necessary and proper for carrying into execution the foregoing powers, and all other powers vested by this constitution, in the government of the United States; or in any department or office thereof." And by the 6th article, it is declared "that this constitution, and the laws of the United States, which shall be made in pursuance thereof, and the treaties made, or which shall be made, under the authority of the United States, shall be the supreme law of the land; and the judges in every state shall be bound thereby, any thing in the constitution, or law of any state to the contrary notwithstanding." It appears from these articles that there is no need of any intervention of the state governments, between the Congress and the people, to execute any one power vested in the general government, and that the constitution and laws of every state are nullified and declared void, so far as they are or shall be inconsistent with this constitution, or the laws made in pursuance of it, or with treaties made under the authority of the United States. The government then, so far as it extends, is a complete one, and not a confederation. It is as much one complete government as that of New-York or Massachusetts, has as absolute and perfect powers to make and execute all laws, to appoint officers, institute courts, declare offences, and annex penalties, with respect to every object to which it extends, as any other in the world. So far therefore as its powers reach, all ideas of confederation are given up and lost.

... It has authority to make laws which will affect the lives, the liberty, and property of every man in the United States; nor can the constitution or laws of any state, in any way prevent or impede the full and complete execution of every power given. The legislative power is competent to lay taxes, duties, imposts, and excises; there is no limitation to this power, unless it be said that the clause which directs the use to which those taxes, and duties shall be applied, may be said to be a limitation; but this is no restriction of the power at all, for by this clause they are to be applied to pay the debts and provide for the common defense and general welfare of the United States; but the legislature have authority to contract debts at their discretion; they are the sole judges of what is necessary to provide for the common defense, and they only are to determine what is for the general welfare: this power therefore is neither more nor less, than a power to lay and collect taxes, imposts, and excises, at their pleasure.... In the business therefore of laying and collecting taxes, the idea of confederation is totally lost, and that of one entire republic is embraced. It is proper here to remark, that the authority to lay and collect taxes is the most important of any power that can be granted; it connects with it almost all other powers, or at least will in process of time draw all other after it; it is the great mean of protection, security, and defense, in a good government, and the great engine of oppression and tyranny in a bad one....

The judicial power of the United States is to be vested in a supreme court, and in such inferior courts as Congress may from time to time ordain and establish. The powers of these courts are very extensive; their jurisdiction comprehends all civil causes, except such as arise between citizens of the same state; and it extends to all cases in law and equity arising under the constitution. One inferior court must be established, I presume, in each state at least, with the necessary executive officers appendant thereto. It is easy to see, that in the common course of things, these courts will eclipse the dignity, and take away from the respectability, of the state courts. These courts will be, in themselves, totally independent of the states, deriving their authority from the United States, and receiving from them fixed salaries; and in the course of human events it is to be expected, that they will swallow up all the powers of the courts in the respective states.

How far the clause in the 8th section of the Ist article may operate to do away all idea of confederated states, and to effect an entire consolidation of the whole into one general government, it is impossible to say. The powers given by this article are very general and comprehensive, and it may receive a construction to justify the passing almost any law. A power to make all laws, which shall be necessary and proper, for carrying into execution, all powers vested by the constitution in the government of the United States, or any department or officer thereof, is a power very comprehensive and definite, and may, for ought I know, be exercised in a such manner as entirely to abolish the state legislatures.

...The legislature of the United States are vested with the great and uncontrollable powers, of laying and collecting taxes, duties, imposts, and excises; of regulating trade, raising and supporting armies, organizing, arming, and disciplining the militia, instituting courts, and other general powers. And are by this clause invested with the power of making all laws, proper and necessary, for carrying all these into execution; and they may so exercise this power as entirely to annihilate all the state governments, and reduce this country to one single government. And if they may do it, it is pretty certain they will; for it will be found that the power retained by individual states, small as it is, will be a clog upon the wheels of the government of the United States; the latter therefore will be naturally inclined to remove it out of the way. Besides, it is a truth confirmed by the unerring experience of ages, that every man, and every body of men, invested with power, are ever disposed to increase it, and to acquire a superiority over everything that stands in their way....

Let us now proceed to enquire, as I at first proposed, whether it be best the thirteen United States should be reduced to one great republic, or not? It is here taken for granted, that all agree in this, that whatever government we adopt, it ought to be a free one; that it should be so framed as to secure the liberty of the citizens of America, and such a one as to admit of a full, fair, and equal representation of the people. The question then will be, whether a government thus constituted, and founded on such principles, is practicable, and can be exercised over the whole United States, reduced into one state?...

In every government, the will of the sovereign is the law. In despotic governments, the supreme authority being lodged in one, his will is law, and can be as easily expressed to a large extensive territory as to a small one. In a pure democracy the people are the sovereign, and their will is declared by themselves; for this purpose, they must all come together to deliberate, and decide. This kind of government cannot be exercised, therefore, over a country of any considerable extent; it must be confined to a single city, or at least limited to such bounds as that the people can conveniently assemble, be able to debate, understand the subject submitted to them, and declare their opinion concerning it.

In a free republic, although all laws are derived from the consent of the people, yet the people do not declare their consent by themselves in person, but by representatives, chosen by them, who are supposed to know the minds of their constituents, and to be possessed of integrity to declare this mind.

...If the people are to give their assent to the laws, by persons chosen and appointed by them, the manner of the choice and the number chosen, must be such, as to possess, be disposed, and consequently qualified to declare the sentiments of the people; for if they do not know, or are not disposed to speak the sentiments of the people, the people do not govern, but the sovereignty is in a few. Now, in a large extended country, it is impossible to have a representation, possessing the sentiments, and of integrity, to declare the minds of the people, without having it so numerous and unwieldly, as to be subject in great measure to the inconveniency of a democratic government.

The territory of the United States is of vast extent; it now contains near three millions of souls, and is capable of containing much more than ten times that number. Is it practicable for a country, so large and so numerous as they will soon become, to elect a representation, that will speak their sentiments, without their becoming so numerous as to be incapable of transacting public business? It certainly is not.

In a republic, the manners, sentiments, and interests of the people should be similar. If this be not the case, there will be a constant clashing of opinions; and the representatives of one part will be continually striving against those of the other. This will retard the operations of government, and prevent such conclusions as will promote the public good. If we apply this remark to the condition of the United States, we shall be convinced that it forbids that we should be one government. The United States includes a variety of climates. The productions of the different parts of the union are very variant, and their interests, of consequence, diverse. Their manners and habits differ as much as their climates and productions; and their sentiments are by no means coincident. The laws and customs of the several states are, in many respects, very diverse, and in some opposite; each would be in favor of its own interests and customs, and, of consequence, a legislature, formed of representatives from the respective parts, would not only be too numerous to act with any care or decision, but would be composed of such heterogenous and discordant principles, as would constantly be contending with each other....

...The confidence which the people have in their rulers, in a free republic, arises from their knowing them, from their being responsible to them for their conduct, and from the power they have of displacing them when they misbehave: but in a republic of the extent of this continent, the people in general would be acquainted with very few of their rulers: the people at large would know little of their proceedings, and it would be extremely difficult to change them.... The different parts of so extensive a country could not possibly be made acquainted with the conduct of their representatives, nor be informed of the reasons upon which measures were founded. The consequence will be, they will have no confidence in their legislature, suspect them of ambitious views, be jealous of every measure they adopt, and will not support the laws they pass. Hence the government will be nerveless and inefficient, and no way will be left to render it otherwise, but by establishing an armed force to execute the laws at the point of the bayonet – a government of all others the most to be dreaded.

In a republic of such vast extent as the United-States, the legislature cannot attend to the various concerns and wants of its different parts. It cannot be sufficiently numerous to be acquainted with the local condition and wants of the different districts, and if it could, it is impossible it should have sufficient time to attend to and provide for all the variety of cases of this nature, that would be continually arising....

These are some of the reasons by which it appears, that a free republic cannot long subsist over a country of the great extent of these states. If then this new constitution is calculated to consolidate the thirteen states into one, as it evidently is, it ought not to be adopted.

Source: https://teachingamericanhistory.org/library/document/brutus-i-2/

Document 2 Questions

1. What is the difference between a confederated government and "one great republic"?

> That is the theme of this essay! Is the United States better off as a confederation, as under the Articles, or should it be under a single authority?

2. What is Brutus's main objection to the U.S. government as defined in the new Constitution?

> "This government is to possess absolute and uncontrollable power, legislative, executive and judicial, with respect to every object to which it extends.... It has authority to make laws which will affect the lives, the liberty, and property of every man in the United States; nor can the constitution or laws of any state, in any way prevent or impede the full and complete execution of every power given."

3. What power remains to the state governments?

> "It appears from these articles that there is no need of any intervention of the state governments, between the Congress and the people, to execute any one power vested in the general government, and that the constitution and laws of every state are nullified and declared void, so far as they are or shall be inconsistent with this constitution, or the laws made in pursuance of it, or with treaties made under the authority of the United States. The government then, so far as it extends, is a complete one, and not a confederation."

4. Is there any limit on the power to tax?

> "In the business therefore of laying and collecting taxes, the idea of confederation is totally lost, and that of one entire republic is embraced. It is proper here to remark, that the authority to lay and collect taxes is the most important of any power that can be granted; it is the great means of protection, security, and defense, in a good government, and the great engine of oppression and tyranny in a bad one."

5. What does Brutus think of the "necessary and proper" or "elastic clause"?

> "A power to make all laws, which shall be necessary and proper, for carrying into execution, all powers vested by the constitution in the government of the United States, or any department or officer thereof, is a power very comprehensive and definite, and may, for ought I know, be exercised in a such manner as entirely to abolish the state legislatures."

6. How likely does Brutus think it is that the central government will override the authority of the states?

> "And if they may do it, it is pretty certain they will; for it will be found that the power retained by individual states, small as it is, will be a clog upon the wheels of the government of the United States; the latter therefore

will be naturally inclined to remove it out of the way. Besides, it is a truth confirmed by the unerring experience of ages, that every man, and every body of men, invested with power, are ever disposed to increase it, and to acquire a superiority over everything that stands in their way."

7. What for Brutus is the difference between a democracy and a republic?

"In a pure democracy the people are the sovereign, and their will is declared by themselves; for this purpose, they must all come together to deliberate, and decide. This kind of government cannot be exercised, therefore, over a country of any considerable extent; it must be confined to a single city, or at least limited to such bounds as that the people can conveniently assemble, be able to debate, understand the subject submitted to them, and declare their opinion concerning it.

"In a free republic, although all laws are derived from the consent of the people, yet the people do not declare their consent by themselves in person, but by representatives, chosen by them, who are supposed to know the minds of their constituents, and to be possessed of integrity to declare this mind."

8. What is the problem with representation in large and diverse countries?

"Now, in a large extended country, it is impossible to have a representation, possessing the sentiments, and of integrity, to declare the minds of the people, without having it so numerous and unwieldly, as to be subject in great measure to the inconveniency of a democratic government....

"In a republic, the manners, sentiments, and interests of the people should be similar. If this be not the case, there will be a constant clashing of opinions; and the representatives of one part will be continually striving against those of the other. This will retard the operations of government, and prevent such conclusions as will promote the public good."

9. Does the growth of the country make things better or worse?

"In a republic of such vast extent as the United-States, the legislature cannot attend to the various concerns and wants of its different parts. It cannot be sufficiently numerous to be acquainted with the local condition and wants of the different districts, and if it could, it is impossible it should have sufficient time to attend to and provide for all the variety of cases of this nature, that would be continually arising."

10. *For Thought:* The last two parts of the Bill of Rights, the Ninth and Tenth Amendments, attempt to address some of Brutus's concerns. How effective have they been in doing that? Does this tend to confirm Brutus's point in Question 6?

11. *For Discussion*: Brutus's essay should be considered in direct comparison with Madison's *Federalist* 10. One historian commented that Madison's argument with regard to factions and the advantages of a large and diverse country was more clever; but Brutus's arguments may have proven more valid, particularly with the rise of political parties. What do you think? Ask your students what they think.

CHAPTER SIX

FROM JEFFERSON TO JACKSON

The Rise of the Common Man

Summary

DESPITE THE CONCILIATORY TONE with which it began, the presidency of Thomas Jefferson proved to be more openly partisan than that of any of his predecessors. He consolidated his power by appointing men who shared his partisan affiliation and his political viewpoint and began the process of ushering the Federalist Party down the road toward dissolution. Yet one obstacle remained: the federal judiciary eluded Jefferson's control.

As one of his last acts as president, John Adams hastily passed the Judiciary Act of 1801, creating six new federal circuit courts staffed entirely by Federalists. He also appointed the Federalist John Marshall as chief justice of the U.S. Supreme Court, an act that led to several key Supreme Court decisions setting important legal precedents. Perhaps most notable among these was *Marbury v. Madison* (1803), the landmark case establishing the Court's power of judicial review and holding that Congress does not have authority to pass laws that overstep the Constitution.

The Louisiana Purchase (1803) was one of Jefferson's most spectacular achievements as president. Acquiring the Louisiana Territory meant adding more than eight hundred thousand square miles of land west of the Mississippi River, doubling the size of the country and removing the possibility of a dangerous foreign presence at the mouth of a great river crucial to western commerce.

In 1807, Jefferson persuaded Congress to pass the Embargo Act, prohibiting American merchant ships from sailing into foreign ports due to the ongoing struggle between France and Britain and America's struggle to remain neutral. Unfortunately, this caused more hardship to Americans, and as one of his last acts as president, Jefferson called for its repeal.

In 1808, James Madison was elected to succeed his friend Jefferson as president. Ongoing challenges with the British would dominate his presidency, which finally led the United States into the near-disaster of the War of 1812. The war ended in December 1814 with the Treaty of Ghent, which restored the status quo from the war's start without making any determination of neutral rights or any other questions that had been at issue. But perhaps the greatest casualty of the War of 1812 was the Federalist Party as the national party. By this time, the Republicans and Federalists had switched roles, with the Republicans becoming the party of vigorous nationalism and the Federalists advocating for states' rights and a strict construction of the Constitution. The greatest benefit of the war was the glorious victory of Andrew Jackson against the British at the Battle of New Orleans, even though it occurred after the Treaty of Ghent had been signed and thus did not affect the settlement of the war. It established Jackson as one of the great American military heroes and put him in line for future political greatness.

In December 1823, Madison's successor, James Monroe, delivered a message to Congress that would become known as the Monroe Doctrine. It specified that the western hemisphere was to be considered off limits to further European colonization, and any effort to the contrary would be regarded as "manifestation of an unfriendly disposition toward the United States" and "dangerous to our peace and safety" (p. 105). The Monroe Doctrine was a codification of America's doctrine of neutrality toward European powers; it would become a cornerstone of American foreign policy and represent a sharp distinction to the American way of understanding the relationship between the Old World and the New World.

The postwar economy was quickly developing into a national economy. Representative Henry Clay of Kentucky proposed what would become known as the American System as an instrument for fostering economic growth. This called for protective tariffs, rechartering the national bank, and creating internal improvements (such as roads and canals) to establish an ever more efficient system of national transportation. There was a boom in the construction of inland waterways, such as New York's Erie Canal (completed in 1825), which connected the Great Lakes to New York City, linking the economies of western farms and eastern port cities. In the 1820s, the first railroads were built, and by the 1830s, the railroad was transforming western towns into major centers for commerce and increased population. Meanwhile, the country was experiencing rapid population growth; its population increased from four million in 1790 to almost thirteen million in 1830.

Slavery continued to be an inescapable part of the national debate, sometimes receding for a time, only to be thrust back into view. When the Missouri Territory applied to be admitted to the Union as a slave state, there was concern that the balance of slave states versus free states would become upset. The issue gave rise to fiery debates in Congress over the merits of Missouri's case and whether restrictions on slavery could be imposed by Congress as a condition of that state's admission to the Union. The issue was defused by the admission of Maine as a free counterpart to Missouri, but it was far from resolved.

Still, Andrew Jackson's inauguration as president on March 4, 1829, constituted a moment of symbolic significance, as Jackson's emergence came to be seen as a new aspect of the American story, a representation of the emerging Age of the Common Man. Jackson's presidency was turbulent, marked by his frequent use of veto power, his handling of the Nullification Crisis of 1832–33 (seen as a possible prelude to the Civil War), and his Indian removal policy.

Questions and Answers

1. How did Jefferson's presidential style differ from those of his predecessors? How effective was it? (pp. 93–94)

> Jefferson disdained Washington's formality and ceremony as monarchical, but he played gracious host (with a French chef) to congressmen in the tiny village of Washington, D.C., and was very effective at establishing his party's power – except in the judiciary.

2. Despite controlling the executive and the Congress, Jefferson's party was repeatedly stymied by the judiciary. Be able to write several paragraphs about the Supreme Court decisions of John Marshall, beginning with *Marbury v. Madison*. (p. 95)

> *Marbury v. Madison* was the first (and, for a long time, the only) occasion when the Court ruled a law passed by Congress to be unconstitutional (judicial review); the second time did not come until the (disastrous) *Dred Scott* decision of 1854. Judicial review is not mentioned in the Constitution; the courts have it because they have assumed it, and not without much controversy.
>
> Marshall was a contemporary and ally of Hamilton, with a similar background in the Continental army. In his long tenure as chief justice, he influenced Supreme Court decisions with shrewd logic even when the other justices were Republican appointees. His decisions mainly did two things: they bolstered the central government's power against the states (e.g., *McCulloch v. Maryland*, a state cannot tax an arm of the U.S.

government), and they freed businesses from state regulation (e.g., *Gibbons v. Ogden*, the "steamboat case").

3. How did Jefferson respond to Marshall? How effective was each man in shaping the course and nature of the country? In particular, understand that even though Hamilton was dead and the Jeffersonians triumphant at the polls, Marshall ensured that Hamiltonian principles remained influential. (p. 96)

> Jefferson tried to impeach a series of Federalist judges but, after one success, was unable to do so. Judicial independence from political pressure was established (if not always observed). One historian suggested that the United States "pursues Jeffersonian ends (like liberty and virtue) through Hamiltonian means (like a strong central government and extensive commerce)."

4. How did the Louisiana Purchase come to happen? How was it both a triumph for Jefferson and the nation and also a betrayal of his principles? What are the "layers of irony" in this situation? (pp. 97–99)

> Napoleon was unable to complete his dream of restoring the French Empire in America, suffering a defeat at the hands of insurgents in Santo Domingo. He offered to sell all of the Mississippi Valley to the U.S. delegation that had been sent to purchase New Orleans. (See the map on p. 98.) It was too good a deal to pass up, but there was no authority in the Constitution to purchase land for a new territory. Strict constructionist or not, Jefferson had to do it, and so betrayed one of his basic political principles. In this case and others, such as the Embargo of 1807–9, Jefferson as president acted in disregard of his own philosophy of limited government power.

5. Note that as the case of the Essex Junto (p. 99) shows, it was always the losing, out-of-power faction that appealed to secession or nullification. Perhaps it follows that every party likes a strong government when it is the one controlling the government?

6. What did the Lewis and Clark Expedition signal about America's future? (pp. 99–100)

> It signaled that the main focus of the nation for the next hundred years would be the exploration, conquest, and settlement of the continent.

7. American foreign policy under Jefferson and Madison continued to focus on protecting America's **neutral status** and its assertion of the principle of **free trade.** (p. 100)

8. Both France and Britain interfered with American shipping, but the British also practiced **impressment** of American sailors into the British navy, a far greater and insulting grievance. (p. 101)

9. Why did Jefferson opt for the Embargo in 1807 instead of war? How successful was this? (p. 101)

> Jefferson had slashed spending to the point that the United States had almost no military, so war was not an option. The embargo failed badly, in part because New England resisted it; Congress (even though controlled by Jefferson's party) repealed the embargo, the date to coincide with the end of Jefferson's presidency.

10. Why did Jefferson not seek a third term? (p. 101)

> He approved of and followed Washington's example of only two terms, and in addition, he was weary, debt-ridden, exhausted, defeated, and overwhelmed – and ready to go home.

11. Why did Jefferson consider the University of Virginia one of his most important achievements? (pp. 101–2)

> Jefferson believed rule should be in the hands of a "natural aristocracy" produced by free public education for all.

12. Madison (who was Jefferson's close friend and ally and had been his secretary of state) inherited all of Jefferson's problems. How effectively did he deal with them? (pp. 102–3)

> Not very effectively. He did begin a military buildup but was forced to go to war by public opinion and expansionist interests who wanted an invasion of Canada (Britain being busy fighting Napoleon).

13. What is ironic about the U.S. declaration of war on Britain in 1812? What does this imply about the *real* reasons for the war? (Who were the War Hawks? Who was Tecumseh?) (p. 102)

> The standard explanation for the U.S. declaration of war in 1812 is the "maritime issues" – British seizure of ships and impressment of sailors. But New England opposed the war, even though American shipping was concentrated there. War was favored by the War Hawks, young congress-

men like John C. Calhoun of South Carolina and Henry Clay of Kentucky. Their interest was in western lands, not shipping. Tecumseh was a Shawnee chief who tried to unite the western tribes against American settlement.

14. Trace the destruction of the Federalist Party from the Hartford Convention through Jackson's victory at New Orleans to the election of 1816 and the Era of Good Feeling. (p. 104)

> The Federalists still controlled several New England states and opposed the War of 1812. They met at Hartford to discuss extreme measures, including even secession, just as the war ended with Jackson's victory at New Orleans and a blaze of patriotic emotion. The party disintegrated as politicians switched to the Republicans; Monroe won in 1816, as the Federalists could not even muster a candidate. Monroe's presidency is called the Era of Good Feeling because there was only one party, although plenty of issues still needed to be debated. But the nationalism and unifying patriotism coming out of the war lasted several years.
>
> Teachers should explain that Jackson's victory at New Orleans made him a national hero comparable to Washington to some extent; his election to the presidency did not come until 1828, a dozen years later, but he was the dominating personality throughout that time, as a military leader against the southern Indians and Florida, and as an unsuccessful candidate in 1824.

15. What was the "Virginia Dynasty"? What was the pattern of advancement in terms of who became the next president?

> Of the first five presidents, only John Adams (single term) was not from Virginia. And the path to the presidency was through the office of secretary of state; Jefferson was Washington's; Madison was Jefferson's; Monroe was Madison's; and John Quincy Adams was Monroe's.

16. The story of how the United States acquired Florida is too complex for the author to include in detail but very revealing about John Quincy Adams, Andrew Jackson, and others. You can look it up in a reference source, and it would make a good extra credit question on a test.

> Jackson invaded Florida (a Spanish possession) without orders. Secretary of war Calhoun wanted Jackson court-martialed, but secretary of state Adams was trying to persuade Spain to sell Florida to the United States, and Jackson's aggression gave him a good arguing point: sell to us, or Jackson may take it anyway. Jackson did not know Calhoun had urged

his court-martial and selected Calhoun as vice president for his first term. He learned later, and Calhoun became, for this and other reasons, Jackson's bitter enemy.

17. Be able to write several paragraphs about the Monroe Doctrine: how it came to be, what it said, and what its consequences and implications were. (pp. 105–6)

Many colonies had won independence during the Napoleonic Wars. After those ended, Spain and France wanted to recover their empires. The United States objected and declared itself opposed to any further expansion of European control in the western hemisphere. The United States was, for many decades, too weak to enforce this, but it coincided with British interests; as the leading commercial nation, Britain wanted free trade with former colonies.

In the long run, it established the United States as the "protector" or "guardian" of Latin America, which would in turn prove to be a constant source of friction between the two.

18. The United States "goes not **abroad** in search of **monsters** to destroy." (p. 105)

19. How did Henry Clay's American Plan demonstrate the continuing influence of Hamiltonian ideas? (pp. 106–8)

Clay advocated a new national bank, a protective tariff to encourage American manufacturing, and federally financed internal improvements (canals, paved roads, and, later on, railroads).

20. How were internal improvements mostly financed in the decades after the War of 1812? (pp. 106–8)

Nobody opposed better transportation; the question was who would pay for it. The possible answers were private companies who would charge tolls, state or local governments, or the U.S. government. Although Clay and others wanted a federally financed national system, several presidents vetoed such bills as an unconstitutional expansion of power, and most roads were built by state governments.

21. What did the Erie Canal do? (p. 107)

By connecting Albany to Buffalo, it connected New York City to the Great Lakes. American farm produce could be shipped cheaply from the interior through New York City and thence to anywhere in the world.

22. How did population growth and economic development reshape America after the War of 1812? (p. 108)

> The "transportation revolution" of canals and paved roads and steamboats, and later railroads, was knitting together a society of small, independent farmers into a national marketplace – which allowed regional and sectional specialization.

23. What was the "fire bell in the night"? What did the Missouri Compromise settle? What did it *not* settle? (pp. 108–10)

> The number of slave and free states needed to be kept the same to balance voting in the Senate. Maine wanted to split from Massachusetts and was allowed to do so, as Missouri was admitted as a slave state. The compromise drew a line on the map and prohibited slavery to the north of it (except for Missouri); it settled the issue of slavery's growth into the western territories but did not address the underlying issue of slavery itself.

24. "We have the **wolf** by the **ear,** and we can neither **hold** him, nor **safely let him go.**" (p. 110)

25. How did the election of 1824 destroy the Era of Good Feeling? Who ran? Who won? How? What was the "corrupt bargain"? Do you think it was really that corrupt? (pp. 110–11)

> One-party rule is unstable, as differences of opinion, and conflicting ambitions, must be contained within it. When Monroe's second term ended, five men ran to succeed him, each claiming to be the nominee of the same (Republican) party. Jackson got the most popular votes, but no one got a majority in the Electoral College, so the decision went to the House. Henry Clay threw his support to John Quincy Adams, who was elected and then appointed Clay as secretary of state – presumably making him next in line for the presidency. The Jacksonians labeled it a "corrupt bargain" (as Jackson had won the most popular votes), but that sort of deal making seems less corrupt than normal wheeling-and-dealing.

26. How did politics change in the Jacksonian Era of the Common Man? What happened at Jackson's inauguration? (p. 112)

> Many states (and especially the newer western states) now allowed all adult males to vote, eliminating property requirements. Jackson's appeal was as a military hero, and his campaign relied on symbols and slogans more than on nuanced arguments. Jackson's supporters trashed the White House on Inauguration Day.

27. In what sense was Jackson the first populist? (pp. 112–13)

Jackson saw himself as representing the common man and was suspicious of aristocracy and great wealth. His special enemy was the Bank of the United States, the largest corporation in the country and, in Jackson's eyes, guilty of many injustices.

28. How did Jackson deal with the Nullification Crisis? (pp. 113–14)

After trying to placate both sides in the tariff debate, Jackson determined to crush nullification. He was prepared to use force against South Carolina, which prepared to resist. (Other southern states did not join South Carolina but also likely would not have aided Jackson against it.) A potential civil war was avoided by a compromise tariff guided by Henry Clay, the "great compromiser."

29. Was Indian removal Jackson's idea? (pp. 115–16)

No, that policy had been proposed under previous presidents.

Teachers may ask students to suggest better policies than those implemented by a succession of presidents from Washington to Jackson. They should keep in mind that, in the long run, whatever was done had to be acceptable to the nation's white majority; otherwise, the responsible political leaders would be defeated at the polls. But is there no alternative to Tocqueville's fatalistic view that what happened was a tragic inevitability?

Teachers may also ask students to reflect on the analysis of historian Wilcomb E. Washburn of a once-famous passage from the 1770s called "Logan's Speech." The historical particulars of that speech are not relevant here (although interested students will want to look them up). But Washburn's observations are thought provoking on a number of levels:

Logan's story is the story of the American Indian from Jamestown and Plymouth Rock forward. It symbolizes the death of one society as the Declaration of Independence marks a new one. It is a tragedy because, given human behavior, it was inevitable, though given human ideals, it was unnecessary. The American may not have a material past of castles and monuments, but he has a psychological past of wrongs committed and not expiated. The recency of those wrongs give our emotional past greater strength, as the lack of ruins gives our material past less significance.

30. Tocqueville saw many things in democracy to admire but also some to fear. Explain. (pp. 118–19)

Tocqueville believed democracy was the most powerful system, as it harnessed the energies of all. He admired American religion, practicality, energy, and mobility. The dangers were conformity to the "tyranny of the majority," or public opinion, and "individualism," which isolated people from any sense of a public good as they pursued self-gratification. Why were Americans "so restless in the midst of their prosperity"?

Objective Questions

Answers are in parentheses.

Put in order:

____	Embargo Act	(3)
____	Lewis and Clark Expedition	(2)
____	Louisiana Purchase	(1)

Put in order:

____	Battle of New Orleans	(1)
____	Monroe Doctrine	(2)
____	Nullification Crisis	(3)

Put in order:

____	presidency of Andrew Jackson	(3)
____	presidency of James Monroe	(1)
____	presidency of John Quincy Adams	(2)

Document 1

ALEXIS DE TOCQUEVILLE, "WHY THE AMERICANS ARE SO RESTLESS IN THE MIDST OF THEIR PROSPERITY," FROM *DEMOCRACY IN AMERICA*, VOLUME 2, SECTION 2, CHAPTER 13

In certain remote corners of the Old World you may still sometimes stumble upon a small district that seems to have been forgotten amid the general tumult, and to have remained stationary while everything around it was in motion. The inhabitants, for the most part, are extremely ignorant and poor; they take no part in the business of the country and are frequently oppressed by the government, yet their countenances are generally placid and their spirits light.

In America I saw the freest and most enlightened men placed in the happiest circumstances that the world affords, it seemed to me as if a cloud habitually hung upon their brow, and I thought them serious and almost sad, even in their pleasures.

The chief reason for this contrast is that the former do not think of the ills they endure, while the latter are forever brooding over advantages they do not possess. It is strange to see with what feverish ardor the Americans pursue their own welfare, and to watch the vague dread that constantly torments them lest they should not have chosen the shortest path which may lead to it.

A native of the United States clings to this world's goods as if he were certain never to die; and he is so hasty in grasping at all within his reach that one would suppose he was constantly afraid of not living long enough to enjoy them. He clutches everything, he holds nothing fast, but soon loosens his grasp to pursue fresh gratifications.

In the United States a man builds a house in which to spend his old age, and he sells it before the roof is on; he plants a garden and lets it just as the trees are coming into bearing; he brings a field into tillage and leaves other men to gather the crops; he embraces a profession and gives it up; he settles in a place, which he soon afterwards leaves to carry his changeable longings elsewhere. If his private affairs leave him any leisure, he instantly plunges into the vortex of politics; and if at the end of a year of unremitting labor he finds he has a few days' vacation, his eager curiosity whirls him over the vast extent of the United States, and he will travel fifteen hundred miles in a few days to shake off his happiness. Death at length overtakes him, but it is before he is weary of his bootless chase of that complete felicity which forever escapes him.

At first sight there is something surprising in this strange unrest of so many happy men, restless in the midst of abundance. The spectacle itself, however, is as old as the world; the novelty is to see a whole people furnish an exemplification of it.

Their taste for physical gratifications must be regarded as the original source of that secret disquietude which the actions of the Americans betray and of that inconstancy of which they daily ford fresh examples. He who has set his heart exclusively upon the pursuit of worldly welfare is always in a hurry, for he has but a limited time at his disposal to reach, to grasp, and to enjoy it.

The recollection of the shortness of life is a constant spur to him. Besides the good things that he possesses, he every instant fancies a thousand others that death will prevent him from trying if he does not try them soon. This thought fills him with anxiety, fear, and regret and keeps his mind in ceaseless trepidation, which leads him perpetually to change his plans and his abode.

If in addition to the taste for physical well-being a social condition be added in which neither laws nor customs retain any person in his place, there is a great additional stimulant to this restlessness of temper. Men will then be seen continually to change their track for fear of missing the shortest cut to happiness.

It may readily be conceived that if men passionately bent upon physical gratifications desire eagerly, they are also easily discouraged; as their ultimate object is to enjoy, the means to reach that object must be prompt and easy or the trouble of acquiring the gratification would be greater than the gratification itself. Their prevailing frame of mind, then, is at once ardent and relaxed, violent and enervated. Death is often less dreaded by them than perseverance in continuous efforts to one end.

The equality of conditions leads by a still straighter road to several of the effects that I have here described. When all the privileges of birth and fortune are abolished, when all professions are accessible to all, and a man's own energies may place him at the top of any one of them, an easy and unbounded career seems open to his ambition and he will readily persuade himself that he is born to no common destinies. But this is an erroneous notion, which is corrected by daily experience. The same equality that allows every citizen to conceive these lofty hopes renders all the citizens less able to realize them; it circumscribes their powers on every side, while it gives freer scope to their desires. Not only are they themselves powerless, but they are met at every step by immense obstacles, which they did not at first perceive. They have swept away the privileges of some of their fellow creatures which stood in their way, but they have opened the door to universal competition; the barrier has changed its shape rather than its position. When men are nearly alike and all follow the same track, it is very difficult for any one individual to walk quickly and cleave a way through the dense throng that surrounds and presses on him. This constant strife between the inclination springing from the equality of condition and the means it supplies to satisfy them harasses and wearies the mind.

It is possible to conceive of men arrived at a degree of freedom that should completely content them; they would then enjoy their independence without anxiety and without impatience. But men will never establish any equality with which they can be contented. Whatever efforts a people may make, they will never succeed in reducing all the conditions of society to a perfect level; and even if they unhappily attained that absolute and complete equality of position, the inequality of minds would still remain, which, coming directly from the hand of God, will forever escape the laws of man. However democratic, then, the social state and the political constitution of a people may be, it is certain that every member of the community will always find out several points about him which overlook his own position; and we may foresee that his looks will be doggedly fixed in that direction. When inequality of conditions is the common law of society, the most marked inequalities do not strike the eye; when everything is nearly on the same level, the slightest are marked enough to hurt it. Hence the desire of equality always becomes more insatiable in proportion as equality is more complete.

Among democratic nations, men easily attain a certain equality of condition, but they can never attain as much as they desire. It perpetually retires from before them, yet without hiding itself from their sight, and in retiring draws them on. At every moment they think they are about to grasp it; it escapes at every moment from their hold. They are near enough to see its charms, but too far off to enjoy them; and before they have fully tasted its delights, they die.

To these causes must be attributed that strange melancholy which often haunts the inhabitants of democratic countries in the midst of their abundance, and that disgust at life which sometimes seizes upon them in the midst of calm and easy circumstances. Complaints are made in France that the number of suicides increases; in America suicide is rare, but insanity is said to be more common there than anywhere else. These are all different symptoms of the same disease. The Americans do not put an end to their lives, however disquieted they may be, because their religion forbids it; and among them materialism may be said hardly to exist, notwithstanding the general passion for physical gratification. The will resists, but reason frequently gives way.

In democratic times enjoyments are more intense than in the ages of aristocracy, and the number of those who partake in them is vastly larger: but, on the other hand, it must be admitted that man's hopes and desires are oftener blasted, the soul is more stricken and perturbed, and care itself more keen.

Source: https://www.gutenberg.org/files/816/816-h/816-h.htm

Document 1 Questions and Answers

1. What contrast does Tocqueville see, writing in the 1830s, between the "ignorant and poor inhabitants" of remote Old World locations and the "free and enlightened" Americans? Why are the former so much happier than the latter?

> "the former do not think of the ills they endure, while the latter are forever brooding over advantages they do not possess."

2. What does Tocqueville place at the root of Americans' disquiet and restlessness?

He names the desire for "physical gratifications" and the social mobility of a society in which "neither laws nor customs retain any person in his place."

3. How does Tocqueville relate this to democracy?

Equality of condition (which is what Tocqueville means by democracy) makes men ambitious for the achievement of a status beyond the condition into which they were born; but equality of condition also makes the achievement of such distinctions of rank next to impossible.

4. Tocqueville is often praised as a prophet, and his work often seems to describe the America of today. Does this reading describe features that you can see operating in present-day American life?

Perhaps you see it in our consumerism, acquisitiveness, status competitiveness, or concern with appearances?

Document 2

DAVY CROCKETT, LETTER TO CHARLES SCHULTZ ON INDIAN REMOVAL, 1834

This is a portion of a letter from David Crockett to Charles Schultz, condemning the forced removal of the Cherokee from Georgia. A fierce opponent of Jackson on this issue, Crockett lost his reelection to Congress. As he threatened in this letter, he did leave the United States for Texas. He died at the Alamo in the fight for Texan independence from Mexico. Land of Hope *states that the policy of removal "was also in part a failure of imagination" (p. 116). Crockett may have had the imagination to see the possibility of sovereign tribes existing alongside citizens of the United States. His understanding, however, was not widely held.*

Crockett had a rudimentary education, as seen in the spelling and punctuation in this letter. But a lack of formal education did not dull his ability to think through important questions. The "little Vann" and "vanburen" mentioned in the letter refer to Jackson's vice president, Martin Van Buren.

Washington City 25 Decr 1834

… The time has Come that man is expected to be transfarable and as negotiable as a promisary note of hand, in those days of Glory and – Jackson & reform

& co – little Vann Sets in his chair and [inserted: looks] as Sly as a red fox and I have no doubt but that he thinks Andrew Jackson has full power to transfer the people of these united States at his will, and I am truly affread that a majority of the free Citizens of these united States will Submit to it and Say amen Jackson done it. It is right If we Judge by the past we can make no other Calculations. I have almost given up the Ship as lost. I have gone So far as to declare that if he martin vanburen is elected that I will leave the united States for I never will live under his king dom before I will Submit to his Governmint I will go to the wildes of Texas, I will consider that government a Paridice to what this will be in fait at this time our Republican Governmint has dwindled almost into insignificancy our bosted land of liberty have almost Bowed to the yoke of of Bondage our happy days of Republican principles are near at an end when a few is to transfer the many....

Source: © 2012 The Gilder Lehrman Institute of American History, https://www.gilderlehrman.org/sites/default/files/inline-pdfs/01162_FPS.pdf. For a contemporary glimpse at how the Chickasaw now see Crockett on this issue, see https://www.chickasaw.tv/videos/davy-crockett-an-early-supporter-of-tribal-sovereignty?ref=durl

Document 2 Questions and Answers

1. What does Crockett mean when he says that "the time has Come that man is expected to be transfarable and as negotiable as a promisary note of hand"?

> Crockett means that "man" (in this case, Native Americans) are now to be treated as property that can be negotiated and traded away.

2. What sentences and phrases does Crockett use to indicate his pessimism regarding the republic?

> "I have no doubt that [Van Buren] thinks Andrew Jackson has full power to transfer the people of these united States at his will, and I am truly afraid that a majority of the free Citizens of these united States will submit to it."
>
> > "I have almost given up the Ship as lost."
> >
> > "Our Republican Government has dwindled almost into insignificancy our bosted land of liberty have almost Bowed to the yoke of Bondage our happy days of Republican principles are near at an end when a few is to transfer the many."

3. What assumptions does Crockett seem to make in this letter?

> He assumes that the Native Americans being forced to move have a right to their land. Could more be inferred? That they have sovereignty? That their rights were guaranteed in treaties? That the Supreme Court upheld these rights? This could be a research topic for interested students.

4. What do you think the "republican principles" are that Crockett felt we were losing? Why?

> There are several possible answers, but chief among them seems to be that "a few" have no right to "transfer the many." He is troubled that a majority of Americans support Indian removal.

Special Unit

TEACHING THE TWO-PARTY SYSTEM

The United States has a two-party political system. This is remarkable and surprising, because the men who wrote the Constitution did not like parties, nor did they want them. Yet these same men became leaders of the first two opposing parties, the Federalists and the Democratic Republicans. Parties in general, and the two-party system in particular, have great advantages and also great disadvantages. They are a key part of our democratic system, and what Winston Churchill said of democracy, that it is the *worst* of all possible governments, except for the others, applies as strongly to the two-party system.

A. Jean-Jacques Rousseau and the General Will

The French philosopher Jean-Jacques Rousseau was an intellectual godfather to the French Revolution, just as John Locke was to the American. Rousseau's big idea, expressed in *The Social Contract*, was that there exists a *general will* distinct from all the various particular wills. **This general will wants what is best for everyone and so is always right.** Each individual human shares a tiny part of this general will but is overwhelmingly more motivated by his particular will. That is, to some small degree, I want what is best for everyone, since I am part of everyone; but mainly I want what is good for me, and if necessary, to heck with you. And so I want two contradictory things: that rules exist to restrain everyone and that I be able to ignore or violate those rules when doing so benefits me. The first is an expression of the general will, the second of my particular will.

Rousseau was a nationalist and believed that **each nation had its own general will**; there was no universal human general will but a French general will that was distinct from a Spanish or an English general will.

The problem, according to Rousseau, is knowing what is the national general will and who embodies it at a given moment. The best method is through voting, but without any political parties – because **each party has a particular will of its own distinct from the general will. And the worst number of parties is two**, because one will be a majority and exercise its power in pursuit of its particular will. That is, if we follow Rousseau's reasoning, there is a Republican general will and a Democratic general will, and each wants what is best for itself rather than what is best for the nation as a whole. Rousseau argued that if parties must exist, the more the better, for if a nation with a million voters had a million parties, each with one member, there would in effect be no parties, which he thought best.

It is of enormous significance that the American revolutionaries mostly followed the ideas of John Locke and the English traditions of individual rights and limits on the powers of government. Yet Rousseau's ideas can be detected in America, seen most readily in James Madison's *Federalist* 10. Madison's definition of faction seems straight out of *The Social Contract*: "By a faction, I understand a number of citizens, whether amounting to a majority or a minority of the whole, who are united and actuated by some common impulse of passion, or of interest, adverse to the rights of other citizens, or to **the permanent and aggregate interests of the community**." The boldfaced phrase is a definition of the general will, which wants what is best for everyone. **Note that there can be majority factions, and majority rule is no protection against them.**

George Washington expressed the same idea in his Farewell Address; parties "serve to organize faction, to give it an artificial and extraordinary force; to put, **in the place of the delegated will of the nation the will of a party**, often a small but artful and enterprising minority of the community; and, according to the alternate triumphs of different parties, to make the public administration the mirror of the ill-concerted and incongruous projects of faction, rather than the organ of **consistent and wholesome plans digested by common counsels and modified by mutual interests**." The boldfaced phrases are expressions of Rousseau's idea. Washington was careful to include the leading adherents of opposing philosophies of government – Jefferson and Hamilton – within his cabinet and gave to each a respectful consideration. Yet by the end of his presidency, the first political parties were well on their way to being formed.

Teachers should remind students that until the Twelfth Amendment took effect in 1804, the vice president was the runner-up in the Electoral College.

John Adams defeated Jefferson in 1796, and Jefferson became vice president. This plan clearly did not allow for the existence of political parties but rather assumed that each candidate ran as an individual.

B. The First Party System: Federalists versus Democratic Republicans, 1794–1816

The key to understanding the first party system is to know that neither side believed in parties, and neither believed itself to be one. Each considered itself to embody the general will and its opponents to be a faction. And factions are by Madison's definition bad things that must be crushed.

The issues dividing the two parties were of fundamental importance: was the national government to be strictly limited in power, or strong enough to deal with new threats and needs as they arose? Was America to be modeled more on the British system, or on a rejection of it? Did the future of the country lie eastward, as a member of an Atlantic world dominated by Britain, or westward, turning its back on Europe's wars and corruptions?

But the conflict in values and vision led to **vicious political infighting**, including dueling sex scandals. Both sides' newspapers printed scurrilous personal attacks on rival leaders.

Perhaps more importantly, **each side tried to destroy its rival** by smearing it as unpatriotic to the point of treason. During the Quasi-War with France (1797–98), the Federalists passed the Alien and Sedition Acts targeting the Jeffersonians, and several Jeffersonian newspaper owners were prosecuted for criticizing John Adams's conduct of foreign affairs. Then what the Federalists failed to do against the Jeffersonians they did to themselves in 1815 at the Hartford Convention: New England Federalists opposing the War of 1812 debated secession, just as the war ended with Jackson's victory at New Orleans and a blaze of patriotic fervor. By 1816, the Federalist Party was no more.

C. The Era of Good Feeling

James Monroe's presidency, with no opposing party, is often called the Era of Good Feeling, in which regional interests were (briefly) subordinated to national ones. (The South, with cotton prices high, even went along with a tariff protecting New England textile manufacturers.) The "good feeling" mostly ended with the Panic of 1819 and the depression that followed. But **long-term dominance by one party is untenable in a system with free elections, given human ambitions.** Monroe's successor was chosen in the chaotic election of 1824, which saw five rival candidates, each claiming to be the candidate of the same Democratic-Republican Party. In other words, the collapse of one party, the Federalists in 1816, led within eight years to the disintegration of the other (apparently victorious) party. **Conflicting policies and ambitions will continue to exist, even if there is only one party, and will soon tear it apart.**

D. The Second Party System: The Jacksonian Democrats versus the Whigs, 1833–1856

Andrew Jackson's victory at New Orleans in 1815 made him *the* national hero, and his chosen issue, opposition to the Second Bank of the United States (2BUS), solidified his national appeal. **The second party system is sometimes understood as made up of a "cult of personality" on one side and an in-gathering of its detractors on the other;** that is, one party was based on the appeal of a single man, Jackson, while the other comprised his enemies. This sense of the era as an Age of Jackson does not quite do justice to the forward-looking ideas of the reform-minded Whig Party, which advocated for extensive internal improvements, such as roads, canals, and railroads, to help create a vibrant national economy. But without Jackson to unite them, the Whigs tended to become faction ridden and lacking in national-level political appeal.

By 1824, the nation's politics were mostly sectional and its leaders mostly representatives of regional interests: Henry Clay of Kentucky spoke for the new West; John C. Calhoun of South Carolina for the South; John Quincy Adams of Massachusetts for New England; Martin Van Buren of New York for the rising financial power of Wall Street. The main issues were mostly about money – protective tariffs, and how to sell western lands, and how to finance internal improvements – and each section found different allies in different debates. Candidates for the presidency maneuvered to combine their own sectional support with votes from another section, to achieve an electable coalition. (This is precisely **the way systems with three or more parties typically operate; no party is strong enough to win by itself, so coalition governments are required,** which are inherently unstable and also less accountable – who do the voters credit or blame?)

Jackson was the only politician with a national appeal. His focus was on the bank, which was one of the most important national institutions and deeply unpopular. The bank's bad reputation stemmed from its actions during the Panic of 1819, when it "saved itself but ruined the country," and also from its offensiveness to Jeffersonian doctrine as epitomized in the *McCulloch v. Maryland* Supreme Court decision. It was the largest corporation in the country but also deemed part of the U.S. government, which held 40 percent of its stock; much of the remaining stock was held by British investors.

Though some historians have suggested that Jackson was the pawn of Van Buren, and the Bank War a clash between the Philadelphia-based 2BUS and the emerging New York City banking community on Wall Street, other historians see Jackson as the champion of the common man fighting against the special interests of big business. Whichever interpretation one prefers, it is certainly true that Jackson cast himself in that role, terming the bank "the Monster" that he would slay.

Jackson's rise to power corresponded with an expansion of the suffrage; many states, especially in the West, relaxed or abandoned property requirements for voting. Jackson's campaigns emphasized slogans and symbols and torchlit parades and lots of hard cider. **Voters did not need to understand the issues;** they needed only to identify with Jackson as the hero who defended them against enemies both foreign (the British) and domestic (the Monster Bank).

The Whig Party coalesced during Jackson's second term and had in common chiefly their opposition to him; that is, the Whigs were as much focused on a single personality as the Democrats. When in 1840 the Whigs actually won an election, defeating Van Buren's attempt to win a second term (mostly because of a depression brought on by Jackson's destruction of the bank), they proved to have little in the way of a coherent program that they were all *for*; they had defined themselves as *against* Jackson, who was now gone.

The Whigs won the "log cabin and hard cider" campaign with slogans ("Tippecanoe and Tyler Too!" – whatever that meant), symbols, and mass campaigning, copying what had worked for the Jacksonians, including choosing a war hero as candidate. Here we see several features of the two-party system. **First, it is rare for one party to win the presidency more than three times in a row, and second, any new technique or tactic that proves successful for one will quickly be adapted or adopted by the other.**

The Whig Party eventually fell apart, even as its own man (Millard Fillmore) was in the White House. The party's raison d'être had disappeared with Jackson, and it had no idea how to handle the emerging crises of westward expansion and slavery.

E. The Third-Party System: Democrats versus Republicans, 1856 to the Present

Northern Whigs joined with other antislavery groups, such as the Free Soil Party, to create the Republican Party, which ran its first candidate in 1856. It was initially a strictly sectional party; the Democrats were the last remaining national institution of any importance, as the various Protestant denominations had all split North and South over slavery. And when the Whig collapse left the Democrats briefly as the sole remaining party, they too split among three regional candidates in 1860, as had happened with the Democratic

Republicans in 1824. Lincoln was able to win the Electoral College with 40 percent of the popular vote, carrying only northern states.

Since the Civil War, however, **the present two parties have always been able to count on at least 40 percent of the popular vote as a base.** Although the Electoral College allows for very lopsided victories (e.g., Nixon's 520–17 win in 1972 or Reagan's 525–13 in 1984), a margin of 20 percent (60–40 percent) in the popular vote is considered a "landslide"; most presidential elections see the opposing popular vote totals within 2 or 3 percent. And in some elections, the popular vote winner fails to win in the Electoral College, where it counts.

It is the winner-take-all nature of the Electoral College that has ensured the continuation of the two-party system. Because voters within each state are really choosing a slate of electors rather than the candidates themselves, the narrowest possible victory in popular votes still results in a candidate receiving all of the state's electoral votes. Political systems with proportional representation (that is, winning 15 percent of the votes yields 15 percent of the delegates or representatives) allow and even encourage third and fourth parties, but in the United States, the presidency is the only national office (senators are selected by their states' voters and representatives from districts within a state), and the all-or-nothing nature of the Electoral College guarantees that the winner will be either the Democratic or the Republican nominee.

Third parties can and do exist, but seldom for long, unless they command only a few percent of the popular vote. **Any third party that begins to gain support sufficient to decide the outcome between the two major parties will soon see one or both of them adopting the third party's ideas and luring its voters back.** Third parties can influence policy by demonstrating the appeal of ideas or interests being ignored by both major parties, but as soon as one of the majors adopts its ideas, the third party will see its support abandon it. The best example of this is the Populist Party in its relations with the Democratic Party in the late 1800s.

If there is one thing that Democrats and Republicans agree on, it is that the best number of parties is two. **There are really fifty separate state political systems, each controlling voting and ballot access and candidate selection, and most have erected procedural barriers that make it difficult for newer and smaller parties to emerge.** (For example, getting on a ballot often requires either getting a certain percentage of the votes in the previous election or submitting a large number of signatures – an expensive and time-consuming requirement.)

Political parties may be considered "brands" that allow voters to decide between individual candidates about whom they may know nothing

else. This makes possible a mass democracy, with millions of voters who are largely ignorant of policy details. On the whole, such mass participation is considered a good thing.

However, **the consequence of a two-party system is a limited number of choices.** American voters are very accustomed to having to choose between two candidates, neither of whom they like. And it may happen that Candidate A supports the voter's views on some issues, while Candidate B supports the voter's views on other and different issues. But each candidate has to be taken as a whole, as a bundle of positions, some of which a voter may like and some of which she may reject.

Another feature is that each vote counts the same, until one candidate wins the state's popular vote; everything above that is "wasted." That is, if the Democratic candidate carries California by one vote or by a million votes, the result in the Electoral College is the same – she gets all of California's electors. This has a direct application to how parties spend their money in advertising and how candidates spend their time and energy.

Voting by itself cannot measure intensity or information. A passionate voter who has carefully studied an issue has no greater impact on the vote total than someone who shrugs and flips a coin in the voting booth. Both parties draw on their committed activists or "base" for money (especially early in the process, as candidates are being chosen within each party) and for time and energy in get-out-the-vote activities.

The ideological makeup of the two major parties has varied a great deal over the 150 years since they emerged. There have been periods when both were **"umbrella" or "big tent" coalitions across a wide spectrum of beliefs.** During the 1950s, for example, many conservative Democrats, and more than a few liberal Republicans, could be found. This made compromise easier, particularly within Congress.

In 1964, however, the Goldwater conservatives took over the Republican Party, and in 1972, the McGovern liberals likewise took over the Democratic Party, in each case changing rules to perpetuate their control. The result today is **two increasingly ideological parties, with less middle ground for compromise and more partisan animosity.**

The closest historical precedent to the current partisanship may be the bitter Hamilton–Jefferson rivalry of the 1790s – which the nation did survive, with each side getting part of what it wanted.

It is possible, however, that the best analogy for understanding today is the period between 1876 and 1900, when the two parties were very close in power (control of Congress changing regularly) and neither really had a good grasp on the nation's problems stemming from industrialization, urbanization, immigration, and so forth. Teachers may want to alert students to the emergence of these themes in chapter 10.

In any case, while it is very possible that one or both current parties will be restructured in very fundamental ways – which seems to be happening now – it is likely that the shells of the two present parties will remain even as their contents may change dramatically.

CHAPTER SEVEN

THE CULTURE OF DEMOCRACY

Summary

I N HIS CLASSIC ACCOUNT of democracy in America, Tocqueville was not interested merely in studying democracy as a political form. He argued that democracy would manifest in every facet of human life: not merely in public institutions but also in family life, in literature, in philosophy, in manners, in language usage, in marriage, in mores, in male–female relations, in ambition, in friendship, in love, and in attitudes toward war and peace. He grasped the fact that a society's political arrangements, far from being matters that merely skate on the surface of life, are in fact influences that reach deep down into the very souls of society's inhabitants. Democracy is not just about politics; it is also a matter of culture, of a people's sensibility and way of life: their habits, convictions, morals, tastes, and spiritual lives. What then did this emerging culture of democracy in America look like?

Because religion lies at the very roots of culture, one can begin there. One of the first things one notices is that both elite and popular expressions of religion were moving away from orthodox Calvinism. The elites were drawn to Deism and Unitarianism, the broad populace toward evangelicalism and revivalism, but both shared a robust belief in human capabilities. In 1821, the young lawyer Charles Grandison Finney would undergo a conversion experience and become the greatest revivalist of his day, espousing a view of evangelism that openly rejected Calvinist ideas of human depravity and irremediable sin. His approach faithfully reflected the expansive individualism of the Jacksonian moment in American culture.

The era was also a time of social experimentation, confident of the possibility of reshaping society and the human soul through discipline and education. Some communities that formed were short-lived (for example, the Brook Farm experiment in Massachusetts, New Harmony in Indiana, and the "Phalanxes" of the French socialist Charles Fourier). Some communities were more durable (for example, the Rappites, a group of German Lutherans in Butler County, Pennsylvania; the Shakers; and the Oneida community).

The Temperance Movement was also an outgrowth of a belief in the possibility of moral perfection, which also sought to address the negative effects of alcohol consumption on workers, families, and children.

Some of the humanitarian causes that captured America's attention during the 1830s also included women's rights; public education; dietary reform; and humane treatment of the mentally ill, the blind, and the deaf.

But the most important cause of all was the opposition to slavery. Opposition to slavery had been growing since the 1780s, but it increased after the Missouri controversy (chapter 6), and by the 1830s, the movement began to coalesce as a primarily religious movement against slavery. Revivalists of the Second Great Awakening, such as Finney, encouraged antislavery reform, while William Lloyd Garrison, a leading abolitionist and fervent Quaker, began publishing his abolitionist newspaper *The Liberator*. Perhaps most notable of all was Harriet Beecher Stowe's *Uncle Tom's Cabin; or, Life among the Lowly* (published in 1852), a best-selling novel that shifted northern antebellum opinion in the direction of antislavery.

One lingering question, however, was whether America was capable of producing a distinctive literary and artistic culture that was fully and unapologetically American, the equal of the nation's distinctive political democracy. Much of the literary and artistic production of the early Republic was highly imitative and derivative in character, taking its bearings from English and European examples, and showing precious little Americannness. Tocqueville predicted that it would always be thus. But he was proved wrong. By the 1850s, there was a thriving literary community in the country, producing an American literature of high quality, epitomized by the works of Ralph Waldo Emerson, Nathaniel Hawthorne, Henry David Thoreau, Bronson Alcott, Herman Melville, Walt Whitman, and Margaret Fuller, among others.

Many of these writers shared a certain fascination with the cluster of ideas and ideals called Transcendentalism, a romantic variant that stressed the glories of the vast, the mysterious, and the intuitive. Yet perhaps the best at expressing the emerging culture of democracy was Whitman, who sang of the Open Road, a doctrine of human freedom and dignity, of the infinite worth of the single and individual soul – which was in turn the deepest aspiration of the age it represented.

Questions and Answers

1. Is democracy merely a political system? Or an entire culture? (p. 120)

   It is both. It is a way of organizing popular government, that is, a form of government that maximizes the active political participation of all the citizenry, but the term also describes the culture of societies in which democratic political institutions have become embedded in the way of life, a culture that is likely to emphasize equality of various levels of society and forms of expression.

2. "The first thing to notice is that the remarkable partnership of **Protestantism** and **Enlightenment** rationalism, that easy harmony of potential antagonists ... was beginning to fray." (p. 120)

3. Established churches were "increasingly drawn to more rational and Enlightened offshoots of Christianity, such as Deism and Unitarianism." How did these offshoots differ from orthodox Christianity? (p. 121)

   They rejected the divinity of Christ and God as a person who miraculously intervenes in his creation.

4. Meanwhile, on "the other side of the religious divide, the **revivalist** side, came the **Second Great Awakening.**" Be able to write several paragraphs about the key persons, events, and institutions of this movement. (pp. 121–23)

   The First Great Awakening split the existing churches (Anglican, Presbyterian, and Congregational); the Second saw the rise of new denominations, particularly the Methodists and the Baptists, who became the two largest churches in the nation. The Methodist "circuit riders" in particular were good at carrying the Gospel out into frontier areas. Churches often were organized before civil governments and served some of the same functions.

   Charles Grandison Finney combined "unabashed showmanship with a rather flexible form of Christian theology" in what has since become a very familiar American style. Finney's optimism about the efficacy of human effort was contrary to Christian doctrine yet very congenial to his listeners and suited the age.

5. Yet the two sides of this new religious divide were not so far apart when considered in light of the old Calvinist doctrine of *human depravity*. What important belief did Deists and followers of Charles Grandison Finney have in common? (p. 123)

> Both were optimistic about human nature.

6. The America of the Jacksonian years became a magnet for utopian political and social movements. What were the specific beliefs and practices of the Millerites? The Fox sisters? Brook Farm? Robert Owen? The French socialist Charles Fourier? The Rappites? The Shakers? The Oneida community? (pp. 123–25)

> Millerites preached the imminent end of the world; the Fox sisters claimed to speak with the dead; Owen and Fourier attempted various forms of utopian communities; the Rappites and Shakers held different theories about the Second Coming and the end times but shared a belief in celibacy; the Oneida community, in contrast, practiced group marriage.

7. Be able to write one or several paragraphs on the origin and history of the Mormons; why have they proven to be a permanent part of American society? (pp. 123–24)

> Their very strong emphasis on group solidarity enabled them to survive the hostility of neighbors – but moving to Utah away from neighbors was also crucial.

8. "Perhaps the most visible and popular of all these reform movements was **the temperance crusade against alcohol.**" Why? (p. 126)

> Alcoholism affected many people and contributed to many other social problems like unemployment and abuse.

9. What was the average annual consumption of alcohol around the year 1830? How does that compare to today? (p. 126)

> The average annual consumption was 7.1 gallons of pure alcohol per year, about three times more than today.
>
> Teachers may note that since colonial days, many American rural families consumed homemade hard liquor with meals, as today we might drink tea or coffee. (Lack of pure water was a factor.)

10. What reforms did each of the following promote: Horace Mann, Dorothea Dix, Thomas Gallaudet, Samuel Gridley Howe? (p. 127)

Horace Mann led the movement for public education; Dix for humane treatment of the mentally ill; Gallaudet for schools for the deaf; Howe for schools for the blind.

11. What was the greatest of all antebellum American reform causes? Was it primarily a secular or a religious cause? (pp. 127–28)

Antislavery was both a religious and a secular movement. Christians might stress the basic equality of all humans created in God's image, while secular reformers might point to the ill effects on free workers who had to compete with slaves. On balance, though, it has to be considered far more a religious movement than a secular one, and a religious movement specifically of evangelical Protestants (and especially Quakers). Crusaders against slavery had come to believe that it was a great national sin and that its abolition was of imperative importance.

12. Why did the early abolitionist movement lack political effectiveness? (pp. 127–28)

William Lloyd Garrison in particular argued that slavery was so integral to American society that only revolutionary changes could root it out; he believed that the Constitution protected slavery and that therefore the Constitution had to be discarded. This position was logical but extreme and lacked widespread appeal even in the North.

13. Did the antislavery movement make things better or worse? Explain each side's argument. (p. 128)

The antislavery crusade certainly heightened southern fears, especially after the Nat Turner revolt in 1831. And southern states tightened restrictions on slaves as a result, by, for example, prohibiting teaching a slave to read.

On the other hand, one can argue that slavery was so entrenched that without strong and uncompromising opposition on moral grounds, the blight of slavery might have lingered on indefinitely.

14. Explain Max Weber's distinction between the ethic of moral conviction and the ethic of responsibility. Which did William Lloyd Garrison espouse? Which did Lincoln? (p. 128)

> Moral conviction is often individualistic and indifferent to consequences; "tell the truth though the heavens fall!" Being right is the main thing; other people's errors are their own responsibility. Responsibility sees morality as in part a corporate act and suggests that practical consequences do matter. Garrison was the first, Lincoln the second.
>
> Teachers may point out that slavery was a very great evil, but a civil war in which at least six hundred thousand died (equivalent to about four million Americans in proportion to today's population) was also a very great evil. Might slavery have been ended without that bloodbath? It is impossible to answer counterfactual questions of this sort, but political leaders like Lincoln were surely justified in trying to ameliorate the situation without war.

15. Why did *Uncle Tom's Cabin* have such an impact? (p. 129)

> Imaginative literature – stories – carry great power and are accessible to far more people.

16. What did Tocqueville think of American high culture? Why was the freshness of America a disadvantage for writers? (p. 129)

> Tocqueville saw no evidence of any high American culture. American writers had few reserves of tradition and allusion to draw on to nourish their imaginations.

17. How and why did American culture change between the 1830s and the 1850s? (p. 130)

> American writers began to find their voice, to find American topics worthy of exploring. A distinctive national culture was forming.

18. "Both romanticism and religious piety and emotionalism derived from a shared suspicion of and weariness with the **intellectualism of the Enlightenment.**" (p. 131)

19. What are some key ideas associated with romanticism?

> Some key ideas are the exaltation of the individual, the love of nature and the primitive, the distrust of sophistication, the preference for the organic over the mechanical, the extolling of folk cultures, the glorification of the ordinary and everyday. (p. 131)

20. Emerson, Hawthorne, Thoreau, Alcott, and Fuller all knew one another, living in or near Concord. Overall, their ideas and ideals are called Transcendentalism, characterized by what? (p. 132)

> Transcendentalism "sought to replace the sin-soaked supernaturalist dogma of orthodox Christianity and the tidy rationalism of Unitarianism with a sprawling romantic and eclectic form of natural piety that bordered on pantheism."

21. How did the Transcendentalists view nature and subjective experience, and society? (p. 132)

> They were contemptuous of society. "Instead, the Transcendental Self enjoyed an **absolute liberty**, free of any external restraint or law other than that of its own nature." (p. 132)

22. "In Transcendentalism, the mysticism of **Jonathan Edwards** was turned loose.... Nature took the place of **God** and the sense of sin itself had begun to evaporate. This sounds very much like a highbrow version of Finney's theology." (p. 133)

23. The specific establishment against which Transcendentalism was rebelling was Unitarianism, which was characterized by what? (p. 133)

> It was a highly intellectual and refined approach to religion that rejected the doctrine of the Trinity and most forms of Christian supernaturalism and was almost entirely associated with the cultured upper reaches of Boston society. Although Unitarians were at the forefront of many reform efforts, including the common-school movement, they came to be disparaged as figures of smugness and complacency. A wag commented that Unitarians believe in the fatherhood of God, the brotherhood of Man, and the neighborhood of Boston. As for Emerson, he complained bitterly of the "corpse-cold Unitarianism of Brattle Street and Harvard College."

24. Why was Emerson America's first great intellectual? His address "The American Scholar" was seen as America's **intellectual Declaration of Independence.** (pp. 134–35)

> Emerson was America's first freelance intellectual, unconnected to any church or university. His lectures and essays were widely enjoyed, challenging but not overwhelming a nonprofessional audience. Emerson's idea of democratic culture was to include the grandeur of the uncoerced and unconforming mind with a tender respect for the details of everyday existence, admitting no conflict between them.

25. Be able to write a sentence or two about the work of Thoreau, Hawthorne, Melville, and Whitman. What similarities does their writing exhibit? (pp. 136–38)

> Thoreau's *Walden* extols self-reliance. Hawthorne's *The Scarlet Letter* was the first great American novel, drawing on the Puritans' focus on sin and guilt. Melville's *Moby Dick* is "a masterpiece of psychological insight and metaphysical ambiguity." Whitman's poetry was original and untamed. Each drew on American themes and experiences and emphasized the infinite worth and dignity of the single and individual soul.

Objective Questions

Answers are in parentheses.

Matching:

____ Emerson	(E)	A. *Moby Dick*
____ Hawthorne	(C)	B. *Leaves of Grass*
____ Melville	(A)	C. *The Scarlet Letter*
____ Thoreau	(D)	D. *Walden*
____ Whitman	(B)	E. "The American Scholar"

Matching:

____ Dorothea Dix	(D)	A. public education
____ Horace Mann	(A)	B. schools for the blind
____ Samuel Gridley Howe	(B)	C. schools for the deaf
____ Thomas Gallaudet	(C)	D. better treatment for the insane

Matching:

____ Brook Farm	(H)	A. multiple marriages
____ Charles Fourier	(F)	B. Joseph Smith
____ Fox sisters	(D)	C. predicted the end of the world
____ Millerites	(C)	D. spoke with the dead
____ Mormons	(B)	E. English socialist
____ Oneida community	(A)	F. French socialist
____ Robert Owen	(E)	G. practiced celibacy
____ Shakers	(G)	H. Transcendentalists

RALPH WALDO EMERSON, *SELF-RELIANCE* (EXCERPT), FROM *ESSAYS: FIRST SERIES* (1847 EDITION)

I read the other day some verses written by an eminent painter which were original and not conventional. The soul always hears an admonition in such lines, let the subject be what it may. The sentiment they instill is of more value than any thought they may contain. **To believe your own thought, to believe that what is true for you in your private heart is true for all men, – that is genius.** Speak your latent conviction, and it shall be the universal sense; for the inmost in due time becomes the outmost, – and our first thought is rendered back to us by the trumpets of the Last Judgment. Familiar as the voice of the mind is to each, the highest merit we ascribe to Moses, Plato, and Milton is, that they set at naught books and traditions, and spoke not what men but what they thought. A man should learn to detect and watch that gleam of light which flashes across his mind from within, more than the lustre of the firmament of bards and sages. Yet he dismisses without notice his thought, because it is his. In every work of genius we recognize our own rejected thoughts: they come back to us with a certain alienated majesty. Great works of art have no more affecting lesson for us than this. They teach us to abide by our spontaneous impression with good-humored inflexibility than most when the whole cry of voices is on the other side. Else, to-morrow a stranger will say with masterly good sense precisely what we have thought and felt all the time, and we shall be forced to take with shame our own opinion from another.

There is a time in every man's education when he arrives at the conviction that envy is ignorance; that imitation is suicide; that he must take himself for better, for worse, as his portion; that though the wide universe is full of good, no kernel of nourishing corn can come to him but through his toil bestowed on that plot of ground which is given to him to till. The power which resides in him is new in nature, and none but he knows what that is which he can do, nor does he know until he has tried. Not for nothing one face, one character, one fact, makes much impression on him, and another none. This sculpture in the memory is not without preestablished harmony. The eye was placed where one ray should fall, that it might testify of that particular ray. We but half express ourselves, and are ashamed of that divine idea which each of us represents. It may be safely trusted as proportionate and of good issues, so it be faithfully imparted, but God will not have his work made manifest by cowards. A man is relieved and gay when he has put his heart into his work and done his best; but what he has said or done otherwise, shall give him no peace. It is a deliverance which does not deliver. In the attempt his genius deserts him; no muse befriends; no invention, no hope.

Trust thyself: every heart vibrates to that iron string. Accept the place the divine providence has found for you, the society of your contemporaries, the connection of events. Great men have always done so, and confided themselves childlike to the genius of their age, betraying their perception that the absolutely trustworthy was seated at their heart, working through their hands, predominating in all their being. And we are now men, and must accept in the highest mind the same transcendent destiny; and not minors and invalids in a protected corner, not cowards fleeing before a revolution, but guides, redeemers, and benefactors, obeying the Almighty effort, and advancing on Chaos and the Dark.

What pretty oracles nature yields us on this text, in the face and behaviour of children, babes, and even brutes! That divided and rebel mind, that distrust of a sentiment because our arithmetic has computed the strength and means opposed to our purpose, these have not. Their mind being whole, their eye is as yet unconquered, and when we look in their faces, we are disconcerted. Infancy conforms to nobody: all conform to it, so that one babe commonly makes four or five out of the adults who prattle and play to it. So God has armed youth and puberty and manhood no less with its own piquancy and charm, and made it enviable and gracious and its claims not to be put by, if it will stand by itself. Do not think the youth has no force, because he cannot speak to you and me. Hark! in the next room his voice is sufficiently clear and emphatic. It seems he knows how to speak to his contemporaries. Bashful or bold, then, he will know how to make us seniors very unnecessary.

The nonchalance of boys who are sure of a dinner, and would disdain as much as a lord to do or say aught to conciliate one, is the healthy attitude of human nature. A boy is in the parlour what the pit is in the playhouse; independent, irresponsible, looking out from his corner on such people and facts as pass by, he tries and sentences them on their merits, in the swift, summary way of boys, as good, bad, interesting, silly, eloquent, troublesome. He cumbers himself never about consequences, about interests: he gives an independent, genuine verdict. You must court him: he does not court you. But the man is, as it were, clapped into jail by his consciousness. As soon as he has once acted or spoken with eclat, he is a committed person, watched by the sympathy or the hatred of hundreds, whose affections must now enter into his account. There is no Lethe for this. Ah, that he could pass again into his neutrality! Who can thus avoid all pledges, and having observed, observe again from the same unaffected, unbiased, unbribable, unaffrighted innocence, must always be formidable. He would utter opinions on all passing affairs, which being seen to be not private, but necessary, would sink like darts into the ear of men, and put them in fear.

These are the voices which we hear in solitude, but they grow faint and inaudible as we enter into the world. Society everywhere is in conspiracy against the manhood of every one of its members. Society is a joint-stock company, in which the members agree, for the better securing of his bread to each share-holder, to surrender the liberty and culture of the eater. The virtue in most request is conformity. Self-reliance is its aversion. It loves not realities and creators, but names and customs.

Whoso would be a man must be a nonconformist. He who would gather immortal palms must not be hindered by the name of goodness, but must explore if it be goodness. Nothing is at last sacred but the integrity of your own mind. Absolve you to yourself, and you shall have the suffrage of the world. I remember an answer which when quite young I was prompted to make to a valued adviser, who was wont to importune me with the dear old doctrines of the church. On my saying, What have I to do with the sacredness of traditions, if I live wholly from within? my friend suggested, – "But these impulses may be from below, not from above." I replied, "They do not seem to me to be such; but if I am the Devil's child, I will live then from the Devil." No law can be sacred to me but that of my nature. Good and bad are but names very readily transferable to that or this; the only right is what is after my constitution, the only wrong what is against it. A man is to carry himself in the presence of all opposition, as if every thing were titular and ephemeral but he. I am ashamed to think how easily we capitulate to badges and names, to large societies and dead institutions. Every decent and well-spoken individual affects and sways me more than is right. I ought to go upright and vital, and speak the rude truth in all ways. If malice and vanity wear the coat of philanthropy, shall that pass? If an angry bigot assumes this bountiful cause of Abolition, and comes to me with his last news from Barbadoes, why should I not say to him, "Go love thy infant; love thy wood-chopper: be good-natured and modest: have that grace; and never varnish your hard, uncharitable ambition with this incredible tenderness for black folk a thousand miles off. Thy love afar is spite at home." Rough and graceless would be such greeting, but truth is handsomer than the affectation of love. Your goodness must have some edge to it, – else it is none. The doctrine of hatred must be preached as the counteraction of the doctrine of love when that pules and whines. I shun father and mother and wife and brother, when my genius calls me. I would write on the lintels of the door-post, Whim. I hope it is somewhat better than whim at last, but we cannot spend the day in explanation. Expect me not to show cause why I seek or why I exclude company.

Then, again, do not tell me, as a good man did to-day, of my obligation to put all poor men in good situations. Are they my poor? I tell thee, thou foolish philanthropist, that I grudge the dollar, the dime, the cent, I give to such men as do not belong to me and to whom I do not belong. There is a class of persons to whom by all spiritual affinity I am bought and sold; for them I will go to prison, if need be; but your miscellaneous popular charities; the education at college of fools; the building of meeting-houses to the vain end to which many now stand; alms to sots; and the thousandfold Relief Societies; – though I confess with shame I sometimes succumb and give the dollar, it is a wicked dollar which by and by I shall have the manhood to withhold....

Source: https://en.wikisource.org/wiki/Essays:_First_Series/Self-Reliance

Document 1 Questions

1. How does Emerson embody the culture of democracy?

    He exults in the infinite worth and potential of each and every individual person.

2. So what does Emerson believe to be the source of all our problems?

    He believes it to be conformity and timidity that society imposes upon us; our unwillingness to "trust thyself"; our inability to practice "self-reliance."

3. Do you see a relationship between Emerson's style of writing (and speaking) and the ideas that he is trying to convey?

    Emerson's style is very free, very casual, obeying no strict pattern of logical reasoning. It would be hard to imagine any other way of writing about Emerson's kind of romanticism, with its attachment to the intuitive and the emotional. But at the same time, Emerson started adult life as a minister, and he was formed by the experience of preaching sermons. Can it be said that "Self-Reliance" is a kind of secular sermon?

4. "Thy love afar is spite at home." What does Emerson mean by this?

    He means that our love for abstractions that are far away from us may be a way of masking our lack of love for the actual, concrete world in which we live. Though look closely at the context in which Emerson says this. He is disparaging a (hypothetical) proponent of the abolition of slavery in Barbados. Does that complicate our reaction to his statement? To be fair, though, it is important to point out that Emerson himself eventually became a strong proponent of abolition and an admirer of the radical abolitionist John Brown.

Document 2

ELIZABETH CADY STANTON, DECLARATION OF SENTIMENTS, JULY 19, 1848

When, in the course of human events, it becomes necessary for one portion of the family of man to assume among the people of the earth a position different from that which they have hitherto occupied, but one to which the laws of nature and of nature's God entitle them, a decent respect to the opinions of mankind requires that they should declare the causes that impel them to such a course.

We hold these truths to be self-evident: that all men and women are created equal; that they are endowed by their Creator with certain inalienable rights; that among these are life, liberty, and the pursuit of happiness; that to secure these rights governments are instituted, deriving their just powers from the consent of the governed. Whenever any form of government becomes destructive of these ends, it is the right of those who suffer from it to refuse allegiance to it, and to insist upon the institution of a new government, laying its foundation on such principles, and organizing its powers in such form, as to them shall seem most likely to effect their safety and happiness. Prudence, indeed, will dictate that governments long established should not be changed for light and transient causes; and accordingly all experience hath shown that mankind are more disposed to suffer, while evils are sufferable, than to right themselves by abolishing the forms to which they were accustomed. But when a long train of abuses and usurpations, pursuing invariably the same object evinces a design to reduce them under absolute despotism, it is their duty to throw off such government, and to provide new guards for their future security. Such has been the patient sufferance of the women under this government, and such is now the necessity which constrains them to demand the equal station to which they are entitled.

The history of mankind is a history of repeated injuries and usurpations on the part of man toward woman, having in direct object the establishment of an absolute tyranny over her. To prove this, let facts be submitted to a candid world.

He has never permitted her to exercise her inalienable right to the elective franchise.

He has compelled her to submit to laws, in the formation of which she had no voice.

He has withheld from her rights which are given to the most ignorant and degraded men–both natives and foreigners.

Having deprived her of this first right of a citizen, the elective franchise, thereby leaving her without representation in the halls of legislation, he has oppressed her on all sides.

He has made her, if married, in the eye of the law, civilly dead.

He has taken from her all right in property, even to the wages she earns.

He has made her, morally, an irresponsible being, as she can commit many crimes with impunity, provided they be done in the presence of her husband. In the covenant of marriage, she is compelled to promise obedience to her husband, he becoming, to all intents and purposes, her master – the law giving him power to deprive her of her liberty, and to administer chastisement.

He has so framed the laws of divorce, as to what shall be the proper causes, and in case of separation, to whom the guardianship of the children shall be given, as to be wholly regardless of the happiness of women – the law, in all cases, going upon a false supposition of the supremacy of man, and giving all power into his hands.

After depriving her of all rights as a married woman, if single, and the owner of property, he has taxed her to support a government which recognizes her only when her property can be made profitable to it.

He has monopolized nearly all the profitable employments, and from those she is permitted to follow, she receives but a scanty remuneration. He closes against her all the avenues to wealth and distinction which he considers most honorable to himself. As a teacher of theology, medicine, or law, she is not known.

He has denied her the facilities for obtaining a thorough education, all colleges being closed against her.

He allows her in Church, as well as State, but a subordinate position, claiming Apostolic authority for her exclusion from the ministry, and, with some exceptions, from any public participation in the affairs of the Church.

He has created a false public sentiment by giving to the world a different code of morals for men and women, by which moral delinquencies which exclude women from society, are not only tolerated, but deemed of little account in man.

He has usurped the prerogative of Jehovah himself, claiming it as his right to assign for her a sphere of action, when that belongs to her conscience and to her God.

He has endeavored, in every way that he could, to destroy her confidence in her own powers, to lessen her self-respect, and to make her willing to lead a dependent and abject life.

Now, in view of this entire disfranchisement of one-half the people of this country, their social and religious degradation – in view of the unjust laws above mentioned, and because women do feel themselves aggrieved, oppressed, and fraudulently deprived of their most sacred rights, we insist that they have immediate admission to all the rights and privileges which belong to them as citizens of the United States.

In entering upon the great work before us, we anticipate no small amount of misconception, misrepresentation, and ridicule; but we shall use every instrumentality within our power to effect our object. We shall employ agents, circulate tracts, petition the State and National legislatures, and endeavor to enlist the pulpit and the press in our behalf. We hope this Convention will be followed by a series of Conventions embracing every part of the country.

Source: https://teachingamericanhistory.org/library/document/declaration-of-sentiments/

Document 2 Questions

1. Ask students to list some of the ways that this Declaration mimics the Declaration of Independence. Why did Stanton choose to pattern this document in this way? In your opinion, was this a wise choice? Do you think that she might, in part, have meant the document to be humorous?

> She chose to write the document in this way because she wanted to call attention to how closely the demands of her generation of American feminists could be correlated with the demands made by the spokesmen of the American Revolution, some seventy-two years before. It is a bold, witty, and penetrating way to make her case. Like great American reformers before and since, she argues for her reforms on the basis of their continuity with fundamental American documents. But the Declaration is unique in its also including a subtle vein of satirical humor.

2. What does she mean in saying that man "has made [woman], morally, an irresponsible being"?

> She is pointing here toward the close relationship between rights and
> responsibilities. A person without rights is also a person without
> responsibilities.

3. How does Stanton's picture of the ideal social environment compare to
Emerson's?

> In many respects they are nearly identical. Both extol the idea of the
> independent and autonomous individual, unconditioned by and unan-
> swerable to other social obligations. Both give us a window onto the
> heightened sense of individualism in the second quarter of the nine-
> teenth century.

4. Stanton has almost nothing to say about the rights and responsibilities of mothers. Is this an important omission on her part? Or are such considerations irrelevant
to her larger concerns?

> There is no obvious right answer to these questions, but they are well
> worth raising, as a way of thinking about the difference between a con-
> ception of feminism that treats men and women as strict equals and a
> conception of feminism that insists upon a form of equality that also rec-
> ognizes women's differences from men.

CHAPTER EIGHT

THE OLD SOUTH AND SLAVERY

Summary

WHEN DID "THE SOUTH" crystallize as a distinct region within the new nation? It may not have been until Jefferson's "fire bell in the night," the 1819–21 crisis over the admission of Missouri to the Union. But the South had a certain unifying distinctiveness from the beginning. At the bottom of it all was a certain combination of climate and economics, a combination that made it ideal territory for the profitable cultivation of cash crops, such as cotton, tobacco, rice, sugar, and indigo, which could in turn be exported as a source of income.

The South also was a more insular area, more self-contained, more drawn in upon itself, more conscious of its own identity, and increasingly aware of its potential minority status within the nation. Unlike the North, it did not experience great waves of immigration from Europe, such as the influx of Irish and German refugees who streamed into northern cities during the 1840s, fleeing from poverty, famine, and political instability in their native lands. As time passed, these trends tended to perpetuate one another; immigrants avoided the South because it was too insular, because there was so little nonagricultural work, and because they didn't want to be forced to compete with slave labor. And so the South became ever more committed to slave labor, in what turned into a self-reinforcing cycle. As a consequence, the region's population growth would come mainly from internal sources.

Thus the South remained an overwhelmingly agricultural society, in which the production and sale of cotton constituted the central form of economic activity and in which cities were few and far between and economic diversification outside of agriculture was almost nonexistent. It was also a very wealthy region, but with wealth concentrated in a very few hands, individuals who were perched atop a very precarious social and economic structure, ultimately dependent on the price of cotton and the use of forced labor for their lofty standing.

Cotton enjoyed phenomenal success in establishing itself as a commodity avidly sought around the world, especially in Great Britain, where southern cotton became the force powering the British textile industry. That success made the planter class overconfident about their standing and their prospects. As world demand for cotton continued to rise inexorably, the South's future prosperity seemed assured, so long as it was firmly wedded to cotton. With cotton as its chief weapon, the southern economy would be unbeatable and could call the tune for the rest of the world, for long into the foreseeable future. As the South Carolina planter James Henry Hammond boasted, if the South were to choose to deprive England of a steady supply of southern cotton, "England would topple headlong and carry the whole civilized world with her.... No, you dare not make war on cotton. No power on earth dares to make war upon it. Cotton is king."

Such words smacked of hubris, the excessive pride that goes before a fall. And so they would turn out to be, expressing a mistaken vision that would lead to cruel and tragic consequences for the South. Lulled into a false sense of economic security by the illusion that cotton was invincible and its prices would never fall, the South would become fatally committed to a brutal social and economic system that was designed for the lucrative production of cotton on a massive scale but that achieved such productivity at an incalculable cost in human and moral terms and placed the region on a collision course with fundamental American ideals.

The practice of slavery in North America was resistant to easy generalizations, varying greatly depending on the time and place. Slavery in North America had begun in 1619 as something not always clearly distinct from indentured servitude, and as it spread, it changed and adapted to circumstances. For the century and a half of British colonial rule, it existed as a system of forced or coerced labor that had not been thoroughly defined and codified, and it was practiced in all the colonies, New England as well as the South. After the Revolution, however, it became more regularized and regulated, and its practice became localized to the South, as the northern states gradually abolished it.

Religion was at the center of slaves' communal life, and it was the crucial resource that made it possible for them to sustain communities and families at all. The forces against their doing so were immense, especially in the closed circumstances of the large plantations. The slave religion taught the same lesson that many previous generations of Christians, as well as Stoics like the Roman slave Epictetus, had learned: the soul can remain free even when the body is bound. While it would be wrong to minimize the psychological ravages of slavery, it would be equally wrong to deny the heroism and resiliency that slaves showed, guarding their hearts and keeping hope alive under hopeless conditions.

There were only three major slave rebellions attempted in nineteenth-century America, and only one of them, the Nat Turner Rebellion in Southampton County, Virginia, in August 1831, managed to move from plan to action. But that one rebellion, the bloodiest in American history, would have enormous consequences.

The ferocity of the Nat Turner Rebellion sent chills of terror down the spines of white southerners, as rumors traveled far and wide about other such rebellions under way or in the making. Such changes in attitude led to a tightening of the institution of slavery and to growing respectability granted to a "pro-slavery" argument that slavery was a "positive good" – a view that underscored the extent to which the South was becoming hopelessly dependent on slavery for its economic well-being. And yet, in the view of the Virginian George Fitzhugh, perhaps the most influential of the pro-slavery apologists, the paternalism of slavery was far preferable to the "wage slavery" of northern industrial society, in which, he maintained, greedy, profit-oriented capitalists took no responsibility for the comprehensive well-being of their workers but instead exploited them freely and then cast them aside like used tissues when their labor was no longer useful.

It is hard to know how widespread acceptance of such ideas was. But their appearance was an ominous portent for the future cohesiveness of the American nation. They were a sign that the South was in the process of cutting itself off from the rest of the nation, and from the nation's shared political heritage, in a multitude of ways that all traced back to the need to defend and protect its "peculiar institution."

Questions and Answers

1. What factors of climate and geography caused the South to focus on commercial or staple crop agriculture? (pp. 139–40)

> The climate produces long growing seasons, and the rivers remain navigable far into the interior, providing easy transportation to overseas markets.

2. How important to the U.S. and world economies was cotton? What were the requirements for successful mass production of this cash crop? (p. 140)

> Cotton accounted for two-thirds of all U.S. exports and was the raw material for the textile industries of Europe and the North. Cotton (and tobacco) exhausts the soil after four or five crops, so planters had to constantly be acquiring new fields. As a consequence, the labor force also had to be easily moved, which slaves were.

3. Unlike the North, the South attracted little immigration from Europe; why? What was the effect of this on southern demographics, society, and culture? (p. 140)

> There was little nonagricultural work, and the existence of slave labor tainted the status of free labor. This became a self-reinforcing trend, keeping the South from gaining population, except from natural increase. Society was dominated by a relatively small number of very wealthy planters; the southern middle class was small compared to that in the North, and there was less interchange of ideas within the South.

4. Southern society was biracial but also, paradoxically, characterized by a certain commonality of culture between whites and blacks. What were the causes and elements of this common culture? (p. 140)

> "The amount of exchange and interchange between and among white and black Southerners, in speech patterns, foodways, music, worship, folklore, and literary expression was enormous." The practice of single-crop agriculture was a factor, focusing the life of the community around a single economic activity. Also, black servants lived in close proximity to planter-class whites; white children on a plantation were not infrequently raised by a black woman, often alongside her own child or children.

5. Is the "Old South" myth or history? Yes. Explain. (pp. 142–43)

> Is *Gone with the Wind* or *Uncle Tom's Cabin* a more accurate portrait of the Old South, which "had many elements of beauty and graciousness, learning and high culture, piety and devotion, all mixed with elements of ugliness and brutal dehumanization"? Is the truth one or the other? Both? Neither? Somewhere in between? Be prepared to defend your position in class or in writing.

6. Why was the planter class so confident that cotton was king, even though it "placed the region on a collision course with changing moral sensibilities in the world, and with fundamental American ideals"? (p. 142)

Cotton was enormously profitable, and shortsighted planters and regional politicians like James Henry Hammond could not imagine that it would not always be just as profitable, if not more so. Pride blinded them to economic realities; they could not imagine, for example, that southern cotton would soon find itself in competition with cotton from other countries. Pride precedes a fall, and so too do inertia and isolation; what the South believed, virtually everyone had believed less than a century before. But the world changed, and the South didn't.

7. "The majority of slave-holders were ordinary farmers who owned fewer than twenty slaves and worked in the field with their slaves." How many southern whites owned no slaves at all? How many were wealthy planters? (p. 143)

> Three-fourths of whites owned no slaves; the white middle class, about 20 percent, owned fewer than twenty slaves. The wealthy planters who owned a hundred or more slaves numbered about twenty-three hundred, about 4 percent of the white population.

8. What characteristics of a medieval feudal society did the South exhibit – and embrace? (p. 143)

> Planters had an often prickly sense of masculine honor; a respect for culture and learning; a taste for grand estates and hospitality; loyalty to family and locality; veneration of womanhood and feminine purity and strict deference to elders; and a strong sense of social hierarchy, which included dutiful respect toward one's "betters," combined with a patriarchal and paternalistic attitude toward "inferiors," including slaves.

9. Why is it difficult to tell the story of black southerners under slavery? (pp. 144–45)

> Sources are relatively few, in part due to the paucity of written materials. But also, the patterns of slavery were as diverse as the larger society; rural slavery differed from urban, small farms from large plantations, house servants from field hands, the upper South from the lower.

10. How did Christianity shape, and how was it shaped by, the slave experience?

> The stories in the Bible, such as the Exodus of the enslaved Hebrews from Egypt, spoke powerfully to African American slaves and provided the crucial resource that enabled them to sustain family and community under harsh conditions. And the African style of music and worship in turn affected American evangelical Christianity.

11. Why was the Underground Railroad successful in freeing many thousands of slaves, while slave revolts were rare and uniformly unsuccessful? (p. 146)

> Insurrections could not succeed when whites so outnumbered slaves. But escaping to Canada (necessary because of the federal Fugitive Slave Act) was feasible for small numbers.

12. How and why did Nat Turner's revolt change slavery and the South? Include discussion of the debate in the Virginia General Assembly of 1831–32. What new laws did the assembly finally pass?

> The revolt terrified the South, particularly as Turner himself testified that his master had not been unkind. It was the system itself he wanted to destroy. The debate about gradual emancipation ended in favor of more strict controls. The South now saw itself as under attack and adopted a defensive mentality. Criticism of slavery, previously very common, was now much less acceptable.

13. How did southerners like George Fitzhugh and John C. Calhoun defend slavery? How did this make civil war increasingly likely?

> They argued that chattel slaves were actually better off than the "wage slaves" of the North and that slavery was not an evil necessity but a positive good.

Objective Question

Answers are in parentheses.

Put in order:

____ "Gag rule" in House prohibits discussion of slavery   (3)
____ Nat Turner's uprising   (1)
____ Virginia Assembly rejects plan for gradual emancipation   (2)

THE SONGS OF AFRICAN AMERICAN SLAVERY

The African American scholar and activist W. E. B. Du Bois produced one of the most beautiful and most penetrating accounts of the songs from the days of slavery, often called "spirituals," in a chapter called "The Sorrow Songs," appearing in his 1903 book The Souls of Black Folk. *Interested students will want to read the whole chapter, which can be found at https://www.bartleby.com/114/14.html. But for our purposes, we will consider only a few small parts of the text:*

> *What are these songs, and what do they mean? I know little of music and can say nothing in technical phrase, but I know something of men, and knowing them, I know that these songs are the articulate message of the slave to the world. They tell us in these eager days that life was joyous to the black slave, careless and happy. I can easily believe this of some, of many. But not all the past South, though it rose from the dead, can gainsay the heart-touching witness of these songs. They are the music of an unhappy people, of the children of disappointment; they tell of death and suffering and unvoiced longing toward a truer world, of misty wanderings and hidden ways.*

Du Bois is warning us that surfaces can be deceiving, and the seeming joyfulness of the songs is always laced with deep currents of sadness and longing. The songs could serve many purposes; they could be work songs, celebratory songs, commemorative songs, the means by which a captive people unable to read or write managed nevertheless to communicate and share memories. Some songs contained coded information about means of escape, about safe houses. Many borrowed from the imagery of the Bible, comparing themselves to the enslaved Israelites who were bound, eventually, for the Promised Land of freedom.

The lyrics are, of course, much diminished when presented without the music. But here are a few of the more famous songs; lyrics are taken from the website Negrospirituals.com.

SOMETIMES I FEEL LIKE A MOTHERLESS CHILD

The profound sadness and uprootedness of slavery are captured in a "relatable" way by being compared to the experience of a homeless orphan.

Sometimes I feel like a motherless child
Sometimes I feel like a motherless child
Sometimes I feel like a motherless child
A long ways from home
A long ways from home
True believer
A long ways from home
Along ways from home

Sometimes I feel like I'm almos' gone
Sometimes I feel like I'm almos' gone
Sometimes I feel like I'm almos' gone
Way up in de heab'nly land
Way up in de heab'nly land
True believer
Way up in de heab'nly land
Way up in de heab'nly land

Sometimes I feel like a motherless child
Sometimes I feel like a motherless child
Sometimes I feel like a motherless child
A long ways from home
There's praying everywhere

WADE IN THE WATER

Harriet Tubman used "Wade in the Water" to tell escaping slaves that they could get into the water to avoid being apprehended.

Chorus: Wade in the Water, wade in the water children.

Wade in the Water. God's gonna trouble the water.
Who are those children all dressed in Red?
God's gonna trouble the water.
Must be the ones that Moses led.
God's gonna trouble the water.

Chorus

Who are those children all dressed in White?
God's gonna trouble the water.
Must be the ones of the Israelites.
God's gonna trouble the water.

Chorus

Who are those children all dressed in Blue?
God's gonna trouble the water.
Must be the ones that made it through.
God's gonna trouble the water.

Chorus

STEAL AWAY

This song has an overtly religious message but also a more worldly undercurrent: the person singing it is planning to escape.

Chorus: steal away, steal away!

Steal away to Jesus?
Steal away, steal away home!
I ain't got long to stay here!

My Lord calls me!
He calls me by the thunder!
The trumpet sound it in my soul!
I ain't got long to stay here!

Chorus

My Lord calls me!
He calls me by the lighting!
The trumpet sound it in my soul!
I ain't got long to stay here!

Chorus

Go Down Moses

Here, too, the enslaved singers found a precedent and a hope in the story of ancient Israel.

> When Israel was in Egypt's land
> Let my people go
> Oppressed so hard they could not stand
> Let my people go
>
> Go down Moses
> Way down in Egypt land
> Tell old Pharaoh
> "Let my people go"
>
> "Thus spoke the Lord" bold Moses said
> Let my people go
> "If not I'll smite your first born dead
> Let my people go
>
> No more in bondage shall they toil
> Let my people go
> Let them come out with Egypt's spoil"
> Let my people go

Sweet Chariot

A slave hearing this song would ready himself to escape – a band of angels is coming to take him to freedom. The Underground Railroad (the sweet chariot) was coming South (swing low) to take the slave to the North or freedom (carry me home).

> Swing low, sweet chariot,
> Coming for to carry me home,
> Swing low, sweet chariot,
> Coming for to carry me home.
>
> I looked over Jordan and what did I see
> Coming for to carry me home,
> A band of angels coming after me,
> Coming for to carry me home.

If you get there before I do,
Coming for to carry me home,
Tell all my friends that I'm coming, too,
Coming for to carry me home.

Returning to Du Bois's essay, he argues that hope was an animating force in the hearts of even those to whom the Land of Hope had given little reason for hope – indeed, he argues that those hearts had made an inestimable contribution to what is best in America.

> *Through all the sorrow of the Sorrow Songs there breathes a hope – a faith in the ultimate justice of things. The minor cadences of despair change often to triumph and calm confidence. Sometimes it is faith in life, sometimes a faith in death, sometimes assurance of boundless justice in some fair world beyond. But whichever it is, the meaning is always clear: that sometime, somewhere, men will judge men by their souls and not by their skins. Is such a hope justified? Do the Sorrow Songs sing true?*
>
> *.... Your country? How came it yours? Before the Pilgrims landed we were here. Here we have brought our three gifts and mingled them with yours: a gift of story and song – soft, stirring melody in an ill-harmonized and unmelodious land; the gift of sweat and brawn to beat back the wilderness, conquer the soil, and lay the foundations of this vast economic empire two hundred years earlier than your weak hands could have done it; the third, a gift of the Spirit. Around us the history of the land has centred for thrice a hundred years; out of the nation's heart we have called all that was best to throttle and subdue all that was worst; fire and blood, prayer and sacrifice, have billowed over this people, and they have found peace only in the altars of the God of Right. Nor has our gift of the Spirit been merely passive. Actively we have woven ourselves with the very warp and woof of this nation, – we fought their battles, shared their sorrow, mingled our blood with theirs, and generation after generation have pleaded with a headstrong, careless people to despise not Justice, Mercy, and Truth, lest the nation be smitten with a curse. Our song, our toil, our cheer, and warning have been given to this nation in blood-brotherhood. Are not these gifts worth the giving? Is not this work and striving? Would America have been America without her Negro people?*

Document Questions

1. What were the multiple uses of their songs for African American slaves?

   They were work songs but also songs of togetherness and shared stories and memories, particularly important to a nonliterate people that had no way of recording its memories on paper. They also often served as coded messages regarding the means of escape from their enslaved condition.

2. How do the songs borrow from the Bible?

   They borrow from the Bible through frequent allusions to the ancient Israelites' escape from slavery in Egypt and by invoking the name and person of Jesus as a source of salvation and ultimate protection.

3. Where and how does Du Bois find hope emerging in the Sorrow Songs? Does he share this hope?

   He sees in them a consistent appeal to a standard of justice, in this life or the next, in some place or time, and a hopeful faith that such justice exists. It is not clear whether he entirely shares the hope himself, since he leaves his own question unanswered. But it would not make sense for him to admire the songs so much while believing them to be based entirely upon illusion.

4. Du Bois seems to be insisting at the end that America would not have been America without her "Negro people," her African Americans. What does he mean by that? What are the "three gifts" to which he refers earlier in the paragraph?

   The three gifts are the gifts of story and song, the gift of labor, and the gift of the Spirit. Without those gifts, he argues, the country would not have become what it is.

5. Why is the image of feeling like a "motherless child, a long ways from home" so piercing?

   A child without a mother is a child that feels itself thrown into the world without any past or any source of moral or emotional support. Being fatherless is bad enough, but to be motherless is far worse. And to be homeless on top of that – it is a very haunting picture of complete estrangement and isolation, expressed in an image of surpassing simplicity.

CHAPTER NINE

THE GATHERING STORM

Summary

MEXICO WON ITS INDEPENDENCE from Spain in the 1820s, and its government welcomed immigrants from the American South to settle and farm the sparsely settled northern province called Texas. But the gesture was too successful. By 1836, the waves of American immigration had been so powerful that they led to a successful movement for the independence of Texas from Mexico. Texas then appealed to the U.S. government to be admitted as a state. War with Mexico would eventually ensue and concluded in a decisive American victory. With the signing of the Treaty of Guadalupe Hidalgo on February 2, 1848, Mexico abandoned its claims to Texas above the Rio Grande River and ceded the territories of California, Utah, and New Mexico to the United States. Taken along with the United States' acquisition of the Oregon Territory two years earlier, this meant that the United States was now a sprawling transcontinental nation.

The addition of this new land, however, brought the slavery question back to the surface, specifically the question of how the United States would control the expansion of slavery into the newly acquired territories. In 1846, Pennsylvania congressman David Wilmot, while endorsing annexation of Texas as a slave state, proposed that Congress forbid the introduction of slavery to any of the territories acquired in the Mexican War. The *Wilmot Proviso* passed the House but was rejected by the Senate. Senator John C. Calhoun of South Carolina responded to the Wilmot Proviso with disdain, arguing that slaveholders had a constitutional right to take their slaves into territories if they wished. Future battle lines were being drawn.

Then something quite unexpected happened. In 1848, gold was discovered in California, luring some three hundred thousand people to California over a seven-year period – one of the greatest mass migrations in American history. The resulting chaos created a desperate need for organized government to bring law and order. California statehood was now on a very fast track. But the admission of California as a free state would undermine the delicate balance between slave and free states in the Senate and consign the slave South to a permanently shrinking minority. How to resolve this problem?

In response, Henry Clay of Kentucky fashioned a complex, multifaceted package of eight different resolutions, known collectively as the Compromise of 1850. California would be admitted as a free state, but the status of slavery in the other territories acquired after the Mexican War was left to be decided by popular sovereignty. The Compromise crucially included also the passing of a strengthened Fugitive Slave Law, to compensate the South for its permanent loss of parity between slave and free states. Northerners opposed to slavery, however, rejected the Fugitive Slave Law because it forced their active and direct support for the institution of slavery by requiring that they cooperate in tracking, capturing, and extraditing men and women. The Wisconsin Supreme Court declared it to be unconstitutional, and Vermont passed laws nullifying it.

The push for a transcontinental railroad linking the two coasts also complicated matters between northern and southern states. Illinois senator Stephen A. Douglas proposed that the land west of Missouri be organized into two territories, the Kansas Territory and the Nebraska Territory, with each being allowed to settle by popular sovereignty the question of whether slavery would be permitted. In effect, Douglas proposed the repeal of the Missouri Compromise (see chapter 6). After passage of the Kansas–Nebraska Act of 1854, the Republican Party rose in direct response, drawing its membership from anti-slavery elements in the Democratic, Whig, and Free Soil Parties, unifying around the issue of opposing the extension of slavery into the territories. By 1856, the Republican Party was the second largest party in the country.

Two days after James Buchanan's inauguration as president, the U.S. Supreme Court published *Dred Scott v. Sandford* (1857), an explosive decision in which the Supreme Court ruled that (1) Scott, a black man, did not have legal standing to sue because he was not recognized as a citizen; (2) Congress lacked power to deprive any person of his property without due process of law, and slaves were property; and (3) the Missouri Compromise was not merely rendered moot by the Kansas–Nebraska Act but had been unconstitutional all along.

Following *Dred Scott*, the eyes of the nation turned to Senator Stephen Douglas of Illinois, who was the last remaining prominent Democrat running for reelection to the Senate in 1858 as a possible candidate for the presidency in 1860. In the 1858 Illinois Senate election, Douglas faced a formidable challenge in a rising star of the Republican Party: Abraham Lincoln.

Lincoln lost the Senate election to Douglas, but his strong showing in the race brought him to the attention of the whole nation and made him a formidable Republican candidate for the presidency in 1860. Lincoln won the presidency that fall but, ominously, without attracting a single Electoral College vote from the South.

Soon after Lincoln's election, South Carolina dissolved its union with the other states, citing the election of Lincoln as justification. By February 1, 1861, six other southern states had followed suit (Mississippi, Florida, Texas, Georgia, Louisiana, and Alabama). By February 7, the seven states had formed into the Confederate States of America, adopting a Constitution nearly identical to the U.S. Constitution, but with added limits on government's power to impose tariffs and protections for slavery.

The ingredients for an explosion were now in place; all that was needed was an event to light the fuse.

Questions and Answers

1. What is the problem with historical hindsight? (p. 151)

> It makes what happened seem inevitable, when in fact few things are, and contemporaries probably didn't think they were.

2. "History is only rarely the story of **inevitabilities**, and it almost never appears in that form to its participants. It is more often a story of **contingencies** and **possibilities**." (p. 151)

3. "What we can say, though, is that there were landmark moments in which a blood-stained outcome became much more likely." At *what point* do you think civil war became all but unavoidable? Be prepared to defend your answer in class or in writing. (p. 152)

> Teachers may point out the series of compromises regarding slavery, from the three-fifths agreement in the Constitution through the Missouri Compromise to the Compromise of 1850 to the election of Lincoln and secession and war. Point out that the earlier agreements lasted a long time; the Missouri Compromise settled the issue of slavery in the West until the Mexican War added territory not covered by it – twenty-five years. But the Compromise of 1850 broke down almost immediately. Was this due to the existence of slavery becoming a moral issue, as opposed to the issue being the expansion of slavery? Or, as some historians have suggested, did a generation of great compromisers (Clay,

Calhoun, Daniel Webster) retire in 1850, with their replacements being less able and more fanatical?

4. What were the consequences of the Mexican War? (p. 152)

It added immense new territories, in which the status of slavery had to be newly determined, as the old Missouri Compromise would not necessarily apply.

5. Be able to write a short description of the role and significance of Stephen F. Austin, Antonio Lopez de Santa Anna, the Mexican Constitution of 1824, Sam Houston, and the battles of the Alamo, Goliad, and San Jacinto. (Note that in proportion to numbers engaged, the Texas Revolution was one of the bloodiest wars ever fought, in large part because each of the three battles listed was in some respect a massacre.) (pp. 152–53)

The Mexican government invited Austin to bring in Anglo-Americans to settle in Texas, as a buffer between Mexico and the Comanche and other hostile tribes. Mexico adopted a liberal constitution in 1824, which General Santa Anna overthrew. When the Texans resisted, Santa Anna invaded and destroyed Texan forces at the Alamo and Goliad. Sam Houston retreated toward the United States while building an army, Santa Anna pursued to drive the Texans out of the land, and Houston turned and defeated Santa Anna's army at San Jacinto. The captured dictator agreed to Texan independence, although his government repudiated him later. Texas remained at war with Mexico for the next ten years, as an independent republic when the United States refused its admission as a state.

6. The Texans wanted to become part of the United States. Why did this not happen for ten years? (p. 153)

Northerners and opponents of slavery did not want more slave states, and there was (justified) fear that annexing Texas as a state would ignite a war with Mexico.

7. Why did the British want Texas to remain an independent republic? (p. 154)

The British could buy cotton from Texas, in tariff-free markets, more easily than from the United States, and Texas might need her protection. It also weakened the United States as a potential British enemy.

8. Annexation of Texas by the United States seems to be the first occasion for the use of the term *Manifest Destiny* (by journalist John L. O'Sullivan). What did Americans of the 1840s mean by that term? (p. 154)

> They believed it was God's will or plan for the United States to extend from sea to sea. This is often presented in strictly negative terms, as a project of imperialist domination. But that is only part of the story. O'Sullivan's Manifest Destiny was an idealistic vision springing from the spirit of Jacksonian democracy but recalling American dreams of previous generations, of America as a land of hope. He said of his country that "we are the nation of progress, of individual freedom, of universal enfranchisement … of the great experiment of liberty … an Union of many Republics, comprising hundreds of happy millions, calling, owning no man master, but governed by God's natural and moral law of equality, the law of brotherhood."

9. Mexico still refused to recognize Texan independence in 1845. Could war with the United States, following annexation, have been avoided? Did either side try very hard? (pp. 154–55)

> Probably not, and no.

10. Although most Americans supported the Mexican War, there was some opposition. From whom, and why? (p. 155)

> Opponents of slavery opposed it; John Quincy Adams labeled it "a most unrighteous war."
>
> Teachers might also mention the San Patricios, a unit of Irish Catholics, many of them deserters from the U.S. Army, who fought courageously as part of the Mexican forces.

11. What and where are the "halls of Montezuma"? (p. 155)

> Montezuma was the last Aztec emperor, killed by Cortez's *conquistadores*. His "halls" are the capital of Mexico captured by the U.S. Army (and U.S. Marines) in 1847.

12. By how much, and how, did the United States grow between 1846 and 1848? How was the event at Sutter's Mill the icing on the cake? (p. 155)

> The United States added Texas, Oregon (split with the British), and the "Mexican cession from Texas to California." (See the map on p. 158.) The Gadsden Purchase was made in 1852 to provide better land for a southern transcontinental railroad. The discovery of gold was the icing on the cake.

13. How did the growth of the United States in 1846–48 upset the delicate political balance of the nation? (pp. 156–59)

> The number of free and slave states needed to be kept equal; otherwise, one section would control the U.S. Senate. California's rapid admission as a free state upset that.

14. What antithetical positions were argued by David Wilmot and John C. Calhoun? A possible solution was the idea of *popular sovereignty* offered by Lewis Cass. Explain that idea. (pp. 156–57)

> Wilmot wanted no slavery in the new territories; Calhoun wanted slavery all the way to California. Cass suggested letting the voters within each new territory decide whether the state would be free or open to slavery. (A territory submits a state constitution to Congress; when it is accepted, the territory is admitted as a new state.)
>
> Teachers may find this a perfect moment to discuss the pros and cons of popular sovereignty as a doctrine of governance.

15. Who was the main architect of the Compromise of 1850? What were its elements? What did it settle? What did it *not* settle? (pp. 158–60)

> Henry Clay was the "great compromiser," but this one was hard to cobble together and had to be passed as individual measures, by slim margins, rather than as an omnibus bill. The North got California as a free state, upsetting the Senate balance, and in recompense, the South got a strengthened Fugitive Slave Act. This was the last political act for Clay, Calhoun, and Daniel Webster, sectional spokesmen who nevertheless had been willing to compromise when necessary. The Compromise did not settle any underlying issues, but it bought time – if only a short time.

16. We tend to think primarily of the South as appealing to states' rights and nullification, and even secession, though those ideas had been espoused in New England in opposition to the War of 1812. How did northern states react to the new Fugitive Slave Law? (p. 160)

> They passed laws attempting to nullify its effect.

17. Did the rise of antislavery as a moral crusade rather than a political cause make compromise more difficult? Impossible? Was this a good thing or a bad thing? Be prepared to discuss in class or on paper. (pp. 159–60)

> It made compromise all but impossible. Whether this was good or bad in effect depends on something unknowable: whether slavery might

somehow have been abolished, perhaps later in the century, without the bloodbath of the Civil War.

18. Debate over the possible route of a **transcontinental railroad** led to the Kansas–Nebraska Act of 1854, which showed the weakness of popular sovereignty and led to **Bleeding Kansas,** where deadly violence first erupted between pro- and anti-slavery forces. (p. 162)

19. What and when were John Brown's two acts of violence? (pp. 162, 168)

He murdered five pro-slavery settlers at Pottawatomie Creek in Kansas in 1854 (and fought in the guerilla war there), and he led a raid to capture the U.S. rifle works, hoping then to spark a slave revolt at Harpers Ferry in Virginia in 1859.

Teachers may point out that Brown did not act alone; he had at least twenty men with him in Kansas and at Harpers Ferry, and he received financial support and encouragement from abolitionists in Boston. He was the tip of the abolitionist spear.

20. How did violence spread to the halls of Congress? (p. 162)

Senator Sumner of Massachusetts made disparaging comments about Senator Butler of South Carolina. Butler's cousin, Congressman Brooks, beat Sumner senseless as he sat in the Senate chamber.

21. When and why did the Republican Party emerge? It was the first entirely sectional party, confined almost entirely to the North. (p. 163)

The Free Soil Party had earlier opposed the expansion of slavery into the West. As the Whig Party broke up (it had been formed to oppose Jackson, who was now gone), its northern members formed the new party. The Republicans were careful to distinguish themselves from the abolitionists; they focused on preventing the spread of slavery into the West and were prepared to tolerate it where it already existed.

22. President Buchanan was ineffective in dealing with the crisis in Kansas, but the Supreme Court made things far worse with the *Dred Scott* decision. What was its effect? (p. 165)

It declared the Missouri Compromise's restriction on slavery in the territories to be unconstitutional, which threw open the whole question once again, and worse. (Contrast the maps on pp. 161 and 164.)

23. If your opponents have a fear of you approaching paranoia, how do you reassure them of your good intentions? What happens if *both* sides have similar irrational ideas about the other?

> You cannot reassure them, as they fear you are deceiving them, "setting us up." If both sides are paranoid, then communication, especially negotiation in good faith, is impossible.
>
> Teachers may encourage students to think what *they* might have done in such a situation to encourage constructive dialogue between the opposing parties.

24. Why were the Lincoln–Douglas debates important? Who won the election? (pp. 166–67)

> Douglas won the Senate seat, but the debates made Lincoln the rising star of the Republican Party. The debates are an excellent example of how complex issues should be argued. They also illustrate the democratic dilemma of reconciling popular sentiments with enduring principles.

25. Were Lincoln's objections to slavery moral or political? Was he an abolitionist? (pp. 166–67)

> Lincoln hated slavery but was unwilling to risk war to abolish it where it already existed. He was glad to be able to act against it, midway through the war to restore the Union, but he was politically shrewd and understood that politics is "the art of the possible."

26. Be able to describe the election of 1860. Who ran? Who won? Why? (pp. 168–69)

> Lincoln won with 40 percent of the vote because the Democrats split three ways: a Northern Democrat (Douglas), a Southern Democrat (Breckenridge), and a border state Democrat (Bell of Kentucky). Lincoln carried every free state, and *only* those states.

27. How did the southern states respond to Lincoln's election? (p. 169)

> The lower seven states seceded and formed the Confederacy. The upper South, including Virginia and Tennessee, remained in the Union for the time being.

28. It is widely and (for the most part) correctly argued that slavery caused the Civil War. Yet how then does one explain support by Lincoln and other Republicans for the Corwin Amendment? And how does one explain the southern states' clinging to secession if they had such a guarantee of protection of slavery where it already existed? (p. 170)

> Things had gone too far, there was too much distrust, and the South saw itself as prey to the North in economic terms through such things as the tariff, and so needing full independence.
>
> Historians generally adhere to the principle of "multiple causation" – nothing ever just has a single cause, and complex events have complex causes. The Civil War was as complex as it gets. So while there is no doubt that the expansion of slavery into the western territories was the great issue that could not be settled permanently (given the growth of the nation) or peaceably (given escalating mutual distrust), it is also fair to point out that northerners were not willing to go to war to free slaves.

Objective Questions

Answers are in parentheses.

Put in order:

_____ "Bleeding Kansas"	(2)
_____ Kansas–Nebraska Act	(1)
_____ John Brown's raid on Harpers Ferry	(3)

Put in order:

_____ *Dred Scott* decision	(2)
_____ Missouri Compromise	(1)
_____ Lincoln–Douglas debates	(3)

Put in order:

_____ Corwin Amendment passes Congress	(3)
_____ Lincoln is elected	(1)
_____ South Carolina secedes	(2)

Put in order:

_____ Alamo battle   (2)
_____ San Jacinto battle   (3)
_____ Santa Anna overthrows Mexican Constitution   (1)

Put in order:

_____ caning of Sumner   (3)
_____ Compromise of 1850   (1)
_____ Kansas–Nebraska Act   (2)

Document

LINCOLN'S SPEECH ON THE *DRED SCOTT* DECISION, JUNE 26, 1857 (ABRIDGED)

FELLOW CITIZENS: I am here to-night, partly by the invitation of some of you, and partly by my own inclination. Two weeks ago Judge Douglas spoke here on the several subjects of Kansas, the Dred Scott decision, and Utah. I listened to the speech at the time, and have read the report of it since. It was intended to controvert opinions which I think just, and to assail (politically, not personally,) those men who, in common with me, entertain those opinions. For this reason I wished then, and still wish, to make some answer to it, which I now take the opportunity of doing.

.... And now as to the Dred Scott decision. That decision declares two propositions – first, that a negro cannot sue in the U.S. Courts; and secondly, that Congress cannot prohibit slavery in the Territories. It was made by a divided court-dividing differently on the different points. Judge Douglas does not discuss the merits of the decision; and, in that respect, I shall follow his example, believing I could no more improve on McLean and Curtis, than he could on Taney.

He denounces all who question the correctness of that decision, as offering violent resistance to it. But who resists it? Who has, in spite of the decision, declared Dred Scott free, and resisted the authority of his master over him?

Judicial decisions have two uses – first, to absolutely determine the case decided, and secondly, to indicate to the public how other similar cases will be decided when they arise. For the latter use, they are called "precedents" and "authorities."

We believe, as much as Judge Douglas, (perhaps more) in obedience to, and respect for the judicial department of government. We think its decisions on Constitutional questions, when fully settled, should control, not only the particular cases decided, but the general policy of the country, subject to be disturbed only by amendments of the Constitution as provided in that instrument itself. More than this would be revolution. But we think the Dred Scott decision is erroneous. We know the court that made it, has often over-ruled its own decisions, and we shall do what we can to have it to over-rule this. We offer no resistance to it.

Judicial decisions are of greater or less authority as precedents, according to circumstances. That this should be so, accords both with common sense, and the customary understanding of the legal profession.

If this important decision had been made by the unanimous concurrence of the judges, and without any apparent partisan bias, and in accordance with legal public expectation, and with the steady practice of the departments throughout our history, and had been in no part, based on assumed historical facts which are not really true; or, if wanting in some of these, it had been before the court more than once, and had there been affirmed and re-affirmed through a course of years, it then might be, perhaps would be, factious, nay, even revolutionary, to not acquiesce in it as a precedent.

But when, as it is true we find it wanting in all these claims to the public confidence, it is not resistance, it is not factious, it is not even disrespectful, to treat it as not having yet quite established a settled doctrine for the country – But Judge Douglas considers this view awful. Hear him:

> "The courts are the tribunals prescribed by the Constitution and created by the authority of the people to determine, expound and enforce the law. Hence, whoever resists the final decision of the highest judicial tribunal, aims a deadly blow to our whole Republican system of government – a blow, which if successful would place all our rights and liberties at the mercy of passion, anarchy and violence. I repeat, therefore, that if resistance to the decisions of the Supreme Court of the United States, in a matter like the points decided in the Dred Scott case, clearly within their jurisdiction as defined by the Constitution, shall be forced upon the country as a political issue, it will become a distinct and naked issue between the friends and the enemies of the Constitution – the friends and the enemies of the supremacy of the laws."

Why this same Supreme court once decided a national bank to be constitutional; but Gen. Jackson, as President of the United States, disregarded the decision, and vetoed a bill for a re-charter, partly on constitutional ground, declaring that each public functionary must support the Constitution, "as he understands it." But hear the General's own words. Here they are, taken from his veto message:

> "It is maintained by the advocates of the bank, that its constitutionality, in all its features, ought to be considered as settled by precedent, and by the decision of the Supreme Court. To this conclusion I cannot assent. Mere precedent is a dangerous source of authority, and should not be regarded as deciding questions of constitutional power, except where the acquiescence of the people and the States can be considered as well settled. So far from this being the case on this subject, an argument against the bank might be based on precedent. One Congress in 1791, decided in favor of a bank; another in 1811, decided against it. One Congress in 1815 decided against a bank; another in 1816 decided in its favor. Prior to the present Congress, therefore the precedents drawn from that source were equal. If we resort to the States, the expressions of legislative, judicial and executive opinions against the bank have been probably to those in its favor as four to one. There is nothing in precedent, therefore, which if its authority were admitted, ought to weigh in favor of the act before me."

I drop the quotations merely to remark that all there ever was, in the way of precedent up to the Dred Scott decision, on the points therein decided, had been against that decision. But hear Gen. Jackson further –

> "If the opinion of the Supreme court covered the whole ground of this act, it ought not to control the co-ordinate authorities of this Government. The Congress, the executive and the court, must each for itself be guided by its own opinion of the Constitution. Each public officer, who takes an oath to support the Constitution, swears that he will support it as he understands it, and not as it is understood by others."

Again and again have I heard Judge Douglas denounce that bank decision, and applaud Gen. Jackson for disregarding it. It would be interesting for him to look over his recent speech, and see how exactly his fierce philippics against us for resisting Supreme Court decisions, fall upon his own head. It will call to his mind a long and fierce political war in this country, upon an issue which, in his own language, and, of course, in his own changeless estimation, was "a distinct and naked issue between the friends and the enemies of the Constitution," and in which war he fought in the ranks of the enemies of the Constitution.

I have said, in substance, that the Dred Scott decision was, in part, based on assumed historical facts which were not really true; and I ought not to leave the subject without giving some reasons for saying this; I therefore give an instance or two, which I think fully sustain me. Chief Justice Taney, in delivering the opinion of the majority of the Court, insists at great length that negroes were no part of the people who made, or for whom was made, the Declaration of Independence, or the Constitution of the United States.

On the contrary, Judge Curtis, in his dissenting opinion, shows that in five of the then thirteen states, to wit, New Hampshire, Massachusetts, New York, New Jersey and North Carolina, free negroes were voters, and, in proportion to their numbers, had the same part in making the Constitution that the white people had. He shows this with so much particularity as to leave no doubt of its truth; and, as a sort of conclusion on that point, holds the following language:

"The Constitution was ordained and established by the people of the United States, through the action, in each State, of those persons who were qualified by its laws to act thereon in behalf of themselves and all other citizens of the State. In some of the States, as we have seen, colored persons were among those qualified by law to act on the subject. These colored persons were not only included in the body of 'the people of the United States' – by whom the Constitution was ordained and established; but in at least five of the States they had the power to act, and, doubtless, did act, by their suffrages, upon the question of its adoption."

Again, Chief Justice Taney says: "It is difficult, at this day to realize the state of public opinion in relation to that unfortunate race, which prevailed in the civilized and enlightened portions of the world at the time of the Declaration of Independence, and when the Constitution of the United States was framed and adopted." And again, after quoting from the Declaration, he says: "The general words above quoted would seem to include the whole human family, and if they were used in a similar instrument at this day, would be so understood."

In these the Chief Justice does not directly assert, but plainly assumes, as a fact, that the public estimate of the black man is more favorable now than it was in the days of the Revolution. This assumption is a mistake. In some trifling particulars, the condition of that race has been ameliorated; but, as a whole, in this country, the change between then and now is decidedly the other way; and their ultimate destiny has never appeared so hopeless as in the last three or four years. In two of the five States – New Jersey and North Carolina – that then gave the free negro the right of voting, the right has since been taken away; and in a third – New York – it has been greatly abridged; while it has not been extended, so far as I know, to a single additional State, though the number of the States has more than doubled. In those days, as I understand, masters could, at their own pleasure, emancipate their slaves; but since then, such legal restraints have been made upon emancipation, as to amount almost to prohibition. In those days, Legislatures held the unquestioned power to abolish slavery in their respective States; but now it is becoming quite fashionable for State Constitutions to withhold that power from the Legislatures. In those days, by common consent, the spread of the black man's bondage to new countries was prohibited; but now, Congress decides that it will not continue the prohibition, and the Supreme Court decides that it could not if it would. In those days, our Declaration of Independence was held sacred by all, and thought to include all; but now, to aid in making the bondage of the negro universal and eternal, it is assailed, and sneered at, and construed, and hawked at, and torn, till, if its framers could rise from their graves, they could not at all recognize it. All the powers of earth seem rapidly combining against him. Mammon is after him; ambition follows, and philosophy follows, and the Theology of the day is fast joining the cry. They have him in his prison house; they have searched his person, and left no prying instrument with him. One after another they have closed the heavy iron doors upon him, and now they have him, as it were, bolted in with a lock of a hundred keys, which can never be unlocked without the concurrence of every key; the keys in the hands of a hundred different men, and they scattered to a hundred different and distant places; and they stand musing as to what invention, in all the dominions of mind and matter, can be produced to make the impossibility of his escape more complete than it is.

It is grossly incorrect to say or assume, that the public estimate of the negro is more favorable now than it was at the origin of the government.

Three years and a half ago, Judge Douglas brought forward his famous Nebraska bill. The country was at once in a blaze. He scorned all opposition, and carried it through Congress. Since then he has seen himself superseded in a Presidential nomination, by one indorsing the general doctrine of his measure, but at the same time standing clear of the odium of its untimely agitation, and its gross breach of national faith; and he has seen that successful rival Constitutionally elected, not by the strength of friends, but by the division of adversaries, being in a popular minority of nearly four hundred thousand votes. He has seen his chief aids in his own State, Shields and Richardson, politically speaking, successively tried, convicted, and executed, for an offense not their own, but his. And now he sees his own case, standing next on the docket for trial.

There is a natural disgust in the minds of nearly all white people, to the idea of an indiscriminate amalgamation of the white and black races; and Judge Douglas evidently is basing his chief hope, upon the chances of being able to appropriate the benefit of this disgust to himself. If he can, by much drumming and repeating, fasten the odium of that idea upon his adversaries, he thinks he can struggle through the storm. He therefore clings to this hope, as a drowning man to the last plank. He makes an occasion for lugging it in from the opposition to the Dred Scott decision. He finds the Republicans insisting that the Declaration of Independence includes ALL men, black as well as white; and forth-with he boldly denies that it includes negroes at all, and proceeds to argue gravely that all who contend it does, do so only because they want to vote, and eat, and sleep, and marry with negroes! He will have it that they cannot be consistent else. Now I protest against that counterfeit logic which concludes that, because I do not want a black woman for a slave I must necessarily want her for a wife. I need not have her for either, I can just leave her alone. In some respects she certainly is not my equal; but in her natural right to eat the bread she earns with her own hands without asking leave of any one else, she is my equal, and the equal of all others.

Chief Justice Taney, in his opinion in the Dred Scott case, admits that the language of the Declaration is broad enough to include the whole human family, but he and Judge Douglas argue that the authors of that instrument did not intend to include negroes, by the fact that they did not at once, actually place them on an equality with the whites. Now this grave argument comes to just nothing at all, by the other fact, that they did not at once, or ever afterwards, actually place all white people on an equality with one or another. And this is the staple argument of both the Chief Justice and the Senator, for doing this obvious violence to the plain unmistakable language of the Declaration. I think the authors of that notable instrument intended to include all men, but they did not intend to declare all men equal in all respects. They did not mean to say all were equal in color, size, intellect, moral developments, or social capacity. They defined with tolerable distinctness, in what respects they did consider all men created equal – equal in "certain inalienable rights, among which are life, liberty, and the pursuit of happiness." This they said, and this meant. They did not mean to assert the obvious untruth, that all were then actually enjoying that equality, nor yet, that they were about to confer it immediately upon them. In fact they had no power to confer such a boon. They meant simply to declare the right, so that the enforcement of it might follow as fast as circumstances should permit. They meant to set up a standard maxim for free society, which should be familiar to all, and revered by all; constantly looked to, constantly labored for, and even though never perfectly attained, constantly approximated, and thereby constantly spreading and deepening its influence, and augmenting the happiness and value of life to all people of all colors everywhere. The assertion that "all men are created equal" was of no practical use in effecting our separation from Great Britain; and it was placed in the Declaration, nor for that, but for future use. Its authors meant it to be, thank God, it is now proving itself, a stumbling block to those who in after times might seek to turn a free people back into the hateful paths of despotism. They knew the proneness of prosperity to breed tyrants, and they meant when such should re-appear in this fair land and commence their vocation they should find left for them at least one hard nut to crack.

I have now briefly expressed my view of the meaning and objects of that part of the Declaration of Independence which declares that "all men are created equal."

Now let us hear Judge Douglas's view of the same subject, as I find it in the printed report of his late speech. Here it is:

> "No man can vindicate the character, motives and conduct of the signers of the Declaration of Independence except upon the hypothesis that they referred to the white race alone, and not to the African, when they declared all men to have been created equal – that they were speaking of British subjects on this continent being equal to British subjects born and residing in Great Britain – that they were entitled to the same inalienable rights, and among them were enumerated life, liberty and the pursuit of happiness. The Declaration was adopted for the purpose of justifying the colonists in the eyes of the civilized world in withdrawing their allegiance from the British crown, and dissolving their connection with the mother country."

My good friends, read that carefully over some leisure hour, and ponder well upon it – see what a mere wreck – mangled ruin – it makes of our once glorious Declaration.

"They were speaking of British subjects on this continent being equal to British subjects born and residing in Great Britain!" Why, according to this, not only negroes but white people outside of Great Britain and America are not spoken of in that instrument. The English, Irish and Scotch, along with white Americans, were included to be sure, but the French, Germans and other white people of the world are all gone to pot along with the Judge's inferior races. I had thought the Declaration promised something better than the condition of British subjects; but no, it only meant that we should be equal to them in their own oppressed and unequal condition. According to that, it gave no promise that having kicked off the King and Lords of Great Britain, we should not at once be saddled with a King and Lords of our own.

I had thought the Declaration contemplated the progressive improvement in the condition of all men everywhere; but no, it merely "was adopted for the purpose of justifying the colonists in the eyes of the civilized world in withdrawing their allegiance from the British crown, and dissolving their connection with the mother country." Why, that object having been effected some eighty years ago, the Declaration is of no practical use now – mere rubbish – old wadding left to rot on the battle-field after the victory is won.

I understand you are preparing to celebrate the "Fourth," tomorrow week. What for? The doings of that day had no reference to the present; and quite half of you are not even descendants of those who were referred to at that day. But I suppose you will celebrate; and will even go so far as to read the Declaration. Suppose after you read it once in the old fashioned way, you read it once more with Judge Douglas's version. It will then run thus: "We hold these truths to be self-evident that all British subjects who were on this continent eighty-one years ago, were created equal to all British subjects born and then residing in Great Britain."

And now I appeal to all – to Democrats as well as others, – are you really willing that the Declaration shall be thus frittered away? – thus left no more at most, than an interesting memorial of the dead past? thus shorn of its vitality, and practical value; and left without the germ or even the suggestion of the individual rights of man in it?

But Judge Douglas is especially horrified at the thought of the mixing blood by the white and black races: agreed for once – a thousand times agreed. There are white men enough to marry all the white women, and black men enough to marry all the black women; and so let them be married. On this point we fully agree with the Judge; and when he shall show that his policy is better adapted to prevent amalgamation than ours we shall drop ours, and adopt his. Let us see. In 1850 there were in the United States, 405,751, mulattoes. Very few of these are the offspring of whites and free blacks; nearly all have sprung from black slaves and white masters. A separation of the races is the only perfect preventive of amalgamation but as an immediate separation is impossible the next best thing is to keep them apart where they are not already together. If white and black people never get together in Kansas, they will never mix blood in Kansas. That is at least one self-evident truth. A few free colored persons may get into the free States, in any event; but their number is too insignificant to amount to much in the way of mixing blood. In 1850 there were in the free states, 56,649 mulattoes; but for the most part they were not born there – they came from the slave States, ready made up. In the same year the slave States had 348,874 mulattoes all of home production. The proportion of free mulattoes to free blacks – the only colored classes in the free states – is much greater in the slave than in the free states. It is worthy of note too, that among the free states those which make the colored man the nearest to equal the white, have, proportionably the fewest mulattoes the least of amalgamation. In New Hampshire, the State which goes farthest towards equality between the races, there are just 184 Mulattoes while there are in Virginia – how many do you think? 79,775, being 23,126 more than in all the free States together. These statistics show that slavery is the greatest source of amalgamation; and next to it, not the elevation, but the degeneration of the free blacks. Yet Judge Douglas dreads the slightest restraints on the spread of slavery, and the slightest human recognition of the negro, as tending horribly to amalgamation.

This very Dred Scott case affords a strong test as to which party most favors amalgamation, the Republicans or the dear Union-saving Democracy. Dred Scott, his wife and two daughters were all involved in the suit. We desired the court to have held that they were citizens so far at least as to entitle them to a hearing as to whether they were free or not; and then, also, that they were in fact and in law really free. Could we have had our way, the chances of these black girls, ever mixing their blood with that of white people, would have been diminished at least to the extent that it could not have been without their consent. But Judge Douglas is delighted to have them decided to be slaves, and not human enough to have a hearing, even if they were free, and thus left subject to the forced concubinage of their masters, and liable to become the mothers of mulattoes in spite of themselves – the very state of case that produces nine tenths of all the mulattoes – all the mixing of blood in the nation.

Of course, I state this case as an illustration only, not meaning to say or intimate that the master of Dred Scott and his family, or any more than a percentage of masters generally, are inclined to exercise this particular power which they hold over their female slaves.

I have said that the separation of the races is the only perfect preventive of amalgamation. I have no right to say all the members of the Republican party are in favor of this, nor to say that as a party they are in favor of it. There is nothing in their platform directly on the subject. But I can say a very large proportion of its members are for it, and that the chief plank in their platform – opposition to the spread of slavery – is most favorable to that separation.

Such separation, if ever effected at all, must be effected by colonization; and no political party, as such, is now doing anything directly for colonization. Party operations at present only favor or retard colonization incidentally. The enterprise is a difficult one; but "when there is a will there is a way"; and what colonization needs most is a hearty will. Will springs from the two elements of moral sense and self-interest. Let us be brought to believe it is morally right, and, at the same time, favorable to, or, at least, not against, our interest, to transfer the African to his native clime, and we shall find a way to do it, however great the task may be. The children of Israel, to such numbers as to include four hundred thousand fighting men, went out of Egyptian bondage in a body.

How differently the respective courses of the Democratic and Republican parties incidentally bear on the question of forming a will – a public sentiment – for colonization, is easy to see. The Republicans inculcate, with whatever of ability they can, that the negro is a man; that his bondage is cruelly wrong, and that the field of his oppression ought not to be enlarged. The Democrats deny his manhood; deny, or dwarf to insignificance, the wrong of his bondage; so far as possible, crush all sympathy for him, and cultivate and excite hatred and disgust against him; compliment themselves as Union-savers for doing so; and call the indefinite outspreading of his bondage "a sacred right of self-government."

The plainest print cannot be read through a gold eagle; and it will be ever hard to find many men who will send a slave to Liberia, and pay his passage while they can send him to a new country, Kansas for instance, and sell him for fifteen hundred dollars, and the rise.

Document Questions

1. What are two uses for judicial decisions, according to Lincoln?

> First, to decide the case; second, to indicate to the public how similar cases will be decided (thus setting precedence).

2. Why does Lincoln argue that the *Dred Scott* decision should not be considered as having set a legitimate precedent?

> It was not unanimous (it was a closely divided court); it was decided on a partisan basis; it was not "in accordance with legal public expectation"; and it was based on faulty history – it could have overcome some of these objections if it had followed established precedents that had been reaffirmed over time, but it did not do that.

3. Why does Lincoln quote at length arguments that Andrew Jackson made when Jackson vetoed a renewal of the charter for the Bank of the United States?

> Jackson argued that just because the Supreme Court ruled the bank as constitutional, it did not mean that he had to renew its charter. The precedents, he argued, were mixed according to various congresses and states. He asserted that he also had a role in deciding whether to approve something based on his own view of the Constitution. Lincoln used this, because Stephen A. Douglas had approved Jackson's reasoning. But now, Lincoln says, Douglas insists that everyone must approve of the *Dred*

Scott decision because the Supreme Court has the final say, and any criticism of the Supreme Court is dangerous and will lead to anarchy. He is using this example to assert that Douglas is a hypocrite on this issue.

4. Why does Lincoln say that the decision was based on faulty history?

Justice Taney declared that the Declaration of Independence and the Constitution were never intended to apply to African Americans. In refuting this argument, Lincoln quotes the dissenting opinion of Justice Curtis, who showed that free African Americans in five states had the right to vote at the time of the adoption of the Constitution and were very much a part of the electorate who voted for the adoption of the Constitution.

Lincoln also refutes Taney's assertion that the Declaration of Independence could not possibly have been meant to apply to African Americans. This is a very powerful part of Lincoln's speech, in which he argues that the state of African Americans has become much worse since the time of the Declaration of Independence:

In these the Chief Justice does not directly assert, but plainly assumes, as a fact, that the public estimate of the black man is more favorable now than it was in the days of the Revolution. This assumption is a mistake. In some trifling particulars, the condition of that race has been ameliorated; but, as a whole, in this country, the change between then and now is decidedly the other way; and their ultimate destiny has never appeared so hopeless as in the last three or four years. In two of the five States – New Jersey and North Carolina – that then gave the free negro the right of voting, the right has since been taken away; and in a third – New York – it has been greatly abridged; while it has not been extended, so far as I know, to a single additional State, though the number of the States has more than doubled. In those days, as I understand, masters could, at their own pleasure, emancipate their slaves; but since then, such legal restraints have been made upon emancipation, as to amount almost to prohibition. In those days, Legislatures held the unquestioned power to abolish slavery in their respective States; but now it is becoming quite fashionable for State Constitutions to withhold that power from the Legislatures. In those days, by common consent, the spread of the black man's bondage to new countries was prohibited; but now, Congress decides that it will not continue the prohibition, and the Supreme Court decides that it could not if it would. In those days, our Declaration of Independence was held sacred by all, and thought to include all; but now, to aid in making the bondage of the negro universal and eternal, it is assailed, and sneered at, and construed, and hawked at, and torn, till, if its framers could rise from their graves, they could not at all recognize it. All the powers of earth seem rapidly combining against him. Mammon is after him; ambition follows, and philosophy follows, and the Theology of the day is fast joining the cry. They have him in his prison house; they have searched his person, and left no prying instrument with him. One after another they have closed the heavy iron doors upon him, and now they have him, as it were, bolted in with a lock of a hundred keys, which can never be unlocked without the concurrence of every key; the keys in the hands of a hundred different men, and they scattered to a hundred different and distant places; and they stand musing as to what invention, in all the dominions of mind and matter, can be produced to make the impossibility of his escape more complete than it is.

It is grossly incorrect to say or assume, that the public estimate of the negro is more favorable now than it was at the origin of the government.

5. What can be understood as Lincoln's view of equality?

Lincoln believed that certain fundamental rights applied equally to all Americans. Lincoln stated that the Declaration of Independence applied to all Americans; it was affirmed that all men were created equal "in certain inalienable rights, among which are life, liberty, and the pursuit of happiness." This was for all; the framers "meant to set up a standard maxim for free society, which should be familiar to all, and revered by all; constantly looked to, constantly labored for, and even though never perfectly attained, constantly approximated, and thereby constantly spreading and deepening its influence, and augmenting the happiness and value of life to all people of all colors everywhere."

But it is true that Lincoln held back from proclaiming a belief in racial equality and took seriously the idea that the well-being of African Americans might be better served by the creation of a colony in Africa. These are positions that are likely to trouble us today. But it is important to keep in mind that Lincoln was a man of his times and that although we cannot know his heart, we can know that no politician can ever get too far out in front of public sensibilities and expect to be successful. As it was, Lincoln was bravely pushing the envelope for many in his audience.

Moreover, we should remember that the very idea of interracial sexual relations was widely regarded as scandalous in the United States, and this continued to be the case up until the mid-twentieth century. Hence the accusation of Lincoln's favoring racial "amalgamation" was a loaded charge used to try to discredit the different, and more fundamental, Republican contention that the promises of the Declaration of Independence applied to all Americans, including African Americans. The latter part of this speech is a reply to Douglas's use of that very charge. Lincoln states that he is not in favor of that but then goes on to assert that most of the mixed-race children born in the United States were born to slave mothers who were coerced into sexual relations by slave owners. Thus did Lincoln return the focus, as he always did, to the domineering and dehumanizing evils of slavery.

CHAPTER TEN

THE HOUSE DIVIDES

Summary

LINCOLN'S FIRST INAUGURAL ADDRESS on March 4, 1861, was conciliatory, informing the South that it had nothing to fear regarding the protection of slavery where it existed. In his address, Lincoln also communicated that he would enforce the Fugitive Slave Act, that he was willing to accept the Corwin Amendment, and that he would not use force against the South unless the South took up arms in an insurrection against the government.

And yet the war came, and Lincoln managed to maneuver the South into firing the first shot in the siege of Fort Sumter, a federal facility located on a small island in the harbor of Charleston, South Carolina. Lincoln then called on the Northern states to supply seventy-five thousand militiamen to battle against the Confederacy. For Lincoln, the restoration and preservation of the Union would be the war's chief goal.

The Northern forces had many obvious advantages over the South: a larger population (twenty-two million to nine million); more states (twenty-three to eleven); a larger economy; control of the nation's banking, financial systems, and industry; most of the iron and coal production; advantages in transportation (70 percent of the railroads and more ships, horses, and wagons); and the navy. The South, on the other hand, needed only to play defense on familiar ground. In addition, some of the nation's most brilliant military men, including Robert E. Lee, Joseph E. Johnston, and Thomas J. "Stonewall" Jackson, were Southerners who had joined the Confederate cause. One of Lincoln's greatest challenges was the volatility of public opinion; without a series of conspicuous Northern victories, political considerations might force him to settle for a negotiated peace settlement.

General-in-Chief Winfield Scott was tasked with developing the Union strategy, and he devised the Anaconda Plan, which would rely on denying trade and resources to squeeze the Confederacy into submission. The challenge with this plan, however, was that it took too long for visible effect. When Scott retired and General George C. McClellan replaced him, there was increasing pressure for progress on the battlefield. On September 17, 1862, twenty-two thousand men were killed or wounded at the battle at Antietam. McClellan's indecisive leadership led to Lincoln replacing him with General Ambrose Burnside. But Burnside would prove a reckless leader and was replaced by General Joseph Hooker. Lincoln's search for a general would continue.

By July 1862, Lincoln had resolved that the national government would take a strong antislavery position justified on both military and diplomatic grounds. On September 22, 1862, he issued the first part of the Emancipation Proclamation, announcing that slaves in the Confederate-held "States and parts of States" would be "then, thenceforward and forever free" on January 1, 1863. The Emancipation was a war measure, but it also had the effect of enlarging the war's purpose.

In June 1863, the Confederacy suffered serious defeats at Vicksburg and Gettysburg. At Gettysburg, Lincoln would deliver one of his greatest speeches, which would read the U.S. Constitution through the lens of the Declaration of Independence. This speech would come to redefine the war as not only a war for the preservation of the Union but a war for the preservation of the democratic idea.

In 1864, General Ulysses S. Grant was given command of the Union army and turned out to be the military leader Lincoln had been seeking. A series of military successes in 1864 ensured Lincoln's reelection in that year, and on March 4, 1865, he was inaugurated for his second term.

On April 3, 1865, the Confederate stronghold of Richmond fell to Union forces, and on April 9, General Lee surrendered to General Grant at Appomattox Court House. Thus ended America's bloodiest conflict, but not without the added horror of Lincoln's assassination by a pro-Confederate zealot on April 15. Like the biblical Moses, Lincoln was cruelly denied entry into the Promised Land of a restored Union. That would be a task for others.

Questions and Answers

1. How did President-Elect Lincoln spend the four months between his election and his inauguration? (p. 171)

> He moved quietly and cautiously, assembling a cabinet and pondering what actions he would take once in office.

2. What were Lincoln's goals in his first inaugural address? What was his tone? (pp. 171–72)

> His goal was to preserve the Union. His tone was mostly conciliatory; he was willing to accept the Corwin Amendment and even to enforce the Fugitive Slave Act – but there could be no secession.

3. How did Lincoln handle the crisis of Fort Sumter? What resulted? (pp. 172–73)

> He out-maneuvered South Carolina into firing the first shot – a huge political victory. It unified the North behind Lincoln, though Lincoln's call for volunteers to suppress the rebellion also led the four states of the upper South to secede.

4. What, and which, were the "border states"? How important were they to Lincoln? (see Question 11)

> Kentucky, Missouri, Delaware, and Maryland were all slave-holding states whose populations divided on the issues. Keeping them from secession was vital.
>
> Teachers may add that Maryland was kept from secession only by the U.S. Army; Kentucky declared its neutrality until the Confederates moved into its territory to build a key fort; and Missouri's rural area was strongly pro-Confederate, but the German population of St. Louis was equally pro-Union. All three states provided thousands of men to both sides during the war and were the scenes of several battles.

5. What was Lincoln's chief objective in launching a war against the Confederacy? (p. 173)

> His chief objective at the war's outset was to restore and preserve the Union. At that time, the North would not likely have accepted a bloody war merely to abolish slavery where it already existed. However, by the time of the Gettysburg Address, Lincoln's thinking on the subject had changed, and the abolition of slavery had become thinkable as a national war goal.

6. What were the relative advantages of North and South in the war? Which side would win a draw? (pp. 173–74)

> The North had far more population, finances, industry, and material resources. But the South had some excellent commanders, was fighting a defensive war, and would win a draw.
>
> Teachers may be asked, could the South possibly have won? From a military standpoint, probably not, but they hoped (not without some reason) for foreign intervention by the British and French (King Cotton diplomacy). And northern war weariness could well have cost Lincoln his reelection in 1864, which would have meant a Confederate victory.

7. How important were military victories to Lincoln politically? (p. 174)

> He was a minority president whose support was neither deep nor wide. Victories were essential to keep morale up. In particular, Lincoln's reelection in 1864 was very much in doubt due to war weariness; without victories like Sherman's capture of Atlanta during the summer before the election, he might well have lost.

8. At the start of the war, the United States had no true national army. That is the context for what image in the gallery following p. 224?

> The Grand Review of the Union Armies down Pennsylvania Avenue.

9. Trace the course of the war in the east from First Bull Run through Appomattox. How many of Lincoln's generals did Robert E. Lee defeat before Lincoln found Grant? (pp. 175–88)

> Lee defeated McClellan, Pope, Burnside, and Hooker. He failed to win in his two invasions of the North (1862 ending at Antietam and 1863 ending at Gettysburg), but in both cases, he was able to retreat back to Virginia with his army intact. Grant in 1864 finally proved his equal and wore Lee's army down, first in the Overland Campaign beginning with the battle of the Wilderness, and then in the nine-month-long siege of Petersburg. Lee was never really defeated until the very end, but Grant "pinned him down" for the final year of the war, while Sherman and other Union commanders destroyed the Confederates in the western theater.

10. Describe Grant's background, character, and methods as a commander. (pp. 182–84)

> Grant was personally unimpressive, just getting by as a West Pointer but also unsuited for civilian life. He was widely suspected of alcoholism. Yet

he was very effective as a commander, winning a string of victories in the West, culminating in his capture, after multiple failed efforts, of the key fortress of Vicksburg. He was unshakable in determination. His tactics were more often hammer blows than artful maneuvers such as Lee (and Jackson before his death) had excelled in. He lost fifty thousand soldiers in two months, driving Lee back to Richmond. He has been called the first modern general.

11. Explain the political, military, and diplomatic context of the Emancipation Proclamation. What did it do? What did it not do? (pp. 178–79)

It turned the war into a fight against slavery, blocking sympathy for the Confederacy in Europe. It struck at the Confederacy's economy through its labor force. It had to be issued after a military victory – though Antietam barely qualified. And it freed only the slaves inside Confederate territory as of January 1, 1863. This left the border states' slaves alone, as their owners' political and economic support for the war was needed.

12. What was the constitutional status of slavery? How did Lincoln accommodate this? (pp. 179–80)

Lincoln hated slavery but believed the Constitution protected it. He freed what slaves he could with the Emancipation Proclamation as a war measure, but full freedom required amending the Constitution, which Lincoln was able to persuade Congress to do not long before his death.

13. For all of its problematical nature, the Emancipation Proclamation did enlarge the war's purpose; it was no longer just about the **preservation** of the **Union.** (p. 180)

14. What happened during the first four days of July 1863? (p. 181)

The battle of Gettysburg ended Lee's invasion of the North, and Grant captured Vicksburg and split the Confederacy along the line of the Mississippi.

15. What did Lincoln achieve in the very short Gettysburg Address? (pp. 181–82)

He gave a "crisp and memorable statement of national purpose and national identity," providing a higher meaning for a war that had grown beyond its original purpose.

16. Modern war is characterized by the full mobilization of each society's resources, so the goal must be to destroy the enemy's **ability and willingness** to fight, and to break the **confidence** of enemy civilians in the ability of their own government to protect them. (p. 183)

17. Why did General Sherman come to be hated in the postwar South? (pp. 184–85)

> His march to the sea targeted civilians, burning plantations. He said he meant to "make Georgia howl."
>
> *Hurrah, hurrah, we bring the Jubilee;*
> *Hurrah, hurrah, the flag makes you free!*
> *So we sang the chorus from Atlanta to the sea,*
> *While we were marching through Georgia.*
>
> However, in Sherman's defense, he had understood and absorbed completely the logic of modern total warfare and that the defeat of the South would involve not only the defeat of Southern armies in the field of battle but the destruction of the Southern will to resist.

18. What did it take for Lincoln to win reelection in 1864? (pp. 185–86)

> He needed to persuade the voters that the end of the war was in sight. That was achieved when Sherman captured Atlanta and Admiral Farragut captured Mobile. Lincoln did get most of the votes from the Union soldiers, who were allowed to cast ballots from camp.

19. How was Lincoln perceived by his contemporaries? (pp. 185–86)

> He was widely disparaged and ridiculed. His elevation to heroic status as "Father Abraham" and the "Great Emancipator" came after his death.

20. How did Lincoln see the hand of God in the war and its outcome? (pp. 186–87)

> "Both read the same Bible and pray to the same God, and each invokes His aid against the other.... The prayers of both could not be answered. That of neither has been answered fully. The Almighty has His own purposes ... [to give] to both North and South this terrible war as the woe due to those by whom the offense [of slavery] came."

21. Lincoln's goal at the end of the war was not to punish the wicked but to **restore the Union.** (p. 187)

22. How did Grant deal with Lee's army after the surrender at Appomattox? (p. 188)

> He dealt with them gently, by Grant's inclination and on Lincoln's orders. Officers kept their side arms, and soldiers who claimed a horse or mule as personal property were allowed to take it home for plowing. The warriors on each side admired each other.

23. What was the death toll of the war? In proportion to population, what would such a war cost today? (p. 188)

> There were at least six hundred thousand and maybe seven hundred thousand deaths, the majority from disease. In proportion to population, that would be four million deaths today.

24. Why was Lincoln's assassination such a tragedy for the defeated South? (p. 189)

> "In his absence, the factions he had managed to keep at bay for so long would no longer be held back by his reasonableness and constraining moderation." A desire for punishment and radical change took hold in their place, a spirit that would make a reconciliation between the sections that much more difficult.

Objective Questions

Answers are in parentheses.

In the blank beside each name, Put a U if he served the Union or a C if he served the Confederacy:

_____ Robert E. Lee	(C)
_____ Stonewall Jackson	(C)
_____ U. S. Grant	(U)
_____ William T. Sherman	(U)

Put in order:

_____ Battle of Antietam	(1)
_____ Battle of Gettysburg	(3)
_____ Emancipation Proclamation	(2)

Put in order:

    ____ Lincoln calls for militia volunteers   (2)
    ____ South Carolina bombards Fort Sumter   (1)
    ____ Virginia secedes   (3)

Put in order:

    ____ Grant captures Richmond   (3)
    ____ Grant captures Vicksburg   (1)
    ____ Sherman captures Atlanta   (2)

Document

LINCOLN, THE GETTYSBURG ADDRESS, NOVEMBER 19, 1863

Four score and seven years ago our fathers brought forth on this continent, a new nation, conceived in Liberty, and dedicated to the proposition that all men are created equal.

Now we are engaged in a great civil war, testing whether that nation, or any nation so conceived and so dedicated, can long endure. We are met on a great battle-field of that war. We have come to dedicate a portion of that field, as a final resting place for those who here gave their lives that that nation might live. It is altogether fitting and proper that we should do this.

But, in a larger sense, we can not dedicate – we can not consecrate – we can not hallow – this ground. The brave men, living and dead, who struggled here, have consecrated it, far above our poor power to add or detract. The world will little note, nor long remember what we say here, but it can never forget what they did here. It is for us the living, rather, to be dedicated here to the unfinished work which they who fought here have thus far so nobly advanced. It is rather for us to be here dedicated to the great task remaining before us – that from these honored dead we take increased devotion to that cause for which they gave the last full measure of devotion – that we here highly resolve that these dead shall not have died in vain – that this nation, under God, shall have a new birth of freedom – and that government of the people, by the people, for the people, shall not perish from the earth.

Document Questions

1. Why does Lincoln begin his speech with the archaic numbering "four score and seven years" rather than saying "in 1776"?

> He is evoking the language of the Bible, a way of underscoring the sacredness of the moment, and giving the American story a mythic dimension, by lifting it out of the flow of mere history. It is all a part of the speech's effort to emphasize the very high stakes in the outcome of the Civil War.

2. In what way is the Civil War a "testing"?

> It is testing the durability of the ideals that undergirded the American Founding. Lincoln strongly suggests that the future of these ideas, not just for America but for the world, is riding on the war's outcome. The war is testing not only whether the American nation can endure but whether "any nation so conceived and so dedicated" can.

3. Why does Lincoln insist that "we cannot dedicate … consecrate … hallow this ground"?

> He wishes to give the fullest possible credit to the soldiers who died for the Union. It is an illustration of Lincoln's democratic impulses, to say that these individuals do not need the authority of government to pronounce upon the nobility of their deed. He also wishes to intensify the sense of obligation and proclaim that we best honor the dead by making sure that the "great task" they began is finished.

4. What is that "great task"?

> Here is one of the interesting ambiguities in the speech. Lincoln of course means the winning of the war and the reunification of the country. But he also means more. Part of what is meant by ensuring that the dead do not "die in vain" is that the nation needs to experience a "new birth of freedom," which surely refers to the abolition of slavery, as well as rededicate itself to the idea of a democracy itself, as "government of the people, by the people, for the people." In other words, the nature of the "task" has changed since the beginning of the war.

CHAPTER ELEVEN

THE ORDEAL OF RECONSTRUCTION

Summary

I hope there will be no persecution, no bloody work, after the war is over....
Enough lives have been sacrificed. We must extinguish our resentment if we
expect harmony and union.

ABRAHAM LINCOLN

THE REUNION AND RECONSTRUCTION of the nation after so devastating a war would be an overwhelming task, and there were opposing views on how to proceed with reunification of the fractured nation. Some wanted to reincorporate the South with few complications and recriminations. Others argued for severe punishment for the South, accompanied by a complete social transformation. In 1864, the Wade–Davis Bill had passed, which required that a majority of voters swear loyalty and that only those who had never been loyal to the Confederacy would be able to vote for the new state constitutions. Lincoln, who favored a less punitive approach, pocket-vetoed the bill, infuriating Republicans. After Lincoln's assassination on April 14, 1865, the national mood toward the South grew even darker. Upon Lincoln's assassination, Andrew Johnson assumed the presidency. He turned out to be ill equipped for the position, lacking the political skills, temperament, and judgment for the job. The road ahead was about to become very rocky indeed.

Johnson quickly found himself at odds with the Republicans. In May 1865, he put forward a Reconstruction plan only slightly more demanding than Lincoln's and excluded from the general pardon property owners with more than $20,000 in taxable assets. In early 1866, Johnson vetoed a bill to extend the life of the Freedman's Bureau, arguing that it had been a wartime measure and its extension into a time of peace would be unconstitutional. He also vetoed a Civil Rights Act that had been designed to counter the Black Codes and other forms of blatantly unequal treatment of freedmen being reinstitutionalized in the postwar South. Both of these would prove inflammatory, and Johnson's Civil Rights Act veto was overridden – the first time in American history that a piece of legislation was enacted into law over the veto of a president. A new Freedman's Bureau bill also passed. Johnson's authority as president was ebbing away, and Congress was taking the lead role in Reconstruction.

The Fourteenth Amendment was passed by Congress in June 1866 and was ratified by the states in July 1868. It was the first attempt to give greater constitutional definition and breadth to the concept of citizenship by declaring all persons born or naturalized in the United States and legally subject to its jurisdiction to be citizens. It also obligated the states to respect and uphold those rights and to give equal protection; states could not remove those rights without due process of law.

In early 1867, Congress passed three Reconstruction Acts treating the South as a conquered province and abolishing state government, dividing the territory into five military districts, and placing it under military occupation. Congress also made the requirements for readmission to the Union more stringent: the ex-Confederate states had to ratify the Fourteenth Amendment and incorporate into their state constitutions a clause that adult males, irrespective of race, would not be denied the right to vote. Congress also passed the Tenure of Office Act, which prohibited the president from removing federal officials from office without the Senate's consent.

When Johnson challenged the act by firing secretary of war Edwin Stanton, the House of Representatives impeached Johnson on February 24, 1868. The trial before the Senate lasted three months; the removal of Johnson failed by a single, unexpected vote against impeachment from Republican senator Edmund Ross of Kansas. But Johnson's presidency lay in ruins nonetheless, and the way seemed clear for the more reform-minded Republicans.

The Republicans went on to win the presidency in 1868 with General Ulysses S. Grant as their nominee. With the passage of the Fifteenth Amendment, which ensured the ex-slaves' right to vote, the reformers seemed to have gotten their way. But had they? Grant insisted that Congress pass three Enforcement Acts in 1870–71 to combat such white supremacist groups as the Ku Klux Klan and to protect the rights of blacks in the South. However, the acts suffered from weak and inconsistent enforcement, and the terroristic groups only grew in strength, a serious blow to the Reconstruction movement. Moreover, there was a growing silence as the North's antislavery zeal was ebbing; the nation seemed to be growing weary. In 1873, a business panic set in, producing a deep economic depression and distracting many Americans from the failing condition of Reconstruction in the South.

The final blow to Reconstruction came during the 1876 presidential election, one of the most corrupt and controverted in American history. The Republicans nominated Rutherford B. Hayes, and the Democrats nominated Samuel J. Tilden. Neither candidate supported the Radical agenda, and both were lenient in their approach to the South. When the electoral votes were inconclusive, Congress set up an electoral commission to decide the outcome. The Compromise of 1877 was worked out between the Republicans and a group of southern Democrats who were willing to defect if the Republicans promised that Hayes, if president, would withdraw the last federal troops from the South and allow the last two Republican state governments (Louisiana and South Carolina) to collapse and commit to the construction of a southern transcontinental railroad. In return, the Democrats would drop their opposition to Hayes and would accept the three Reconstruction amendments to the Constitution (the Thirteenth, Fourteenth, and Fifteenth). In the end, Hayes became president, and the Compromise of 1877 marked an inglorious end to the Reconstruction era – with much left undone and a great many gaping wounds remaining unhealed.

Questions and Answers

1. What was the condition of the South when the war ended? What was the situation of the freedmen? (pp. 190–91)

> The South was devastated: railroads and cities were destroyed, and a quarter of a million men were dead. The freedmen were jubilant but had nowhere to go; "he was free from the old plantation," wrote Frederick Douglass of the liberated slave, "but he had nothing but the dusty road under his feet."

2. How had the North fared during the war? Why? (pp. 191–92)

> It had prospered, particularly in that with the southern congressmen gone, many much-wanted laws were enacted: protective tariffs, the Homestead Act providing free land in the West, a National Banking Act, and easier requirements for immigrants to become citizens. The much-debated transcontinental railroad would be built on a northern route.

3. Why did Charles A. Beard call the war a "second American revolution"? What is the weakness of Beard's argument? (p. 191)

> "Beard saw that the capitalists, laborers, and farmers of the North drove from power the planting aristocracy of the South." That is valid, but the changes in fact were far deeper and broader than Beard suggested.
>
> Teachers may also point out that within ten to fifteen years, the planter class (though many now were becoming industrialists) was once again in control in the southern states and well on their way (because of the one-party system of the post-Reconstruction South and the seniority rule in Congress) to once again strongly influencing, if not dominating, national politics.

4. What questions did the victorious North have to answer in dealing with the defeated South? (pp. 191–92)

> Broadly, they had to determine what to do with the defeated white southerners and what to do with the freed slaves. Were the ex-Confederates to be punished harshly, or reintegrated smoothly back into the nation? The freedman were no longer slaves, but what were they instead? Citizens? Would they be elevated to be equal to, or even placed above, their former masters? Would the devastated South be rebuilt? If so, who would pay for it?

5. Was the South to be treated as **returning states** or as **conquered territories?** (The first gave them many rights, including representation in Congress; the second subjected them to being ruled *by* Congress.) (p. 192)

6. What was Lincoln's plan for Reconstruction? How far was he able to go in implementing it before his death? (p. 192)

> Once 10 percent of the citizens of a state (remember there had been a census in 1860) swore an oath of allegiance to the United States, their rights as citizens would be restored, and they could elect state governments and send senators and representatives to Congress. Several states did this. The U.S. Army, which controlled conquered southern territory, took its orders from the president and implemented Lincoln's plan.

7. How did the Republicans in Congress feel about Lincoln's policy? (p. 193)

> Congress disapproved, considering Lincoln's plan far too lenient, and refused to seat the southern representatives. The Wade–Davis Bill required a majority, not 10 percent, to swear an oath of allegiance and excluded ex-Confederates from voting for new state constitutions.

8. Why was Lincoln's assassination such a disaster for the South? (pp. 193–94)

> Lincoln was disposed to mercy, charity, and reconciliation; the Radical Republicans wanted a dramatic restructuring, even revolutionizing, of the social order.

9. How did Andrew Johnson become vice president and then, on Lincoln's death, president? What were his goals? Why was he unable to achieve them? (pp. 195–96)

> Johnson was a Democrat from Tennessee, chosen as running mate because Lincoln wanted to show the war to be not a northern or Republican affair but a bipartisan effort to restore the Union. Johnson identified with poor whites and hated the wealthy planter class, but he was deeply prejudiced against blacks and had no interest in raising the freedmen toward equality. He issued thousands of pardons and quickly accepted the new state governments – many controlled by former Confederates – back into full participation in the government.

10. What was the situation in the South when Congress reconvened in December 1865? (They had been in session throughout the war and needed the vacation.) (p. 195)

> All eleven former Confederate states had met the criteria to be restored to the Union; all had ratified the Thirteenth Amendment and elected senators and representatives. None, however, had extended the vote to the freedmen, and many had set up "Black Codes" that restricted the movements of former slaves.

11. How did the Radical Republicans take control of Reconstruction policy? What policy did they impose on the South? (pp. 195–97)

> Congress refused to seat the members elected from the southern states and set up a Joint Committee on Reconstruction, which determined that Congress should control Reconstruction and that the southern states had the status of conquered provinces. Eventually the Joint Committee proposed the Fourteenth and Fifteenth Amendments.

12. In what two ways did Johnson try to oppose Congress in this? How successful was he? (pp. 196–97)

> He vetoed two key bills, and he campaigned against Congress. But the Republicans could override his vetoes and also won the congressional elections of 1866.

13. Why was Johnson impeached? Why was he not convicted? (pp. 198–99)

He violated the Tenure in Office Act, which declared that the president could not dismiss without Senate approval any subordinate whose appointment had required Senate approval. This was probably unconstitutional, but Johnson took the bait and fired secretary of war Stanton, a leading Radical. Johnson was acquitted by one vote, by a senator who feared the precedent being set.

14. There are three "Reconstruction amendments": the Thirteenth, Fourteenth, and Fifteenth. Be sure to know when each was passed and what each said or did. (p. 197)

The Thirteenth (1865) abolished slavery, and the Fifteenth (passed 1866, ratified 1868) was designed to protect freedmen from being denied the vote. The Fourteenth (same dates as the Fifteenth) was longer and more complex; it defined citizenship in such a way that the former slaves qualified, and it prohibited any state from denying citizens the "equal protection of the laws" and assured that their rights could not be taken away without "due process."

15. The First Amendment begins "Congress shall make no law" and so did not apply to the states. Today it *does* apply. Why? (p. 197)

The Fourteenth Amendment *incorporates* much of the Bill of Rights, making it apply to states as well as to the national government.

16. What was Johnson's last official act as president? (p. 199)

He pardoned Jefferson Davis.

17. What were the problems facing Reconstruction governments in southern states? How successful were they in addressing those problems? (pp. 199–201)

They had little money and faced widespread devastation. But there were many accomplishments, in areas such as civil rights, internal improvements, hospital building, and the creation of public school systems. There also were failures, evidenced both in the spread of corrupt practices in the awarding of state contracts and in the paucity of good and efficient political leadership. Under the circumstances, spectacular successes were too much to hope for; even a minor success represented a major achievement.

18. What replaced slavery as a labor system in much of the South? (p. 200)

Slavery was replaced by sharecropping (which both whites and blacks practiced). The landowner got most of the profit when the crop was sold, but the worker got a specific percentage as his share. Sharecroppers were often kept in debt and so under the control of the landowner.

19. How did the South resist Reconstruction? (p. 200)

The Ku Klux Klan and similar organizations intimidated and suppressed the freedmen and their "carpetbagger" allies. More importantly, in the long run, many ex-Confederates received pardons and restored voting rights. And employers and landowners had ways of influencing the voting of people who were economically dependent on them.

20. Why was Grant ineffective as president? (p. 201)

Though personally honorable, Grant showed poor judgment in selecting subordinates, many of whom were corrupt. A postwar depression began in 1873, and Grant had few ways to deal with it.

21. Be able to define *carpetbaggers*, *scalawags*, and *redeemers*. What do these terms imply about who was setting the terms of the controversies over Reconstruction? (p. 199)

Carpetbaggers were northerners who came to the South to live. Scalawags were native southerners (white or black) who voted Republican. Redeemers were the former Confederates who overthrew Reconstruction. Obviously the terms were coined by southerners.

22. Why did the North lose much of its prewar zeal for reform? (p. 201)

War weariness combined with distractions like railroad construction and the influx of new immigration from southern and eastern Europe contributed to the loss of reform energy. Maintaining an army in the southern states was expensive and unpopular. And as the new immigration changed the racial and ethnic composition of the North, especially in its big cities, where Democratic political machines like Tammany Hall controlled immigrants' votes, some northern Republicans found themselves in sympathy with the idea that the southern whites should be left to deal with their own social problems.

23. Be able to recount the story of the election of 1876 and the compromise that settled it. (p. 202)

Democratic candidate Samuel J. Tilden won the popular vote but was one vote short in the Electoral College. Several southern states had contested outcomes. A commission voted 8–7 along party lines to give every disputed elector to Republican Rutherford B. Hayes. Northern Democrats were outraged and threatened violence. The Republicans persuaded the southern states to recognize Hayes by promising to withdraw troops from the South (thus ending Reconstruction) and by supporting construction of a southern transcontinental railroad.

Teachers should point out that a President Tilden would have withdrawn the troops also. But northern Democrats opposed any new subsidies for railroad construction, as those had become thoroughly corrupted during Grant's administration. But the South objected that the North had gotten all the railroads it needed (and then some), while the South was still not well provided for. The Republicans were willing to help build a southern line, while the Democrats were not.

24. Be able to assess the degree of success and failure of Reconstruction. (pp. 203–4)

The three amendments represented genuine achievement, though, in some cases, delayed a generation or several in being felt. The problems were overwhelming, so failures are easily explained. The what-ifs, such as whether Lincoln might have done better had he survived, are fascinating but unanswerable. There were many missed opportunities, perhaps – if they really were opportunities.

Objective Questions

Answers are in parentheses.

Put in order:

_____	Johnson is impeached	(2)
_____	Johnson pardons Jefferson Davis	(3)
_____	Johnson vetoes the Tenure in Office Act	(1)

Put in order:

    _____ Fourteenth Amendment is proposed   (3)
    _____ Lincoln is assassinated   (2)
    _____ Wade–Davis Bill   (1)

Put in order:

    _____ Compromise of 1877   (1)
    _____ Hayes becomes president   (2)
    _____ U.S. troops withdrawn from the South   (3)

Document

THE FOURTEENTH AMENDMENT

Amendment XIV

Section 1.

    All persons born or naturalized in the United States, and subject to the jurisdiction thereof, are citizens of the United States and of the state wherein they reside. No state shall make or enforce any law which shall abridge the privileges or immunities of citizens of the United States; nor shall any state deprive any person of life, liberty, or property, without due process of law; nor deny to any person within its jurisdiction the equal protection of the laws.

Section 2.

    Representatives shall be apportioned among the several states according to their respective numbers, counting the whole number of persons in each state, excluding Indians not taxed. But when the right to vote at any election for the choice of electors for President and Vice President of the United States, Representatives in Congress, the executive and judicial officers of a state, or the members of the legislature thereof, is denied to any of the male inhabitants of such state, being twenty-one years of age, and citizens of the United States, or in any way abridged, except for participation in rebellion, or other crime, the basis of representation therein shall be reduced in the proportion which the number of such male citizens shall bear to the whole number of male citizens twenty-one years of age in such state.

Section 3.

No person shall be a Senator or Representative in Congress, or elector of President and Vice President, or hold any office, civil or military, under the United States, or under any state, who, having previously taken an oath, as a member of Congress, or as an officer of the United States, or as a member of any state legislature, or as an executive or judicial officer of any state, to support the Constitution of the United States, shall have engaged in insurrection or rebellion against the same, or given aid or comfort to the enemies thereof. But Congress may by a vote of two-thirds of each House, remove such disability.

Section 4.

The validity of the public debt of the United States, authorized by law, including debts incurred for payment of pensions and bounties for services in suppressing insurrection or rebellion, shall not be questioned. But neither the United States nor any state shall assume or pay any debt or obligation incurred in aid of insurrection or rebellion against the United States, or any claim for the loss or emancipation of any slave; but all such debts, obligations and claims shall be held illegal and void.

Section 5.

The Congress shall have power to enforce, by appropriate legislation, the provisions of this article.

Document Questions

1. How is U.S. citizenship defined in Section 1? Why is this important?

Citizenship is defined in Section 1 as "All persons born or naturalized in the United States and subject to the jurisdiction thereof."

This aspect of the amendment is especially important because, up to then, U.S. citizenship had not been defined in the Constitution. This portion of the amendment thus represents a direct repudiation of the *Dred Scott* decision, since Scott clearly fulfilled these requirements. Section 1 in its entirety was intended to enshrine the terms of the Civil Rights Law of 1866 in the Constitution, and it did so for a very good reason. President Johnson had vetoed that law, and even though it was passed into law over his veto – the first time that had ever happened with a significant piece of legislation in American history – the Republicans feared that without the solid backstop of a constitutional amendment, those protections would be rolled back, if not by Johnson, then by some future leader.

2. According to Section 1, what may states not do?

> States may not abridge certain rights of U.S. citizens; they may not deprive persons of life, liberty, or property without due process; and they cannot deny U.S. citizens the equal protection of the laws.

3. Why was this amendment directed at the states?

> The Civil Rights Act of 1866 had been passed because the former Confederate states were enacting laws that denied African Americans basic civil and political liberties (as in the Black Codes, for example). These were state actions. As congressional Reconstruction progressed, the primary focus was dealing with the actions of former Confederate states.

4. What about the actions of private (nonstate) individuals?

> Because of the language of Section 1, the amendment is directed at the states. In 1875, Congress passed the Civil Rights Act of 1875, which sought to ensure access to public accommodations regardless of race. This was ruled unconstitutional by the Supreme Court in 1883, because the Fourteenth Amendment did not give power to Congress to outlaw acts of private, individual discrimination.

5. What else did the Fourteenth Amendment do?

> It did almost too much to itemize here. It had the effect of greatly enlarging federal authority, transferring large areas of what had been state responsibility to the national government. It fundamentally altered the balance between the two.
>
> Section 2 also repealed the original Constitution's three-fifths rule, while penalizing states in the event that they failed to extend the right to vote to all citizens. The rationale for that needs explaining. With slavery now abolished by the Thirteenth Amendment, former slaves no longer counted as three-fifths of a person for arriving at representation in Congress. This had the potential to give the former Confederate states a vastly increased number of representatives in Congress. To counter the possible influence of former Confederates, Republicans wanted to ensure that the newly freed former slaves would not be denied the right to vote. So this section gave them a weapon against that, stating that representation in those states would be reduced if people were denied the right to vote. However, this was never used.
>
> Sections 3 and 4 barred certain ex-Confederate officials from public office and repudiated Confederate war debts as well as compensation

claims for slaves emancipated by the Emancipation Proclamation.

Teachers may want to point out that many of the provisions of the Fourteenth Amendment that were most important to the Reconstruction Congress turned out to be less important in subsequent history, while the interpretation of "due process" and "equal protection" has proved to be productive of an enormous amount of jurisprudential activity and controversy, especially in the post–World War II era.

Teachers may also wish to point out that the Fifteenth Amendment, which was phrased in a way that did not extend the right of suffrage in positive terms – "The right of citizens of the United States to vote shall not be denied or abridged by the United States or by any State on account of race, color, or previous condition of servitude" – unintentionally left open the possibility of denying the right to vote on other terms (literacy tests, poll taxes, and the like).

CHAPTER TWELVE

A NATION TRANSFORMED

Summary

THE CIVIL WAR marks the boundary between early America and modern America. Prior to the Civil War, the United States was a decentralized agrarian country, with a few cities, many relatively autonomous communities, and a weak national government. By the end of the nineteenth century, however, the United States was a powerfully unified national state, one of the world's great commercial and industrial powers, with great cities linked by a formidable national transportation system. It was a dramatic change, and it occurred in a mere thirty-five years – the blink of an eye.

The Grand Review of the Union Armies at the conclusion of the Civil War was a perfect symbol for this change. In a solemn but also celebratory procession ordered by the War Department for May 18, 1865, two hundred thousand Union soldiers marched for two days through the streets of Washington, D.C., in a line that stretched for twenty-five miles. There had never been a display of this kind in all of American history. The Grand Review affirmed the ascent of national power, national unity, national governance, and national consciousness.

All these changes raised important questions though, perhaps the most pressing of which was whether the U.S. Constitution – an eighteenth-century document designed for a small, decentralized, agrarian republic – was now outdated in meeting the needs of a great urban and industrial power: the leading industrial power in the world.

The growth of the postbellum American economy makes for a fascinating story. Railroads were the single most important drivers of American economic development, and by 1881, they purchased 94 percent of the rolled steel manufactured in the United States. They were the first American businesses to become a powerful magnet for international and American investors and entrepreneurs, such as Cornelius Vanderbilt. The railroads also promoted vertically integrated corporate business models, suitable for a continent-spanning enterprise.

It was an age of prodigious invention, with hundreds of thousands of patents granted during this dynamic period. The petroleum industry also expanded. At first, petroleum was used for kerosene, but by the 1870s, it was being used for naphtha, gasoline, and various lubricants and waxes. John D. Rockefeller incorporated the Standard Oil Company of Ohio in 1870, and by 1879, he controlled 90 percent of the nation's refining capacity, becoming the richest man in America. Also playing a key role in economic development was J. Pierpont Morgan, an investment banker who financed and stabilized the fast-growing American industrial economy. Morgan became so wealthy and influential that in 1895 and 1907, the president of the United States called upon Morgan to rescue the government and national economy. Such developments called into question the extent to which American democracy itself had been bypassed by the fabulous new fortunes that the industrial economy had produced.

American industrialization led to an increase in the number of industrial wage laborers – from 885,000 in 1860 to more than 3.2 million in 1890 – in a work environment that was often both dangerous and exploitative. It was a turbulent time for American labor, with notable and often bloody actions, such as the great Railroad Strike of 1877, the Haymarket riot in 1886, the Homestead steel strike of 1892, and the Pullman strike of 1894.

Industrialization and urban growth also changed the character of American cities. Prior to 1870, American cities had been "walking cities" with compact and diverse urban cores. With the dramatic economic changes in the postbellum era, sprawling cities came into being that were structured around segregated rings of affluence, with the greatest wealth at the furthest extensions of the urban environment. The living conditions of impoverished urban centers deteriorated rapidly as the poor were crammed into densely packed neighborhoods and lived in crowded tenement buildings. A new brand of urban politics arose to address these problems, revolving around a new generation of urban "bosses" and their "machines," designed to address the most pressing material circumstances, although doing so in ways that would not have appealed much to the American Founders.

The massive waves of immigration that helped to populate the new American cities also constituted an important element in postwar industrialization, urbanization, and modernization. America had always been a nation of immigrants, a land of hope for them. But the character of its immigrant population changed dramatically toward the end of the nineteenth century. Up until the 1870s, the majority of immigrants had always been Protestants from Northern and Western Europe. Between 1880 and 1920, an estimated twenty million immigrants came to America, with the bulk of them being from Eastern and Southern Europe, their religion being Roman Catholic, Orthodox, or Jewish. The new urban environment would become the crucible of a new culture.

Questions and Answers

1. The Civil War marks the boundary between the earlier **decentralized agrarian** republic and a larger, more **unified,** more **consolidated,** and more **powerful** nation-state. (p. 205)

2. What did the Grand Review symbolize? (p. 206)

> It symbolized national power, national unity, national governance, and national consciousness.
>
> Teachers may remind students that most men in 1860 had never traveled more than a few miles from their place of birth. The war brought them together into armies of thousands and moved them, by railroad or steamboat as well as by marches, to places they would never otherwise have been. It was undoubtedly the most important formative experience in many lives – and the Grand Review pulled all of that together and gave it powerful meaning.
>
> Teachers may also point out that army camps were scenes of religious revivals; examine the second and subsequent verses of "The Battle Hymn of the Republic":

I have seen Him in the watch-fires of a hundred circling camps;
They have builded Him an altar in the evening dews and damps;
I can read His righteous sentence by the dim and flaring lamps,
His day is marching on.

I have read His fiery gospel writ in rows of burnished steel!
"As ye deal with my contemners, so with you My grace shall deal!
Let the Hero, born of woman, crush the serpent with his heel,"
Since God is marching on.

He has sounded forth the trumpet that shall never call retreat;
He is sifting out the hearts of men before His judgment seat;

Oh, be swift, my soul, to answer Him; be jubilant, my feet!
Our God is marching on.

In the beauty of the lilies Christ was born across the sea,
With a glory in His bosom that transfigures you and me;
As He died to make men holy, let us die to make men free!
While God is marching on.

Some historians credit a wave of revivals in Confederate armies both for turning the South into the "Bible Belt" and also for strengthening soldiers' resolve to fight on as the war turned against them.

3. What were the great constitutional questions following the war? (p. 207)

Was a consolidation of power incompatible with self-rule and republicanism? Was the Constitution outdated? Could it meet the needs of an emerging major industrial power?

4. How, why, and when did the United States become the world's leading industrial power? (pp. 207–9)

In 1865, the U.S. economy was inferior to the economies of the European powers, but by 1900, the United States had surpassed in gross national product (GNP) major European powers like Britain, Germany, and France.

Why? The United States had lavish natural resources, a growing population providing cheap labor, access to copious amounts of capital both domestic and from foreign sources, an excellent transportation system, and a legal and political system that respected private property and regulated and taxed business only lightly.

The war may or may not have stimulated growth in the North – it was happening there long before – but it certainly stimulated industrial growth in the South, first to fight a modern war, and then as an alternative to staple crop agriculture. Teachers may point out that Birmingham, Alabama, did not even exist before the war but became a major industrial center soon after it.

5. How important were railroads after the war? (pp. 209–11)

Railroads are the nineteenth-century equivalent of the space program of the 1960s or the internet today. They dominate everything and stimulate technological innovation. Automobiles did not yet exist, and steamboats could only go where the rivers and oceans were; railroads could go anywhere, and soon did. And everywhere a railroad line went, so did a telegraph line, essential to keeping trains from running into each other – but able to carry other information at the speed of electricity. Congress encouraged (and indeed overencouraged) railroad construction by paying subsidies for every mile of track built – so a lot of track was built to get the government money rather than because a line was needed there. In the long run, this produced too many railroad companies competing for too little business, weakening that industry and also the banks that financed them. The financial panics and recessions after the war were in part a consequence of a weakened banking system overinvested in railroads.

6. How did business organization change after the war? (p. 209)

Railroads are an "all-or-nothing" enterprise requiring massive capital investment. Only the modern corporation whereby many investors pool capital could provide that. Also, corporations are immortal and limit liability and risk; the most an investor can lose is the cost of the stock. So corporations replaced individual proprietorships and partnerships to a great extent.

7. Be able to describe the careers and impact of Cornelius Vanderbilt, Andrew Carnegie, John D. Rockefeller, and J. Pierpont Morgan. Why were political leaders, including presidents, relatively insignificant in comparison? (pp. 209–12)

Business leaders commanded vast amounts of resources and met the needs of millions of people. Also, politicians come and go, while corporations and their leaders are more permanent. Businessmen could easily "buy" influence in Congress and throughout government.

Vanderbilt was railroads, Rockefeller was oil, Carnegie was steel, and Morgan was banking. In each case, a number of smaller economic units, and resources, were brought into alignment to produce larger and more efficient organizations.

Teachers may illustrate this with oil; would a business requiring petroleum want to depend for its supply on an oil company with just one well? No, because wells run dry, and new drilling attempts sometimes fail to find more. A reliable supply can come only from a company with many wells. And businesses need a relatively stable price for essential raw materials like petroleum; only a larger company can achieve this by controlling supply. These are called *economies of scale*; McDonald's pays much less for a pound of beef than you do.

8. Big business might be perceived as a threat to democracy or republican government, but it also provided great prosperity, which was widely enjoyed. The best example of this is the **mail order** business pioneered by **Montgomery Ward** and then by **Sears and Roebuck** Company. (p. 213)

9. What are *communities of consumption*? How do they contrast with *island communities*? (pp. 213–14)

> Everyone who buys fast food at McDonald's is a member of the McDonald's consumption community. This may seem trivial but is profound. Consider that only mass markets of consumer goods require mass advertising, and without advertising, there would be no mass media. Brands, advertising, and mass media (first magazines like the *Saturday Evening Post*, begun in 1897, and the *Ladies Home Journal*, begun in 1883) grew together, as each required the other two.
>
> Island communities are small towns and surrounding farms with a railroad running through. They are not totally isolated as long as the railroad runs, but otherwise they are very self-contained. Farmers come into town, typically weekly, to get mail that comes by rail and to buy manufactured goods either from local merchants or by mail order. Churches, government, medical treatment, school, and other services for the surrounding farms are centered in the town.
>
> Everything is filtered through the island community. For example, the town newspaper probably comes out once a week, on market day, when the farmers come in to get their mail and shop. The newspaper editor probably subscribes to New York, Chicago, and even London newspapers, delivered by rail, and reprints anything from them that *he* thinks his local readers will be interested in.
>
> Consumption communities gradually eroded and replaced island communities. Consider the impact of a Walmart that suddenly comes into a small town and places that town's small, locally owned shops into competition with a global big business.

10. How did the lives of workers change? (pp. 214–16)

> Workers did benefit from the general prosperity, but working conditions in factories were often unpleasant, even dehumanizing. Child labor was common. The machines had the "skill" and did much of the "work"; the role of many workers was to tend the machines. Workers were interchangeable, which kept wages low.

11. Why were labor unions weak and often ineffective? (p. 215)

Many Americans resisted joining unions. Also, "craft unions" composed of skilled workers often conflicted with "industrial unions" attempting to represent all the workers in an industry. The Brotherhood of Electrical Workers represents electricians, while the United Auto Workers (UAW) represents workers in the auto industry. But does an electrician who works for Ford join the electricians (craft) union or the UAW? He prefers to join with other skilled workers for better pay and conditions, but that leaves the UAW representing only the unskilled workers, who are easily replaced. The American Federation of Labor was composed of craft unions, while the Congress of Industrial Unions (founded 1935) was composed of, well, industrial unions. The two joined in 1955, forming the AFL-CIO.

12. What did Thomas Jefferson think of cities and farmers? (p. 216)

He thought big cities were wicked places where people got their living in unvirtuous ways, while farming, especially the subsistence agriculture of farmers who owned their own land, was a uniquely virtuous activity. Farmers, he once wrote, are God's chosen people. But this outlook created a psychological problem when the mechanization of agriculture (Cyrus McCormick, John Deere, etc.) meant that fewer farmers could grow more food – so surplus farmers had to move to the cities. They did not *want* to move to the cities, however necessary it was to do so.

13. Before roughly 1870, the American city was a **walking city** with a compact urban core. Suburbs did not exist. People needed to live near to where they worked. Technological innovations like streetcars changed this, and the urban core deteriorated as more people lived farther out. (p. 217)

14. Why were cities so dreadful? (p. 218)

Living conditions in the urban cores deteriorated rapidly as cities grew. The poor lived in crowded tenement buildings, which maximized the number of living units but created unhealthy conditions that were a constant fire hazard and became breeding grounds for disease and crime. Infectious diseases, such as tuberculosis and measles, were rampant, as were gangs and street crime in chaotic and lightly policed neighborhoods. Public sanitation was very poor, with many places relying on cesspools rather than sewer systems to manage waste, resulting in water supplies being subject to pollution.

15. How did immigration change after the Civil War? What technological innovation contributed by making ocean voyages faster and cheaper? (p. 219)

> Steamships allowed Eastern and Southern Europeans to travel to America. Prewar immigrants had been mostly from Britain and Germany and other Western European nations, some of whom spoke English and most of whom were Protestant. Now immigrants were from places like Italy, Poland, and Russia and generally either Roman Catholic or Jewish.

16. "Thus did the three great *-ations* converge – **industrialization, urbanization,** and **immigration.**" (p. 220)

17. Most of these people were **dual** immigrants, moving from Europe to America and from rural to city life. No wonder they are called the "**uprooted.**" (pp. 220–21)

18. What is a better metaphor than "melting pot"? (p. 221)

> A better metaphor is a salad bowl, in which different ingredients are tossed together without losing individual identities.
>
> To some extent, there was a religious-based "triple melting pot," Protestant/Catholic/Jew, as Irish and Polish Catholics changed into American Catholics and Russian Jews changed into American Jews.

19. In 1890, four out of **five** residents of New York City were foreign born. (p. 221)

20. Why were native Americans suspicious and fearful of these immigrants? (pp. 221–22)

> There were questions about their loyalty to American ideals (e.g., the accusation that Catholics' main loyalty is to the Pope) and also concern that they kept wages low and prevented unions from organizing (Samuel Gompers). (The latest wave of immigrants could be recruited as strike breakers.) There were also the corrupt big-city political machines, mostly Democratic, such as New York's Tammany Hall, which traded assistance to immigrants for votes and power.

21. How much of the West does the U.S. government own? (p. 222)

> It owns roughly half (except for Texas, which wisely demanded that all public lands be state owned when it joined the United States in 1845).

22. How did the U.S. government deal with 250,000 Plains Indians? (pp. 222–23)

It dealt with Indians brutally at worst and with ham-handed attempts to "Americanize" them at best, uprooting them onto reservations which are still today among the poorest spots in the country.

23. What was Frederick Jackson Turner's thesis about America? (pp. 223–24)

His thesis was that the frontier – which had just disappeared from the census when he wrote in 1893 – had been the key to shaping America, providing opportunity, fresh starts, and democracy and acting as a "safety valve" for the East by draining away excess population and thereby keeping wages relatively higher than they would otherwise have been.

Teachers should point out that Turner's thesis was widely accepted until he died, then subjected to much criticism. He failed to define *frontier* clearly, and other nations, such as Russia and Brazil, that have had frontiers did not develop as America did.

David Potter argued in *People of Plenty* (1954) that Turner was right for the wrong reason; American optimism and democracy are a product of economic prosperity, and for much of our history, the frontier – all that free land out there – was the main source of economic abundance. But there are other sources of wealth, and we remain a nation of great prosperity even if the frontier no longer exists.

Objective Question

Answers are in parentheses.

Matching:

____ Andrew Carnegie	(D)	A. banking
____ John D. Rockefeller	(B)	B. oil
____ J. Pierpont Morgan	(A)	C. railroads
____ Cornelius Vanderbilt	(C)	D. steel

EMMA LAZARUS, "THE NEW COLOSSUS," 1883

"The New Colossus" is a Petrarchan sonnet by American poet Emma Lazarus (1849–87), who wrote the poem in 1883 to raise money for the construction of a pedestal for the Statue of Liberty. In 1903, the poem was cast onto a bronze plaque and mounted inside the pedestal's lower level. The great statue, a gift from the people of France to the people of the United States, was originally meant to symbolize the international spirit of enlightened republicanism; indeed, its name was Liberty Enlightening the World. *Emma Lazarus's poem had the effect of transforming the statue's meaning into a symbol of America's openness to immigrants.*

THE NEW COLOSSUS

Not like the brazen giant of Greek fame,
With conquering limbs astride from land to land;
Here at our sea-washed, sunset gates shall stand
A mighty woman with a torch, whose flame
Is the imprisoned lightning, and her name
Mother of Exiles. From her beacon-hand
Glows world-wide welcome; her mild eyes command
The air-bridged harbor that twin cities frame.
"Keep, ancient lands, your storied pomp!" cries she
With silent lips. "Give me your tired, your poor,
Your huddled masses yearning to breathe free,
The wretched refuse of your teeming shore.
Send these, the homeless, tempest-tost to me,
I lift my lamp beside the golden door!"

Document Questions and Answers

1. What do you think Lazarus is getting at with the contrast that she makes in the first four lines between the "brazen giant" of antiquity (probably referring to the Colossus of Rhodes) and the "mighty woman with a torch" who is Mother of Exiles?

> The brazen giant is a conquering and domineering man; the "new Colossus" is a generous and welcoming woman, who opens her arms to the suffering of the world.

2. Why is she the "Mother of Exiles"?

> Lazarus is pointing here to one element of American identity, as an asylum for those, like the German 48ers and the Jews of Czarist Russia, who suffered from political and religious persecution.

3. Why does she invite "the wretched refuse" and the "homeless, tempest-tost" to be sent to her?

> She affirms the biblical (and American) idea of the infinite worth and potentiality of all human beings, irrespective of their social class or national origin.

4. In what ways is the poem consistent with the original concept of the sculpture, and in what ways is it inconsistent?

> It is consistent with the sculpture in that it reinforces the idea that the Old World, especially in antiquity, fostered divisions by class that cruelly imprisoned men and women in the conditions of their birth. It is perhaps inconsistent with the original concept in that it does not give the same emphasis to the *intellectual* freedom implied by "enlightenment." A poem that was truer to the sculpture's original intent might have emphasized the blessings of freedom of inquiry and freedom of speech rather than the compassion of a mighty Mother who embraces the lowly and the homeless. It's an open question, though, which of the two we most admire in today's America. It is entirely possible to admire both.

CHAPTER THIRTEEN

BECOMING A WORLD POWER

Summary

FOR MOST OF the nineteenth century, the United States enjoyed a long respite from involvement in world affairs. Many at the time believed such "apartness" to be America's ideal and natural state. John Quincy Adams, in an 1821 address celebrating the Declaration of Independence, proclaimed that America "goes not abroad in search of monsters to destroy" and that while she is a "well-wisher to the freedom and independence of all," she remains "the champion and vindicator only of her own."

These resounding words stood in an uncertain relationship with others that Adams would articulate two years later in his drafting of the Monroe Doctrine, which declared that the United States would not accept any further European colonization of the western hemisphere but would instead regard itself as the dominant power in that sphere. The two perspectives are not entirely contradictory, but there is certainly a tension between them. How would the United States assert its hegemony over the western hemisphere without ever "going abroad," likely in a southerly direction, to support republicanism and perhaps destroy a few monsters in the process?

The concept of imperialism was in the air, all around the world. Most of the major European nations, and a few minor ones, as well as Japan in the Far East were aggressively seeking out imperial acquisitions in Africa and Asia. But for Americans, there was a problem: how was one to reconcile such actions with fundamental American principles of inherent human equality and liberty?

Some imperialists simply ignored those principles by drawing on doctrines of "scientific" racism; others embraced the paternalistic concept of imperial rule as a "civilizing mission." But the driving force behind such expansion was a small but influential group of elite thinkers and public officials who came to believe that the acquisition of overseas possessions by the United States was necessary to the nation's commercial and political interests. This group included such figures as naval officer Alfred Thayer Mahan; Senator Henry Cabot Lodge of Massachusetts; Theodore Roosevelt, then assistant secretary of the navy; and Indiana attorney Albert Beveridge, whose soaring 1898 Senate campaign speech "The March of the Flag" expertly wove together all the elements – religious, strategic, humanitarian, commercial, national greatness – in the pro-imperial case.

Asia was always a particular target of expansionists, who ultimately had their eyes on the limitless markets of China and the rest of the Far East, and the first American steps toward expansion occurred in that direction, with the acquisition of Alaska from Russia and then the islands of Samoa and Hawai'i. But then came Cuba, still a Spanish colony, although one rocked periodically by unsuccessful revolts against increasingly ruthless Spanish rule. The United States looked on with interest, partly because of extensive American commercial interests in Cuba but also because the cause of Cuban independence was one for which Americans felt instinctive sympathy. When an insurrection broke out on February 24, 1895, and the Spanish government put it down brutally, the American public was outraged. If there were ever a monster worth going abroad to destroy, this seemed to be one.

Such public outrage is hard for elected officials to contain. After the destruction of the American battleship *Maine* on February 15, 1898, in Havana harbor, with a loss of most of her crew, President McKinley faced the heat of an inflamed American public demanding vengeance. On April 20, Congress recognized the independence of Cuba by joint resolution and authorized use of the armed forces to drive out the Spanish. Two days later, McKinley announced a blockade of Cuba's northern coast and the southeastern port of Santiago. That was an act of war, and the Spanish promptly declared war in response.

The war itself was brief and one-sided, as disastrous for Spain as can be imagined, a dizzying example of a world turned upside down. After a mere 114 days, the United States found itself elevated to the ranks of the certifiable world powers, and Spain had lost that status forever, in a war that became known simply as El Desastre (the Disaster). But the peace to follow would present the United States with far greater difficulties than it had imagined. With the collapse of Spanish rule, Spain's colonial possessions were also plunged into crisis. The Philippines needed stable and humane governance, but it was not clear how that was to be done in a way consistent with American principles. The stage was set for a great national debate.

McKinley finally concluded that there was no alternative to annexation.

But this position put the United States in opposition to an indigenous anti-Spanish insurrectionary movement that saw itself as the rightful successor to Spanish colonial rule in the Philippines. The ensuing conflict lasted until spring 1902 and cost many more lives than had been required to defeat the Spanish.

The Philippines were not the only problem facing the newly imperial United States. The principles of the Founding were being fudged left and right, as in the case of Puerto Rico, ceded to the United States by Spain, where an indeterminate and intermediate status, somewhere between colonial dependency and fully incorporated statehood, would be settled on. In addition, relations with Cuba, the original cause for the war, became tense and complicated, with interventionist policies like the Platt Amendment and the Roosevelt Corollary as chief elements in that tension.

There was always a divided heart in the American approach to imperial rule, which helps explain why most of the lands acquired in the Spanish–American War were soon devolved toward independent status. It was not easy to recognize what was wise and proper in John Quincy Adams's admonitions and at the same time recognize that the growth of American wealth and power naturally begot responsibilities for the well-being of the rest of the world.

Questions and Answers

1. From the end of the War of 1812 through the rest of the nineteenth century, the United States "enjoyed a long **respite** from any major involvement in **the affairs of the rest of the world.**" (p. 225)

> Teachers may point out that this period of eighty or ninety years did see the expansion of the United States across the continent; we were mostly looking west.

2. Why is it not exactly accurate to call America isolationist during this time? (pp. 225–26)

> We welcomed immigrants, paid attention to cultural trends from Europe, and traded extensively with the rest of the world. Mostly we avoided involvement in foreign wars.
>
> Teachers may also point out that the period 1815–1914 is called the *pax Britannica*, the "British peace," when the Royal Navy dominated the world. There were several small wars but no general or "world wars" during this time, so it was relatively easy to stay out of them.

3. America "goes not abroad in search of **monsters to destroy**. She is the well-wisher to the freedom and independence of all. She is the champion and vindicator **only of her own.**" – John Quincy Adams, July 4, 1821 (pp. 226–27)

4. Yet Adams also was responsible two years later for the **Monroe Doctrine,** declaring that the United States would not accept any further colonization by Europe of the western hemisphere. (Many Spanish colonies in the New World had gained independence during the Napoleonic Wars, and Spain and France wanted to reconquer them.) The United States lacked the power to enforce this doctrine, but it was consistent with **British** interests, who wanted to see Latin America independent and so open to **British** trade. But there was tension between the ideas of staying out of European wars while asserting what would gradually become an American hegemony over the western hemisphere. (pp. 227–28)

5. "In very rough terms, *imperial* tends to refer to the activity of **domination,** while *colonial* tends to refer to the activity of **settlement.**" (p. 229)

> In general, the Spanish conquest and colonization of Mexico and Peru were more imperial, while the British approach to North America relied more on colonization.

6. European nations had practiced imperialism since the sixteenth century, but a new form of more paternalistic imperialism developed based to an extent on **Charles Darwin**'s notion of the **"survival of the fittest."** "Superior" races were meant to rule; other races were meant to follow. But imperial rule might also be seen partly as a "civilizing mission" to uplift the "less advanced" cultures. (pp. 229–30)

7. Who was Alfred T. Mahan? (p. 230)

> He was an American naval officer whose book *The Influence of Sea Power upon History* provided a historical and theoretical justification for a stronger navy – which necessarily included bases in colonies around the world where warships could be refueled with pre-positioned coal. His ideas were used by Senators Henry Cabot Lodge and Albert Beveridge, and by Theodore Roosevelt, to justify a naval buildup and also imperial expansion. It is only a slight exaggeration to say that Roosevelt read Mahan and went out and built the Panama Canal.
>
> Teachers may also point out that Mahan's book inspired the German naval buildup that led to World War I. Mahan died in 1914 as the canal was opening, sorrowful that he might have started a great war.

8. Mahan argued that sea power was not just battleships; it was also the **merchant marine**, civilian ships that carried goods and trained a nation's sailors, plus **colonies** that provided raw materials and **naval bases.** That is, sea power was as much an economic as a military concept. Beveridge's speech "The March of the Flag" (p. 231) touches on all of these points.

9. How did America first grow into the Pacific? (p. 231)

> Lincoln's (then Johnson's) secretary of state, William Seward, acquired Alaska from the Russians. Then came Samoa and the Hawaiian Islands, which President McKinley annexed partly to protect American missionaries and business interests and partly to keep the Japanese from taking the islands for themselves.

10. Why was America sympathetic to the Cuban revolution against Spain? (pp. 231–32)

> America had an instinctive sympathy toward colonists seeking independence, as well as substantial commercial interests. Spain's suppression of the Cuban uprising was brutal, and American newspapers (Hearst's and Pulitzer's dueling "yellow journalism") inflamed American opinion against Spain.

11. How was McKinley forced into war? (pp. 232–33)

> He wanted to avoid war and ignored the provocation of the Spanish ambassador's insulting letter, sending the battleship *Maine* to Havana as an expression of concern for American lives and property. An explosion destroying the *Maine*, though the cause was unknown, made war unavoidable. McKinley "would very likely have no choice but to get out in front of the public passions or risk being bulldozed by them."

12. The war started with two spectacular American naval victories, at Manila in the Philippines and at Santiago, the Spanish naval base in Cuba. American troops then occupied Cuba as well as Puerto Rico, Guam, and the Philippines. Suddenly the United States had a far-flung empire and status as a world power. (pp. 233–34)

> Teachers may also point out that the Spanish–American War was a major step toward healing the wounds of the Civil War, as southern troops fought alongside northern against a common enemy. Four U.S. Army commanders during the war with Spain had been generals in the Confederate army: Fitzhugh Lee, Joseph Wheeler, Matthew Butler, and Tom Rosser. (Many Civil War generals, on both sides, were quite young – in their twenties – and so were only in their fifties in 1898.)

13. Who opposed American imperialism? Why? (pp. 235–36)

> Opponents were many and varied, including both industrialist Andrew Carnegie and labor leader Samuel Gompers. Idealistic reasons combined with racial and ethnic prejudices. Some saw the United States as acquiring "subject and vassal states" in "barbarous archipelagoes" and in the process trampling on our own sacred principles.

14. What was the problem in the Philippines? How was it eventually solved? (pp. 236–37)

> The anti-Spanish insurrection led by Emilio Aguinaldo considered itself the rightful government and fought a bloody guerilla war against the United States. McKinley appointed Judge William Howard Taft as governor, and he quickly included Filipinos as partners and social equals. The United States granted the Philippines self-rule and gradual independence, which was finally accomplished in 1946 (after U.S. troops liberated the Philippines from Japanese occupation).

15. How was Cuba dealt with? (p. 237)

> Cuba got independence, but the Platt Amendment guaranteed the right of the United States to intervene in Cuba to protect its independence from any foreign power and to protect life, property, and individual liberty.

16. What was the Roosevelt Corollary to the Monroe Doctrine? (pp. 237–38)

> Theodore Roosevelt extended the idea of the Platt Amendment to the whole Caribbean; the United States would act as a reluctant police power in circumstances when European powers might otherwise intervene. This was done to resolve a financial crisis in the Dominican Republic.

17. How did American imperialism contrast with that of European powers (and increasingly also Japan)? (p. 238)

> At a time when the other imperial powers were dividing up China into "spheres of influence" in which each country would have exclusive trading rights, McKinley's secretary of state, John Hay, asserted the "open door" policy that committed the United States to protecting Chinese territorial integrity. This also benefited the United States commercially, as we otherwise had no sphere.

18. How did Theodore Roosevelt's secretary of war, Elihu Root, sum it up? "We do not want **to take them for ourselves.** We do not want **any foreign nations to take them for themselves.** We want to help them." But helping people is generally more complicated than it first seems. (p. 239)

Objective Questions

Answers are in parentheses.

Put in order:

_____	Mahan writes *Influence of Seapower*	(2)
_____	Monroe Doctrine	(1)
_____	Roosevelt Corollary	(3)

Put in order:

_____	battle of Santiago	(2)
_____	*Maine* explodes	(1)
_____	Platt Amendment	(3)

Document 1

JOHN QUINCY ADAMS, AN ADDRESS CELEBRATING THE DECLARATION OF INDEPENDENCE, JULY 4, 1821

Fellow Citizens,

Until within a few days before that which we have again assembled to commemorate, our fathers, the people of this Union, had constituted a portion of the British nation; a nation, renowned in arts and arms, who, from a small Island in the Atlantic ocean, had extended their dominion over considerable parts of every quarter of the globe. Governed themselves by a race of kings, whose title to sovereignty had originally been founded on conquest, spellbound, for a succession of ages, under that portentous system of despotism and of superstition which, in the name of the meek and humble Jesus, had been spread over the Christian world, the history of this nation had, for a period of seven hundred years, from the days of the conquest till our own, exhibited a conflict almost continued, between the oppressions of power and the claims of right. In the theories of the crown and the mitre, man had no rights. Neither the body nor the soul of the individual was his own....

The religious reformation was an improvement in the science of mind; an improvement in the intercourse of man with his Creator, and in his acquaintance with himself. It was an advance in the knowledge of his duties and his rights. It was a step in the progress of man, in comparison with which the magnet and gunpowder, the wonders of either India, nay the printing press itself, were but as the paces of a pigmy to the stride of a giant....

The corruptions and usurpations of the church were the immediate objects of these reformers; but at the foundation of all their exertions there was a single plain and almost self-evident principle – that man has a right to the exercise of his own reason. It was this principle which the sophistry and rapacity of the church had obscured and obliterated, and which the intestine divisions of that same church itself first restored. The triumph of reason was the result of inquiry and discussion. Centuries of desolating wars have succeeded and oceans of human blood have flowed, for the final establishment of this principle; but it was from the darkness of the cloister that the first spark was emitted, and from the arches of a university that it first kindled into day. From the discussion of religious rights and duties, the transition to that of the political and civil relations of men with one another was natural and unavoidable; in both, the reformers were met by the weapons of temporal power. At the same glance of reason, the tiara would have fallen from the brow of priesthood, and the despotic scepter would have departed from the hand of royalty, but for the sword, by which they were protected; that sword which, like the flaming sword of the Cherubims, turned every way to debar access to the tree of life.

The double contest against the oppressors of church and state was too appalling for the vigor, or too comprehensive for the faculties of the reformers of the European continent. In Britain alone was it undertaken, and in Britain but partially succeeded.

It was in the midst of that fermentation of the human intellect, which brought right and power in direct and deadly conflict with each other, that the rival crowns of the two portions of the British Island were united on the same head. It was then, that, released from the fetters of ecclesiastical domination, the minds of men began to investigate the foundations of civil government. But the mass of the nation surveyed the fabric of their Institutions as it existed in fact. It had been founded in conquest; it had been cemented in servitude; and so broken and molded had been the minds of this brave and intelligent people to their actual conditions, that instead of solving civil society into its first elements in search of their rights, they looked back only to conquest as the origin of their liberties, and claimed their rights but as donations from their kings. This faltering assertion of freedom is not chargeable indeed upon the whole nation. There were spirits capable of tracing civil government to its first foundation in the moral and physical nature of man: but conquest and servitude were so mingled up in every particle of the social existence of the nation, that they had become vitally necessary to them, as a portion of the fluid, itself destructive of life, is indispensably blended with the atmosphere in which we live.

Fellow citizens, it was in the heat of this war of moral elements, which brought one Stuart to the block and hurled another from his throne, that our forefathers sought refuge from its fury, in the then wilderness of this Western World. They were willing exiles from a country dearer to them than life. But they were the exiles of liberty and of conscience: dearer to them even than their country. They came too, with charters from their kings; for even in removing to another hemisphere, they "cast longing, lingering looks behind," and were anxiously desirous of retaining ties of connection with their country, which, in the solemn compact of a charter, they hoped by the corresponding links of allegiance and protection to preserve. But to their sense of right, the charter was only the ligament between them, their country, and their king. Transported to a new world, they had relations with one another, and relations with the aboriginal inhabitants of the country to which they came; for which no royal charter could provide. The first settlers of the Plymouth colony, at the eve of landing from their ship, therefore, bound themselves together by a written covenant; and immediately after landing, purchased from the Indian natives the right of settlement upon the soil.

Thus was a social compact formed upon the elementary principles of civil society, in which conquest and servitude had no part. The slough of brutal force was entirely cast off; all was voluntary; all was unbiased consent; all was the agreement of soul with soul.

Other colonies were successively founded, and other charters granted, until in the compass of a century and a half, thirteen distinct British provinces peopled the Atlantic shores of the North American continent with two millions of freemen; possessing by their charters the rights of British subjects, and nurtured by their position and education, in the more comprehensive and original doctrines of human rights. From their infancy they had been treated by the parent state with neglect, harshness and injustice. Their charters had often been disregarded and violated; their commerce restricted and shackled; their interest wantonly or spitefully sacrificed; so that the hand of the parent had been scarcely ever felt, but in the alternate application of whips and scorpions.

When in spite of all these persecutions, by the natural vigor of their constitution, they were just attaining the maturity of political manhood, a British parliament, in contempt of the clearest maxims of natural equity, in defiance of the fundamental principle upon which British freedom itself had been cemented with British blood; on the naked, unblushing allegation of absolute and uncontrollable power, undertook by their act to levy, without representation and without consent, taxes upon the people of America for the benefit of the people of Britain. This enormous project of public robbery was no sooner made known, than it excited, throughout the colonies, one general burst of indignant resistance. It was abandoned, reasserted and resumed, until fleets and armies were transported, to record in the characters of fire, famine, and desolation, the transatlantic wisdom of British legislation, and the tender mercies of British consanguinity....

For the independence of North America, there were ample and sufficient causes in the laws of moral and physical nature. The tie of colonial subjection is compatible with the essential purposes of civil government, only when the condition of the subordinate state is from its weakness incompetent to its own protection. Is the greatest moral purpose of civil government, the administration of justice? And if justice has been truly defined, the constant and perpetual will of securing to every one his right, how absurd and impracticable is that form of polity, in which the dispenser of justice is in one quarter of the globe, and he to whom justice is to be dispensed is in another.... Are the essential purposes of civil government, to administer to the wants, and to fortify the infirmities of solitary man? To unite the sinews of numberless arms, and combine the councils of multitudes of minds, for the promotion of the well-being of all? The first moral element then of this composition is sympathy between the members of which it consists; the second is sympathy between the giver and the receiver of the law. The sympathies of men begin with the relations of domestic life. They are rooted in the natural relations of domestic life. They are rooted in the natural relations of husband and wife, of parent and child, of brother and sister; thence they spread through the social and moral propinquities of neighbor and friend, to the broader and more complicated relations of countryman and fellow-citizens; terminating only with the circumference of the globe which we inhabit, in the co-extensive charities incident to the common nature of man. To each of these relations, different degrees of sympathy are allotted by the ordinances of nature. The sympathies of domestic life are not more sacred and obligatory, but closer and more powerful, than those of neighborhood and friendship. The tie which binds us to our country is not more holy in the sight of God, but it is more deeply seated in our nature, more tender and endearing, than that common link which merely connects us with our fellow-mortal, man. It is a common government that constitutes our country. But in that association, all the sympathies of domestic life and kindred blood, all the moral ligatures of friendship and of neighborhood, are combined with that instinctive and mysterious connection between man and physical nature, which binds the first perceptions of childhood in a chain of sympathy with the last gasp of expiring age, to the spot of our nativity, and the natural objects by which it is surrounded. These sympathies belong and are indispensable to the relations ordained by nature between the individual and his country. They dwell in the memory and are indelible in the hearts of the first settlers of a distant colony. These are the feelings under which the children of Israel "sat down by the rivers of Babylon, and wept when they remembered Zion." These are the sympathies under which they "hung their harps upon the willow," and instead of songs of mirth, exclaimed, "If I forget thee, O Jerusalem, let my right hand forget her cunning." But these sympathies can never exist for a country, which we have never seen. They are transferred in the hearts of succeeding generations, from the country of human institution, to the country of their birth; from the land of which they have only heard, to the land where their eyes first opened to the day. The ties of neighborhood are broken up, those of friendship can never be formed, with an intervening ocean; and the natural ties of domestic life, the all-subduing sympathies of love, the indissoluble bonds of marriage, the heart-riveted kindliness of consanguinity, gradually wither and perish in the lapse of a few generations. All the elements, which form the basis of that sympathy between the individual and his country, are dissolved.

Long before the Declaration of Independence, the great mass of the people of America and of the people of Britain had become total strangers to each other.... The sympathies therefore most essential to the communion of country were, between the British and American people, extinct. Those most indispensable to the just relation between sovereign and subject, had never existed and could not exist between the British government and the American people. The connection was unnatural; and it was in the moral order no less than in the positive decrees of Providence, that it should be dissolved.

Yet, fellow-citizens, these are not the causes of the separation assigned in the paper which I am about to read. The connection between different portions of the same people and between a people and their government, is a connection of duties as well as rights. In the long conflict of twelve years which had preceded and led to the Declaration of Independence, our fathers had been not less faithful to their duties, than tenacious of their rights. Their resistance had not been rebellion. It was not a restive and ungovernable spirit of ambition, bursting from the bonds of colonial subjection; it was the deep and wounded sense of successive wrongs, upon which complaint had been only answered by aggravation, and petition repelled with contumely, which had driven them to their last stand upon the adamantine rock of human rights.

It was then fifteen months after the blood of Lexington and Bunker's hill, after Charlestown and Falmouth, fired by British hands, were but heaps of ashes, after the ear of the adder had been turned to two successive supplications to the throne; after two successive appeals to the people of Britain, as friends, countrymen, and brethren, to which no responsive voice of sympathetic tenderness had been returned.... Then it was that the thirteen United Colonies of North America, by their delegates in Congress assembled, exercising the first act of sovereignty by a right ever inherent in the people, but never to be resorted to, save at the awful crisis when civil society is solved into its first elements, declared themselves free and independent states; and two days afterwards, in justification of that act, issued this [Declaration].

[*Adams here read the Declaration of Independence*]

...The interest, which in this paper has survived the occasion upon which it was issued; the interest which is of every age and every clime; the interest which quickens with the lapse of years, spreads as it grows old, and brightens as it recedes, is in the principles which it proclaims. It was the first solemn declaration by a nation of the only legitimate foundation of civil government. It was the corner stone of a new fabric, destined to cover the surface of the globe. It demolished at a stroke the lawfulness of all governments founded upon conquest. It swept away all the rubbish of accumulated centuries of servitude. It announced in practical form to the world the transcendent truth of the unalienable sovereignty of the people. It proved that the social compact was no figment of the imagination; but a real, solid, and sacred bond of the social union. From the day of this declaration, the people of North America were no longer the fragment of a distant empire, imploring justice and mercy from an inexorable master in another hemisphere. They were no longer children appealing in vain to the sympathies of a heartless mother; no longer subjects leaning upon the shattered columns of royal promises, and invoking the faith of parchment to secure their rights. They were a nation, asserting as of right, and maintaining by war, its own existence. A nation was born in a day.

> How many ages hence
> Shall this their lofty scene be acted o'er
> In states unborn, and accents yet unknown?

It will be acted o'er, fellow-citizens, but it can never be repeated. It stands, and must forever stand alone, a beacon on the summit of the mountain, to which all the inhabitants of the earth may turn their eyes for a genial and saving light, till time shall be lost in eternity, and this globe itself dissolve, nor leave a wreck behind. It stands forever, a light of admonition to the rulers of men; a light of salvation and redemption to the oppressed. So long as this planet shall be inhabited by human beings, so long as man shall be of social nature, so long as government shall be necessary to the great moral purposes of society, and so long as it shall be abused to the purposes of oppression, so long shall this declaration hold out to the sovereign and to the subject the extent and the boundaries of their respective rights and duties; founded in the laws of nature and of nature's God. Five and forty years have passed away since this Declaration was issued by our fathers; and here are we, fellow-citizens, assembled in the full enjoyment of its fruits, to bless the Author of our being for the bounties of his providence, in casting our lot in this favored land; to remember with effusions of gratitude the sages who put forth, and the heroes who bled for the establishment of this Declaration; and, by the communion of soul in the re-perusal and hearing of this instrument, to renew the genuine Holy Alliance of its principles, to recognize them as eternal truths, and to pledge ourselves and bind our posterity to a faithful and undeviating adherence to them....

...AND NOW, FRIENDS AND COUNTRYMEN, if the wise and learned philosophers of the elder world, the first observers of nutation and aberration, the discoverers of maddening ether and invisible planets, the inventors of Congreve rockets and Shrapnel shells, should find their hearts disposed to enquire what has America done for the benefit of mankind?

Let our answer be this: America, with the same voice which spoke herself into existence as a nation, proclaimed to mankind the inextinguishable rights of human nature, and the only lawful foundations of government. America, in the assembly of nations, since her admission among them, has invariably, though often fruitlessly, held forth to them the hand of honest friendship, of equal freedom, of generous reciprocity.

She has uniformly spoken among them, though often to heedless and often to disdainful ears, the language of equal liberty, of equal justice, and of equal rights.

She has, in the lapse of nearly half a century, without a single exception, respected the independence of other nations while asserting and maintaining her own.

She has abstained from interference in the concerns of others, even when conflict has been for principles to which she clings, as to the last vital drop that visits the heart.

She has seen that probably for centuries to come, all the contests of that Aceldama the European world, will be contests of inveterate power, and emerging right.

Wherever the standard of freedom and Independence has been or shall be unfurled, there will her heart, her benedictions and her prayers be.

But she goes not abroad, in search of monsters to destroy.

She is the well-wisher to the freedom and independence of all.

She is the champion and vindicator only of her own.

She will commend the general cause by the countenance of her voice, and the benignant sympathy of her example.

She well knows that by once enlisting under other banners than her own, were they even the banners of foreign independence, she would involve herself beyond the power of extrication, in all the wars of interest and intrigue, of individual avarice, envy, and ambition, which assume the colors and usurp the standard of freedom.

The fundamental maxims of her policy would insensibly change from liberty to force....

She might become the dictatress of the world. She would be no longer the ruler of her own spirit....

[America's] glory is not dominion, but liberty. Her march is the march of the mind. She has a spear and a shield: but the motto upon her shield is, Freedom, Independence, Peace. This has been her Declaration: this has been, as far as her necessary intercourse with the rest of mankind would permit, her practice.

Document 1 Questions

1. How does Adams feel about kings?

    He sees them as oppressors, blind to the claims of rights.

2. What about the Reformation?

    For Adams it was a great movement forward for the human race, an escape from what he regarded as the corruption and superstitions imposed by the "despotic" Roman Catholic Church, a precursor to the greatness of the American Revolution.

3. How did his era's forefathers come to America?

    They were "exiles of liberty and conscience," fleeing from the "war of moral elements" in their native Britain, willing to seek refuge in "the wilderness of this Western world." The Plymouth settlers embodied the concept of the social compact founded upon free consent with their Mayflower Compact.

4. How did the American Revolution come about?

> Over time, the immediate ties with neighbors took precedence over the ties with a distant country that Americans had never seen, and "long before the Declaration of Independence, the great mass of the people of America and of the people of Britain had become total strangers to each other." But the catalyst came from "a deep and wounded sense of successive wrongs, upon which complaint had been only answered by aggravation … which had driven them to their last stand upon the adamantine rock of human rights."

5. How was the Declaration unique?

> "It was the first solemn declaration by a nation of the only legitimate foundation of civil government. It was the cornerstone of a new fabric, destined to cover the surface of the globe. It demolished at a stroke the lawfulness of all governments founded upon conquest. It swept away all the rubbish of accumulated centuries of servitude. It announced in practical form to the world the transcendent truth of the unalienable sovereignty of the people. It proved that the social compact was no figment of the imagination; but a real, solid, and sacred bond of the social union."

6. What in Adams's view is the best thing that America has done for the world? How might it spoil that?

> The peerless example of American republicanism and democracy is America's greatest gift to the world. America risks undermining that witness by intervening in the affairs of other nations, even with the best of intentions.

Document 2

ALBERT BEVERIDGE, "MARCH OF THE FLAG," 1898

It is a noble land that God has given us; a land that can feed and clothe the world; a land whose coastlines would inclose half the countries of Europe; a land set like a sentinel between the two imperial oceans of the globe, a greater England with a nobler destiny.

It is a mighty people that He has planted on this soil; a people sprung from the most masterful blood of history; a people perpetually revitalized by the virile, man-producing working-folk of all the earth; a people imperial by virtue of their power, by right of their institutions, by authority of their Heaven-directed purposes – the propagandists and not the misers of liberty.

It is a glorious history our God has bestowed upon His chosen people; a history heroic with faith in our mission and our future; a history of statesmen who flung the boundaries of the Republic out into unexplored lands and savage wilderness; a history of soldiers who carried the flag across blazing deserts and through the ranks of hostile mountains, even to the gates of sunset; a history of a multiplying people who overran a continent in half a century; a history of prophets who saw the consequences of evils inherited from the past and of martyrs who died to save us from them; a history divinely logical, in the process of whose tremendous reasoning we find ourselves today.

Therefore, in this campaign, the question is larger than a party question. It is an American question. It is a world question. Shall the American people continue their march toward the commercial supremacy of the world? Shall free institutions broaden their blessed reign as the children of liberty wax in strength, until the empire of our principles is established over the hearts of all mankind?

Have we no mission to perform, no duty to discharge to our fellow man? Has God endowed us with gifts beyond our deserts and marked us as the people of His peculiar favor, merely to rot in our own selfishness, as men and nations must, who take cowardice for their companion and self for their deity – as China has, as India has, as Egypt has?

Shall we be as the man who had one talent and hid it, or as he who had ten talents and used them until they grew to riches? And shall we reap the reward that waits on our discharge of our high duty; shall we occupy new markets for what our farmers raise, our factories make, our merchants sell-aye, and please God, new markets for what our ships shall carry?

Hawaii is ours; Porto Rico is to be ours; at the prayer of her people Cuba finally will be ours; in the islands of the East, even to the gates of Asia, coaling stations are to be ours at the very least; the flag of a liberal government is to float over the Philippines, and may it be the banner that Taylor unfurled in Texas and Fremont carried to the coast.

The Opposition tells us that we ought not to govern a people without their consent. I answer, The rule of liberty that all just government derives its authority from the consent of the governed, applies only to those who are capable of selfgovernment. We govern the Indians without their consent, we govern our territories without their consent, we govern our children without their consent. How do they know what our government would be without their consent? Would not the people of the Philippines prefer the just, humane, civilizing government of this Republic to the savage, bloody rule of pillage and extortion from which we have rescued them?

And, regardless of this formula of words made only for enlightened, self-governing people, do we owe no duty to the world? Shall we turn these peoples back to the reeking hands from which we have taken them? Shall we abandon them, with Germany, England, Japan, hungering for them? Shall we save them from those nations, to give them a selfrule of tragedy?

They ask us how we shall govern these new possessions. I answer: Out of local conditions and the necessities of the case methods of government will grow. If England can govern foreign lands, so can America. If Germany can govern foreign lands, so can America. If they can supervise protectorates, so can America. Why is it more difficult to administer Hawaii than New Mexico or California? Both had a savage and an alien population: both were more remote from the seat of government when they came under our dominion than the Philippines are today.

Will you say by your vote that American ability to govern has decayed, that a century's experience in selfrule has failed of a result? Will you affirm by your vote that you are an infidel to American power and practical sense? Or will you say that ours is the blood of government; ours the heart of dominion; ours the brain and genius of administration? Will you remember that we do but what our fathers did – we but pitch the tents of liberty farther westward, farther southward-we only continue the march of the flag?

The march of the flag! In 1789 the flag of the Republic waved over 4,000,000 souls in thirteen states, and their savage territory which stretched to the Mississippi, to Canada, to the Floridas. The timid minds of that day said that no new territory was needed, and, for the hour, they were right. But Jefferson, through whose intellect the centuries marched; Jefferson, who dreamed of Cuba as an American state, Jefferson, the first Imperialist of the Republic – Jefferson acquired that imperial territory which swept from the Mississippi to the mountains, from Texas to the British possessions, and the march of the flag began!

The infidels to the gospel of liberty raved, but the flag swept on! The title to that noble land out of which Oregon, Washington, Idaho and Montana have been carved was uncertain: Jefferson, strict constructionist of constitutional power though he was, obeyed the AngloSaxon impulse within him, whose watchword is, "Forward!": another empire was added to the Republic, and the march of the flag went on!

Those who deny the power of free institutions to expand urged every argument, and more, that we hear, today; but the people's judgment approved the command of their blood, and the march of the flag went on!

A screen of land from New Orleans to Florida shut us from the Gulf, and over this and the Everglade Peninsula waved the saffron flag of Spain; Andrew Jackson seized both, the American people stood at his back, and, under Monroe, the Floridas came under the dominion of the Republic, and the march of the flag went on! The Cassandras prophesied every prophecy of despair we hear, today, but the march of the flag went on!

Then Texas responded to the bugle calls of liberty, and the march of the flag went on! And, at last, we waged war with Mexico, and the flag swept over the southwest, over peerless California, past the Gate of Gold to Oregon on the north, and from ocean to ocean its folds of glory blazed.

And, now, obeying the same voice that Jefferson heard and obeyed, that Jackson heard and obeyed, that Monroe heard and obeyed, that Seward heard and obeyed, that Grant heard and obeyed, that Harrison heard and obeyed, our President today plants the flag over the islands of the seas, outposts of commerce, citadels of national security, and the march of the flag goes on!

Distance and oceans are no arguments. The fact that all the territory our fathers bought and seized is contiguous, is no argument. In 1819 Florida was farther from New York than Porto Rico is from Chicago today; Texas, farther from Washington in 1845 than Hawaii is from Boston in 1898; California, more inaccessible in 1847 than the Philippines are now. Gibraltar is farther from London than Havana is from Washington; Melbourne is farther from Liverpool than Manila is from San Francisco.

The ocean does not separate us from lands of our duty and desire – the oceans join us, rivers never to be dredged, canals never to be repaired. Steam joins us; electricity joins us – the very elements are in league with our destiny. Cuba not contiguous? Porto Rico not contiguous! Hawaii and the Philippines not contiguous! The oceans make them contiguous. And our navy will make them contiguous.

But the Opposition is right – there is a difference. We did not need the western Mississippi Valley when we acquired it, nor Florida, nor Texas, nor California, nor the royal provinces of the far northwest. We had no emigrants to people this imperial wilderness, no money to develop it, even no highways to cover it. No trade awaited us in its savage fastnesses. Our productions were not greater than our trade There was not one reason for the landlust of our statesmen from Jefferson to Grant, other than the prophet and the Saxon within them. But, today, we are raising more than we can consume, making more than we can use. Therefore we must find new markets for our produce.

And so, while we did not need the territory taken during the past century at the time it was acquired, we do need what we have taken and we need it now. The resources and the commerce of the immensely rich dominions will be increased as much as American energy is greater than Spanish sloth.

In Cuba, alone, there are 15,000,000 acres of forest unacquainted with the ax, exhaustless mines of iron, priceless deposits of manganese, millions of dollars' worth of which we must buy, today, from the Black Sea districts. There are millions of acres yet unexplored.

The resources of Porto Rico have only been trifled with. The riches of the Philippines have hardly been touched by the fingertips of modern methods. And they produce what we consume, and consume what we produce – the very predestination of reciprocity – a reciprocity "not made with hands, eternal in the heavens." They sell hemp, sugar, cocoanuts, fruits of the tropics, timber of price like mahogany; they buy flour, clothing, tools, implements, machinery and all that we can raise and make. Their trade will be ours in time. Do you indorse that policy with your vote?

Cuba is as large as Pennsylvania, and is the richest spot on the globe. Hawaii is as large as New Jersey; Porto Rico half as large as Hawaii; the Philippines larger than all New England, New York, New Jersey, and Delaware combined. Together they are larger than the British Isles, larger than France, larger than Germany, larger than Japan.

If any man tells you that trade depends on cheapness and not on government influence, ask him why England does not abandon South Africa, Egypt, India. Why does France seize South China, Germany, the vast region whose port is Kaouchou?

Our trade with Porto Rico, Hawaii and the Philippines must be as free as between the states of the Union, because they are American territory, while every other nation on earth must pay our tariff before they can compete with us. Until Cuba shall ask for annexation, our trade with her will, at the very least, be like the preferential trade of Canada with England. That, and the excellence of our goods and products; that, and the convenience of traffic; that, and the kinship of interests and destiny, will give the monopoly of these markets to the American people.

The commercial supremacy of the Republic means that this Nation is to be the sovereign factor in the peace of the world. For the conflicts of the future are to be conflicts of trade – struggles for markets – commercial wars for existence. And the golden rule of peace is impregnability of position and invincibility of preparedness. So, we see England, the greatest strategist of history, plant her flag and her cannon on Gibraltar, at Quebec, in the Bermudas, at Vancouver, everywhere.

So Hawaii furnishes us a naval base in the heart of the Pacific; the Ladrones another, a voyage further on; Manila another, at the gates of Asia – Asia, to the trade of whose hundreds of millions American merchants, manufacturers, farmers, have as good right as those of Germany or France or Russia or England; Asia, whose commerce with the United Kingdom alone amounts to hundreds of millions of dollars every year; Asia, to whom Germany looks to take her surplus products; Asia, whose doors must not be shut against American trade. Within five decades the bulk of Oriental commerce will be ours.

No wonder that, in the shadows of coming events so great, free-silver is already a memory. The current of history has swept past that episode. Men understand, today, the greatest commerce of the world must be conducted with the steadiest standard of value and most convenient medium of exchange human ingenuity can devise. Time, that unerring reasoner, has settled the silver question. The American people are tired of talking about money-they want to make it....

There are so many real things to be done – canals to be dug, railways to be laid, forests to be felled, cities to be builded, fields to be tilled, markets to be won, ships to be launched, peoples to be saved, civilization to be proclaimed and the Rag of liberty Hung to the eager air of every sea. Is this an hour to waste upon triflers with nature's laws? Is this a season to give our destiny over to wordmongers and prosperity-wreckers? No! It is an hour to remember our duty to our homes. It is a moment to realize the opportunities fate has opened to us. And so is all hour for us to stand by the Government.

Wonderfully has God guided us Yonder at Bunker Hill and Yorktown. His providence was above us at New Orleans and on ensanguined seas His hand sustained us. Abraham Lincoln was His minister and His was the altar of freedom the Nation's soldiers set up on a hundred battlefields. His power directed Dewey in the East and delivered the Spanish fleet into our hands, as He delivered the elder Armada into the hands of our English sires two centuries ago [actually in 1588]. The American people can not use a dishonest medium of exchange; it is ours to set the world its example of right and honor. We can not fly from our world duties; it is ours to execute the purpose of a fate that has driven us to be greater than our small intentions. We can not retreat from any soil where Providence has unfurled our banner; it is ours to save that soil for liberty and civilization.

Document 2 Questions

1. How would you contrast Beveridge's view of America with John Quincy Adams's?

    Beveridge supports the expansion of American influence in the world, taking precisely the position that Adams so adamantly rejects.

2. On what grounds does Beveridge arrive at his conclusions?

He makes extensive use of religious justifications, citing America's evident "chosenness" by God, a "history divinely logical," its prophetic role as the carrier of free institutions, and its responsibility to use its wealth to care for the needy. He compares the decision before the country to the biblical parable of the talents, in which the man who used his talents was to be preferred to the man who hid his single talent. Students will be able to find other examples of biblical imagery.

3. How does he justify governing without the consent of the governed?

He claims that the principle of consent of the governed only applies to people who are capable of governing themselves. It does not apply to the people of the Philippines, whom he believed America rescued from "the savage, bloody rule of pillage and extortion."

4. What does he mean by the "march of the flag"?

He refers to the process of steady territorial expansion that has characterized American history, a march that has also been the march of liberty, of the expansion of free institutions and enlightened governance.

5. For all their manifest differences, what do Adams's and Beveridge's views have in common?

They share a conviction of the unique virtues of American institutions. Both Adams and Beveridge are intensely patriotic Americans, but they draw radically different conclusions from that uniqueness. Adams would protect that uniqueness by avoiding foreign entanglements and tending to our own virtue at home, thereby serving as an example to humankind. Beveridge sees it as our duty to use our strength and prosperity to transmit the benefits of our way of life to a needful world. This is a dichotomy with which we have struggled throughout the nation's history.

CHAPTER FOURTEEN

THE PROGRESSIVE ERA

Summary

PROGRESSIVISM HAD MANY PREDECESSORS, including visionary writers like Henry George and the prairie reformers who created the Populist Party. But Progressivism itself was a middle-class movement, with its heartbeat in the small towns and growing cities of the upper Midwest, and particularly in states such as Wisconsin, where Progressivism enjoyed a pinnacle of success. It sought not merely to help the poor and oppressed but to change the system that brought about those ills: to correct the abuses, inequities, and inefficiencies that the new industrial economy had created and, in doing so, to restore the preconditions of democracy. In that sense, they were both reformist and conservative: willing to endorse dramatic changes in the service of rescuing and recovering older values.

There was therefore a certain high-mindedness about the Progressives, which reflected their Protestant religious formation. They tended to distrust politics, which they found to be a dishearteningly grubby business of deal making and vote trading, and thought it better to entrust as much of governance as possible to those with the expert knowledge, and the disinterested position, to enable them to govern with complete objectivity and unquestioned authority. The chief task facing the country was the task of proper regulation. If the vast productivity of modern industry was not to be rejected and dismantled, but was instead to be controlled and directed, made to serve the public interest and not private interests alone, then the chief question was how one was to do it.

To that question, there were basically two Progressive answers: the antitrust method, which would use the power of government to break up monopolies and large concentrations of corporate wealth and power, and the consolidation method, which would, instead of breaking up large combinations, seek to actively and vigorously regulate them, with the public interest always in view. With these alternatives came questions about the Constitution itself: Was it still the indispensable foundation of American law and life? Or had the new America passed it by and rendered it outmoded, as a creaking eighteenth-century document no longer able to keep up with the needs of a twentieth-century world?

Progressivism began in the cities and states and worked its way upward. The national phase of Progressivism began in 1901 with the ascent to the presidency of Theodore Roosevelt, upon the assassination of President William McKinley. An activist by temperament, Roosevelt was not inclined to be excessively deferential to the Constitution. His "stewardship" theory of the Constitution interpreted it as a charter, not of enumerated powers, but of enumerated prohibitions. The president was permitted to do anything necessary for the well-being of the people.

Despite his reputation in American folklore as a "trust buster," Roosevelt in fact tended to favor the consolidationist approach to regulation, a preference that would grow stronger over the years of his presidency. Henceforth the government, TR said, must be "the senior partner in every business," which would represent a stunning change in the most fundamental American conceptions about the relationship between business and government.

By the end of 1907, buoyed by his early success and anxiously eyeing the imminent end of his term as president, Roosevelt turned up the heat even more and began calling for radical reforms, such as income and inheritance taxes, federal controls over the stock market, and stricter regulation of interstate corporations, among other things. His rhetoric also became notably more strident, as he denounced the "malefactors of great wealth" for their "predatory" behavior. Such proposals and such rhetoric still fell far short of a socialist vision, but they were strident enough to antagonize the conservative "Old Guard" of the Republican Party and foreshadow a coming division of the Republican Party that would enable the election of Democrat Woodrow Wilson as president in 1912, one of the most exciting and unusual elections in American history, which included the third-party candidacy of TR himself.

Like Roosevelt, Wilson was convinced that the U.S. Constitution was defective and favored something closer to the British parliamentary system, which would draw the executive and legislative branches together more closely and make the president as active in the legislative process as he was in the execution of laws. Even the natural-rights doctrines of human equality and fundamental rights were subject to this counterdoctrine of fluidity: "We are not bound to adhere to the doctrines held by the signers of the Declaration of

Independence," he insisted in a 1907 speech; "we are as free as they were to make and unmake governments."

Despite his inexperience, Wilson enjoyed one of the most impressive beginnings of any president in American history. He moved quickly, putting his theories about a parliamentary-style presidency to the test: lowering tariffs, creating a federal income tax, proposing a central banking system to regulate elements of the national economy, and strengthening the Federal Trade Commission as an antitrust instrument.

There were many other reforms in his first term: advances in labor organizing, creation of a system of federal farmland banks, a Federal Highways Act to stimulate road construction, child labor laws, an eight-hour workday for rail workers – in short, a dazzling array of legislative and executive accomplishment. In addition, the ratification in 1913 of the Sixteenth and Seventeenth Amendments, the latter being a measure to establish that senators be chosen by the direct election of the people and not by the respective state legislatures, seemed to betoken the dawning of a new and more streamlined, more efficient, more nationalized era. It was a moment when Progressivism seemed triumphant and old-fashioned constitutionalism seemed on the way out.

Wilson had enjoyed phenomenal success in promoting his Progressive domestic agenda. That success was about to be tested in the larger and more unforgiving arena of world politics.

Questions and Answers

1. Why can the term "Progressive Era" for the period 1898 to 1917 easily mislead? (p. 240)

> "What we call the Progressive Era was a more concentrated and widely influential phase in a longer and more general response to the great disruptions of industrialization, urbanization, national consolidation, and concentrated wealth and power."

2. Who was Henry George? How are his ideas a precursor to Progressivism? (pp. 240–41)

> In *Progress and Poverty* (1879), he advocated a single tax on land as a solution to inequalities of wealth.
>
> Teachers may explain that George believed in the free market but saw that the market in land did not work as efficiently as the markets of other goods that are movable. If the price of soybeans is higher than normal in a particular place, people will bring in more to get the extra

proceeds off their sale. Eventually, the price will drop to normal, and no more soybeans will be moved in. (High prices in general are never the problem when something is in short supply; high prices are the solution.) But land is different because its value is based on location. A farmer wants to be the first to sell his crops, for the best price. But landowners want to be the last to sell. George contended that this led to underuse of land and advocated a 100 percent tax on unearned appreciation of land. "Unearned" means the land's value went up not because of anything the owner did but because of what the rest of society did.

3. Who was Edward Bellamy? (p. 241)

His book *Looking Backward* (1888) imagined a socialist cooperative commonwealth set in the year 2000. The book was hugely popular, and many "Bellamy clubs" existed.

4. What was the "Social Gospel"? (p. 241)

Christian leaders argued that the essence of Christianity lay not in its supernatural aspects nor in its offer of salvation but rather in its implications for social and economic reform. (Some historians call the rise of the Social Gospel the "third Great Awakening.")

5. How did the lives of farmers change in the decades after the Civil War? (p. 241)

Crop prices were deeply depressed, and farmers struggled as isolated individuals against banks, railroads, and other middlemen and creditors.

Teachers should point out that with the mechanization of agriculture and the opening up of vast amounts of new farmland in the Great Plains, the country simply had too many farmers producing too much. The long-term solution was that millions of farmers needed to move to the city and find something else to do for a living. But this was a very unpopular and difficult solution.

6. Who were the Populists? What did they want? (pp. 241–42)

They began as an agrarian protest movement and organized as a third political party. They wanted a graduated income tax, nationalization of the railroads, coinage of silver (to increase the money supply and bring down interest rates), direct election of senators, and an eight-hour workday.

7. Who was William Jennings Bryan? (His image is in the portrait gallery following p. 224.) (p. 242)

> He was a great orator who, in 1896, ran for president on a combined Populist and Democratic Party ticket, losing to William McKinley by about 51 to 48 percent in the popular vote.
>
> Teachers may mention that we will learn more of Bryan in following chapters.

8. What was the relationship between Populists and Progressives? (pp. 243–44)

> Although both movements wanted many of the same reforms, the Populists were an agrarian movement of poor farmers, while Progressivism was overwhelmingly urban and middle class, drawing heavily on town-dwelling professionals, such as doctors, lawyers, and middle managers in corporations. "Progressives tended to be educated, civic minded, religiously inclined, and morally earnest."
>
> Teachers may remind students of the old island communities and the new consumption communities. The Populists were the doomed defenders of the slowly disappearing island communities. They did not like the new society that was emerging. Progressives embraced the new developments but wanted to regulate them for what they considered to be the good of all. Progressives believed in the rule of experts – and they were the experts.

9. Who were the "muckrakers"? (p. 244)

> They were investigative journalists like Henry Demarest Lloyd, Jacob Riis, Lincoln Steffens, and Ida Tarbell.

10. At what level of government did Progressivism have its first and greatest successes? (p. 244)

> Its first successes were at the level of municipalities, then states, finally spreading to the national level. Progressivism gets the credit for turning American cities into decent places to live, with safe water, building codes, professional fire and police protection, garbage collection, parks and playgrounds, and so forth.

11. Progressives professed **disinterestedness,** avowing to be working for the "public interest" and not from self-interest. "This was admirable; it could also be annoyingly **self-righteous and self-deceiving.**" (p. 245)

12. At the state level, Progressives changed the legislative process to include **initiative, referendum, recall,** and the party **primary system** – all increasing direct popular influence. (p. 245)

13. One of the paradoxes of the Progressive view of things was that they were skeptical of **democratic institutions** and preferred the rule of experts, yet they had expansive faith in the people and their ability to initiate positive change in the public interest, operating outside the legislative process. They had great faith in **democracy** but far less faith in **democratic institutions.** (p. 246)

> Teachers may point out that Progressives' chief opponents in reforming American cities were often corrupt political machines like New York's Tammany Hall. These stayed in power by manipulating the votes of the poor and marginalized.

14. What was the basis for Progressives' support of prohibition? (pp. 246–47)

> They saw abuse of alcohol as underlying many other social problems, such as poverty, but their critique was not primarily moral. (p. 247)

15. "The Progressive view of human nature saw humans as **fundamentally good** and evil as a function of **bad social systems and corrupted institutions,** not something irremediably wrong or sinful deep in the soul of individual persons." (p. 247)

16. John Dewey's philosophy saw the old "**rugged individualism**" as a thing of the past; Progressivism "cared deeply about the common people **and knew, far better than they did, what was best for them.**" (p. 248)

17. Condescension was not the worst of the Progressives' blind spots; **racism** was. **Eugenics** was "not a fringe phenomenon in its time, and it was not confined to the most reactionary elements; it was endorsed by leading scientists and scientific organizations as well as figures such as the feminist Margaret Sanger [and] the African American scholar W. E. B. Du Bois." (p. 248)

18. Eugenics, and the "**gospel of efficiency**" in the workplace, clashed with Christian values, such as the dignity and worth of every human as made in **the image of God.** (pp. 248–49)

19. What two ways did Progressives answer the question of how best to control and direct big business, made to serve the public interest? (p. 249)

> They advocated either using antitrust laws to break up the large concentrations and restore healthy competition *or* accepting bigness as good, encouraging consolidation, and then regulating the resulting monopoly

in the public interest. The Sherman Antitrust Act did the first; the Interstate Commerce Act did the second.

20. What was Theodore Roosevelt's background? (pp. 250–51)

He was a New Yorker, a sickly boy who pushed himself into strength. Homeschooled and then educated at Harvard, he wrote a history of the naval war of 1812 that is still used. He went into politics, interspersed with ranching in North Dakota. He served as police commissioner of New York City, then as assistant secretary of the navy, Rough Rider, and vice president, before becoming the youngest president ever elected.

21. What was TR's political style? (p. 251)

He was an activist and not overly deferential to the Constitution. He had a "stewardship" view of the presidency.

22. Was TR more a trust buster or a consolidator? (p. 252)

He was a bit of both, but he preferred consolidation, of any except "bad" trusts. He strongly supported consumer protection.

23. TR's lasting achievement is his focus on **conservation** and the establishment of **national parks** and the U.S. **Forestry Service.** (p. 252)

24. TR chose his own successor, William Howard Taft, then went off to Africa. But Taft was less a Progressive, and TR was still quite young; he decided in 1912 that he was not through being president. What happened in the election? (pp. 255–56)

Taft and the Old Guard kept control of the Republican Party, so TR started the Progressive or "Bull Moose" Party as a third contender. TR and Taft split the normal 60 percent Republican vote, so Woodrow Wilson won with 40 percent of the vote.

25. Wilson was a convert to Progressivism, of the antitrust variety. He called his program **"the New Freedom"** to contrast with TR's **"New Nationalism."** (p. 255)

26. What was Woodrow Wilson's background? (pp. 255–56)

He was a scholar of the British constitutional system, president of Princeton, and then governor of New Jersey, his only political experience. He was dismissive of the U.S. Constitution, considering it too rigid. He pioneered the field of public administration as outside of politics.

27. What did Wilson accomplish during his first term? (p. 257)

He lowered tariffs, created the Federal Reserve banking system, implemented an income tax, and oversaw ratification of the Sixteenth and Seventeenth Amendments (income tax and direct election of senators).

28. How did Wilson differ from TR on racial matters? (pp. 257–58)

TR invited Booker T. Washington to the White House. Wilson, in contrast, supported racial segregation and the postbellum restoration of white rule in the South.

29. The Progressives were always tempted to cast off constitutional restrictions. But what did G. K. Chesterton say about fences? (p. 258)

Before you think about tearing a fence down, you'd better understand why it was put up in the first place.

Objective Question

Answers are in parentheses.

Put TR or WW in the blank according to whether Theodore Roosevelt or Woodrow Wilson is described:

_____	New Freedom	(WW)
_____	New Nationalism	(TR)
_____	president of Princeton	(WW)
_____	wrote naval history of the War of 1812	(TR)
_____	welcomed Booker T. Washington to the White House	(TR)
_____	was a strong supporter of racial segregation	(WW)

Document

WOODROW WILSON, "WHAT IS PROGRESS?," 1913

In that sage and veracious chronicle, "Alice Through the Looking-Glass," it is recounted how, on a noteworthy occasion, the little heroine is seized by the Red Chess Queen, who races her off at a terrific pace. They run until both of them are out of breath; then they stop, and Alice looks around her and says,

"Why, we are just where we were when we started!" "Oh, yes," says the Red Queen; "you have to run twice as fast as that to get anywhere else."

That is a parable of progress. The laws of this country have not kept up with the change of political circumstances in this country; and therefore we are not even where we were when we started. We shall have to run, not until we are out of breath, but until we have caught up with our own conditions, before we shall be where we were when we started; when we started this great experiment which has been the hope and the beacon of the world. And we should have to run twice as fast as any rational program I have seen in order to get anywhere else.

I am, therefore, forced to be a progressive, if for no other reason, because we have not kept up with our changes of conditions, either in the economic field or in the political field. We have not kept up as well as other nations have. We have not kept our practices adjusted to the facts of the case, and until we do, and unless we do, the facts of the case will always have the better of the argument; because if you do not adjust your laws to the facts, so much the worse for the laws, not for the facts, because law trails along after the facts. Only that law is unsafe which runs ahead of the facts and beckons to it and makes it follow the will-o'-the-wisps of imaginative projects.

Business is in a situation in America which it was never in before; it is in a situation to which we have not adjusted our laws. Our laws are still meant for business done by individuals; they have not been satisfactorily adjusted to business done by great combinations, and we have got to adjust them. I do not say we may or may not; I say we must; there is no choice. If your laws do not fit your facts, the facts are not injured, the law is damaged; because the law, unless I have studied it amiss, is the expression of the facts in legal relationships. Laws have never altered the facts; laws have always necessarily expressed the facts; adjusted interest as they have arisen and have changed toward one another.

Politics in America is in a case which sadly requires attention. The system set up by our law and our usage doesn't work, – or at least it can't be depended on; it is made to work only by a most unreasonable expenditure of labor and pains. The government, which was designed for the people, has got into the hands of bosses and their employers, the special interests. An invisible empire has been set up above the forms of democracy.

There are serious things to do. Does any man doubt the great discontent in this country? Does any man doubt that there are grounds and justifications for discontent? Do we dare stand still? Within the past few months we have witnessed (along with other strange political phenomena, eloquently significant of popular uneasiness) on one side a doubling of the Socialist vote and on the other the posting on dead walls and hoardings all over the country of certain very attractive and diverting bills warning citizens that it was "better to be safe than sorry" and advising them to "let well enough alone." Apparently a good many citizens doubted whether the situation they were advised to let alone was really well enough, and concluded that they would take a chance of being sorry. To me, these counsels of do-nothingism, these counsels of sitting still for fear something would happen, these counsels addressed to the hopeful, energetic people of the United States, telling them that they are not wise enough to touch their own affairs without marring them, constitute the most extraordinary argument of fatuous ignorance I ever heard. Americans are not yet cowards. True, their self-reliance has been sapped by years of submission to the doctrine that prosperity is something that benevolent magnates provide for them with the aid of the government; their self-reliance has been weakened, but not so utterly destroyed that you can twit them about it. The American people are not naturally stand-patters. Progress is the word that charms their ears and stirs their hearts.

There are, of course, Americans who have not yet heard that anything is going on. The circus might come to town, have the big parade and go, without their catching a sight of the camels or a note of the calliope. There are people, even Americans, who never move themselves or know that anything else is moving.

A friend of mind who had heard of the Florida "cracker," as they call a certain ne'er-do-well portion of the population down there, when passing through the State in a train, asked some one to point out a "cracker" to him. The man asked replied, "Well, if you see something off in the woods that looks brown, like a stump, you will know it is either a stump or a cracker; if it moves, it is a stump."

Now, movement has no virtue in itself. Change is not worth while for its own sake. I am not one of those who love variety for its own sake. If a thing is good today, I should like to have it stay that way tomorrow. Most of our calculations in life are dependent upon things staying the way they are. For example, if, when you got up this morning, you had forgotten how to dress, if you had forgotten all about those ordinary things which you do almost automatically, which you can almost do half awake, you would have to find out what you did yesterday. I am told by the psychologists that if I did not remember who I was yesterday, I should not know who I am today, and that, there fore, my very identity depends upon my being able to tally today with yesterday. If they do not tally, then I am confused; I do not know who I am, and I have to go around and ask somebody to tell me my name and where I came from.

I am not one of those who wish to break connection with the past; I am not one of those who wish to change for the mere sake of variety. The only men who do that are the men who want to forget something, the men who filled yesterday with something they would rather not recollect today, and so go about seeking diversion, seeking abstraction in something that will blot out recollection, or seeking to put something into them which will blot out all recollection. Change is not worth while unless it is improvement. If I move out of my present house because I do not like it, then I have got to choose a better house, or build a better house, to justify the change.

It would seem a waste of time to point out that ancient distinction, – between mere change and improvement. Yet there is a class of mind that is prone to confuse them. We have had political leaders whose conception of greatness was to be forever frantically doing something, – it mattered little what; restless, vociferous men, without sense of the energy of concentration, knowing only the energy of succession. Now, life does not consist of eternally running to a fire. There is no virtue in going anywhere unless you will gain something by being there. The direction is just as important as the impetus of motion.

All progress depends on how fast you are going, and where you are going, and I fear there has been too much of this thing of knowing neither how fast we were going or where we were going. I have my private belief that we have been doing most of our progressiveness after the fashion of those things that in my boyhood days we called "treadmills," a treadmill being a moving platform, with cleats on it, on which some poor devil of a mule was forced to walk forever without getting anywhere. Elephants and even other animals have been known to turn treadmills, making a good deal of noise, and causing certain wheels to go round, and I daresay grinding out some sort of product for somebody, but without achieving much progress. Lately, in an effort to persuade the elephant to move, really, his friends tried dynamite. It moved, – in separate and scattered parts, but it moved.

A cynical but witty Englishman said, in a book, not long ago, that it was a mistake to say of a conspicuously successful man, eminent in his line of business, that you could not bribe a man like that, because, he said, the point about such men is that they have been bribed – not in the ordinary meaning of that word, not in any gross, corrupt sense, but they have achieved their great success by means of the existing order of things and therefore they have been put under bonds to see that that existing order of things is not change; they are bribed to maintain the *status quo*.

It was for that reason that I used to say, when I had to do with the administration of an educational institution, that I should like to make the young gentlemen of the rising generation as unlike their fathers as possible. Not because their fathers lacked character or intelligence or knowledge or patriotism, but because their fathers, by reason of their advancing years and their established position in society, had lost touch with the processes of life; they had forgotten what it was to begin; they had forgotten what it was to rise; they had forgotten what it was to be dominated by the circumstances of their life on their way up from the bottom to the top, and, therefore, they were out of sympathy with the creative, formative and progressive forces of society.

Progress! Did you ever reflect that that word is almost a new one? No word comes more often or more naturally to the lips of modern man, as if the thing it stands for were almost synonymous with life itself, and yet men through many thousand years never talked or thought of progress. They thought in the other direction. Their stories of heroisms and glory were tales of the past. The ancestor wore the heavier armor and carried the larger spear. "There were giants in those days." Now all that has altered. We think of the future, not the past, as the more glorious time in comparison with which the present is nothing. Progress, development, – those are modern words. The modern idea is to leave the past and press onward to something new.

But what is progress going to do with the past, and with the present? How is it going to treat them? With ignominy, or respect? Should it break with them altogether, or rise out of them, with its roots still deep in the older time? What attitude shall progressives take toward the existing order, toward those institutions of conservatism, the Constitution, the laws, and the courts?

Are those thoughtful men who fear that we are now about to disturb the ancient foundations of our institutions justified in their fear? If they are, we ought to go very slowly about the processes of change. If it is indeed true that we have grown tired of the institutions which we have so carefully and sedulously built up, then we ought to go very slowly and very carefully about the very dangerous task of altering them. We ought, therefore, to ask ourselves, first of all, whether thought in this country is tending to do anything by which we shall retrace our steps, or by which we shall change the whole direction of our development?

I believe, for one, that you cannot tear up ancient rootages and safely plant the tree of liberty in soil which is not native to it. I believe that the ancient traditions of a people are its ballast; you cannot make a *tabula rasa* upon which to write a political program. You cannot take a new sheet of paper and determine what your life shall be tomorrow. You must knit the new into the old. You cannot put a new patch on an old garment without ruining it; it must be not a patch, but something woven into the old fabric, of practically the same pattern, of the same texture and intention. If I did not believe that to be progressive was to preserve the essentials of our institutions, I for one could not be a progressive.

One of the chief benefits I used to derive from being president of a university was that I had the pleasure of entertaining thoughtful men from all over the world. I cannot tell you how much has dropped into my granary by their presence. I had been casting around in my mind for something by which to draw several parts of my political thought together when it was my good fortune to entertain a very interesting Scotsman who had been devoting himself to the philosophical thought of the seventeenth century. His talk was so engaging that it was delightful to hear him speak of anything, and presently there came out of the unexpected region of his thought the thing I had been waiting for. He called my attention to the fact that in every generation all sorts of speculation and thinking tend to fall under the formula of the dominant thought of the age. For example, after the Newtonian Theory of the universe had been developed, almost all thinking tended to express itself in the analogies of the Newtonian Theory, and since the Darwinian Theory has reigned amongst us, everybody is likely to express whatever he wishes to expound in terms of development and accommodation to environment.

Now, it came to me, as this interesting man talked, that the Constitution of the United States had been made under the dominion of the Newtonian Theory. You have only to read the papers of the *The Federalist* to see that fact written on every page. They speak of the "checks and balances" of the Constitution, and use to express their idea the simile of the organization of the universe, and particularly of the solar system, – how by the attraction of gravitation the various parts are held in their orbits; and then they proceed to represent Congress, the Judiciary, and the President as a sort of imitation of the solar system.

They were only following the English Whigs, who gave Great Britain its modern constitution. Not that those Englishmen analyzed the matter, or had any theory about it; Englishmen care little for theories. It was a Frenchman, Montesquieu, who pointed out to them how faithfully they had copied Newton's description of the mechanism of the heavens.

The makers of our Federal Constitution read Montesquieu with true scientific enthusiasm. They were scientists in their way – the best way of their age – those fathers of the nation. Jefferson wrote of "the laws of Nature" – and then by way of afterthought – "and of Nature's God." And they constructed a government as they would have constructed an orrery – to display the laws of nature. Politics in their thought was a variety of mechanics. The Constitution was founded on the law of gravitation. The government was to exist and move by virtue of the efficacy of "checks and balances."

The trouble with the theory is that government is not a machine, but a living thing. It falls, not under the theory of the universe, but under the theory of organic life. It is accountable to Darwin, not to Newton. It is modified by its environment, necessitated by its tasks, shaped to its functions by the sheer pressure of life. No living thing can have its organs offset against each other, as checks, and live. On the contrary, its life is dependent upon their quick cooperation, their ready response to the commands of instinct or intelligence, their amicable community of purpose. Government is not a body of blind forces; it is a body of men, with highly differentiated functions, no doubt, in our modern day, of specialization, with a common task and purpose. Their cooperation is indispensable, their warfare fatal. There can be no successful government without the intimate, instinctive coordination of the organs of life and action. This is not theory, but fact, and displays its force as fact, whatever theories may be thrown across its track. Living political constitutions must be Darwinian in structure and in practice. Society is a living organism and must obey the laws of life, not of mechanics; it must develop.

All that progressives ask or desire is permission – in an era when "development" "evolution," is the scientific word – to interpret the Constitution according to the Darwinian principle; all they ask is recognition of the fact that a nation is a living thing and not a machine.

Some citizens of this country have never got beyond the Declaration of Independence, signed in Philadelphia, July 4th, 1776. Their bosoms swell against George III, but they have no consciousness of the war for freedom that is going on today.

The Declaration of Independence did not mention the questions of our day. It is of no consequence to us unless we can translate its general terms into examples of the present day and substitute them in some vital way for the examples it itself gives, so concrete, so intimately involved in the circumstances of the day in which it was conceived and written. It is an eminently practical document, meant for the use of practical men; not a thesis for philosophers, but a whip for tyrants; not a theory for government, but a program of action. Unless we can translate it into the questions of our own day, we are not worthy of it, we are not the sons of the sires who acted in response to its challenge.

What form does the contest between tyranny and freedom take to-day? What is the special form of tyranny we now fight? How does it endanger the rights of the people, and what do we mean to do in order to make our contest against it effectual? What are to be the items of our new declaration of independence?

By tyranny, as we now fight it, we mean control of the law, of legislation and adjudication, by organizations which do not represent the people, by means which are private and selfish. We mean, specifically, the conduct of our affairs and the shaping of our legislation in the interest of special bodies of capital and those who organize their use. We mean the alliance, for this purpose, of political machines with selfish business. We mean the exploitation of the people by legal and political means. We have seen many governments under these influences cease to be representative governments, cease to be governments representative of the people, and become governments representative of special interests, controlled by machines, which in their turn are not controlled by the people.

Sometimes, when I think of the growth of our economic system, it seems to me as if, leaving our law just about where it was before any of the modern inventions or developments took place, we had simply at haphazard extended the family residence, added an office here and a workroom there, and a new set of sleeping rooms there, built up higher on our foundations, and put out little lean-tos on the side, until we have a structure that has no character whatever. Now, the problem is to continue to live in the house and yet change it.

Well, we are architects in our time, and our architects are also engineers. We don't have to stop using a railroad terminal because a new station is being built. We don't have to stop any of the processes of our lives because we are rearranging the structures in which we conduct those processes. What we have to undertake is to systematize the foundations of the house, then to thread all the old parts of the structure with the steel which will be laced together in modern fashion, accommodated to all the modern knowledge of structural strength and elasticity, and then slowly change the partitions, relay the walls, let in the light through new apertures, improve the ventilation; until finally, a generation or two from now, the scaffolding will be taken away, and there will be the family in a great building whose noble architecture will at last be disclosed, where men can live as a single community, cooperative as in a perfected, coordinated beehive, not afraid of any storm of nature, not afraid of any artificial storm, any imitation of thunder and lightning, knowing that the foundations go down to the bedrock of principle, and knowing that whenever they please they can change that plan again and accommodate it as they please to the altering necessities of their lives.

But there are a great many men who don't like the idea. Some wit recently said, in view of the fact that most of our American architects are trained in a certain *Ecole* in Paris, that all American architecture in recent years was either bizarre or "Beaux Arts." I think that our economic architecture is decidedly bizarre; and I am afraid that there is a good deal to learn about matters other than architecture from the other side of the water. Men can now hold up against us the reproach that we have not adjusted our lives to modern conditions to the same extent that they have adjusted theirs. I was very much interested in some of the reasons given by our friends across the Canadian border for being very shy about the reciprocity arrangements. They said: "We are not sure whither these arrangements will lead, and we don't care to associate too closely with the economic conditions of the United States until those conditions are as modern as ours." And when I resented it, and asked for particulars, I had, in regard to many matters, to retire from the debate because I found that they had adjusted their regulations of economic development to conditions we had not yet found a way to meet in the United States.

Well, we have started now at all events. The procession is under way. The stand-patter doesn't know there is a procession. He is asleep in the back part of his house. He doesn't know that the road is resounding with the tramp of men going to the front. And when he wakes up, the country will be empty. He will be deserted, and he will wonder what has happened. Nothing has happened. The world has been going on. The world has a habit of going on. The world has a habit of leaving those behind who won't go with it. The world has always neglected stand-patters. And, therefore, the stand-patter does not excite my indignation; he excited my sympathy. He is going to be so lonely before it is all over. And we are good fellows, we are good company; why doesn't he come along? We are not going to do him any harm. We are going to show him a good time. We are going to climb the slow road until it reaches some upland where the air is fresher, where the whole talk of mere politicians is stilled, where men can look in each other's faces and see that there is nothing to conceal, that all they have to talk about they are willing to talk about in the open and talk about with each other; and whence, looking back over the road, we shall see at last that we have fulfilled our promise to mankind. We had said to all the world, "America was created to break every kind of monopoly, and to set men free, upon a footing of equality, upon a footing of opportunity, to match their brains and their energies." And now we have proved that we meant it.

Source: https://teachingamericanhistory.org/library/document/what-is-progress/

Document Questions

1. Why does Wilson say that "I am forced to be a progressive"?

   Because the pace of change in modern times has been so brisk that all the means we use to govern ourselves have been rendered obsolete. Our laws – including, as we will see, the Constitution – are out of touch with the circumstances in which we actually live. We need to make our "practices adjust to the facts of the case."

2. What are some examples of this obsolescence in our national life?

> Businesses are still run as if they were the work of individuals rather than large "combinations." Politics doesn't work, because there is an "invisible empire" set up above the forms of democracy. And yet people are terrified of change. But that is not the American way, Wilson contends. Americans are not "stand-patters."

3. Why does Wilson say that when he was president of Princeton University, he wanted "to make the young gentlemen of the rising generation as unlike their fathers as possible"?

> It was not because the fathers were bad people but because they had "lost touch with the processes of life" and were "out of sympathy with the creative, formative and progressive forces of society."

4. What is Wilson's problem with the Declaration of Independence and the Constitution as political guides?

> They were made in the image of a "Newtonian Theory" of the universe, but that understanding has been superseded. We have outgrown the Founding. We are now in the age of Darwin and have come to understand that "government is not a machine, but a living thing," responding not to physics but to biology. For example, the mechanical theory of checks and balances does not work, Wilson claimed, because it does not describe the actual operation of an organism. A new understanding of society in organismic terms will necessitate an entirely new theory of government.

CHAPTER FIFTEEN

WOODROW WILSON AND THE GREAT WAR

Summary

WHEN THE GREAT WAR descended upon Europe in late summer 1914, it reminded Americans of why they'd wanted to be a nation apart in the first place. How could an isolated terrorist act in the Bosnian capital of Sarajevo lead to a general conflagration engulfing all the nations of Europe and affecting much of the rest of the planet? Who could explain it?

Small wonder that President Wilson immediately issued a Declaration of Neutrality and instructed the nation to remain impartial "in thought, as well as action" with respect to this unfolding conflict. At first, the policy seemed wise. Fueled by the illusion that it could be ended quickly with a master stroke, the war soon spun out of control, descending to levels of hellish mayhem and mass slaughter that were almost surreal in their enormity and horror. Who could wish to take part in such madness?

But a policy of neutrality toward all belligerent parties would prove hard to sustain in the end, for the same reason it was at the time of the Napoleonic wars. The United States wanted to be able to trade with all parties, relying on the principle of "freedom of the seas" to protect its shipping. But such a policy of strict equality would have the effect of denying the British the full benefit of their vastly superior naval power and would thereby in effect favor the Germans.

In the event, the Germans settled on a different tactic to challenge the Allies' control of the seas. They would unleash their fearsome submarine fleet to go after Allied shipping, launching torpedoes without warning at merchant targets, including ships flying neutral flags. This was a risky approach, as became evident with the sinking of the British liner *Lusitania* on May 7, 1915, off the Irish coast, with a loss of 1,200 lives, including 128 Americans. The American public was outraged at the Germans, and Wilson responded accordingly, stiffly extracting a German promise to cease targeting merchant and passenger ships. The issue subsided for the time being, while greatly aiding Wilson's reelection efforts in 1916. "He kept us out of war!" became the Democrats' campaign slogan.

But that alone would not be enough for Wilson. Once reelected, he launched into an effort to assert American moral leadership in the world and broker a settlement to the war in Europe. But he was too late; the Germans had already decided to resume their unrestricted submarine warfare, knowing that in doing so, they would face the likelihood of American entry into the war. But they took the risk, hoping to land a quick and decisive military blow – and for a hesitant and confused mobilization on the American side.

They did not get their wish. Wilson quickly asked Congress for a declaration of war in a speech that bitterly decried Germany's submarine policy as "warfare against mankind" and declared that "the world must be made safe for democracy." A rapid American military mobilization began, coordinated by the War Industries Board, which was granted the power to set production quotas and allocate raw materials, encouraging companies to use mass-production techniques and product standardization to increase efficiency and decrease waste. American forces were in France by July 1917 and by fall 1918 numbered more than a million strong in Europe, injecting badly needed energy into the Allied effort that was finally too much for the weary German army to withstand. The Germans were forced to surrender and sign an armistice on November 11 – the day we now celebrate as Veterans Day.

Wilson grasped that the world now faced a pivotal moment amid the wreckage of this astoundingly costly conflict and believed that his Fourteen Points could be the basis for new international order, a world "fit and safe to live in."

To ensure that his visionary proposals got a fair hearing at the Allies' peace conference, he decided that he would go in person to Paris to lead the American delegation. He arrived in Europe to a hero's welcome; but once the conference got to work, he found it impossible to overcome the obstinacy and cynicism of the other Allied leaders. In the end, he had to sacrifice all his other hopes to gain his final Point, the idea of an "association of nations," what eventually became the League of Nations. All else, he believed, would be possible in due course if such an organization, committed to collective security and mutual accountability, could be established. Wilson was willing to accept that bargain.

It was clear almost from the start that he had made a bad choice. Powerful domestic foes, such as Senator Henry Cabot Lodge, chairman of the powerful Senate Foreign Relations Committee, strongly opposed the League and got thirty-nine Republican senators or senators-elect – enough to block ratification of the treaty – to oppose it. Nevertheless, Wilson brushed their demands aside contemptuously and vowed to "crush" all opposition. He was setting things up for a major confrontation and seemed entirely confident of prevailing.

But Lodge would prove a formidable foe, and Wilson was his own worst enemy, refusing to consider any substantive changes, particularly to the controversial Article X, which seemed to chip away at American national sovereignty. Despite his undertaking a nationwide speaking tour to rally public support, he was unable to budge the disposition of the Senate. The treaty was never ratified.

Questions and Answers

1. Why was what we now call World War I such a shock to Americans? (p. 259)

> They paid little attention to the world – which had been at peace (no general or world wars) for ninety-nine years (1815–1914).

2. "Some of the greatest events in human history are also among the most unfathomable." Explain. (p. 259)

> The war was to some degree an accident, as the rise of Germany led to the creation of two alliances and the proliferation of treaties – some of them secret – such that any small conflict anywhere in Europe had the potential of igniting a general war if one of the major powers became involved.

3. The war "changed Europe and the world forever, ending a long period of **unparalleled optimism** and **confidence** and replacing it with persistent **anxiety** and **doubt** about the very idea of **progress** itself." (p. 259)

4. How did the unification of Germany upset the balance of power? What two alliances resulted? (p. 260)

> Fear of German power led France to ally with Russia, which in turn led Germany to ally with longtime rival Austria: Triple Alliance (Germany, Austria-Hungary, and Italy) and Triple Entente (France, Russia, and Great Britain).
>
> > Teachers may point out that *entente* is a French word and that the Triple Entente is the one that included France.

5. "It was a royal mess, like a game of toppling and exploding dominoes." How did an act of terrorism in the periphery of Europe lead to general war? (pp. 260–61)

> Once Austria attacked Serbia, Russia intervened to defend Serbia, triggering Germany to declare war on Russia, triggering the French alliance against Germany. All of this happened in a few days.

6. What was the response by President Wilson to the outbreak of war? (p. 261)

> He reaffirmed American neutrality, including freedom of neutral nations to trade freely during wartime.

7. Why did the war not end quickly? Why was the slaughter unparalleled? (And why did this shatter optimism based on scientific and technological progress?) (p. 261)

> Mass armies and trench warfare produced a stalemate. Machine guns, poison gas, submarines, aircraft, and so on produced a slaughter. Modern science was quickly applied to destruction.

8. What was the human cost of the Battle of the Somme? What resulted from the battle? (p. 261)

> The British army lost twenty thousand killed and forty thousand wounded on one day, with no decisive result.

9. Where did Americans' sympathies lie? (Is this part of what it means to be a "nation of immigrants"?) (p. 262)

> German Americans tended to favor Germany, and so on.
> Teachers should point out that, unlike in World War II, there was no clear moral distinction between the two sides, between the German or Austrian Empire and the British and French Empires.

10. Germany had the strongest army, while Britain had the strongest navy. How did this asymmetry affect America's desire to remain neutral? "Under these circumstances (what circumstances?) nothing the Americans did could ever be completely impartial." Explain. (p. 262)

> Britain could blockade the German coast, but that did not kill people. German submarines trying to prevent ships from reaching Britain did kill people.

11. How did Wilson respond to German submarine warfare? (pp. 262–63)

> He stopped short of an ultimatum but made it clear that continued submarine warfare would draw an American response.

12. Why was Wilson's reelection in 1916 not easy? (Recall how he was elected in 1912.) How strong was the United States militarily? What slogan did Wilson run on? Why did he manage to win his second term? (p. 263)

> This time Wilson faced only one Republican opponent. "He kept us out of war" was a good slogan and Republican Hughes a weak candidate and campaigner. Even so, Wilson barely won.

13. How did Wilson try to restore peace? Whom did he address in his speech of January 22, 1917? What ideals did he proclaim? (p. 263)

> Wilson spoke to the U.S. Senate but really addressed the people of the countries involved – appealing over the heads of their governments – advocating a "peace without victory" based on a recognition of a "common interest."

14. Why did the Germans decide to "roll the dice" by resuming submarine warfare in February 1917? (p. 264)

> The German economy was collapsing, and they would lose the war otherwise. They knew resuming submarine warfare would bring in the Americans but calculated they might be able to win before American help could be felt.

15. After the U.S. declaration of war, "the race was on between American **preparation** and **the knockout blow** Germany hoped to administer." (p. 265)

16. The Progressive Wilson "proved to be an excellent wartime leader, once he **accepted the fact that war was unavoidable.**" How did Wilson's government respond to the needs of mobilization? (p. 265)

> It responded with typical Progressive efficiency and energy. Many government agencies were created to oversee every part of mobilization.

17. How did America fill the need for workers as four million men entered the military? (p. 266)

> Women took factory jobs, and nearly half a million African Americans moved from the rural South to northern industrial cities.

18. What was the Creel Committee? (p. 266)

It was Wilson's propaganda bureau; it was designed to reinforce the Wilson administration's high-minded conception of the American war effort and convince Americans that their national security depended on the war's outcome.

19. How did civil liberties fare under Wilson's wartime administration? (p. 267)

Poorly. More than a thousand people were convicted under the Sedition Act, including Eugene V. Debs.

20. "Wilson seemed to have an impatience with **dissent** and a reluctance to **pay attention to contrary points of view.**" (p. 267)

21. How did the Progressive movement change as a result of the war? (p. 267)

They decided having everyone working together toward a common purpose was a great thing and looked for a "moral equivalent to war."

22. "How can a liberal political culture, one grounded ultimately in the **free consent** of **rights-bearing individuals,** nevertheless be capable of purposeful **public action** when circumstances call for it?" (p. 268)

23. What is the fundamental conflict between Progressivism and the structures of the U.S. Constitution, such as checks and balances? What opposing views of human nature are involved? (p. 268)

The centralizing, consolidating, harmonizing tendencies of Progressivism fit awkwardly with the constitutional channeling of conflict through checks and balances to protect against concentrated power – which is better suited to a fallible human condition.

24. How close did Germany come to winning in 1917? How did American participation in the war turn it around? (pp. 269–70)

Germany came very close to winning the war in 1917 (knocking Russia out of the war and smashing the Italian army) and in early 1918, driving back the British and French. The American Expeditionary Force arrived just in time, defeating the Germans in the Argonne forest and leading to a German request for an armistice.

25. How did American deaths compare to those of other nations? (p. 270)

The major powers each lost from 1.8 million (Germany) to 400,000 (Italy). American losses from disease and combat were 117,000.

26. Besides wiping out 10 percent of Europe's population, what else did the war destroy? (p. 270)

> The great empires either crumbled or were so weakened that they were dismantled following World War II. The idea of progress was shattered, and the world economy was weakened.

27. What was Wilson's vision for the world, expressed in the Fourteen Points? (pp. 270–71)

> He wanted to restore a just and lasting peace, particularly through rejecting a "winner's peace" and instead creating a League of Nations.

28. How did the Fourteen Points help end the war? What were their internal contradictions? How realistic were they? (pp. 271–72)

> The Germans surrendered partly out of hope that the generosity of the Fourteen Points would prevail in peace negotiations. The contradiction was that nationalism was blamed for the war but the principle of "self-determination" inevitably fired the growth of nationalism. And the British were never going to accept freedom of the seas.

29. "The idea of **self-determination** inevitably fired the growth of **nationalism** – the very same force that Wilson felt needed to be tamped down." (pp. 271–72)

30. How did the Allies respond to Wilson's idealism? (p. 272)

> They responded with obstinacy and cynicism. They insisted Germany admit war guilt and pay reparations.

31. Why did Wilson decide to go to Paris to lead the American peace delegation? Why (several reasons, in Europe and in America) was this a really bad idea?

> He arrogantly thought he could bypass the national leaders and appeal to the people directly. But joining the peace talks lowered him to the level of other national leaders. Plus he was gone six months, and his political coalition back home came apart.

32. Wilson's decision to go to Paris "proceeded from a mixture of **high-mindedness and hubris.**" (p. 272)

33. What was the result of the 1918 midterm elections? (p. 272)

> The Republicans took control of both houses of Congress.

34. Wilson's biggest blunder was failing to take any **Republican senators** along with him. (p. 272)

35. Germany had surrendered in part as a result of Wilson's implied promise that they would not be punished by a "victors' peace." How was Germany in fact treated by the treaty? How did this lay the foundation for World War II twenty years later? (p. 273)

> The "war guilt" and reparations were major German grievances leading directly to the rise of Hitler and the coming of the next war.

36. What one Point of the Fourteen was most important to Wilson? (p. 273)

> The League of Nations was most important.

37. How and why did the Republicans led by Senator Henry Cabot Lodge oppose the treaty and the League? Who refused to delink the two? What resulted? (pp. 73–74)

> Lodge's concern was that America's sovereignty would be threatened and the nation would be dragged into foreign wars where its national interest was not involved. Wilson refused to delink the treaty and the League or to accept the "reservations" desired by some senators. So the treaty was defeated in the Senate.

38. How did Wilson twice appeal to public opinion against Lodge and the Senate Republicans? What resulted? (pp. 274–75)

> He made a nationwide speaking tour and, when that failed, made the election of 1920 a referendum on the League. Both failed.

39. What was the significance of Harding's victory? "After eight years of Wilson, and **twenty** years of **Progressivism,** America was ready for something different." (p. 275) Harding was the first American president to be elected with more than 60 percent of the popular vote.

Answers are in parentheses.

Put in order:

    ____ Germany asks for armistice   (2)
    ____ Versailles Peace Conference   (3)
    ____ Wilson issues the Fourteen Points (1)

Document

WOODROW WILSON, FOURTEEN POINTS, JANUARY 8, 1918

Gentlemen of the Congress, –

Once more, as repeatedly before, the spokesmen of the Central Empires have indicated their desire to discuss the objects of the war and the possible basis of a general peace. Parleys have been in progress at Brest-Litovsk between representatives of the Central Powers to which the attention of all the belligerents has been invited for the purpose of ascertaining whether it may be possible to extend these parleys into a general conference with regard to terms of peace and settlement.

The Russian representatives presented not only a perfectly definite statement of the principles upon which they would be willing to conclude peace, but also an equally definite program of the concrete application of those principles. The representatives of the Central Powers, on their part, presented an outline of settlement which, if much less definite, seemed susceptible of liberal interpretation until their specific program of practical terms was added. That program proposed no concessions at all either to the sovereignty of Russia or to the preferences of the populations with whose fortunes it dealt, but meant, in a word, that the Central Empires were to keep every foot of territory their armed forces had occupied, – every province, every city, every point of vantage, – as a permanent addition to their territories and their power. It is a reasonable conjecture that the general principles of settlement which they at first suggested originated with the more liberal statesmen of Germany and Austria, the men who have begun to feel the force of their own peoples' thought and purpose, while the concrete terms of actual settlement came from the military leaders who have no thought but to keep what they have got. The negotiations have been broken off. The Russian representatives were sincere and in earnest. They cannot entertain such proposals of conquest and domination.

The whole incident is full of significance. It is also full of perplexity. With whom are the Russian representatives dealing? For whom are the representatives of the Central Empires speaking? Are they speaking for the majorities of their respective parliaments or for the minority parties, that military and imperialistic minority which has so far dominated their whole policy and controlled the affairs of Turkey and of the Balkan states which have felt obliged to become their associates in this war? The Russian representatives have insisted, very justly, very wisely, and in the true spirit of modern democracy, that the conferences they have been holding with the Teutonic and Turkish statesmen should be held within open, not closed doors, and all the world has been audience, as was desired.

To whom have we been listening, then? To those who speak the spirit and intention of the Resolutions of the German Reichstag on the 9th of July last, the spirit and intention of the liberal leaders and parties of Germany, or to those who resist and defy that spirit and intention and insist upon conquest and subjugation? Or are we listening, in fact, to both, unreconciled and in open and hopeless contradiction? These are very serious and pregnant questions. Upon the answer to them depends the peace of the world. But, whatever the results of the parleys at Brest-Litovsk, whatever the confusions of counsel and of purpose in the utterances of the spokesmen of the Central Empires, they have again attempted to acquaint the world with their objects in the war and have again challenged their adversaries to say what their objects are and what sort of settlement they would deem just and satisfactory. There is no good reason why that challenge should not be responded to, and responded to with the utmost candor. We did not wait for it. Not once, but again and again, we have laid our whole thought and purpose before the world, not in general terms only, but each time with sufficient definition to make it clear what sort of definitive terms of settlement must necessarily spring out of them.

Within the last week Mr. Lloyd George has spoken with admirable candor and in admirable spirit for the people and Government of Great Britain. There is no confusion of counsel among the adversaries of the Central Powers, no uncertainty of principle, no vagueness of detail. The only secrecy of counsel, the only lack of fearless frankness, the only failure to make definite statement of the objects of the war, lies with Germany and her Allies. The issues of life and death hang upon these definitions. No statesman who has the least conception of his responsibility ought for a moment to permit himself to continue this tragical and appalling outpouring of blood and treasure unless he is sure beyond a peradventure that the objects of the vital sacrifice are part and parcel of the very life of Society and that the people for whom he speaks think them right and imperative as he does.

There is, moreover, a voice calling for these definitions of principle and of purpose which is, it seems to me, more thrilling and more compelling than any of the many moving voices with which the troubled air of the world is filled. It is the voice of the Russian people. They are prostrate and all but helpless, it would seem, before the grim power of Germany, which has hitherto known no relenting and no pity. Their power, apparently, is shattered. And yet their soul is not subservient. They will not yield either in principle or in action. Their conception of what is right, of what is humane and honorable for them to accept, has been stated with a frankness, a largeness of view, a generosity of spirit, and a universal human sympathy which must challenge the admiration of every friend of mankind; and they have refused to compound their ideals or desert others that they themselves may be safe.

They call to us to say what it is that we desire, – in what, if in anything, our purpose and our spirit differ from theirs; and I believe that the people of the United States would wish me to respond, with utter simplicity and frankness. Whether their present leaders believe it or not, it is our heartfelt desire and hope that some way may be opened whereby we may be privileged to assist the people of Russia to attain their utmost hope of liberty and ordered peace.

It will be our wish and purpose that the processes of peace, when they are begun, shall be absolutely open and that they shall involve and permit henceforth no secret understandings of any kind. The day of conquest and aggrandizement is gone by; so is also the day of secret covenants entered into in the interest of particular governments and likely at some unlooked-for moment to upset the peace of the world. It is this happy fact, now clear to the view of every public man whose thoughts do not still linger in an age that is dead and gone, which makes it possible for every nation whose purposes are consistent with justice and the peace of the world to avow now or at any other time the objects it has in view.

We entered this war because violations of right had occurred which touched us to the quick and made the life of our own people impossible unless they were corrected and the world secured once for all against their recurrence. What we demand in this war, therefore, is nothing peculiar to ourselves. It is that the world be made fit and safe to live in; and particularly that it be made safe for every peace-loving nation which, like our own, wishes to live its own life, determine its own institutions, be assured of justice and fair dealing by the other peoples of the world as against force and selfish aggression. All the peoples of the world are in effect partners in this interest, and for our own part we see very clearly that unless justice be done to others it will not be done to us.

The program of the world's peace, therefore, is our program; and that program, the only possible program, as we see it, is this:

1. Open covenants of peace, openly arrived at, after which there shall be no private international understandings of any kind but diplomacy shall proceed always frankly and in the public view.

2. Absolute freedom of navigation upon the seas, outside territorial waters, alike in peace and in war, except as the seas may be closed in whole or in part by international action for the enforcement of international covenants.

3. The removal, so far as possible, of all economic barriers and the establishment of an equality of trade conditions among all the nations consenting to the peace and associating themselves for its maintenance.

4. Adequate guarantees given and taken that national armaments will be reduced to the lowest point consistent with domestic safety.

5. A free, open-minded, and absolutely impartial adjustment of all colonial claims, based upon a strict observance of the principle that in determining all such questions of sovereignty the interests of the populations concerned must have equal weight with the equitable claims of the government whose title is to be determined.

6. The evacuation of all Russian territory and such a settlement of all questions affecting Russia as will secure the best and freest cooperation of the other nations of the world in obtaining for her an unhampered and unembarrassed opportunity for the independent determination of her own political development and national policy and assure her of a sincere welcome into the society of free nations under institutions of her own choosing; and, more than a welcome, assistance also of every kind that she may need and may herself desire. The treatment accorded Russia by her sister nations in the months to come will be the acid test of their good will, of their comprehension of her needs as distinguished from their own interests, and of their intelligent and unselfish sympathy.

7. Belgium, the whole world will agree, must be evacuated and restored, without any attempt to limit the sovereignty which she enjoys in common with all other free nations. No other single act will serve as this will serve to restore confidence among the nations in the laws which they have themselves set

and determined for the government of their relations with one another. Without this healing act the whole structure and validity of international law is forever impaired.

8. All French territory should be freed and the invaded portions restored, and the wrong done to France by Prussia in 1871 in the matter of Alsace-Lorraine, which has unsettled the peace of the world for nearly fifty years, should be righted, in order that peace may once more be made secure in the interests of all.

9. A readjustment of the frontiers of Italy should be effected along clearly recognizable lines of nationality.

10. The peoples of Austria-Hungary, whose place among the nations we wish to see safeguarded and assured, should be accorded the freest opportunity of autonomous development.

11. Rumania, Serbia, and Montenegro should be evacuated; occupied territories restored; Serbia accorded free and secure access to the sea; and the relations of the several Balkan states to one another determined by friendly counsel along historically established lines of allegiance and nationality; and international guarantees of the political and economic independence and territorial integrity of the several Balkan states should be entered into.

12. The Turkish portions of the present Ottoman Empire should be assured a secure sovereignty, but the other nationalities which are now under Turkish rule should be assured an undoubted security of life and an absolutely unmolested opportunity of autonomous development, and the Dardanelles should be permanently opened as a free passage to the ships and commerce of all nations under international guarantees.

13. An independent Polish state should be erected which should include the territories inhabited by indisputably Polish populations, which should be assured a free and secure access to the sea, and whose political and economic independence and territorial integrity should be guaranteed by international covenant.

14. A general association of nations must be formed under specific covenants for the purpose of affording mutual guarantees of political independence and territorial integrity to great and small states alike.

In regard to these essential rectifications of wrong and assertions of right we feel ourselves to be intimate partners of all the governments and peoples associated together against the Imperialists. We cannot be separated in interest or divided in purpose. We stand together until the end.

For such arrangements and covenants we are willing to fight and to continue to fight until they are achieved; but only because we wish the right to prevail and desire a just and stable peace such as can be secured only by removing the chief provocations to war, which this program does remove. We have no jealousy of German greatness, and there is nothing in this program that impairs it. We grudge her no achievement or distinction of learning or of pacific enterprise, such as have made her record very bright and very enviable. We do not wish to injure her or to block in any way her legitimate influence or power. We do not wish to fight her either with arms or with hostile arrangements of trade if she is willing to associate herself with us and the other peace-loving nations of the world in covenants of justice and law and fair dealing. We wish her only to accept a place of equality among the peoples of the world, – the new world in which we now live, – instead of a place of mastery.

Neither do we presume to suggest to her any alteration or modification of her institutions. But it is necessary, we must frankly say, and necessary as a preliminary to any intelligent dealings with her on our part, that we should know whom her spokesmen speak for when they speak to us, whether for the Reichstag majority or for the military party and the men whose creed is imperial domination.

We have spoken now, surely, in terms too concrete to admit of any further doubt or question. An evident principle runs through the whole program I have outlined. It is the principle of justice to all peoples and nationalities, and their right to live on equal terms of liberty and safety with one another, whether they be strong or weak.

Unless this principle be made its foundation no part of the structure of international justice can stand. The people of the United States could act upon no other principle; and to the vindication of this principle they are ready to devote their lives, their honor, and everything they possess. The moral climax of this the culminating and final war for human liberty has come, and they are ready to put their own strength, their own highest purpose, their own integrity and devotion to the test.

Source: https://teachingamericanhistory.org/library/document/fourteen-points/

Document Questions

1. Note how many times Wilson distinguishes between governments and peoples. In which does he seem to have more faith, and with whose welfare is he most concerned? Does the overall tendency of this speech tend to undermine the legitimacy of the international political system?

> This statement does that most clearly: "the principle that in determining all such questions of sovereignty the interests of the populations concerned must have equal weight with the equitable claims of the government whose title is to be determined."

2. What political entities does Wilson envision ending? What new nations and governments does he wish to create?

> The Ottoman Empire will be dismantled, and Turkey is to lose control of the Dardanelles. The Austro-Hungarian Empire is likewise to be broken up. Poland is to be created as a new nation, and new governments are to be created in Russia and possibly in the Balkans.

3. What territory does Wilson envision changing hands?

> France gets Alsace-Lorraine from Germany, and the boundaries of Italy and the Balkan states are to be redrawn along lines of nationality.

4. Which of the Fourteen Points seem realistic and which idealistic, perhaps to the point of fantasy?

> Point 1 seems contrary to all of human history and unenforceable. The British would never agree to Point 2. Implementing free trade as Point 3 recommends would require every government to subordinate its own interests to those of the world. Point 5 seems hopelessly idealistic, as terms like "open-minded" and "absolutely impartial" have no agreed-upon, objective meaning. The Austrian and Ottoman Empires were defeated and already breaking up, so Points 10 and 12 reflect reality. Whether an association of nations would work remained to be seen.

5. What assurances did Wilson offer Germany, which at this point had not yet surrendered?

> He assured "a just and stable peace" and "a place of equality among the nations of the world," in which "German greatness" in peaceable pursuits would be honored.

6. *For Thought:* Does Wilson seem arrogant or high-handed here? Are these recommendations likely to find favor among the winners (Britain and France in particular)? Is the task of drawing boundaries along national or ethnic lines even possible in areas like the Balkans? And does Wilson see nationalism as a good thing or a bad thing? If national rivalries caused the war, and yet the plan is to give every ethnic group its own nation …?

CHAPTER SIXTEEN

FROM BOOM TO BUST

Summary

"THEY WON THE WAR, but lost the peace"; never was that adage more applicable than as a description of what the Allies accomplished, and failed to accomplish, during their months of deliberation in Paris. The British economist John Maynard Keynes observed it all with sour resignation from his ringside seat as a British delegate to the Paris Conference and came away all but predicting that the treaty would lead to another and far worse war. He was not wrong about that.

Keynes's discouragement would be echoed in the disillusionment felt by a great many Americans in the wake of the war. The grand rhetoric from Wilson's presidential podium about the nation's noble war aims, making the world safe for democracy, self-determination, open agreements openly arrived at, freedom of the seas, and so on – all of these now rang pitiably hollow. Some Americans even went so far as to suspect that American intervention in the war had occurred under false pretenses and was promoted primarily for the benefit of financial and banking interests associated with the munitions industry.

The roller-coaster ride of an unstable economy was another source of anxiety. Returning vets eager to get on with their lives found housing, autos, and consumer goods to be in very short supply, causing huge spikes in prices. There was widespread labor unrest, as unions sought to hold on to their wartime gains or otherwise cope in the savagely inflationary postwar environment. Racial and ethnic tensions, fed by the tight labor and housing markets, led to some twenty-five urban riots erupting in 1919, notably a July riot in Chicago that left thirty-eight dead and more than five hundred injured. And there was the Spanish influenza epidemic, which killed almost seven hundred thousand Americans.

When Harding called for a "return to normalcy," he was offering the American public a time of relief from such things. Small wonder his message was so welcome.

Things got off to a rough start for Harding, though, as he inherited a deep economic downturn beginning in July 1920 and lasting through 1921, during which time commodity prices, particularly for agricultural products, fell sharply and unemployment soared. But Mellon's insistence that high war-time taxes be reduced without delay proved to be the right medicine for the economy. By the end of 1922, real GNP was already inching up, and by 1923, it was up sharply and would continue to rise through most of the decade. It was the beginning of what would prove to be one of the most concentrated periods of economic growth and general prosperity in the nation's history. The economy grew 42 percent over the 1920s, with an average rate of GNP for the decade of 4.7 percent per year. In addition, Mellon's policies were successful in halving the national debt, from $33 billion in 1919 to $16 billion by 1929.

The sheer size of the American economy was simply astounding. It truly was becoming the economic colossus of the world, the source of nearly half the world's output. Automobiles became to the economy of the 1920s, and much of the twentieth century, what textiles had been early in the previous century and what railroads had been after the Civil War: a centrally important industry that was not only a big business in its own right but also a powerful economic multiplier that gave rise to important by-products, including additional big businesses, subsidiary industries, and various other ripple effects through the economy.

Many historians consider the 1920s to be the first decade of "our times." What they mean by this is that a great many of the standard features of American life as we know it today – pervasive mass communications, personal automobiles, motion pictures, a consumer-oriented economy, professional sports, celebrity culture, readily available consumer credit, the widespread availability of cheap electrical power, and so on – first began to become commonplace during those years. The chapter provides extensive examples of each of these developments.

Harding's administration had been markedly successful in lifting the economy out of the postwar recession and getting it aloft. But it struggled with corruption in its ranks. Fortunately for the country, Harding would be succeeded by Calvin Coolidge, a man of high probity who continued the taxation policies of Andrew Mellon, further reducing income tax rates and keeping spending low, to continue retiring the national debt. By 1927, income taxes affected only the wealthiest 2 percent of Americans – others paid no federal income tax – and the economy continued to thrive.

Coolidge chose not to run for a second term in 1928 but would be succeeded by Herbert Hoover, his and Harding's commerce secretary, a brilliant former businessman and mining engineer. In the 1928 election, Hoover cruised to victory, smashing the Democratic candidate Al Smith and riding the continuing wave of Coolidge prosperity. As he took office in 1929, the stock market was booming.

But in retrospect, we can see that the country was in the grip of a speculative mania, a bull market that had begun in 1927 and showed no signs of quitting. Caught up in a classic economic bubble, many investors forgot what every wise investor needs to remember: no boom lasts forever, and what goes up must eventually come down.

On September 3, those laws of nature began to assert themselves, and by Tuesday, October 29, the bottom fell out, as 16.5 million stock shares changed hands and prices collapsed.

It is important to understand that, although this great stock market crash was a herald of the coming Great Depression, it was not its principal cause. Stock markets rise and fall, sometimes with extreme volatility, but their activity is largely self-corrective over time, like any market. This was the case even in 1929. Stocks would rally later in the year, and business activity did not begin to decline notably until spring 1930. But once depression had taken hold, it did not yield its grip – not until a second world war had begun in Europe.

Questions and Answers

1. What did Harding mean by a "return to normalcy," and why did his words resonate with voters? (pp. 276, 279)

> The war was now regarded as a "self-evident mistake" and the peace as "lost."
>
> Teachers may also point out that the Wilson administration had suppressed dissent with the Sedition Act and also centralized control of important sectors of the economy, such as the railroads. Americans were reluctantly willing to accept such actions as temporary necessities in wartime, but they were not normal.
>
> And the postwar disruptions were very great (see later). Wilson was blamed for that.

2. What did economist John Maynard Keynes think of the peace treaty and its likely consequences? (pp. 276–77)

> He thought that it was unjust and would lead to another war.
>
> Keynes's argument can be summarized as this: Europe is the heart of the world economy, and Germany is the heart of Europe's economy. To wreck Germany's economy, as reparations would do, would ultimately bring economic ruin to the whole world.
>
> Teachers may note that the rebuilding of Europe under the Marshall Plan after World War II, including the defeated Germany, was based in part on the correct perception that Keynes had been right.

3. All of Wilson's grand rhetoric now **"rang pitiably hollow."** (p. 277)

4. What motives did Americans suspect were really behind the American entry into war? (We will return to this later with the Nye Committee.) (p. 277)

> The suspicion was that the United States entered the war to protect American business interests, such as banks and the munitions industry.

5. How well planned was demobilization and the reduction of wartime economic regulations? What happened to the cost of living? (p. 278)

> Demobilization was chaotic, veterans frequently could not find work, and the cost of living soared.

6. What different types of violent unrest erupted during 1919? (pp. 278–79)

> Race riots and violent strikes erupted, plus the letter bombs leading to the Palmer raids (see later).

7. What did the Spanish flu do to the world? To America? (p. 278)

> It killed more than 22 million people around the world, including 675,000 Americans.

8. What events led to the Palmer raids? (Palmer was Woodrow Wilson's attorney general.) Why did support for them finally stop? (p. 279)

> The Bolshevik Revolution in Russia was ongoing, and threatening. Someone (who turned out to be an Italian American radical) was sending bombs to prominent business and political leaders; thirty-six were intercepted, and eight went off. Palmer responded by rounding up thousands of anarchists and other radicals; any who were not citizens were quickly deported. But eventually the unconstitutionality of the raids, and the subsiding of fears, led to their halt.

9. Why did politicians in the 1920s loom less large in the American story? What group takes their place? ("The business of America is business.") (p. 280)

> Businessmen, and particularly industrial leaders, commanded vast resources of capital and labor and satisfied the wants of millions of Americans. Politicians come and go; presidents serve a limited number of years; but big business is a permanent fixture.

10. How did Andrew Mellon advise President Harding to deal with the economic crisis created by the end of the war? What resulted? (p. 280)

> Mellon advised Harding to cut taxes – this would stimulate the economy and (paradoxically) increase government revenue. The result of Mellon's economic policies was the boom of the 1920s.
>
> Teachers should be sure that students understand that tax revenues depend on two things: the tax rate and the amount being taxed at that rate. If lower rates produce economic growth, revenues can increase.

11. How did Harding improve the government's attitude toward and treatment of African Americans? (p. 281)

> He reversed Wilson's policy of excluding African Americans from federal positions and spoke out against the scandal of lynching.

12. By how much did the economy grow under the Harding/Mellon policies? (p. 281)

> The economy grew 42 percent during the decade, while the national debt was halved from $33 billion to $16 billion by 1929.

13. We know what Henry Ford did; *how* did he do it? (pp. 281–83)

> He emphasized low costs, allowing low prices, achieved by concentrating all processes of production under one large roof on an "assembly line," and he understood that high wages allowed workers to buy his products. Ford's wages were as much as double those paid by his competitors.

14. **Automobiles** became the centrally important industry that was not only a big business in its own right but also a powerful economic multiplier that gave rise to important by-products, which included additional big businesses, subsidiary industries, and various other ripple effects. Explain. (p. 282)

> Service stations, roadside restaurants, and tourist attractions added jobs. More cars required more steel, more gasoline – more of many things.

15. How did automobiles transform the American landscape and American life in general? (p. 282)

> Automobiles and highways changed the relationship between cities, suburbs, and countryside, allowing families and commerce to move easily between and among them.

16. Why did Ford pay his workers so well? (two reasons) (p. 282)

> He needed to reduce turnover, which was high in boring factory jobs, and he realized that consumers and workers, taken together, are the same people. If businesses pay workers more, consumers have more to spend on their products.

17. What contradictions and complexities did Ford's personality contain? (pp. 282–83)

> Although brilliant as an innovating entrepreneur, he was not very skilled as an executive, and he sometimes did strange things, such as snooping around in his employees' private lives. Though he declared famously that history was "bunk," he had a nostalgic passion for early Americana – the same Americana that was being forever altered by the automobile.

18. The 1920s were the first decade of "our times," in which the basic structures of life are essentially like what we have today. Explain. (pp. 283–85)

> For the first time, the majority of Americans lived in houses with electricity and running water. By 1929, 60 percent of American families owned a radio. Movies, professional sports, and recorded music provided entertainment.

19. How did American culture develop during the 1920s?

> Hollywood, and Hollywood stars, became important. Music developed into now-familiar categories like jazz, blues, and country.

20. **Sports** became a model of how the new mass communications not only reflected events but **created** them. (p. 285)

21. How and why did Charles Lindbergh become an American hero? (pp. 285–86)

> He was first to fly solo across the Atlantic. Lindbergh was modest and humble but tough, an admirable person – but his fame was in large part a product of the way the new national media amplified an event into a story.

22. "These events became elements of a shared national experience," but "there was always the danger" that what? (Can you think of people who are "famous for being famous," whose fame does not seem to rest on any genuine achievement?) (pp. 286–87)

> With enough "spin," almost any event can be hyped into seeming consequential when it really is not. And the media who control this are motivated to sell papers or advertising or otherwise profit from keeping people excited.
>
> Teachers may simply do an internet search for "famous for being famous." Examples abound.

23. *Is* journalism the "**first draft** of history"? (pp. 286–87)

> This is a statement of which we should be wary. First impressions are frequently mistaken, and the press often provides accounts that are sensational, one-sided, oversimplified, and misleading. Time is necessary for reflection, and "the news" seldom allows for that.

24. "**Seeing** is believing." But "things **are not always as they seem.**" What peacetime industry is based on the same manipulative techniques used by the Creel Committee? (p. 287)

> Advertising

25. Frederick Lewis Allen's influential 1931 book *Only Yesterday* was "in many respects a summation of the journalistic images of the Roaring Twenties." But *was* Allen's judgment correct that the 1920s saw a "revolution in manners and morals"? (pp. 287–88)

> That revolution was largely confined to a relatively small number of wealthy – often newly wealthy – families. Most people retained their traditional attitudes. But the decade did see the beginnings of a bifurcation of culture that has continued until the present time.

26. What is the risk in generalizing about culture based on only a small part of society – especially on the rich and famous? (p. 288)

> We miss a great deal of complexity in doing so.

27. Many of Fitzgerald's characters "are **displaced** Midwesterners filled with **nihilism** and foreboding about the possible moral consequences of the very prosperity their characters were craving and enjoying." (p. 288)

28. The 1920s were a time of cultural bifurcation. Explain. (pp. 299–89)

"Action and reaction tracked with each other." Experimentation in the arts and in manners and morals paralleled a resurgence of nativism, the reemergence of the Ku Klux Klan as a national organization (incorporating prejudice against Roman Catholics as much as against blacks), and other reactionary tendencies.

29. How did American Christianity split during the 1920s? (p. 289)

Fundamentalism emerged as a counter to modernists within denominations like the Presbyterian Church. Fundamentalists identified certain beliefs as nonnegotiable and were suspicious of new methods of biblical criticism and interpretation.

Teachers may need to explain to students the difference between fundamentalism – strictly adhering to basic Christian doctrines, such as the authority of the Bible – and evangelism, which is outreach intended to produce conversions. Many Christians are both, but this is not logically required. Charles Finney was very evangelical but not particularly fundamentalist (though that term was not in use during his day – *orthodox* is better).

30. For William Jennings Bryan, Darwinism was to be resisted because **it eliminated any basis for affirming the dignity of all humans.** (p. 289)

31. The textbook Scopes taught from "was indeed an openly and unapologetically **racist** text, in line with Bryan's claims." (p. 289)

Teachers should help students understand that while ethnocentrism and racial prejudice have been nearly universal throughout human history, modern "scientific" racism, such as that culminating in Hitler's National Socialism, also drew upon the faulty biological science of the time, which contended that some races were more "evolved" and so more civilized and advanced.

32. Who supported Prohibition? Why? Who opposed it? Why? (p. 290)

It divided the Progressive movement and contributed to its decline. Reformers saw alcohol as underlying many social ills, while many Christians saw it as a moral issue. But many recent immigrants came from cultures where wine or beer was an important family beverage and saw (with some justification) Prohibition as an attack on their status as Americans.

33. How did the "noble experiment" of Prohibition turn out? (pp. 290–91)

> It was a disaster: widely disobeyed, hard to enforce, and undermining respect for the law. It enabled the rise of organized crime. Even its supporters seemed relieved when it was repealed.

34. Despite some excellent appointments like Mellon, Taft, and Hoover, Harding's administration was rife with corruption. Know the story of Teapot Dome. (p. 291)

> Teapot Dome was an oil field on public land held as part of the strategic national reserve (in case we run out during a war). Oilmen bribed secretary of the interior Albert Fall to lease it to them. In separate trials, the oilmen were acquitted of paying the bribes, but Fall was convicted of accepting them!

35. How did Calvin Coolidge become president? What were his personality and style? (pp. 291–92)

> Harding died unexpectedly of a heart attack. Coolidge was a reticent, modest, and self-disciplined Yankee, deeply committed to American ideals.

36. Why was Coolidge's Philadelphia address in July 1926 "a speech for the ages"? "If all men are created equal, that is **final.** If they are endowed with inalienable rights, that is **final.** If governments derive their just powers from the consent of the governed, that is **final.**" (p. 292)

> The principles of American self-government are not subject to being displaced by newer and more "modern" theories.

37. Describe Herbert Hoover's early life and career. (p. 293)

> Trained as an engineer, he organized relief efforts for Wilson during and after the war (and saved millions from starvation). He was a very effective secretary of commerce during the 1920s.

38. Why was the Democratic Party much stronger than it seemed during the Republican decade of the 1920s? (pp. 293–94)

> Working-class ethnic Catholics favored the Democrats, and the South was solidly Democratic after Reconstruction.

39. Why was the stock market a bubble? When and why did it burst? (p. 294)

> It was a speculative spiral, as rising prices seemed to go on forever, leading to increased demand for stocks, leading to still higher prices. Bubbles

of that sort inevitably burst when something pricks the public's optimism. This happened in October 1929.

40. Was the stock market crash the main cause of the Great Depression? If not, what was? (pp. 294–95)

> Despite much folklore to the contrary, the stock market crash was not the cause of the Depression. Other factors, such as overproduction in the economy and unwise policies adopted by the Federal Reserve Board, played a much larger role. Moreover, the Depression was a worldwide affair, a delayed effect of the dislocations of the Great War. The stock market was more of a symptom than a cause.

41. What are the two schools of thought about the causes of the Great Depression? (p. 295)

> Some blame underconsumption (or overproduction); unsold goods may drive prices down below a sustainable level for the manufacturer. Others point to errors in government policy, especially by the Federal Reserve, and to the high protective tariffs (culminating in the Hawley–Smoot Tariff of 1930) that strangled international trade. There is some truth in all of these; complex events have complex causes.

42. "But the truth of the matter is that, as with the origins of the First World War, so with the Great Depression, we live in the immense shadow of a great event that remains, in some crucial aspects, a **mystery**." (p. 296)

Objective Question

Answers are in parentheses.

Put in order:

_____ Lindbergh's flight	(3)
_____ Mellon tax cuts	(2)
_____ Palmer raids	(1)

CALVIN COOLIDGE, SPEECH ON THE 150TH ANNIVERSARY OF THE DECLARATION OF INDEPENDENCE, JULY 5, 1926

We meet to celebrate the birthday of America. The coming of a new life always excites our interest. Although we know in the case of the individual that it has been an infinite repetition reaching back beyond our vision, that only makes it the more wonderful. But how our interest and wonder increase when we behold the miracle of the birth of a new nation. It is to pay our tribute of reverence and respect to those who participated in such a mighty event that we annually observe the fourth day of July. Whatever may have been the impression created by the news which went out from this city on that summer day in 1776, there can be no doubt as to the estimate which is now placed upon it. At the end of 150 years the four corners of the earth unite in coming to Philadelphia as to a holy shrine in grateful acknowledgement of a service so great, which a few inspired men here rendered to humanity, that it is still the preeminent support of free government throughout the world.

Although a century and a half measured in comparison with the length of human experience is but a short time, yet measured in the life of governments and nations it ranks as a very respectable period. Certainly enough time has elapsed to demonstrate with a great deal of thoroughness the value of our institutions and their dependability as rules for the regulation of human conduct and the advancement of civilization. They have been in existence long enough to become very well seasoned. They have met, and met successfully, the test of experience.

It is not so much, then, for the purpose of undertaking to proclaim new theories and principles that this annual celebration is maintained, but rather to reaffirm and reestablish those old theories and principles which time and the unerring logic of events have demonstrated to be sound. Amid all the clash of conflicting interests, amid all the welter of partisan politics, every American can turn for solace and consolation to the Declaration of Independence and the Constitution of the United States with the assurance and confidence that those two great charters of freedom and justice remain firm and unshaken. Whatever perils appear, whatever dangers threaten, the Nation remains secure in the knowledge that the ultimate application of the law of the land will provide an adequate defense and protection.

It is little wonder that people at home and abroad consider Independence Hall as hallowed ground and revere the Liberty Bell as a sacred relic. That pile of bricks and mortar, that mass of metal, might appear to the uninstructed as only the outgrown meeting place and the shattered bell of a former time, useless now because of more modern conveniences, but to those who know they have become consecrated by the use which men have made of them. They have long been identified with a great cause. They are the framework of a spiritual event. The world looks upon them, because of their associations of one hundred and fifty years ago, as it looks upon the Holy Land because of what took place there nineteen hundred years ago. Through use for a righteous purpose they have become sanctified.

It is not here necessary to examine in detail the causes which led to the American Revolution. In their immediate occasion they were largely economic. The colonists objected to the navigation laws which interfered with their trade, they denied the power of Parliament to impose taxes which they were obliged to pay, and they therefore resisted the royal governors and the royal forces which were sent to secure obedience to these laws. But the conviction is inescapable that a new civilization had come, a new spirit had arisen on this side of the Atlantic more advanced and more developed in its regard for the rights of the individual than that which characterized the Old World. Life in a new and open country had aspirations which could not be realized in any subordinate position. A separate establishment was ultimately inevitable. It had been decreed by the very laws of human nature. Man everywhere has an unconquerable desire to be the master of his own destiny.

We are obliged to conclude that the Declaration of Independence represented the movement of a people. It was not, of course, a movement from the top. Revolutions do not come from that direction. It was not without the support of many of the most respectable people in the Colonies, who were entitled to all the consideration that is given to breeding, education, and possessions. It had the support of another element of great significance and importance to which I shall later refer. But the preponderance of all those who occupied a position which took on the aspect of aristocracy did not approve of the Revolution and held toward it an attitude either of neutrality or open hostility. It was in no sense a rising of the oppressed and downtrodden. It brought no scum to the surface, for the reason that colonial society had developed no scum. The great body of the people were accustomed to privations, but they were free from depravity. If they had poverty, it was not of the hopeless kind that afflicts great cities, but the inspiring kind that marks the spirit of the pioneer. The American Revolution represented the informed and mature convictions of a great mass of independent, liberty-loving, God-fearing people who knew their rights, and possessed the courage to dare to maintain them.

The Continental Congress was not only composed of great men, but it represented a great people. While its Members did not fail to exercise a remarkable leadership, they were equally observant of their representative capacity. They were industrious in encouraging their constituents to instruct them to support independence. But until such instructions were given they were inclined to withhold action.

While North Carolina has the honor of first authorizing its delegates to concur with other Colonies in declaring independence, it was quickly followed by South Carolina and Georgia, which also gave general instructions broad enough to include such action. But the first instructions which unconditionally directed its delegates to declare for independence came from the great Commonwealth of Virginia. These were immediately followed by Rhode Island and Massachusetts, while the other Colonies, with the exception of New York, soon adopted a like course.

This obedience of the delegates to the wishes of their constituents, which in some cases caused them to modify their previous positions, is a matter of great significance. It reveals an orderly process of government in the first place; but more than that, it demonstrates that the Declaration of Independence was the result of the seasoned and deliberate thought of the dominant portion of the people of the Colonies. Adopted after long discussion and as the result of the duly authorized expression of the preponderance of public opinion, it did not partake of dark intrigue or hidden conspiracy. It was well advised. It had about it nothing of the lawless and disordered nature of a riotous insurrection. It was maintained on a plane which rises above the ordinary conception of rebellion. It was in no sense a radical movement but took on the dignity of a resistance to illegal usurpations. It was conservative and represented the action of the colonists to maintain their constitutional rights which from time immemorial had been guaranteed to them under the law of the land.

When we come to examine the action of the Continental Congress in adopting the Declaration of Independence in the light of what was set out in that great document and in the light of succeeding events, we can not escape the conclusion that it had a much broader and deeper significance than a mere secession of territory and the establishment of a new nation. Events of that nature have been taking place since the dawn of history. One empire after another has arisen, only to crumble away as its constituent parts separated from each other and set up independent governments of their own. Such actions long ago became commonplace. They have occurred too often to hold the attention of the world and command the admiration and reverence of humanity. There is something beyond the establishment of a new nation, great as that event would be, in the Declaration of Independence which has ever since caused it to be regarded as one of the great charters that not only was to liberate America but was everywhere to ennoble humanity.

It was not because it was proposed to establish a new nation, but because it was proposed to establish a nation on new principles, that July 4, 1776, has come to be regarded as one of the greatest days in history. Great ideas do not burst upon the world unannounced. They are reached by a gradual development over a length of time usually proportionate to their importance. This is especially true of the principles laid down in the Declaration of Independence. Three very definite propositions were set out in its preamble regarding the nature of mankind and therefore of government. These were the doctrine that all men are created equal, that they are endowed with certain inalienable rights, and that therefore the source of the just powers of government must be derived from the consent of the governed.

If no one is to be accounted as born into a superior station, if there is to be no ruling class, and if all possess rights which can neither be bartered away nor taken from them by any earthly power, it follows as a matter of course that the practical authority of the Government has to rest on the consent of the governed. While these principles were not altogether new in political action, and were very far from new in political speculation, they had never been assembled before and declared in such a combination. But remarkable as this may be, it is not the chief distinction of the Declaration of Independence. The importance of political speculation is not to be underestimated, as I shall presently disclose. Until the idea is developed and the plan made there can be no action.

It was the fact that our Declaration of Independence containing these immortal truths was the political action of a duly authorized and constituted representative public body in its sovereign capacity, supported by the force of general opinion and by the armies of Washington already in the field, which makes it the most important civil document in the world. It was not only the principles declared, but the fact that therewith a new nation was born which was to be founded upon those principles and which from that time forth in its development has actually maintained those principles, that makes this pronouncement an incomparable event in the history of government. It was an assertion that a people had arisen determined to make every necessary sacrifice for the support of these truths and by their practical application bring the War of Independence to a successful conclusion and adopt the Constitution of the United States with all that it has meant to civilization.

The idea that the people have a right to choose their own rulers was not new in political history. It was the foundation of every popular attempt to depose an undesirable king. This right was set out with a good deal of detail by the Dutch when as early as July 26, 1581, they declared their independence of

Philip of Spain. In their long struggle with the Stuarts the British people asserted the same principles, which finally culminated in the Bill of Rights deposing the last of that house and placing William and Mary on the throne. In each of these cases sovereignty through divine right was displaced by sovereignty through the consent of the people. Running through the same documents, though expressed in different terms, is the clear inference of inalienable rights. But we should search these charters in vain for an assertion of the doctrine of equality. This principle had not before appeared as an official political declaration of any nation. It was profoundly revolutionary. It is one of the corner stones of American institutions.

But if these truths to which the Declaration refers have not before been adopted in their combined entirety by national authority, it is a fact that they had been long pondered and often expressed in political speculation. It is generally assumed that French thought had some effect upon our public mind during Revolutionary days. This may have been true. But the principles of our Declaration had been under discussion in the Colonies for nearly two generations before the advent of the French political philosophy that characterized the middle of the eighteenth century. In fact, they come from an earlier date. A very positive echo of what the Dutch had done in 1581, and what the English were preparing to do, appears in the assertion of the Rev. Thomas Hooker, of Connecticut, as early as 1638, when he said in a sermon before the General Court that –

"The foundation of authority is laid in the free consent of the people."

"The choice of public magistrates belongs unto the people by God's own allowance."

This doctrine found wide acceptance among the nonconformist clergy who later made up the Congregational Church. The great apostle of this movement was the Rev. John Wise, of Massachusetts. He was one of the leaders of the revolt against the royal governor Andros in 1687, for which he suffered imprisonment. He was a liberal in ecclesiastical controversies. He appears to have been familiar with the writings of the political scientist, Samuel Pufendorf, who was born in Saxony in 1632. Wise published a treatise, entitled "The Church's Quarrel Espoused," in 1710, which was amplified in another publication in 1717. In it he dealt with the principles of civil government. His works were reprinted in 1772 and have been declared to have been nothing less than a textbook of liberty for our Revolutionary fathers.

While the written word was the foundation, it is apparent that the spoken word was the vehicle for convincing the people. This came with great force and wide range from the successors of Hooker and Wise. It was carried on with a missionary spirit which did not fail to reach the Scotch-Irish of North Carolina, showing its influence by significantly making that Colony the first to give instructions to its delegates looking to independence. This preaching reached the neighborhood of Thomas Jefferson, who acknowledged that his "best ideas of democracy" had been secured at church meetings.

That these ideas were prevalent in Virginia is further revealed by the Declaration of Rights, which was prepared by George Mason and presented to the general assembly on May 27, 1776. This document asserted popular sovereignty and inherent natural rights, but confined the doctrine of equality to the assertion that "All men are created equally free and independent." It can scarcely be imagined that Jefferson was unacquainted with what had been done in his own Commonwealth of Virginia when he took up the task of drafting the Declaration of Independence. But these thoughts can very largely be traced back to what John Wise was writing in 1710. He said, "Every man must be acknowledged equal to every man." Again, "The end of all good government is to cultivate humanity and promote the happiness of all and the good of every man in all his rights, his life, liberty, estate, honor, and so forth...." And again, "For as they have a power every man in his natural state, so upon combination they can and do bequeath this power to others and settle it according as their united discretion shall determine." And still again, "Democracy is Christ's government in church and state." Here was the doctrine of equality, popular sovereignty, and the substance of the theory of inalienable rights clearly asserted by Wise at the opening of the eighteenth century, just as we have the principle of the consent of the governed stated by Hooker as early as 1638.

When we take all these circumstances into consideration, it is but natural that the first paragraph of the Declaration of Independence should open with a reference to Nature's God and should close in the final paragraphs with an appeal to the Supreme Judge of the world and an assertion of a firm reliance on Divine Providence. Coming from these sources, having as it did this background, it is no wonder that Samuel Adams could say "The people seem to recognize this resolution as though it were a decree promulgated from heaven."

No one can examine this record and escape the conclusion that in the great outline of its principles the Declaration was the result of the religious teachings of the preceding period. The profound philosophy which Jonathan Edwards applied to theology, the popular preaching of George Whitefield, had aroused the thought and stirred the people of the Colonies in preparation for this great event. No doubt the speculations which had been going on in England, and especially on the Continent, lent their influence to the general sentiment of the times. Of course, the world is always influenced by all the experience and all the thought of the past. But when we come to a contemplation of the immediate conception of the principles of human relationship which went into the Declaration of Independence we are not required to extend our search beyond our own shores. They are found in the texts, the sermons, and the writings of the early colonial clergy who were earnestly undertaking to instruct their congregations in the great mystery of how to live. They preached equality because they believed in the fatherhood of God and the brotherhood of man. They justified freedom by the text that we are all created in the divine image, all partakers of the divine spirit.

Placing every man on a plane where he acknowledged no superiors, where no one possessed any right to rule over him, he must inevitably choose his own rulers through a system of self-government. This was their theory of democracy. In those days such doctrines would scarcely have been permitted to flourish and spread in any other country. This was the purpose which the fathers cherished. In order that they might have freedom to express these thoughts and opportunity to put them into action, whole congregations with their pastors had migrated to the Colonies. These great truths were in the air that our people breathed. Whatever else we may say of it, the Declaration of Independence was profoundly American.

If this apprehension of the facts be correct, and the documentary evidence would appear to verify it, then certain conclusions are bound to follow. A spring will cease to flow if its source be dried up; a tree will wither if its roots be destroyed. In its main features the Declaration of Independence is a great spiritual document. It is a declaration not of material but of spiritual conceptions. Equality, liberty, popular sovereignty, the rights of man – these are not elements which we can see and touch. They are ideals. They have their source and their roots in the religious convictions. They belong to the unseen world. Unless the faith of the American people in these religious convictions is to endure, the principles of our Declaration will perish. We can not continue to enjoy the result if we neglect and abandon the cause.

We are too prone to overlook another conclusion. Governments do not make ideals, but ideals make governments. This is both historically and logically true. Of course the government can help to sustain ideals and can create institutions through which they can be the better observed, but their source by their very nature is in the people. The people have to bear their own responsibilities. There is no method by which that burden can be shifted to the government. It is not the enactment, but the observance of laws, that creates the character of a nation.

About the Declaration there is a finality that is exceedingly restful. It is often asserted that the world has made a great deal of progress since 1776, that we have had new thoughts and new experiences which have given us a great advance over the people of that day, and that we may therefore very well discard their conclusions for something more modern. But that reasoning can not be applied to this great charter. If all men are created equal, that is final. If they are endowed with inalienable rights, that is final. If governments derive their just powers from the consent of the governed, that is final. No advance, no progress can be made beyond these propositions. If anyone wishes to deny their truth or their soundness, the only direction in which he can proceed historically is not forward, but backward toward the time when there was no equality, no rights of the individual, no rule of the people. Those who wish to proceed in that direction can not lay claim to progress. They are reactionary. Their ideas are not more modern, but more ancient, than those of the Revolutionary fathers.

In the development of its institutions America can fairly claim that it has remained true to the principles which were declared 150 years ago. In all the essentials we have achieved an equality which was never possessed by any other people. Even in the less important matter of material possessions we have secured a wider and wider distribution of wealth. The rights of the individual are held sacred and protected by constitutional guaranties, which even the Government itself is bound not to violate. If there is any one thing among us that is established beyond question, it is self-government – the right of the people to rule. If there is any failure in respect to any of these principles, it is because there is a failure on the part of individuals to observe them. We hold that the duly authorized expression of the will of the people has a divine sanction. But even in that we come back to the theory of John Wise that "Democracy is Christ's government." The ultimate sanction of law rests on the righteous authority of the Almighty.

On an occasion like this a great temptation exists to present evidence of the practical success of our form of democratic republic at home and the ever-broadening acceptance it is securing abroad. Although these things are well known, their frequent consideration is an encouragement and an inspiration. But it is not results and effects so much as sources and causes that I believe it is even more necessary constantly to contemplate. Ours is a government of the people. It represents their will. Its officers may sometimes go astray, but that is not a reason for criticizing the principles of our institutions. The real heart of the American Government depends upon the heart of the people. It is from that source that we must look for all genuine reform. It is to that cause that we must ascribe all our results.

It was in the contemplation of these truths that the fathers made their declaration and adopted their Constitution. It was to establish a free government, which must not be permitted to degenerate into the unrestrained authority of a mere majority or the unbridled weight of a mere influential few. They undertook the balance of these interests against each other and provide the three separate independent branches, the executive, the legislative, and the judicial departments of the Government, with checks against each other in order that neither one might encroach upon the other. These are our guaranties of liberty. As a result of these methods enterprise has been duly protected from confiscation, the people have been free from oppression, and there has been an ever-broadening and deepening of the humanities of life.

Under a system of popular government there will always be those who will seek for political preferment by clamoring for reform. While there is very little of this which is not sincere, there is a large portion that is not well informed. In my opinion very little of just criticism can attach to the theories and principles of our institutions. There is far more danger of harm than there is hope of good in any radical changes. We do need a better understanding and comprehension of them and a better knowledge of the foundations of government in general. Our forefathers came to certain conclusions and decided upon certain courses of action which have been a great blessing to the world. Before we can understand their conclusions we must go back and review the course which they followed. We must think the thoughts which they thought. Their intellectual life centered around the meeting-house. They were intent upon religious worship. While there were always among them men of deep learning, and later those who had comparatively large possessions, the mind of the people was not so much engrossed in how much they knew, or how much they had, as in how they were going to live. While scantily provided with other literature, there was a wide acquaintance with the Scriptures. Over a period as great as that which measures the existence of our independence they were subject to this discipline not only in their religious life and educational training, but also in their political thought. They were a people who came under the influence of a great spiritual development and acquired a great moral power.

No other theory is adequate to explain or comprehend the Declaration of Independence. It is the product of the spiritual insight of the people. We live in an age of science and of abounding accumulation of material things. These did not create our Declaration. Our Declaration created them. The things of the spirit come first. Unless we cling to that, all our material prosperity, overwhelming though it may appear, will turn to a barren sceptre in our grasp. If we are to maintain the great heritage which has been bequeathed to us, we must be like-minded as the fathers who created it. We must not sink into a pagan materialism. We must cultivate the reverence which they had for the things that are holy. We must follow the spiritual and moral leadership which they showed. We must keep replenished, that they may glow with a more compelling flame, the altar fires before which they worshiped.

Source: https://teachingamericanhistory.org/library/document/speech-on-the-occasion-of-the-one-hundred-and-fiftieth-anniversary-of-the-declaration-of-independence/

Document Questions

1. What does Coolidge see as the purpose of the annual celebration of national independence (the Fourth of July)?

> "It is not so much, then, for the purpose of undertaking to proclaim new theories and principles that this annual celebration is maintained, but rather to reaffirm and reestablish those old theories and principles which time and the unerring logic of events have demonstrated to be sound. Amid all the clash of conflicting interests, amid all the welter of partisan politics, every American can turn for solace and consolation to the Declaration of Independence and the Constitution of the United States with the assurance and confidence that those two great charters of freedom and justice remain firm and unshaken."
>
> In other words, Coolidge's view of the matter is exactly opposite to that of Wilson, who thought the Declaration and Constitution were outmoded.

2. How have the Liberty Bell and Independence Hall become "consecrated" objects? Does this resemble Lincoln's words about the "consecration" of Gettysburg's battlefield?

> "They have become consecrated by the use which men have made of them." And yes, they do remind us of Lincoln's famous words.

3. Why does Coolidge say that the Declaration was not "a movement from the top"?

> He contends that it represented "a movement of a people," not of the elites alone (because many of them were inclined toward Loyalism anyway), but of "a great mass of independent, liberty-loving, God-fearing people who knew their rights, and possessed the courage to dare to maintain them."

4. Why is July 4, 1776, regarded as one of the great days of history?

> "It was not because it was proposed to establish a new nation, but because it was proposed to establish a nation on new principles … the doctrine that all men are created equal, that they are endowed with certain inalienable rights, and that therefore the source of the just powers of government must be derived from the consent of the governed."

5. In what way was the Declaration a product of the religious teachings of the times?

> "They are found in the texts, the sermons, and the writings of the early colonial clergy who were earnestly undertaking to instruct their congregations in the great mystery of how to live. They preached equality because they believed in the fatherhood of God and the brotherhood of man. They justified freedom by the text that we are all created in the divine image, all partakers of the divine spirit."

6. What does Coolidge mean by the "finality" of the Declaration? Are his words an answer to Wilson and other critics of the Founding?

> "If all men are created equal, that is final. If they are endowed with inalienable rights, that is final. If governments derive their just powers from the consent of the governed, that is final. No advance, no progress can be made beyond these propositions. If anyone wishes to deny their truth or their soundness, the only direction in which he can proceed historically is not forward, but backward toward the time when there was no equality, no rights of the individual, no rule of the people. Those who wish to proceed in that direction can not lay claim to progress. They are reactionary. Their ideas are not more modern, but more ancient, than those of the Revolutionary fathers."

> And yes, he absolutely was answering the critiques of the Declaration and Constitution offered by Wilson and other Progressives. Given Coolidge's advanced views on racial equality, and Wilson's retrograde views on that subject, it is hard not to think of Wilson in the last three sentences of the preceding quotation.

CHAPTER SEVENTEEN

THE NEW DEAL

Summary

THE STOCK MARKET CRASH of 1929, and the separate economic collapse that became known as the Great Depression, seemed an unprecedented disaster for the country, with steep losses in productivity and employment in the American economy and the near-collapse of the banking sector. Despite the efforts of Presidents Herbert Hoover and Franklin Roosevelt, nothing that the federal government tried could turn the economy around. What began as a sharp recession in 1930 settled into a decade-long economic depression.

To revive the economy, Herbert Hoover advocated policies that stopped short of direct payments to individual citizens, believing that such action was unconstitutional. Nevertheless, he tried a number of measures meant to prop up segments of the economy and signed the Smoot–Hawley Tariff in the hope of protecting American jobs and manufacturing. (This turned out to be an extremely harmful tariff in a number of ways.) The economy continued to spiral downward, however, and in 1932, the nation elected Franklin Delano Roosevelt as president. Roosevelt (FDR) would remain president until his death in 1945.

If the New Deal did not succeed in pulling the United States out of the Great Depression, then why is it of such significance? For one thing, FDR was willing to cross the line that Hoover was not and willing to push the boundaries of executive action to a degree that was unprecedented in peacetime. His approach was experimental and pragmatic, ready to try a variety of approaches, discarding what did not work and embracing what did. His first hundred days in office saw a multitude of programs aimed at settling down the banking industry (FDIC), providing temporary government employment (WPA, CCC,

CWA), controlling wages and prices in industry, and stabilizing supply and demand in the agricultural sector. The early New Deal also saw the creation of the Tennessee Valley Authority and the Securities and Exchange Commission. The most enduringly significant program to come out of FDR's first term, however, was the Social Security Act, a program that clearly and irreversibly crossed Hoover's line.

This flood of New Deal programs, despite their varying successes, seemed to lift the nation's spirits and give Americans the sense that at least their government was trying something to address the situation. This, combined with FDR's optimistic persona and his highly effective use of his radio fireside chats, seemed to give much of the nation hope. He roared to reelection in 1936 with the largest margin of victory yet seen in American history.

But he had problems with the Constitution and the Court. Parts of his New Deal programming were struck down by the Supreme Court, and as his second term got under way, challenges to other of his programs were making their way through the courts. In response to this, and confident in his overwhelming electoral victory in 1936, FDR proposed legislation that would increase the number of Supreme Court justices so that his programs would survive. This "court packing" scheme was very unpopular, and FDR had to back away from it. It diminished his popularity, but it also had the apparent effect of intimidating the Court, which did not strike down any of his other programs. Still, soon into his his second term, there would be no more innovative programs and policies as there had been in the early New Deal. FDR, following in the tradition of many Progressives, had attempted to frame the battle against the Great Depression as the moral equivalent of war. Yet it would turn out that war itself, and not its moral equivalent, would pull the nation out of the Great Depression.

Questions and Answers

1. How might Calvin Coolidge have responded to the stock market crash had he still been president? (p. 297)

> He might have responded with a laissez-faire, "hands-off" policy to allow normal market corrections.

2. Hoover's views "reflected the can-do problem-solving spirit of his own profession of engineering, and his activist tendencies were far closer to the **Progressive** tradition than to the *laissez-faire* tradition embraced by Harding and Coolidge." (pp. 297–98)

3. What was associationalism? (p. 298)

It was the idea of promoting an alliance between government and business.

Teachers may point out that close association between business and government was a popular idea in Europe and America; Italian fascism included it, as did both Hoover's RFC and FDR's NRA.

4. "Like the Progressives, Hoover was quite comfortable with the idea that government should play an active role in fostering a **collective and coordinated response to public needs.**" (p. 298)

5. How did the economy spiral downward between 1929 and 1932?

"The national income dropped by a staggering **40** percent." (p. 298)

6. What were Hoovervilles? (pp. 298–99)

They were shantytowns built by unemployed homeless.

7. How did Hoover go about trying to restore prosperity? (pp. 299–301)

Energetically – but not much that he did worked. He sought tax reduction, public works projects to create jobs and stimulate the economy, federal aid to banks and corporations threatened with failure, aid to homeowners threatened with mortgage foreclosure, and limited revision upward of the tariff to help American farmers and manufacturers against foreign competition.

8. Why was the Smoot–Hawley Tariff such a disaster? (p. 299)

Other nations retaliated, and American exports suffered.

Some historians also blame the tariff (which became law in June 1930) for the stock market crash of October 1929. This seems odd, as causes normally precede rather than follow effects! But a bill moves through Congress to become a law (or not) in stages, and the key Senate Finance Committee approved the Smoot–Hawley bill in September 1939. So fear that the tariff would eventually become law (as it did) was likely a factor in the loss of confidence leading to the stock market crash.

9. How successful was the Reconstruction Finance Corporation (RFC)? What phrase did Will Rogers coin about it? (p. 300)

It had modest success in "bailing out" some large companies (who would also be major employers), but the perception was that it favored the rich and powerful. Will Rogers called it "trickle down."

10. What part of federal government emergency relief did Hoover adamantly oppose? Why? How did the public perceive this? How did Democrats in Congress take advantage of it? (pp. 300–301)

> Hoover disliked the idea of federal direct aid to the poor and believed it to be unconstitutional. (State and local governments could of course do that, and many did.) This was perceived as hard-hearted, and the Democrats took full advantage.

11. What is the tragedy (and irony) of Herbert Hoover's policies toward the Great Depression and their effect on his reputation? (pp. 300–301)

> He was a brilliant man, a skilled administrator, and had in fact organized several relief efforts that saved many from starvation during and after World War I. His reputation as uncaring is undeserved.

12. What was the Bonus Expeditionary Force? What happened to it? (pp. 301–2)

> It was veterans who wanted benefits early. Hoover used troops under General MacArthur to disperse them.

13. The Republicans were resigned to defeat in 1932. Who did the Democrats pick to win? (p. 302)

> Franklin Delano Roosevelt (FDR)

14. Describe FDR's background and personality. (pp. 302–3)

> Born to privilege, he was a career politician, governor of New York, and crippled at age thirty-nine by something that looked like polio. He had a sunny disposition and was a tough, determined, very pragmatic, and brilliant politician.

15. FDR possessed "a second-class **intellect,** but a first-class **temperament.**" (p. 303)

16. The term "New Deal" was not carefully thought out but proved to resonate with voters. Why? (p. 303)

> The idea of "a good deal" or a bargain is very American, and it did not sound like some new radical, revolutionary program.

17. What sort of campaign did FDR run and win on? (p. 303)

> "Happy Days Are Here Again!" He succeeded in restoring confidence and promised to keep trying things until something worked – a very American, pragmatic approach.

18. What happened to the economy between the election and FDR's inauguration? (p. 304)

> The Depression deepened, and the banking system was close to collapse.

19. What were the tone and the content of FDR's inaugural address? (p. 305)

> It was upbeat ("the only thing we have to fear is fear itself") but also promised sweeping change.

20. What did Congress do during the Hundred Days? Why (two reasons) was the result a "hodgepodge of conflicting tendencies"? (pp. 305–6)

> Congress passed pretty much anything FDR asked for. Some of FDR's advisors wanted stricter enforcement of antitrust laws; others wanted them waived. FDR did not choose one approach over others, and he had to keep various parts of his coalition happy – especially southern congressmen. But "much of it reflected Roosevelt's own mind and its unsystematic, unideological, and episodic way of proceeding."

21. How did FDR deal with the bank crisis? (p. 306)

> A "bank holiday" closed banks until they could safely reopen; eventually, he instituted federal insurance of bank deposits.

22. What were the "fireside chats"? How important were they? (p. 306)

> They were weekly radio talks that made the president and his administration seem very close and accessible to ordinary people.

23. What were the main elements of FDR's relief program? How effective were they? Was the effect more psychological than real? (pp. 306–7)

> The Civilian Conservation Corps, the Civil Works Administration, and the Works Progress Administration were more about putting people on a payroll than getting work done – though some useful projects were completed. The effect was mostly psychological.

24. The key program of the first New Deal was the NIRA that created the NRA. Describe the plan. What happened to it? Why was it an anticlimax when the Supreme Court declared the NRA unconstitutional?

> It created industry-wide boards, including labor unions, to set prices and "fair competition." The antitrust laws were suspended. The job was overwhelming, as no human agency can keep track of economic needs the way the price mechanism (supply and demand) does. Big business benefited

at the expense of smaller competitors. The whole thing was increasingly corrupt as well as ineffective, and the Supreme Court decision saved FDR from having to admit to the failure.

25. The AAA was "somewhat more successful." Explain. Who benefited most? What happened to the AAA? (pp. 309–10)

The Agricultural Adjustment Administration tried to raise farm prices by reducing production. Some farmers were helped, though mostly the larger ones at the expense of the smaller. And destroying food seemed counterintuitive. The Supreme Court declared its funding source to be unconstitutional.

26. What were the TVA, the SEC, and the FHA? (p. 310)

They were three of the more successful and permanent New Deal agencies: the Tennessee Valley Authority brought electric power to the South, the Securities and Exchange Commission regulated the stock market, and the Federal Housing Authority encouraged homeownership.

27. Although the Democrats prevailed in the midterm elections of 1934 (an unusual event, as the party in power normally loses seats in Congress in midterms), FDR faced increasing criticism both from the Republicans and within his own party. Who led the American Liberty League? Who was Huey P. Long? Who was Francis Townsend? Charles Coughlin? Was FDR attacked from both the Left and the Right? (pp. 310–12)

He was opposed from both sides. The ALL was bipartisan and believed FDR had moved too far to the left, too fast. The other three were radio personalities (and Long was a serious political rival) who critiqued the New Deal from the left.

28. The centerpiece of the Second New Deal was **Social Security.** (p. 312)

29. How did Social Security "follow a very American pattern"? (p. 312)

It was modest, and the funds came from workers and employers, so no one needed to feel like a charity case.

30. What did the Wagner Act do? (p. 312)

It created the National Labor Relations Board and gave unions protection and power.

31. What did the Revenue Act of 1935 do? How effective was it? (pp. 312–13)

    It raised taxes on the rich and was theatrical but produced little revenue.

32. By how much did FDR and the Democrats win in 1936? (p. 313)

    They won overwhelmingly; FDR had full control of government.

33. Why was there no Third New Deal? "Pride goes before a fall." (p. 313)

    FDR's overconfidence led to sharply increased opposition even within his own party.

34. Why did the court packing plan fail? FDR was seen as "**brazen, unprincipled, and too clever by half.**" (pp. 313–14)

    It would have upset permanently the balance of power and "checks and balances." Even FDR's own party rejected it.

35. What happened to the economy in 1937? It was fairly labeled the "Roosevelt Recession." (p. 314)

    There was a serious downturn, including increased unemployment

36. What happened to the Executive Reorganization Act? Why? (p. 314)

    Congress rejected it as giving too much power to the president.

37. What happened in the midterm elections of 1938? (p. 315)

    Republicans won many seats in Congress, governorships, and so on. A conservative coalition of Republicans and anti–New Deal Democrats dominated Congress.

38. "Roosevelt's New Deal had made **dramatic and permanent changes** in the landscape of American life and had eased the effects of **a very great economic calamity.** His spirit and his words had restored the **nation's spirit.** But his policies had not solved the problems of the economy and had not returned the country to full employment." (p. 315)

Answers are in parentheses.

Put in order:

____	National Recovery Administration	(2)
____	Reconstruction Finance Corporation	(1)
____	Wagner Act	(3)

Put in order:

____	Executive Reorganization Act	(3)
____	Smoot–Hawley Tariff	(1)
____	Civilian Conservation Corps	(2)

Matching:

____ AAA	(E)	A.	Made work to increase employment
____ FHA	(F)	B.	Dams and flood control and electricity
____ NRA	(D)	C.	Regulated stock market
____ SEC	(C)	D.	Industry councils to fix prices
____ TVA	(B)	E.	Reduced crop production to raise prices
____ WPA	(A)	F.	Insured bank loans for housing construction

Document

FRANKLIN ROOSEVELT, COMMONWEALTH CLUB ADDRESS, SEPTEMBER 23, 1932

The issue of Government has always been whether individual men and women will have to serve some system of Government or economics, or whether a system of Government and economics exists to serve individual men and women. This question has persistently dominated the discussion of government for many generations. On questions relating to these things men have differed, and for time immemorial it is probable that honest men will continue to differ.

The final word belongs to no man; yet we can still believe in change and in progress. Democracy, as a dear old friend of mine in Indiana, Meredith Nicholson, has called it, is a quest, a never-ending seeking for better things, and in the seeking for these things and the striving for them, there are many roads to follow. But, if we map the course of these roads, we find that there are only two general directions.

When we look about us, we are likely to forget how hard people have worked to win the privilege of government. The growth of the national Governments of Europe was a struggle for the development of a centralized force in the Nation, strong enough to impose peace upon ruling barons. In many instances the victory of the central Government, the creation of a strong central Government, was a haven of refuge to the individual. The people preferred the master far away to the exploitation and cruelty of the smaller master near at hand.

But the creators of national Government were perforce ruthless men. They were often cruel in their methods, but they did strive steadily toward something that society needed and very much wanted, a strong central State able to keep the peace, to stamp out civil war, to put the unruly nobleman in his place, and to permit the bulk of individuals to live safely. The man of ruthless force had his place in developing a pioneer country, just as he did in fixing the power of the central Government in the development of Nations. Society paid him well for his services and its development. When the development among the Nations of Europe, however, had been completed, ambition and ruthlessness, having served their term, tended to overstep their mark.

There came a growing feeling that Government was conducted for the benefit of a few who thrived unduly at the expense of all. The people sought a balancing – a limiting force. There came gradually, through town councils, trade guilds, national parliaments, by constitution and by popular participation and control, limitations on arbitrary power.

Another factor that tended to limit the power of those who ruled, was the rise of the ethical conception that a ruler bore a responsibility for the welfare of his subjects.

The American colonies were born in this struggle. The American Revolution was a turning point in it. After the Revolution the struggle continued and shaped itself in the public life of the country. There were those who because they had seen the confusion which attended the years of war for American independence surrendered to the belief that popular Government was essentially dangerous and essentially unworkable. They were honest people, my friends, and we cannot deny that their experience had warranted some measure of fear. The most brilliant, honest and able exponent of this point of view was Hamilton. He was too impatient of slow-moving methods. Fundamentally he believed that the safety of the republic lay in the autocratic strength of its Government, that the destiny of individuals was to serve that Government, and that fundamentally a great and strong group of central institutions, guided by a small group of able and public spirited citizens, could best direct all Government.

But Mr. Jefferson, in the summer of 1776, after drafting the Declaration of Independence turned his mind to the same problem and took a different view. He did not deceive himself with outward forms. Government to him was a means to an end, not an end in itself; it might be either a refuge and a help or a threat and a danger, depending on the circumstances. We find him carefully analyzing the society for which he was to organize a Government. "We have no paupers. The great mass of our population is of laborers, our rich who cannot live without labor, either manual or professional, being few and of moderate wealth. Most of the laboring class possess property, cultivate their own lands, have families and from the demand for their labor, are enabled to exact from the rich and the competent such prices as enable them to feed abundantly, clothe above mere decency, to labor moderately and raise their families."

These people, he considered, had two sets of rights, those of "personal competency" and those involved in acquiring and possessing property. By "personal competency" he meant the right of free thinking, freedom of forming and expressing opinions, and freedom of personal living, each man according to his own Rights. To insure the first set of rights, a Government must so order its functions as not to interfere with the individual. But even Jefferson realized that the exercise of the property rights might so interfere with the rights of the individual that the Government, without whose assistance the property rights could not exist, must intervene, not to destroy individualism, but to protect it.

You are familiar with the great political duel which followed; and how Hamilton, and his friends, building toward a dominant centralized power were at length defeated in the great election of 1800, by Mr. Jefferson's party. Out of that duel came the two parties, Republican and Democratic, as we know them today.

So began, in American political life, the new day, the day of the individual against the system, the day in which individualism was made the great watchword of American life. The happiest of economic conditions made that day long and splendid. On the Western frontier, land was substantially free. No one, who did not shirk the task of earning a living, was entirely without opportunity to do so. Depressions could, and did, come and go; but they could not alter the fundamental fact that most of the people lived partly by selling their labor and partly by extracting their livelihood from the soil, so that starvation and dislocation were practically impossible. At the very worst there was always the possibility of climbing into a covered wagon and moving west where the untilled prairies afforded a haven for men to whom the East did not provide a place. So great were our natural resources that we could offer this relief not only to our own people, but to the distressed of all the world; we could invite immigration from Europe, and welcome it with open arms. Traditionally, when a depression came a new section of land was opened in the West; and even our temporary misfortune served our manifest destiny.

It was in the middle of the nineteenth century that a new force was released and a new dream created. The force was what is called the industrial revolution, the advance of steam and machinery and the rise of the forerunners of the modern industrial plant. The dream was the dream of an economic machine, able to raise the standard of living for everyone; to bring luxury within the reach of the humblest; to annihilate distance by steam power and later by electricity, and to release everyone from the drudgery of the heaviest manual toil. It was to be expected that this would necessarily affect Government. Heretofore, Government had merely been called upon to produce conditions within which people could live happily, labor peacefully, and rest secure. Now it was called upon to aid in the consummation of this new dream. There was, however, a shadow over the dream. To be made real, it required use of the talents of men of tremendous will and tremendous ambition, since by no other force could the problems of financing and engineering and new developments be brought to a consummation.

So manifest were the advantages of the machine age, however, that the United States fearlessly, cheerfully, and, I think, rightly, accepted the bitter with the sweet. It was thought that no price was too high to pay for the advantages which we could draw from a finished industrial system. This history of the last half century is accordingly in large measure a history of a group of financial Titans, whose methods were not scrutinized with too much care and who were honored in proportion as they produced the results, irrespective of the means they used. The financiers who pushed the railroads to the Pacific were always ruthless, often wasteful, and frequently corrupt; but they did build railroads, and we have them today. It has been estimated that the American investor paid for the American railway system more than three times over in the process; but despite this fact the net advantage was to the United States. As long as we had free land; as long as population was growing by leaps and bounds; as long as our industrial plants were insufficient to supply our own needs, society chose to give the ambitious man free play and unlimited reward provided only that he produced the economic plant so much desired.

During this period of expansion, there was equal opportunity for all and the business of Government was not to interfere but to assist in the development of industry. This was done at the request of business men themselves. The tariff was originally imposed for the purpose of "fostering our infant industry," a phrase I think the older among you will remember as a political issue not so long ago. The railroads were subsidized, sometimes by grants of money, oftener by grants of land; some of the most valuable oil lands in the United States were granted to assist the financing of the railroad which pushed through the Southwest. A nascent merchant marine was assisted by grants of money, or by mail subsidies, so that our steam shipping might ply the seven seas. Some of my friends tell me that they do not want the Government in business. With this I agree; but I wonder whether they realize the implications of the past. For while it has been American doctrine that the Government must not go into business in competition with private enterprises, still it has been traditional, particularly in Republican administrations, for business urgently to ask the Government to put at private disposal all kinds of Government assistance. The same man who tells you that he does not want to see the Government interfere in business – and he means it, and has plenty of good reasons for saying so – is the first to go to Washington and ask the Government for a prohibitory tariff on his product. When things get just bad enough as they did two years ago, he will go with equal speed to the United States Government and ask for a loan; and the Reconstruction Finance Corporation is the outcome of it. Each group has sought protection from the Government for its own special interests, without realizing that the function of Government must be to favor no small group at the expense of its duty to protect the rights of personal freedom and of private property of all its citizens.

In retrospect we can now see that the turn of the tide came with the turn of the century. We were reaching our last frontier; there was no more free land and our industrial combinations had become great uncontrolled and irresponsible units of power within the State. Clear-sighted men saw with fear the danger that opportunity would no longer be equal; that the growing corporation, like the feudal baron of old, might threaten the economic freedom of individuals to earn a living. In that hour, our antitrust laws were born. The cry was raised against the great corporations. Theodore Roosevelt, the first great Republican Progressive, fought a Presidential campaign on the issue of "trust busting" and talked freely about malefactors of great wealth. If the government had a policy it was rather to turn the clock back, to destroy the large combinations and to return to the time when every man owned his individual small business.

This was impossible; Theodore Roosevelt, abandoning the idea of "trust busting," was forced to work out a difference between "good" trusts and "bad" trusts. The Supreme Court set forth the famous "rule of reason" by which it seems to have meant that a concentration of industrial power was permissible if the method by which it got its power, and the use it made of that power, were reasonable.

Woodrow Wilson, elected in 1912, saw the situation more clearly. Where

Jefferson had feared the encroachment of political power on the lives of individuals, Wilson knew that the new power was financial. He saw, in the highly centralized economic system, the despot of the twentieth century, on whom great masses of individuals relied for their safety and their livelihood, and whose irresponsibility and greed (if they were not controlled) would reduce them to starvation and penury. The concentration of financial power had not proceeded so far in 1912 as it has today; but it had grown far enough for Mr. Wilson to realize fully its implications. It is interesting, now, to read his speeches. What is called "radical" today (and I have reason to know whereof I speak) is mild compared to the campaign of Mr. Wilson. "No man can deny," he said, "that the lines of endeavor have more and more narrowed and stiffened; no man who knows anything about the development of industry in this country can have failed to observe that the larger kinds of credit are more and more difficult to obtain unless you obtain them upon terms of uniting your efforts with those who already control the industry of the country, and nobody can fail to observe that every man who tries to set himself up in competition with any process of manufacture which has taken place under the control of large combinations of capital will presently find himself either squeezed out or obliged to sell and allow himself to be absorbed." Had there been no World War – had Mr. Wilson been able to devote eight years to domestic instead of to international affairs – we might have had a wholly different situation at the present time. However, the then distant roar of European cannon, growing ever louder, forced him to abandon the study of this issue. The problem he saw so clearly is left with us as a legacy; and no one of us on either side of the political controversy can deny that it is a matter of grave concern to the Government.

A glance at the situation today only too clearly indicates that equality of opportunity as we have known it no longer exists. Our industrial plant is built; the problem just now is whether under existing conditions it is not overbuilt. Our last frontier has long since been reached, and there is practically no more free land. More than half of our people do not live on the farms or on lands and cannot derive a living by cultivating their own property. There is no safety valve in the form of a Western prairie to which those thrown out of work by the Eastern economic machines can go for a new start. We are not able to invite the immigration from Europe to share our endless plenty. We are now providing a drab living for our own people.

Our system of constantly rising tariffs has at last reacted against us to the point of closing our Canadian frontier on the north, our European markets on the east, many of our Latin-American markets to the south, and a goodly proportion of our Pacific markets on the west, through the retaliatory tariffs of those countries. It has forced many of our great industrial institutions which exported their surplus production to such countries, to establish plants in such countries, within the tariff walls. This has resulted in the reduction of the operation of their American plants, and opportunity for employment.

Just as freedom to farm has ceased, so also the opportunity in business has narrowed. It still is true that men can start small enterprises, trusting to native shrewdness and ability to keep abreast of competitors; but area after area has been pre-empted altogether by the great corporations, and even in the fields which still have no great concerns, the small man starts under a handicap. The unfeeling statistics of the past three decades show that the independent business man is running a losing race. Perhaps he is forced to the wall; perhaps he cannot command credit; perhaps he is "squeezed out," in Mr. Wilson's words, by highly organized corporate competitors, as your corner grocery man can tell you. Recently a careful study was made of the concentration of business in the United States. It showed that our economic life was dominated by some six hundred odd corporations who controlled two-thirds of American industry. Ten million small business men divided the other third. More striking still, it appeared that if the process of concentration goes on at the same rate, at the end of another century we shall have all American industry controlled by a dozen corporations, and run by perhaps a hundred men. Put plainly, we are steering a steady course toward economic oligarchy, if we are not there lready.

Clearly, all this calls for a re-appraisal of values. A mere builder of more industrial plants, a creator of more railroad systems, an organizer of more corporations, is as likely to be a danger as a help. The day of the great promoter or the financial Titan, to whom we granted anything if only he would build, or develop, is over. Our task now is not discovery or exploitation of natural resources, or necessarily producing more goods. It is the soberer, less dramatic business of administering resources and plants already in hand, of seeking to reestablish foreign markets for our surplus production, of meeting the problem of underconsumption, of adjusting production to consumption, of distributing wealth and products more equitably, of adapting existing economic organizations to the service of the people. The day of enlightened administration has come.

Just as in older times the central Government was first a haven of refuge, and then a threat, so now in a closer economic system the central and ambitious financial unit is no longer a servant of national desire, but a danger. I would draw the parallel one step farther. We did not think because national Government had become a threat in the 18th century that therefore we should abandon the principle of national Government. Nor today should we abandon the principle of strong economic units called corporations, merely because their power is susceptible of easy abuse. In other times we dealt with the problem of an unduly ambitious central Government by modifying it gradually into a constitutional democratic Government. So today we are modifying and controlling our economic units.

As I see it, the task of Government in its relation to business is to assist the development of an economic declaration of rights, an economic constitutional order. This is the common task of statesman and business man. It is the minimum requirement of a more permanently safe order of things.

Happily, the times indicate that to create such an order not only is the proper policy of Government, but it is the only line of safety for our economic structures as well. We know, now, that these economic units cannot exist unless prosperity is uniform, that is, unless purchasing power is well distributed throughout every group in the Nation. That is why even the most selfish of corporations for its own interest would be glad to see wages restored and unemployment ended and to bring the Western farmer back to his accustomed level of prosperity and to assure a permanent safety to both groups. That is why some enlightened industries themselves endeavor to limit the freedom of action of each man and business group within the industry in the common interest of all; why business men everywhere are asking a form of organization which will bring the scheme into balance, even though it may in some measure qualify the freedom of action of individual units within the business.

The exposition need not further be elaborated. It is brief and incomplete, but you will be able to expand it in terms of your own business or occupation without difficulty. I think everyone who has actually entered the economic struggle – which means everyone who was not born to safe wealth – knows in his own experience and his own life that we have now to apply the earlier concepts of American Government to the conditions of today.

The Declaration of Independence discusses the problem of Government in terms of a contract. Government is a relation of give and take, a contract, perforce, if we would follow the thinking out of which it grew. Under such a contract rulers were accorded power, and the people consented to that power on consideration that they be accorded certain rights. The task of statesmanship has always been the re-definition of these rights in terms of a changing and growing social order. New conditions impose new requirements upon Government and those who conduct Government.

I held, for example, in proceedings before me as Governor, the purpose of which was the removal of the Sheriff of New York, that under modern conditions it was not enough for a public official merely to evade the legal terms of official wrongdoing. He owned a positive duty as well. I said in substance that if he had acquired large sums of money, he was when accused required to explain the sources of such wealth. To that extent this wealth was colored with a public interest. I said that in financial matters, public servants should, even beyond private citizens, be held to a stern and uncompromising rectitude.

I feel that we are coming to a view through the drift of our legislation and our public thinking in the past quarter century that private economic power is, to enlarge an old phrase, a public trust as well. I hold that continued enjoyment of that power by any individual or group must depend upon the fulfillment of that trust. The men who have reached the summit of American business life know this best; happily, many of these urge the binding quality of this greater social contract.

The terms of that contract are as old as the Republic, and as new as the new economic order.

Every man has a right to life; and this means that he has also a right to make a comfortable living. He may by sloth or crime decline to exercise that right; but it may not be denied him. We have no actual famine or dearth; our industrial and agricultural mechanism can produce enough and to spare. Our Government formal and informal, political and economic, owes to everyone an avenue to possess himself of a portion of that plenty sufficient for his needs, through his own work.

Every man has a right to his own property; which means a right to be assured, to the fullest extent attainable, in the safety of his savings. By no other means can men carry the burdens of those parts of life which, in the nature of things, afford no chance of labor: childhood, sickness, old age. In all thought of property, this right is paramount; all other property rights must yield to it. If, in accord with this principle, we must restrict the operations of the speculator, the manipulator, even the financier, I believe we must accept the restriction as needful, not to hamper individualism but to protect it.

These two requirements must be satisfied, in the main, by the individuals who claim and hold control of the great industrial and financial combinations which dominate so large a part of our industrial life. They have undertaken to be, not business men, but princes of property. I am not prepared to say that the system which produces them is wrong. I am very clear that they must fearlessly and competently assume the responsibility which goes with the power. So many enlightened business men know this that the statement would be little more than a platitude, were it not for an added implication.

This implication is, briefly, that the responsible heads of finance and industry instead of acting each for himself, must work together to achieve the common end. They must, where necessary, sacrifice this or that private advantage; and in reciprocal self-denial must seek a general advantage. It is here that formal Government – political Government, if you choose – comes in. Whenever in the pursuit of this objective the lone wolf, the unethical competitor, the reckless promoter, the Ishmael or Insull whose hand is against every man's, declines to join in achieving an end recognized as being for the public welfare, and threatens to drag the industry back to a state of anarchy, the Government may properly be asked to apply restraint. Likewise, should the group ever use its collective power contrary to the public welfare, the Government must be swift to enter and protect the public interest.

The Government should assume the function of economic regulation only as a last resort, to be tried only when private initiative, inspired by high responsibility, with such assistance and balance as Government can give, has finally failed. As yet there has been no final failure, because there has been no attempt; and I decline to assume that this Nation is unable to meet the situation.

The final term of the high contract was for liberty and the pursuit of happiness. We have learned a great deal of both in the past century. We know that individual liberty and individual happiness mean nothing unless both are ordered in the sense that one man's meat is not another man's poison. We know that the old "rights of personal competency," the right to read, to think, to speak, to choose and live a mode of life, must be respected at all hazards. We know that liberty to do anything which deprives others of those elemental rights is outside the protection of any compact; and that Government in this regard is the maintenance of a balance, within which every individual may have a place if he will take it; in which every individual may find safety if he wishes it; in which every individual may attain such power as his ability permits, consistent with his assuming the accompanying responsibility.

All this is a long, slow talk. Nothing is more striking than the simple innocence of the men who insist, whenever an objective is present, on the prompt production of a patent scheme guaranteed to produce a result. Human endeavor is not so simple as that. Government includes the art of formulating a policy, and using the political technique to attain so much of that policy as will receive general support; persuading, leading, sacrificing, teaching always, because the greatest duty of a statesman is to educate. But in the matters of which I have spoken, we are learning rapidly, in a severe school. The lessons so learned must not be forgotten, even in the mental lethargy of a speculative upturn. We must build toward the time when a major depression cannot occur again; and if this means sacrificing the easy profits of inflationist booms, then let them go; and good riddance.

Faith in America, faith in our tradition of personal responsibility, faith in our institutions, faith in ourselves demand that we recognize the new terms of the old social contract. We shall fulfill them, as we fulfilled the obligation of the apparent Utopia which Jefferson imagined for us in 1776, and which Jefferson,

Roosevelt and Wilson sought to bring to realization. We must do so, lest a rising tide of misery, engendered by our common failure, engulf us all. But failure is not an American habit; and in the strength of great hope we must all shoulder our common load.

Source: https://teachingamericanhistory.org/library/document/commonwealth-club-address/

Document Questions

1. Is FDR's analysis more optimistic or pessimistic about the current state of the nation? How important is Turner's "frontier thesis" in FDR's analysis? What are its implications?

> Turner was very pessimistic. The closing of the frontier removed the "safety valve" of free and empty land and the chance to make a good living through ordinary labor. The whole focus of FDR's speech is the need to reevaluate and renegotiate fundamental relationships among people, labor, and property. In this view, economic opportunity as we had known it no longer exists.

2. What does FDR see as the proper relationship between business and government?

> He advocated continuing partnership, but with government as the ultimate arbiter and with the interests of the people protected against the large corporations and monied interests. Government had often helped business (through tariffs and railroad subsidies, etc.); the time had come for government to help ordinary people.

3. FDR sees the Democrats as Jeffersonians and the Republicans as Hamiltonians. Is this accurate?

> This is accurate in part, if "Hamiltonian" means sympathetic to commercial and industrial development and "Jeffersonian" means suspicious of corporations and sympathetic to the common man of modest means. But Jefferson was suspicious of the sort of powerful and active central authority that FDR lauds.

4. Does FDR distinguish between "property rights" and "human rights"?

> He doesn't use the second phrase, but he does emphasize rights of "personal competency" as distinct from and superior to property rights. He

emphasizes a right to labor and a right to save money as basic (human) property rights.

5. What about the social contract?

It is time for it to be renegotiated. We must recognize the new terms of the old social contract. "We know that individual liberty and individual happiness mean nothing unless both are ordered in the sense that one man's meat is not another man's poison. We know that the old 'rights of personal competency' – the right to read, to think, to speak to choose and live a mode of life, must be respected at all hazards. We know that liberty to do anything which deprives others of those elemental rights is outside the protection of any compact; and that government in this regard is the maintenance of a balance."

6. *For Thought:* What is radical about FDR's analysis, and what is conservative?

Renegotiating the social contract seems pretty radical, but he accepts the existence of large corporations, banks, and so on as necessary and on the whole as good. FDR would consider himself a capitalist rather than a socialist. He clearly sees his "new deal" as consistent with historic American ideals rather than as a radical break with the past.

CHAPTER EIGHTEEN

THE FINEST HOUR

World War II

Summary

AMERICANS' ATTENTION had been riveted to their own massive domestic problems through the 1930s. But in the meantime, the situation in Europe and Asia had deteriorated markedly, with the rise of brutal and aggressive dictatorships in Germany, Italy, and Japan. Soon the world was once again at war. By 1940, Nazi Germany occupied or controlled almost all of Continental Europe, with only the British Isles remaining free of its grasp – for the time being. In Asia, Imperial Japan attacked and occupied parts of China and other areas of Southeast Asia. The United States, meanwhile, sought to maintain its historic position of neutrality, a position that enjoyed broad popular support.

But such a position was difficult to sustain, and the United States gradually moved toward helping to arm Britain and protect British shipping from German submarine warfare. Americans were deeply impressed by the valor shown by British pilots in the Battle of Britain, and ancestral ties to Britain tugged at many American heartstrings. But each step away from neutrality was highly controversial. In the end, what brought the United States fully into the war was not an emerging national consensus but instead the coordinated Japanese attacks on U.S. naval bases in Hawai'i, the Philippines, Wake Island, and Guam on December 7, 1941. The once-divided Americans quickly united behind a declaration of war against Japan, and against the other Axis powers, Germany and Italy, as well.

Despite the fact that Japanese acts of aggression were the catalyst for the

American war effort, American leaders gave priority to defeating Hitler, reasoning that Germany posed a more immediate threat to the most vital American allies (Great Britain and the Soviet Union). Major military campaigns and strategy are sketched in the chapter, with particular attention paid to the D-Day invasion of Normandy on June 6, 1944 – a monumental accomplishment and a turning point in the defeat of Germany. The chapter then discusses the Pacific theater, with key battles and the strategy behind those battles. Even after the huge victories at Leyte Gulf in 1944 – and there was no doubt that the Allies would defeat the Japanese – the prospect of invading the Japanese mainland was regarded with dread. The Battle of Okinawa alone, for example, had seen more than 250,000 deaths and the unleashing of unprecedented kamikaze attacks. Given the fierce determination of Japanese defenders, the invasion of the mainland was certain to be much, much worse. Estimates ranged as high as a million Allied deaths from such an invasion and many more Japanese. The final victory was likely to be purchased at a horrifying cost.

Such was the situation when President Roosevelt died in office in 1945 and his vice president, Harry Truman, succeeded him. It was not until Truman became president that he learned of the secret Manhattan Project and the production of a fearsome new weapon, the atomic bomb, which could be a game-changer in bringing the war to a less bloody conclusion. Truman did not hesitate to use that weapon. He made the decision to demand unconditional surrender of Japan or face terrible consequences. On August 6, the United States dropped an atomic bomb on Hiroshima. With no surrender forthcoming three days later, a second bomb was dropped on Nagasaki. With the second bomb, Japan surrendered. The chapter weighs this decision in terms of the alternatives that Truman had available to him at the time.

With the conclusion of this devastating war, the United States would have no choice but to become a self-conscious leader of the world. There was no other candidate for the job. And yet, it was an unaccustomed role for America, deeply at odds with much of the American past. Would taking up that role necessitate a complete departure from that past? Or would it represent a fulfillment of that past, the acceptance of a destiny that had been implicit all along? The answer remained to be seen.

1. Besides being preoccupied with the Great Depression, why else did Americans largely ignore foreign developments during the 1930s? (p. 316)

> The consensus was that involvement in the Great War (World War I) had been a big mistake and that involvement in ongoing or future wars would be equally bad or worse.

2. Why is "isolationist" not the best way to describe American sentiment? (pp. 316–17)

> First, the United States might well have joined the League of Nations had Wilson been less stubborn and inflexible. Second, Americans were thoroughly involved in worldwide commerce. Third, the United States played a leading role in disarmament conferences, such as the Washington Conference of 1921, and the treaties that followed, and the Kellogg–Briand Pact outlawing war.

3. "It would be more accurate to say, instead, that in the interwar years, the US was reverting to a traditional policy of acting **selectively** and **unilaterally,** with the **national interest** foremost in mind." (p. 317)

4. What part of the world experienced a marked improvement in relations with the United States in the interwar years? (p. 317)

> Latin America

5. In the meantime, what were Germany, Italy, and Japan all up to? (pp. 317–18)

> They were authoritarian and expansionist regimes, each trying to build an empire.
>
> Teachers may also point out that the Soviet Union, once the Communists had achieved control after the Bolshevik Revolution (which overthrew the democratic regime that had overthrown the czar) and had won the bloody Russian Civil War (in which the United States intervened, ineffectually), set out to restore the Russian Empire. Stalin's Russia became as authoritarian and expansionist as the other three.

6. Why was the response of the Western democracies to these expanding threats weak and/or negligible? (p. 318)

> Nations like Britain and France were exhausted by the devastation of the Great War. They had lost their will as much or more than their ability to deal with threats.

7. What acts of aggression occurred in 1936–38? (p. 318)

> Hitler reoccupied the Rhineland; the Spanish Civil War began; Japan went to war against China and joined Germany and Italy in the Rome–Berlin–Tokyo Axis.

8. What happened to the Chinese city of Nanking? (p. 318)

> In the Rape of Nanking, the Japanese army massacred as many as three hundred thousand Chinese and raped tens of thousands of women.

9. How did the Western democracies respond to these events? (pp. 318–19)

> They did little or nothing.

10. How did British and French appeasement of Hitler lead to the outbreak of World War II in Europe in September 1939? (War was already going on in China.) (p. 319)

> Hitler successively annexed Austria, then the ethnically German Sudeten region in Czechoslovakia, then the rest of Czechoslovakia; Germany then invaded Poland, at which point the British and French finally acted.

11. What did the Nye Committee report about why the United States entered World War I? How did this shape American reactions to foreign crises? (p. 319)

> Nye reported that we entered the war to protect American banks that had made loans to belligerent nations and to sell munitions. A series of neutrality acts (1935–37) prohibited such American involvement in foreign wars. These acts turned out to be harmful in several instances.

12. "A Gallup poll in March 1937 found that 94% ... preferred efforts to keep America out of any foreign war over efforts to keep such wars from breaking out – a sentiment that can justly be described as **isolationist** since it meant foreswearing any attempt by America to influence the flow of events in the world." (p. 319)

13. How did the neutrality acts play into the hands of the Axis aggressors? (pp. 319–320)

> They enabled aggressors to act without fear of American action, and the prohibitions on aid to either side might mean that the poorly armed victim of aggression would be prevented from acquiring American weapons that the militaristic aggressors did not need.

14. What are the elements of Blitzkrieg? (pp. 320–21)

> It comprises mobile attackers supported by aircraft attacking on a narrow front to penetrate enemy lines and sow confusion and panic in the enemy rear areas. The target was as much enemy morale and confidence as it was material assets.
>
> Teachers may point out that the Germans used infiltration tactics successfully in 1918 and came close to winning a German victory before American intervention prevailed. British historian B. H. Liddell-Hart developed the theory of this "expanding torrent" attack strategy during the interwar years, drawing extensively on Sherman's march through Georgia. As is commonly the case, it was the losers from the previous war who were eager to try new techniques that might let them win the next one. Tanks and dive bombers provided the key technologies, but it was the idea behind it that mattered. (France actually had more and stronger tanks than the Germans did in 1940, but the German tanks all had radios and massed to achieve superiority on a small front, while the French tanks were scattered along the entire front.)

15. By June 1940, all of Western Europe was **effectively in Hitler's hands.** Britain stood alone behind its twenty-mile-wide moat, the English Channel. (p. 321)

16. What did the British save at Dunkirk? (p. 321)

> They saved 350,000 troops but no heavy equipment.

17. As Churchill rallied the British people, what was FDR's response? (p. 321)

> He could not yet abandon neutrality, but he did initiate a military buildup and began to make arms and aircraft available to the British.

18. How close was Hitler to winning in 1940? (pp. 321–22)

> If he had been able to defeat the Royal Air Force in the Battle of Britain, he could have invaded England and secured the domination of Europe. It was a close call.

19. What strategy did Hitler adopt after the defeat of the Luftwaffe? (p. 322)

He adopted the Blitz, bombing London to destroy British morale, combined with submarine warfare to starve Britain.

20. What did American ambassador Joseph Kennedy (father of president John F. Kennedy) advocate? Why? (p. 322)

"Democracy is finished in England," and no aid should be provided by America.

21. How did American public opinion about aiding Britain break? (pp. 322–23)

The change was split between the influences of the Committee to Defend America by Aiding the Allies versus the America First Committee (eight hundred thousand members) led by Charles Lindbergh.

Teachers may at this point again remind students of the dangers of 20/20 historical hindsight. We know the Holocaust was coming and that the Nazi regime was thoroughly evil. That evil was much less visible in 1940, while the idea was very fresh that American intervention in the previous war had been a big mistake. Learning lessons from the past is all well and good, but it is often far from clear which lessons best apply in immediate circumstances.

22. On what slogan did FDR run for a third term? What was the Republican position on the world war? (p. 323)

"Don't switch horses in the middle of the stream." Republican candidate Wendell Willkie also supported aid to Britain.

23. Upon reelection, FDR pledged to make the United States the "**arsenal of democracy**" – providing aid to Britain, building up American power, and stimulating the economy. (p. 323)

Teachers may point, perhaps with some irony, to the contrast between FDR's phrase "arsenal of democracy" and Eisenhower's warning, twenty years later, of the danger of the "military–industrial complex."

24. After laying a principled foundation for war in the **Four Freedoms** speech, FDR asked for and Congress passed the **Lend–Lease Act,** which effectively abandoned neutrality and committed the United States to aiding Britain in almost every way. (p. 324)

25. Beginning in September 1940, FDR issued "shoot on sight" orders to American ships, launching a **secret naval war** against German submarines. Isolationist sentiment was still strong, and FDR would have been severely criticized had the public known. (p. 324)

26. Why did Japan have to expand? What did it lack and have to import? (p. 325)

> Japan has very little land for its population; it depends heavily on fishing to feed its people. It lacks oil, rubber, and other strategic materials.

27. Why did Roosevelt's oil embargo push the Japanese toward war with America? (p. 325)

> The alternative for Japan was to give up its dream of empire, for example, by ending the war in China.

28. The United States had **broken** some of the Japanese **codes.** They knew by November 1941 that an attack was coming – but not **where.** (p. 325)

29. What was the target of the Japanese carrier strike on Pearl Harbor? Why was the attack, although devastating, really a failure? (pp. 325–26)

> Pearl Harbor is the main U.S. naval base in the Pacific, and the U.S. battleships there were sunk or damaged. But the three U.S. aircraft carriers were at sea, and carriers would prove to be the key weapons in the naval war.

30. How did the American people respond to the Pearl Harbor attack? (p. 326)

> They responded with unified outrage. Sentiment favoring neutrality was gone in an instant. Contemplate the folly of the Japanese in launching a surprise attack against a moralistic country whose economic weakness was hundreds of factories with no goods to make and millions of men with no work to do.

31. Contemplate the folly of Hitler and Mussolini in declaring war on the United States – a war FDR wanted (and was already secretly fighting) but which many Americans still wanted to stay out of.

32. Teachers will want to note that Stalin's Soviet Union was as much a totalitarian aggressor as Germany (Stalin had in fact invaded Poland from the east when Hitler invaded it from the west) but became an American ally when Hitler betrayed Stalin – they had sworn a pact of alliance – and invaded Russia in June 1941. This made the moral calculus a bit tricky; the Axis were clearly the Bad Guys, but the Allies included one of the Bad Guys too. This moral murkiness lasted through the Nuremberg trials,

in which Nazi war criminals were condemned by judges including Soviet leaders whose guilt was as great.

33. FDR changed from Dr. **New Deal** into Dr. **Win the War.** How did American war production increase between 1942 and 1944? (pp. 327–28)

> It equaled the combined production of Germany, Italy, and Japan by the end of the first year and was double that by 1944.

34. How many Americans served in the armed forces? (p. 328)

> Just under sixteen million served, mostly men.

35. What was frozen and rationed? (p. 328)

> Prices and rents were frozen, and items including meat, gasoline, and tires were rationed.

36. What did Henry J. Kaiser contribute to the war effort? (p. 328)

> He contributed liberty ships. Kaiser knew nothing about shipbuilding, but he knew how to organize a massive construction project. By 1944 he was launching one ship per day. "We can build them faster than you can sink them."

37. As during World War I, many **women** and **minorities** entered the workforce. Many African Americans moved from the **rural South** to **northern cities** to work in factories. (pp. 328–29)

38. How were Japanese Americans treated? (p. 329)

> Unjustly – they were interned away from the coast in California, many losing all their property.

39. Why was the strategy to defeat Germany first? (p. 329)

> Hitler was regarded as the more dangerous opponent, and distance provided some protection against Japanese attacks.

40. How did the United States deal with the submarine threat? (pp. 329–31)

> Convoys with air cover from land bases and intelligence intercepts of U-boat communications were used.

41. Although the Allies drove the enemy out of Africa and then Sicily, Italy was not a "soft underbelly" but rather "one tough gut." (p. 331)

> However, opening a southern front did relieve some pressure on Russia, and overthrowing Mussolini and driving Italy out of the war was an achievement. Also, bases in northern Italy were used in the American bombing campaign against Germany.

42. Why is strategic bombing so controversial? (p. 331)

> It promised to end the war quickly by targeting industrial bottlenecks, but the effect was slow, and the Germans adjusted. Morally, such bombing entailed killing many enemy civilians.
>
> If students want more detailed information, teachers may cite the Schweinfurt raids. German ball bearing production was concentrated in several factories in a single city, and since every modern weapon needs them, these factories were a bottleneck. A single American raid on October 14, 1943, reduced ball bearing production by 34 percent, but at a cost of sixty B-17 bombers, each with a crew of ten highly trained men. Losses were so great that the United States could not return to the same targets for another four months.
>
> Teachers may also raise the question of the morality of bombing. If attacks on enemy weapons are morally permissible, then presumably so too are attacks on factories producing weapons, even though the workers in those factories are technically civilians – and the factories themselves are surrounded by homes and hospitals and schools and other civilians who may become "collateral damage."
>
> But preserving one's own aircraft and crews may require night-time or high-altitude attacks that cannot target specific buildings but only an enemy city in general. The Germans began this when they shifted to terror attacks on London in the Blitz. By 1944, the British especially were determined to protect their bomber crews and so attacked only at night. The United States had accurate bombsights and attacked from a high altitude by day but willingly joined the British in the around-the-clock firebombing of Dresden (February 1945), creating artificial firestorms that destroyed the city and killed twenty thousand to thirty thousand civilians. The attacking air forces suffered only minimal losses.
>
> In a war, even the Good Guys may do bad things. And teachers may point out that modern science can destroy entire cities in a number of ways, even without nuclear bombs.

43. Why was Stalin desperate for his allies to invade first Italy and then France? (pp. 331–32)

> To open a second front and divide the German army, which had been focused on Russia.

44. The **Normandy invasion** (D-Day) was "not only a masterwork of large-scale military and logistical planning but also a mosaic of countless individual acts of unbelievable valor and daring." (p. 332)

> Teachers may inform students that, in fact, every invasion has a D-day (and an H-hour and even an M-minute). These are used for planning purposes when the actual invasion date is not yet known – but planners need to know, for example, exactly what troops and supplies will be landed on the day following the invasion, which would be D+1. But *the* D-Day will always be the Normandy invasion, the largest and most complex D-day ever.

45. Patton's sweep across France "**mirrored the rapidity with which Hitler had captured France in 1940.**" (p. 333)

46. What did the Battle of the Bulge achieve for Germany? (p. 333)

> It only delayed the inevitable.

47. Why did it matter who captured Berlin first? (pp. 333–34)

> It shaped the postwar world and especially control of Germany and Eastern Europe.

48. What did the Big Three decide at Yalta? (p. 333)

> They decided how to divide Germany and Berlin and to set up a free government in Poland.
>
> Teachers may add that the Yalta agreements proved very unfavorable to the United States after the war. FDR was in declining health, and Churchill's warnings about Soviet untrustworthiness went unheeded.
>
> The United States did get something from Stalin that was thought to be crucial at the time but turned out later to be not only unnecessary but counterproductive: a pledge to attack the Japanese army in China. Russia had not been at war with Japan, and the bulk of the Japanese army was in China. The United States anticipated invading Japan and wanted its troops kept in China and not transferred home.
>
> As it turned out, the atomic bombs brought Japanese surrender without an invasion, and the Russian attack into China put Stalin in

position to provide weapons to the Chinese Communists, who would defeat the Nationalists supported by the United States shortly after World War II ended.

49. Who made the decision to let the Russians capture Berlin? Why? (p. 333)

Eisenhower made this decision, to save American lives (but in fact, many Germans who fought to the death against the Russians would have surrendered to Americans).

50. How did their victories in 1942 lead the Japanese to overextend themselves? (p. 334)

They aimed to cut off Australia and finish the destruction of the U.S. fleet.

51. What happened first at the Coral Sea and then at Midway? (p. 334)

The Japanese lost four aircraft carriers and never recovered. American codebreaking was crucial.

Teachers may tell the story of Torpedo Squadron Eight, flying obsolete bombers off the USS *Hornet*. At Midway they attacked straight into the Japanese fleet; all fifteen planes were shot down, and only one of thirty crewmen survived. But their sacrifice diverted Japanese attention from the U.S. dive bombers arriving overhead from the *Enterprise* and the *Yorktown*, which destroyed all four Japanese carriers.

52. The first large-scale battle between the U.S. Marines and U.S. Army against the Japanese army was on **Guadalcanal.** (pp. 335–36)

53. The United States launched a two-pronged offensive against Japan: General MacArthur drove across northern new Guinea toward the Philippines, while Admiral Nimitz **island-hopped** to the north. (p. 336)

54. FDR met with MacArthur and Nimitz and decided the next target should be the Philippines. An enormous air/sea battle, **Leyte Gulf,** destroyed the remaining Japanese fleet. (p. 336)

55. What new tactic did the Japanese introduce at Leyte Gulf? (p. 336)

They introduced kamikaze or "suicide" bombers, who inflicted serious losses on the American fleet.

56. Describe the Battle of Okinawa. What were the implications for an invasion of Japan? (p. 336)

> The Japanese army made suicidal resistance, and the battle led to 250,000 deaths, many of them Okinawans, but with almost no Japanese surrendering; U.S. planners anticipated that an invasion of the home islands would encounter similarly ferocious resistance and lead to many millions of deaths.

57. FDR died as the war in Europe was ending. He was succeeded by **Harry Truman.** (p. 336)

58. What did Eisenhower do when he saw the death camp at Ohrdruf? (p. 337)

> He ordered all American troops nearby to visit and see the horrors they had been fighting against.

59. What were the alternatives to an invasion of Japan? (pp. 337–38)

> Theoretically, a naval blockade would have starved the Japanese, but it would have taken a long time to force surrender and resulted in millions of deaths. The only real alternative was the atomic bomb.

60. Why didn't the United States drop a demonstration bomb and demand surrender? (p. 338)

> We only had two, with two more coming, and we weren't sure they would work.

61. How many people died at Hiroshima? (p. 338)

> Eighty thousand were killed in the initial blast.

62. Why was the war such a shock to ideas of progress and morality? (p. 339)

> Science was used to destroy whole cities. Germany had long been considered, correctly, one of the most advanced societies in the world and now was revealed to have killed six million in the Holocaust genocide.

63. How did the war permanently change America? (p. 339)

> The "Pearl Harbor generation" could never again ignore the rest of the world. The United States was now the leader of the world, like it or not.

Objective Questions

Answers are in parentheses.

Put in order:

_____	Battle of Okinawa	(2)
_____	Hiroshima bombing	(3)
_____	Pearl Harbor attack	(1)

Put in order:

_____	Battle of Britain	(2)
_____	Blitz on London	(3)
_____	Dunkirk	(1)

Put in order:

_____	Battle of the Bulge	(2)
_____	Fall of Berlin	(3)
_____	Normandy invasion	(1)

Document

FRANKLIN D. ROOSEVELT, STATE OF THE UNION ADDRESS, "THE FOUR FREEDOMS," 1941

January 6, 1941

Mr. President, Mr. Speaker, Members of the Seventy-seventh Congress:

I address you, the Members of the Seventy-seventh Congress, at a moment unprecedented in the history of the Union. I use the word "unprecedented," because at no previous time has American security been as seriously threatened from without as it is today....

Even when the World War broke out in 1914, it seemed to contain only small threat of danger to our own American future. But, as time went on, the American people began to visualize what the downfall of democratic nations might mean to our own democracy.

We need not overemphasize imperfections in the Peace of Versailles. We need not harp on failure of the democracies to deal with problems of world reconstruction. We should remember that the Peace of 1919 was far less unjust than the kind of "pacification" which began even before Munich, and which is being carried on under the new order of tyranny that seeks to spread over every continent today. The American people have unalterably set their faces against that tyranny.

Every realist knows that the democratic way of life is at this moment being directly assailed in every part of the world – assailed either by arms, or by secret spreading of poisonous propaganda by those who seek to destroy unity and promote discord in nations that are still at peace.

During sixteen long months this assault has blotted out the whole pattern of democratic life in an appalling number of independent nations, great and small. The assailants are still on the march, threatening other nations, great and small.

Therefore, as your President, performing my constitutional duty to "give to the Congress information of the state of the Union," I find it, unhappily, necessary to report that the future and the safety of our country and of our democracy are overwhelmingly involved in events far beyond our borders.

Armed defense of democratic existence is now being gallantly waged in four continents. If that defense fails, all the population and all the resources of Europe, Asia, Africa and Australasia will be dominated by the conquerors. Let us remember that the total of those populations and their resources in those four continents greatly exceeds the sum total of the population and the resources of the whole of the Western Hemisphere – many times over.

In times like these it is immature – and incidentally, untrue – for anybody to brag that an unprepared America, single-handed, and with one hand tied behind its back, can hold off the whole world.

No realistic American can expect from a dictator's peace international generosity, or return of true independence, or world disarmament, or freedom of expression, or freedom of religion – or even good business.…

The need of the moment is that our actions and our policy should be devoted primarily – almost exclusively – to meeting this foreign peril. For all our domestic problems are now a part of the great emergency.

Just as our national policy in internal affairs has been based upon a decent respect for the rights and the dignity of all our fellow men within our gates, so our national policy in foreign affairs has been based on a decent respect for the rights and dignity of all nations, large and small. And the justice of morality must and will win in the end. Our national policy is this:

First, by an impressive expression of the public will and without regard to partisanship, we are committed to all-inclusive national defense.

Second, by an impressive expression of the public will and without regard to partisanship, we are committed to full support of all those resolute peoples, everywhere, who are resisting aggression and are thereby keeping war away from our Hemisphere. By this support, we express our determination that the democratic cause shall prevail; and we strengthen the defense and the security of our own nation.

Third, by an impressive expression of the public will and without regard to partisanship, we are committed to the proposition that principles of morality and considerations for our own security will never permit us to acquiesce in a peace dictated by aggressors and sponsored by appeasers.

We know that enduring peace cannot be bought at the cost of other people's freedom.

In the recent national election there was no substantial difference between the two great parties in respect to that national policy. No issue was fought out on this line before the American electorate. Today it is abundantly evident that American citizens everywhere are demanding and supporting speedy and complete action in recognition of obvious danger.

Therefore, the immediate need is a swift and driving increase in our armament production....

A free nation has the right to expect full cooperation from all groups. A free nation has the right to look to the leaders of business, of labor, and of agriculture to take the lead in stimulating effort, not among other groups but within their own groups.

The best way of dealing with the few slackers or trouble makers in our midst is, first, to shame them by patriotic example, and, if that fails, to use the sovereignty of Government to save Government.

As men do not live by bread alone, they do not fight by armaments alone. Those who man our defenses, and those behind them who build our defenses, must have the stamina and the courage which come from unshakable belief in the manner of life which they are defending. The mighty action that we are calling for cannot be based on a disregard of all things worth fighting for.

The Nation takes great satisfaction and much strength from the things which have been done to make its people conscious of their individual stake in the preservation of democratic life in America. Those things have toughened the fiber of our people, have renewed their faith and strengthened their devotion to the institutions we make ready to protect.

Certainly this is no time for any of us to stop thinking about the social and economic problems which are the root cause of the social revolution which is today a supreme factor in the world.

For there is nothing mysterious about the foundations of a healthy and strong democracy. The basic things expected by our people of their political and economic systems are simple. They are:

Equality of opportunity for youth and for others.

Jobs for those who can work.

Security for those who need it.

The ending of special privilege for the few.

The preservation of civil liberties for all.

The enjoyment of the fruits of scientific progress in a wider and constantly rising standard of living.

These are the simple, basic things that must never be lost sight of in the turmoil and unbelievable complexity of our modern world. The inner and abiding strength of our economic and political systems is dependent upon the degree to which they fulfill these expectations.

Many subjects connected with our social economy call for immediate improvement. As examples:

We should bring more citizens under the coverage of old-age pensions and unemployment insurance.

We should widen the opportunities for adequate medical care.

We should plan a better system by which persons deserving or needing gainful employment may obtain it.

I have called for personal sacrifice. I am assured of the willingness of almost all Americans to respond to that call.

A part of the sacrifice means the payment of more money in taxes. In my Budget Message I shall recommend that a greater portion of this great defense program be paid for from taxation than we are paying today. No person should try, or be allowed, to get rich out of this program; and the principle of tax payments in accordance with ability to pay should be constantly before our eyes to guide our legislation.

If the Congress maintains these principles, the voters, putting patriotism ahead of pocketbooks, will give you their applause.

In the future days, which we seek to make secure, we look forward to a world founded upon four essential human freedoms.

The first is freedom of speech and expression – everywhere in the world.

The second is freedom of every person to worship God in his own way – everywhere in the world.

The third is freedom from want – which, translated into world terms, means economic understandings which will secure to every nation a healthy peacetime life for its inhabitants – everywhere in the world.

The fourth is freedom from fear – which, translated into world terms, means a world-wide reduction of armaments to such a point and in such a thorough fashion that no nation will be in a position to commit an act of physical aggression against any neighbor – anywhere in the world.

That is no vision of a distant millennium. It is a definite basis for a kind of world attainable in our own time and generation. That kind of world is the very antithesis of the so-called new order of tyranny which the dictators seek to create with the crash of a bomb.

To that new order we oppose the greater conception – the moral order. A good society is able to face schemes of world domination and foreign revolutions alike without fear.

Since the beginning of our American history, we have been engaged in change – in a perpetual peaceful revolution – a revolution which goes on steadily, quietly adjusting itself to changing conditions – without the concentration camp or the quick-lime in the ditch. The world order which we seek is the cooperation of free countries, working together in a friendly, civilized society.

This nation has placed its destiny in the hands and heads and hearts of its millions of free men and women; and its faith in freedom under the guidance of God. Freedom means the supremacy of human rights everywhere. Our support goes to those who struggle to gain those rights or keep them. Our strength is our unity of purpose. To that high concept there can be no end save victory.

Document Questions

1. What is the situation in the world at the time of this speech (January 6, 1941?)

> Germany has conquered France and much of Western Europe (but has not yet invaded Russia). Japan has invaded China but is at peace with the United States; Pearl Harbor is eleven months ahead. Britain is standing almost alone against Hitler and the Nazis.

2. Is this a wartime speech?

> Yes, the emphasis is on military preparation for war, even though the United States is technically still at peace. FDR is very concerned with overcoming isolationist sentiment – arguing, for instance, that the oceans no longer protect us as much as they once did – and with motivating a national effort aimed at aiding the democratic nations that are actually fighting.

3. How will the United States assist the democratic nations?

> We will be their arsenal, and we will defer payment until after the war. "We Americans are vitally concerned in your defense of freedom. We are putting forth our energies, our resources and our organizing powers to

give you the strength to regain and maintain a free world. We shall send you, in ever-increasing numbers, ships, planes, tanks, guns. This is our purpose and our pledge."

4. What is the United States' diplomatic stance toward "the dictators"?

No more appeasement – we will help the democracies whether they object or not.

5. What domestic programs does FDR mention – briefly?

"We should bring more citizens under the coverage of old-age pensions and unemployment insurance, widen the opportunities for adequate medical care, and should plan a better system by which persons deserving or needing gainful employment may obtain it."

But the speech is overwhelmingly concerned with the international danger and America's response to it.

6. This is called the "Four Freedoms" speech. Why does FDR end with those principles?

"That is no vision of a distant millennium. It is a definite basis for a kind of world attainable in our own time and generation. That kind of world is the very antithesis of the so-called new order of tyranny which the dictators seek to create with the crash of a bomb. To that new order we oppose the greater conception – the moral order. A good society is able to face schemes of world domination and foreign revolutions alike without fear."

CHAPTER NINETEEN

ALL THOUGHTS AND THINGS WERE SPLIT

The Cold War

Summary

POSTWAR AMERICA was both jubilant and prosperous but also full of anxiety about the state of the world and our role in it. Major factors in feeding this anxiety were the development of atomic weapons and the emerging hostility between the Soviet Union and the United States, which came to be called the Cold War.

Although there is some discussion in the chapter of domestic policy, the presidencies of both Truman and Eisenhower were preoccupied with foreign affairs. The American–Soviet rivalry stood over all else. After the war, the Soviet Union quickly took control of much of Eastern Europe, setting up puppet dictatorships in violation of agreements made with the United States and England during the war. Communism came to be seen as a lethal threat to liberal democracy, and the aggressive tactics of the Soviet Union in particular were seen as a geopolitical threat. In a variety of ways, the United States sought to bolster weakened Europe (through the Marshall Plan, for example) and to counter Soviet aggression (as in the Berlin Airlift). In 1949, the United States entered into a formal defensive alliance with twelve Western democracies, known as the North Atlantic Treaty Organization (NATO), the primary purpose of which was to allow these nations to stand together against the Soviet threat.

By 1949, however, the Soviet Union also had workable atomic weapons. Because of the unprecedented threat of nuclear weapons, the United States increasingly chose to follow a policy known as containment – an approach that favored stopping Soviet (and, later, Chinese) expansion, but without waging open warfare to defeat Communist-controlled governments and "roll back" Communist domination where it existed. An era of limited war, stalemates, and war by proxies ensued. The greatest military test of this doctrine was the Korean War. American involvement in Vietnam also had its roots in this policy of containment.

The American role in the world was now dramatically and irrevocably different from what it had been prior to World War II. Clearly now the leader of the free world, the United States had an important say about the foreign policy of its allies. It was at the center of a huge web of entangling alliances and rapidly developing a national-security apparatus that included a capacity and willingness to engage in covert operations all over the world – all of this with the threat of nuclear war hovering in the background. How could the republican values on which the nation was founded survive this vast expansion?

In addition to providing biographical sketches of Truman and Eisenhower, this chapter closes with a look ahead to the civil rights movement. The war gave added impetus to a movement that had been building for some time. Quoting Gunnar Myrdal, "America is continually struggling for its soul" – which he took to mean a struggle to more fully live out the American creed of equality, freedom, and opportunity. The struggle for full civil liberties for African Americans would be the next great step in that struggle.

Questions and Answers

1. The end of the war was also the end of the Depression. What was the fear? (pp. 341–42)

> The fear was that turmoil like that of 1919 might break out and that the wartime economic recovery might falter as demobilization restored millions of men to the workforce.

2. Were those fears realized? (p. 342)

> Briefly, with some major strikes, a housing shortage, and a sharp but brief recession – but not in the long run.

3. The forced savings of **rationing** (e.g., no new automobiles, as Detroit was making military vehicles) meant lots of pent-up **demand,** which American business was eager to meet. (p. 342)

4. What happened to GNP between 1945 and 1970? (p. 343)

> It more than doubled, from $355 billion to $723 billion, while per capita income before taxes increased from $1,870 to $3,050 in steady 1958 dollars (i.e., no inflation).

5. How did the automobile industry fare? (p. 343)

> It produced eight million new cars a year, up from one million produced during the war. There was massive highway construction, including the interstate system.

6. How did housing patterns change? (p. 343)

> Far more Americans now lived in suburbs than in cities. Levittowns featured small, easily affordable houses suited for young families.

7. What did the GI Bill do for veterans? (p. 344)

> It provided low-cost mortgage loans and free education. This was the beginning of widespread college education.

8. Between the end of the war and 1960, the American population increased by **30 percent,** almost all from the "baby boom." (p. 344)

9. What psychological stresses did Americans, and especially returning veterans, face? (pp. 344–45)

> All Americans now lived in the shadow of possible nuclear warfare, and veterans had to cope with what we now call posttraumatic stress disorder and other postwar challenges, economic and psychological.

10. What is the theme of Sloan Wilson's *The Man in the Grey Flannel Suit*? (pp. 345–46)

> All seems well on the surface, but only because of a cloak of denial of wartime trauma.

11. Why was the Cold War always especially frightening? (p. 346)

> Because it could become nuclear, with unimaginable destruction.

12. One historian called postwar America a "**troubled feast.**" (p. 346)

13. What was Truman's personal background and early career? How did he overcome his earlier association with the corrupt **Pendergast** machine and become respected enough to be chosen to succeed FDR? (pp. 346–47)

> Truman chaired a Senate committee rooting out corruption in wartime spending.

14. FDR "had been formed in the well-pedigreed political tradition of Jefferson and Wilson; Truman was a product of the great **unpedigreed tradition** of Jackson and Lincoln, both of them **uncommon common men.**" (p. 348)

15. What happened in the midterm elections of 1946? (p. 348)

> Republicans won majorities in both houses of Congress.

16. The Republicans overrode a Truman veto to pass in 1947 the **Taft–Hartley Act,** designed to pare back the power of labor unions. (p. 348)

17. Why was the wartime alliance between Stalin's Soviet Union and the Western democracies short-lived? (pp. 348–49)

> The Red Army occupied most of Eastern Europe, installing puppet Communist governments, in flagrant violation of the Yalta agreement.

18. Who coined the widely accepted term or metaphor for the division between the free world and the Communist? (p. 349)

> Winston Churchill did, at a speech in Missouri with Truman in the audience: an "iron curtain" has fallen dividing the free world from the Communist.

19. Did the Russians have legitimate grievances against the Americans and British? Did those grievances justify Soviet deceptions and broken promises? (pp. 349–50)

> Russia bore the brunt of the fighting against Hitler for more of the war and had historical reasons for fear of invasion. But no, Stalin was a committed Marxist–Leninist with an ambitious program of expansion.

20. Stalin tried to dominate **Turkey and Greece,** gaining control of the eastern Mediterranean and threatening the **Suez Canal.** (p. 350)

21. How did George Kennan lay the theoretical basis for the Cold War? (pp. 350–51)

> He argued that Soviet instability and insecurity would fuel a ceaseless drive toward expansion, though with a certain caution. The proper

strategy was not to try to roll back Soviet power from where it existed but to contain it and prevent its further growth, as the Soviet system "bears within itself the seeds of its own decay."

22. Why did "containment" of Soviet power have to include an economic as well as a political and diplomatic and military component? (p. 351)

Europe was devastated by the war, and Communist parties in both Italy and France were gaining influence. Only America was in a position to supply the needed help.

23. Who would the Marshall Plan have helped? Who refused the help? (pp. 351–52)

It would have helped all European countries, including the Soviet Union, but Stalin refused aid for Russia and for the Communist satellite countries.

24. How much money did the Marshall Plan provide to Europe? What was the result? (p. 352)

It provided $13 billion, rebuilding the Western European economy and cementing American leadership.

25. Where is Berlin located in respect to East and West Germany? How did Stalin threaten the Western occupation of West Berlin? How did the United States respond? (p. 352)

Berlin is well inside East Germany, and Stalin cut off communications, hoping to starve the city into submission. Truman avoided armed conflict but resupplied Berlin by air – a massive airlift no one thought possible.

26. What is NATO? (p. 353)

The North Atlantic Treaty Organization is an alliance of Western nations, including West Germany; an attack by the Soviets on one was considered an attack on all.

Teachers should point out that NATO represents the complete abandonment of Washington's principle of avoiding "entangling alliances."

27. What role did Truman play in the creation of Israel? (p. 353)

He recognized Israel eleven minutes after it declared independence. He saw Israel as a moral necessity after the Holocaust.

28. Why was Truman's reelection in 1948 an uphill fight? (p. 354)

The Democrats split into three factions, including southern "Dixiecrats" and a Progressive group who thought Truman was not going far enough in reform.

29. How did Truman win? (p. 354)

Republican Thomas Dewey ran a "lackadaisical campaign," while Truman made a whistle-stop tour of the country by train.

30. What was happening in China? How did the United States respond? (pp. 355–56)

The Communists under Mao Zedong took control, defeating U.S.-backed Nationalists under Chang Kai-shek, who retreated to Formosa (Taiwan). The United States rethought its strategy in NSC-68, proposing a massive increase in defense spending and alliances with non-Communist nations around the world.

31. To what extent was the second "Red Scare" justified? (pp. 356–57)

It was an overreaction in an atmosphere of fear – but we now know that espionage really had been a serious problem, affecting in particular rapid acquisition of nuclear weapons by Stalin.

Teachers may mention in particular the case of Alger Hiss, a very high-ranking U.S. diplomat who was convincingly accused of being a Communist agent.

32. Why did Korea become a hot battlefield in the Cold War? (p. 357)

Korea was divided North (Communist) and South. The North invaded the South.

33. How did Truman respond? (p. 357)

He committed to defending South Korea under the doctrine of containment, but under the auspices of the United Nations rather than as a unilateral U.S. war.

34. How did the war go? (pp. 357–58)

North Korea almost conquered the South initially, then MacArthur's Inchon landing drove the Communists back. MacArthur ignored Chinese warnings, and they entered the war, driving U.S. troops back again. The battle lines stabilized, and the war became a stalemate.

35. Why did Truman fire MacArthur? (p. 358)

MacArthur's ego led him to criticize Truman and containment strategy in public – an act of insubordination.

35. What did firing MacArthur cost Truman? (p. 358)

His popularity dropped a lot, and he knew better than to run for another term.

37. Who was right? (p. 359)

MacArthur's strategy risked expanding the war, possibly even into nuclear war. Truman's course was prudent. On the other hand, the Korean situation remained (and is still today) a frustrating stalemate and a confirmation of the difficulties of containment.

38. What was Eisenhower's background before being elected president? (p. 359)

He was supreme U.S. commander in Europe, the hero of D-Day.

39. What was Eisenhower's domestic program? (p. 360)

Consolidation – the New Deal was accepted rather than being removed, but it was administered more effectively and less expensively by business executives.

40. What was Eisenhower's Cold War strategy? (pp. 360–63)

He wanted continued commitment to containment, even though secretary of state John Foster Dulles talked of "rolling back" Communism.

41. American goals in the Cold War were to effectively **position and project American power** but also **to win hearts and minds in Third World countries.** These were often incompatible. (p. 361)

42. Why did the CIA's actions in Iran produce favorable short-term success but have far less favorable long-term consequences? (p. 361)

Reza Pahlavi became a staunch American ally but was eventually overthrown by a regime that was very anti-American.

43. Why did the United States take France's side in Indochina? (pp. 361–62)

France was essential to keeping the Soviets out of Western Europe. Asia was a secondary concern.

44. How was Indochina divided? (p. 362)

It was divided into Laos, Cambodia, and North and South Vietnam. North Vietnam (capital Hanoi) was Communist; South Vietnam (capital Saigon), which included many Catholics, was non-Communist.

45. Who did Eisenhower support in South Vietnam? (p. 362)

He supported Ngo Dinh Diem, a corrupt and unreliable ally.

46. What happened in the Suez Crisis? (p. 362)

Egypt seized the canal; Britain, France, and Israel recaptured it; America backed Egypt and made its allies give the canal back. This demonstrated America's power.

47. How did Cuba change from Batista's dictatorship to Castro's? (p. 363)

Batista was a corrupt dictator who accommodated American business interests. When Fidel Castro, a young revolutionary who successfully fought a guerrilla war against Batista's regime, came to power in 1959, Eisenhower quickly extended diplomatic recognition to the new government, and many Americans applauded Castro and hoped he would be an instrument of democratic reform. They miscalculated badly. Instead, Castro declared himself a Communist and made it clear that he was hostile to the United States, aligning himself with the Soviet Union.

48. Is it just coincidence that the civil rights movement gained strength and eventually prevailed during the Cold War? (p. 363)

No. The Holocaust discredited racism and made groups like American Jews natural allies to civil right activists. It was difficult to criticize Communist mistreatment of their peoples when blacks were treated unfairly in the segregated South, particularly after the distinguished service and sacrifices of so many African Americans in World War II. The time was right for the civil rights movement to prevail.

Answers are in parentheses.

Put in order:

____ Marshall Plan	(1)
____ Korean War	(2)
____ Suez Crisis	(3)

Document

GEORGE KENNAN, THE SOURCES OF SOVIET CONDUCT, 1947

PART I

The political personality of Soviet power as we know it today is the product of ideology and circumstances: ideology inherited by the present Soviet leaders from the movement in which they had their political origin, and circumstances of the power which they now have exercised for nearly three decades in Russia. There can be few tasks of psychological analysis more difficult than to try to trace the interaction of these two forces and the relative role of each in the determination of official Soviet conduct. yet the attempt must be made if that conduct is to be understood and effectively countered.

It is difficult to summarize the set of ideological concepts with which the Soviet leaders came into power. Marxian ideology, in its Russian-Communist projection, has always been in process of subtle evolution. The materials on which it bases itself are extensive and complex. But the outstanding features of Communist thought as it existed in 1916 may perhaps be summarized as follows: (a) that the central factor in the life of man, the factor which determines the character of public life and the "physiognomy of society," is the system by which material goods are produced and exchanged; (b) that the capitalist system of production is a nefarious one which inevitably leads to the exploitation of the working class by the capital-owning class and is incapable of developing adequately the economic resources of society or of distributing fairly the material good produced by human labor; (c) that capitalism contains the seeds of its own destruction and must, in view of the inability of the capital-owning class to adjust itself to economic change, result eventually and inescapably in a revolutionary transfer of power to the working class; and (d) that imperialism, the final phase of capitalism, leads directly to war and revolution.

The rest may be outlined in Lenin's own words: "Unevenness of economic and political development is the inflexible law of capitalism. It follows from this that the victory of Socialism may come originally in a few capitalist countries or even in a single capitalist country. The victorious proletariat of that country, having expropriated the capitalists and having organized Socialist production at home, would rise against the remaining capitalist world, drawing to itself in the process the oppressed classes of other countries." It must be noted that there was no assumption that capitalism would perish without proletarian revolution. A final push was needed from a revolutionary proletariat movement in order to tip over the tottering structure. But it was regarded as inevitable that sooner or later that push be given.

For 50 years prior to the outbreak of the Revolution, this pattern of thought had exercised great fascination for the members of the Russian revolutionary movement. Frustrated, discontented, hopeless of finding self-expression – or too impatient to seek it – in the confining limits of the Tsarist political system, yet lacking wide popular support or their choice of bloody revolution as a means of social betterment, these revolutionists found in Marxist theory a highly convenient rationalization for their own instinctive desires. It afforded pseudo-scientific justification for their impatience, for their categoric denial of all value in the Tsarist system, for their yearning for power and revenge and for their inclination to cut corners in the pursuit of it. It is therefore no wonder that they had come to believe implicitly in the truth and soundness of the Marxist–Leninist teachings, so congenial to their own impulses and emotions. Their sincerity need not be impugned. This is a phenomenon as old as human nature itself. It has never been more aptly described than by Edward Gibbon, who wrote in *The Decline and Fall of the Roman Empire*: "From enthusiasm to imposture the step is perilous and slippery; the demon of Socrates affords a memorable instance of how a wise man may deceive himself, how a good man may deceive others, how the conscience may slumber in a mixed and middle state between self-illusion and voluntary fraud." And it was with this set of conceptions that the members of the Bolshevik Party entered into power.

Now it must be noted that through all the years of preparation for revolution, the attention of these men, as indeed of Marx himself, had been centered less on the future form which Socialism would take than on the necessary overthrow of rival power which, in their view, had to precede the introduction of Socialism. Their views, therefore, on the positive program to be put into effect, once power was attained, were for the most part nebulous, visionary and impractical. Beyond the nationalization of industry and the expropriation of large private capital holdings there was no agreed program. The treatment of the peasantry, which, according to the Marxist formulation was not of the proletariat, had always been a vague spot in the pattern of Communist thought: and it remained an object of controversy and vacillation for the first ten years of Communist power.

The circumstances of the immediate post-revolution period – the existence in Russia of civil war and foreign intervention, together with the obvious fact that the Communists represented only a tiny minority of the Russian people – made the establishment of dictatorial power a necessity. The experiment with war Communism and the abrupt attempt to eliminate private production and trade had unfortunate economic consequences and caused further bitterness against the new revolutionary regime. While the temporary relaxation of the effort to communize Russia, represented by the New Economic Policy, alleviated some of this economic distress and thereby served its purpose, it also made it evident that the "capitalistic sector of society" was still prepared to profit at once from any relaxation of governmental pressure, and would, if permitted to continue to exist, always constitute a powerful opposing element to the Soviet regime and a serious rival for influence in the country. Somewhat the same situation prevailed with respect to the individual peasant who, in his own small way, was also a private producer.

Lenin, had he lived, might have proved a great enough man to reconcile these conflicting forces to the ultimate benefit of Russian society, though this is questionable. But be that as it may, Stalin, and those whom he led in the struggle for succession to Lenin's position of leadership, were not the men to tolerate rival political forces in the sphere of power which they coveted. Their sense of insecurity was too great. Their particular brand of fanaticism, unmodified by any of the Anglo-Saxon traditions of compromise, was too fierce and too jealous to envisage any permanent sharing of power. From the Russian–Asiatic world out of which they had emerged they carried with them a skepticism as to the possibilities of permanent and peaceful coexistence of rival forces. Easily persuaded of their own doctrinaire "rightness," they insisted on the submission or destruction of all competing power. Outside the Communist Party, Russian society was to have no rigidity. There were to be no forms of collective human activity or association which would not be dominated by the Party. No other force in Russian society was to be permitted to achieve vitality or integrity. Only the Party was to have structure. All else was to be an amorphous mass.

And within the Party the same principle was to apply. The mass of Party members might go through the motions of election, deliberation, decision and action; but in these motions they were to be animated not by their own individual wills but by the awesome breath of the Party leadership and the over-brooding presence of "the word."

Let it be stressed again that subjectively these men probably did not seek absolutism for its own sake. They doubtless believed – and found it easy to believe – that they alone knew what was good for society and that they would accomplish that good once their power was secure and unchallengeable. But in seeking that security of their own rule they were prepared to recognize no restrictions, either of God or man, on the character of their methods. And until such time as that security might be achieved, they placed far down on their scale of operational priorities the comforts and happiness of the peoples entrusted to their care.

Now the outstanding circumstance concerning the Soviet regime is that down to the present day this process of political consolidation has never been completed and the men in the Kremlin have continued to be predominantly absorbed with the struggle to secure and make absolute the power which they seized in November 1917. They have endeavored to secure it primarily against forces at home, within Soviet society itself. But they have also endeavored to secure it against the outside world. For ideology, as we have seen, taught them that the outside world was hostile and that it was their duty eventually to overthrow the political forces beyond their borders. Then powerful hands of Russian history and tradition reached up to sustain them in this feeling. Finally, their own aggressive intransigence with respect to the outside world began to find its own reaction; and they were soon forced, to use another Gibbonesque phrase, "to chastise the contumacy" which they themselves had provoked. It is an undeniable privilege of every man to prove himself right in the thesis that the world is his enemy; for if he reiterates it frequently enough and makes it the background of his conduct he is bound eventually to be right.

Now it lies in the nature of the mental world of the Soviet leaders, as well as in the character of their ideology, that no opposition to them can be officially recognized as having any merit or justification whatsoever. Such opposition can flow, in theory, only from the hostile and incorrigible forces of dying capitalism. As long as remnants of capitalism were officially recognized as existing in Russia, it was possible to place on them, as an internal element, part of the blame for the maintenance of a dictatorial form of society. But as these remnants were liquidated, little by little, this justification fell away, and when it was indicated officially that they had been finally destroyed, it disappeared altogether. And this fact created one of the most basic of the compulsions which came to act upon the Soviet regime: since capitalism no longer existed in Russia and since it could not be admitted that there could be serious or widespread opposition to the Kremlin springing spontaneously from the liberated masses under its authority, it became necessary to justify the retention of the dictatorship by stressing the menace of capitalism abroad.

This began at an early date. In 1924 Stalin specifically defended the retention of the "organs of suppression," meaning, among others, the army and the secret police, on the ground that "as long as there is a capitalistic encirclement there will be danger of intervention with all the consequences that flow from that danger." In accordance with that theory, and from that time on, all internal opposition forces in Russia have consistently been portrayed as the agents of foreign forces of reaction antagonistic to Soviet power.

By the same token, tremendous emphasis has been placed on the original Communist thesis of a basic antagonism between the capitalist and Socialist worlds. It is clear, from many indications, that this emphasis is not founded in reality. The real facts concerning it have been confused by the existence abroad of genuine resentment provoked by Soviet philosophy and tactics and occasionally by the existence of great centers of military power, notably the Nazi regime in Germany and the Japanese Government of the late 1930s, which indeed have aggressive designs against the Soviet Union. But there is ample evidence that the stress laid in Moscow on the menace confronting Soviet society from the world outside its borders is founded not in the realities of foreign antagonism but in the necessity of explaining away the maintenance of dictatorial authority at home.

Now the maintenance of this pattern of Soviet power, namely, the pursuit of unlimited authority domestically, accompanied by the cultivation of the semi-myth of implacable foreign hostility, has gone far to shape the actual machinery of Soviet power as we know it today. Internal organs of administration which did not serve this purpose withered on the vine. Organs which did serve this purpose became vastly swollen. The security of Soviet power came to rest on the iron discipline of the Party, on the severity and ubiquity of the secret police, and on the uncompromising economic monopolism of the state. The "organs of suppression," in which the Soviet leaders had sought security from rival forces, became in large measures the masters of those whom they were designed to serve. Today the major part of the structure of Soviet power is committed to the perfection of the dictatorship and to the maintenance of the concept of Russia as in a state of siege, with the enemy lowering beyond the walls. And the millions of human beings who form that part of the structure of power must defend at all costs this concept of Russia's position, for without it they are themselves superfluous.

As things stand today, the rulers can no longer dream of parting with these organs of suppression. The quest for absolute power, pursued now for nearly three decades with a ruthlessness unparalleled (in scope at least) in modern times, has again produced internally, as it did externally, its own reaction. The excesses of the police apparatus have fanned the potential opposition to the regime into something far greater and more dangerous than it could have been before those excesses began.

But least of all can the rulers dispense with the fiction by which the maintenance of dictatorial power has been defended. For this fiction has been canonized in Soviet philosophy by the excesses already committed in its name; and it is now anchored in the Soviet structure of thought by bonds far greater than those of mere ideology.

PART II

So much for the historical background. What does it spell in terms of the political personality of Soviet power as we know it today?

Of the original ideology, nothing has been officially junked. Belief is maintained in the basic badness of capitalism, in the inevitability of its destruction, in the obligation of the proletariat to assist in that destruction and to take power into its own hands. But stress has come to be laid primarily on those concepts which relate most specifically to the Soviet regime itself: to its position as the sole truly Socialist regime in a dark and misguided world, and to the relationships of power within it.

The first of these concepts is that of the innate antagonism between capitalism and Socialism. We have seen how deeply that concept has become imbedded in foundations of Soviet power. It has profound implications for Russia's conduct as a member of international society. It means that there can never be on Moscow's side an sincere assumption of a community of aims between the Soviet Union and powers which are regarded as capitalist. It must inevitably be assumed in Moscow that the aims of the capitalist world are antagonistic to the Soviet regime, and therefore to the interests of the peoples it controls. If the Soviet government occasionally sets its signature to documents which would indicate the contrary, this is to be regarded as a tactical maneuver permissible in dealing with the enemy (who is without honor) and should be taken in the spirit of *caveat emptor*. Basically, the antagonism remains. It is postulated. And from it flow many of the phenomena which we find disturbing in the Kremlin's conduct of foreign policy: the secretiveness, the lack of frankness, the duplicity, the wary suspiciousness, and the basic unfriendliness of purpose. These phenomena are there to stay, for the foreseeable future. There can be variations of degree and of emphasis. When there is something the Russians want from us, one or the other of these features of their policy may be thrust temporarily into the background; and when that happens there will always be Americans who will leap forward with gleeful announcements that "the Russians have changed," and some who will even try to take credit for having brought about such "changes." But we should not be misled by tactical maneuvers. These characteristics of Soviet policy, like the postulate from which they flow, are basic to the internal nature of Soviet power, and will be with us, whether in the foreground or the background, until the internal nature of Soviet power is changed.

This means we are going to continue for a long time to find the Russians difficult to deal with. It does not mean that they should be considered as embarked upon a do-or-die program to overthrow our society by a given date. The theory of the inevitability of the eventual fall of capitalism has the fortunate connotation that there is no hurry about it. The forces of progress can take their time in preparing the final coup de grâce. Meanwhile, what is vital is that the "Socialist fatherland" – that oasis of power which has already been won for Socialism in the person of the Soviet Union – should be cherished and defended by all good Communists at home and abroad, its fortunes promoted, its enemies badgered and confounded. The promotion of premature, "adventuristic" revolutionary projects abroad which might embarrass Soviet power in any way would be an inexcusable, even a counter-revolutionary act. The cause of Socialism is the support and promotion of Soviet power, as defined in Moscow.

This brings us to the second of the concepts important to contemporary Soviet outlook. That is the infallibility of the Kremlin. The Soviet concept of power, which permits no focal points of organization outside the Party itself, requires that the Party leadership remain in theory the sole repository of truth. For if truth were to be found elsewhere, there would be justification for its expression in organized activity. But it is precisely that which the Kremlin cannot and will not permit.

The leadership of the Communist Party is therefore always right, and has been always right ever since in 1929 Stalin formalized his personal power by announcing that decisions of the Politburo were being taken unanimously.

On the principle of infallibility there rests the iron discipline of the Communist Party. In fact, the two concepts are mutually self-supporting. Perfect discipline requires recognition of infallibility. Infallibility requires the observance of discipline. And the two go far to determine the behaviorism of the entire Soviet apparatus of power. But their effect cannot be understood unless a third factor be taken into account: namely, the fact that the leadership is at liberty to put forward for tactical purposes any particular thesis which it finds useful to the cause at any particular moment and to require the faithful and unquestioning acceptance of that thesis by the members of the movement as a whole. This means that truth is not a constant but is actually created, for all intents and purposes, by the Soviet leaders themselves. It may vary from week to week, from month to month. It is nothing absolute and immutable – nothing which flows from objective reality. It is only the most recent manifestation of the wisdom of those in whom the ultimate wisdom is supposed to reside, because they represent the logic of history. The accumulative effect of these factors is to give to the whole subordinate apparatus of Soviet power an unshakable stubbornness and steadfastness in its orientation. This orientation can be changed at will by the Kremlin but by no other power. Once a given party line has been laid down on a given issue of current policy, the whole Soviet governmental machine, including the mechanism of diplomacy, moves inexorably along the prescribed path, like a persistent toy automobile wound up and headed in a given direction, stopping only when it meets with some unanswerable force. The individuals who are the components of this machine are unamenable to argument or reason, which comes to them from outside sources. Their whole training has taught them to mistrust and discount the glib persuasiveness of the outside world. Like the white dog before the phonograph, they hear only the "master's voice." And if they are to be called off from the purposes last dictated to them, it is the master who must call them off. Thus the foreign representative cannot hope that his words will make any impression on them. The most that he can hope is that they will be transmitted to those at the top, who are capable of changing the party line. But even those are not likely to be swayed by any normal logic in the words of the bourgeois representative. Since there can be no appeal to common purposes, there can be no appeal to common mental approaches. For this reason, facts speak louder than words to the ears of the Kremlin; and words carry the greatest weight when they have the ring of reflecting, or being backed up by, facts of unchallengeable validity.

But we have seen that the Kremlin is under no ideological compulsion to accomplish its purposes in a hurry. Like the Church, it is dealing in ideological concepts which are of long-term validity, and it can afford to be patient. It has no right to risk the existing achievements of the revolution for the sake of vain baubles of the future. The very teachings of Lenin himself require great caution and flexibility in the pursuit of Communist purposes. Again, these precepts are fortified by the lessons of Russian history: of centuries of obscure battles between nomadic forces over the stretches of a vast unfortified plain. Here caution, circumspection, flexibility and deception are the valuable qualities; and their value finds a natural appreciation in the Russian or the oriental mind. Thus the Kremlin has no compunction about retreating in the face of superior forces. And being under the compulsion of no timetable, it does not get panicky under the necessity for such retreat. Its political action is a fluid stream which moves constantly, wherever it is permitted to move, toward a given goal. Its main concern is to make sure that it has filled every nook and cranny available to it in the basin of world power. But if it finds unassailable barriers in its path, it accepts these philosophically and accommodates itself to them. The main thing is that there should always be pressure, unceasing constant pressure, toward the desired goal. There is no trace of any feeling in Soviet psychology that that goal must be reached at any given time.

These considerations make Soviet diplomacy at once easier and more difficult to deal with than the diplomacy of individual aggressive leaders like Napoleon and Hitler. On the one hand it is more sensitive to contrary force, more ready to yield on individual sectors of the diplomatic front when that force is felt to be too strong, and thus more rational in the logic and rhetoric of power. On the other hand it cannot be easily defeated or discouraged by a single victory on the part of its opponents. And the patient persistence by which it is animated means that it can be effectively countered not by sporadic acts which represent the momentary whims of democratic opinion but only by intelligent long-range policies on the part of Russia's adversaries – policies no less steady in their purpose, and no less variegated and resourceful in their application, than those of the Soviet Union itself.

In these circumstances it is clear that the main element of any United States policy toward the Soviet Union must be that of long-term, patient but firm and vigilant containment of Russian expansive tendencies. It is important to note, however, that such a policy has nothing to do with outward histrionics: with threats or blustering or superfluous gestures of outward "toughness." While the Kremlin is basically flexible in its reaction to political realities, it is by no means unamenable to considerations of prestige. Like almost any other government, it can be placed by tactless and threatening gestures in a position where it cannot afford to yield even though this might be dictated by its sense of realism. The Russian leaders are keen judges of human psychology, and as such they are highly conscious that loss of temper and of self-control is never a source of strength in political affairs. They are quick to exploit such evidences of weakness. For these reasons it is a *sine qua non* of successful dealing with Russia that the foreign government in question should remain at all times cool and collected and that its demands on Russian policy should be put forward in such a manner as to leave the way open for a compliance not too detrimental to Russian prestige.

PART III

In the light of the above, it will be clearly seen that the Soviet pressure against the free institutions of the western world is something that can be contained by the adroit and vigilant application of counter-force at a series of constantly shifting geographical and political points, corresponding to the shifts and maneuvers of Soviet policy, but which cannot be charmed or talked out of existence. The Russians look forward to a duel of infinite duration, and they see that already they have scored great successes. It must be borne in mind that there was a time when the Communist Party represented far more of a minority in the sphere of Russian national life than Soviet power today represents in the world community.

But if the ideology convinces the rulers of Russia that truth is on their side and they can therefore afford to wait, those of us on whom that ideology has no claim are free to examine objectively the validity of that premise. The Soviet thesis not only implies complete lack of control by the west over its own economic destiny, it likewise assumes Russian unity, discipline and patience over an infinite period. Let us bring this apocalyptic vision down to earth, and suppose that the western world finds the strength and resourcefulness to contain Soviet power over a period of ten to fifteen years. What does that spell for Russia itself?

The Soviet leaders, taking advantage of the contributions of modern techniques to the arts of despotism, have solved the question of obedience within the confines of their power. Few challenge their authority; and even those who do are unable to make that challenge valid as against the organs of suppression of the state.

The Kremlin has also proved able to accomplish its purpose of building up Russia, regardless of the interests of the inhabitants, and industrial foundation of heavy metallurgy, which is, to be sure, not yet complete but which is nevertheless continuing to grow and is approaching those of the other major industrial countries. All of this, however, both the maintenance of internal political security and the building of heavy industry, has been carried out at a terrible cost in human life and in human hopes and energies. It has necessitated the use of forced labor on a scale unprecedented in modern times under conditions of peace. It has involved the neglect or abuse of other phases of Soviet economic life, particularly agriculture, consumers' goods production, housing and transportation.

To all that, the war has added its tremendous toll of destruction, death and human exhaustion. In consequence of this, we have in Russia today a population which is physically and spiritually tired. The mass of the people are disillusioned, skeptical and no longer as accessible as they once were to the magical attraction which Soviet power still radiates to its followers abroad. The avidity with which people seized upon the slight respite accorded to the Church for tactical reasons during the war was eloquent testimony to the fact that their capacity for faith and devotion found little expression in the purposes of the regime.

In these circumstances, there are limits to the physical and nervous strength of people themselves. These limits are absolute ones, and are binding even for the cruelest dictatorship, because beyond them people cannot be driven. The forced labor camps and the other agencies of constraint provide temporary means of compelling people to work longer hours than their own volition or mere economic pressure would dictate; but if people survive them at all they become old before their time and must be considered as human casualties to the demands of dictatorship. In either case their best powers are no longer available to society and can no longer be enlisted in the service of the state.

Here only the younger generations can help. The younger generation, despite all vicissitudes and sufferings, is numerous and vigorous; and the Russians are a talented people. But it still remains to be seen what will be the effects on mature performance of the abnormal emotional strains of childhood which Soviet dictatorship created and which were enormously increased by the war. Such things as normal security and placidity of home environment have practically ceased to exist in the Soviet Union outside of the most remote farms and villages. And observers are not yet sure whether that is not going to leave its mark on the over-all capacity of the generation now coming into maturity.

In addition to this, we have the fact that Soviet economic development, while it can list certain formidable achievements, has been precariously spotty and uneven. Russian Communists who speak of the "uneven development of capitalism" should blush at the contemplation of their own national economy. Here certain branches of economic life, such as the metallurgical and machine industries, have been pushed out of all proportion to other sectors of the economy. Here is a nation striving to become in a short period one of the great industrial nations of the world while it still has no highway network worthy of the name and only a relatively primitive network of railways. Much has been done to increase efficiency of labor and to teach primitive peasants something about the operation of machines. But maintenance is still a crying deficiency of all Soviet economy. Construction is hasty and poor in quality. Depreciation must be enormous. And in vast sectors of economic life it has not yet been possible to instill into labor anything like that general culture of production and technical self-respect which characterizes the skilled worker of the west.

It is difficult to see how these deficiencies can be corrected at an early date by a tired and dispirited population working largely under the shadow of fear and compulsion. And as long as they are not overcome, Russia will remain economically as vulnerable, and in a certain sense an impotent, nation, capable of exporting its enthusiasms and of radiating the strange charm of its primitive political vitality but unable to back up those articles of export by the real evidences of material power and prosperity.

Meanwhile, a great uncertainty hangs over the political life of the Soviet Union. That is the uncertainty involved in the transfer of power from one individual or group of individuals to others.

This is, of course, outstandingly the problem of the personal position of Stalin. We must remember that his succession to Lenin's pinnacle of pre-eminence in the Communist movement was the only such transfer of individual authority which the Soviet Union has experienced. That transfer took 12 years to consolidate. It cost the lives of millions of people and shook the state to its foundations. The attendant tremors were felt all through the international revolutionary movement, to the disadvantage of the Kremlin itself.

It is always possible that another transfer of pre-eminent power may take place quietly and inconspicuously, with no repercussions anywhere. But again, it is possible that the questions involved may unleash, to use some of Lenin's words, one of those "incredibly swift transitions" from "delicate deceit" to "wild violence" which characterize Russian history, and may shake Soviet power to its foundations.

But this is not only a question of Stalin himself. There has been, since 1938, a dangerous congealment of political life in the higher circles of Soviet power. The All-Union Congress of Soviets, in theory the supreme body of the Party, is supposed to meet not less often than once in three years. It will soon be eight full years since its last meeting. During this period membership in the Party has numerically doubled. Party mortality during the war was enormous; and today well over half of the Party members are persons who have entered since the last Party congress was held. meanwhile, the same small group of men has carried on at the top through an amazing series of national vicissitudes. Surely there is some reason why the experiences of the war brought basic political changes to every one of the great governments of the west. Surely the causes of that phenomenon are basic enough to be present somewhere in the obscurity of Soviet political life, as well. And yet no recognition has been given to these causes in Russia.

It must be surmised from this that even within so highly disciplined an organization as the Communist Party there must be a growing divergence in age, outlook and interest between the great mass of Party members, only so recently recruited into the movement, and the little self-perpetuating clique of men at the top, whom most of these Party members have never met, with whom they have never conversed, and with whom they can have no political intimacy.

Who can say whether, in these circumstances, the eventual rejuvenation of the higher spheres of authority (which can only be a matter of time) can take place smoothly and peacefully, or whether rivals in the quest for higher power will not eventually reach down into these politically immature and inexperienced masses in order to find support for their respective claims? If this were ever to happen, strange consequences could flow for the Communist Party: for the membership at large has been exercised only in the practices of iron discipline and obedience and not in the arts of compromise and accommodation. And if disunity were ever to seize and paralyze the Party, the chaos and weakness of Russian society would be revealed in forms beyond description. For we have seen that Soviet power is only concealing an amorphous mass of human beings among whom no independent organizational structure is tolerated. In Russia there is not even such a thing as local government. The present generation of Russians have never known spontaneity of collective action. If, consequently, anything were ever to occur to disrupt the unity and efficacy of the Party as a political instrument, Soviet Russia might be changed overnight from one of the strongest to one of the weakest and most pitiable of national societies.

Thus the future of Soviet power may not be by any means as secure as Russian capacity for self-delusion would make it appear to the men of the Kremlin. That they can quietly and easily turn it over to others remains to be proved. Meanwhile, the hardships of their rule and the vicissitudes of international life have taken a heavy toll of the strength and hopes of the great people on whom their power rests. It is curious to note that the ideological power of Soviet authority is strongest today in areas beyond the frontiers of Russia, beyond the reach of its police power. This phenomenon brings to mind a comparison used by Thomas Mann in his great novel *Buddenbrooks*. Observing that human institutions often show the greatest outward brilliance at a moment when inner decay is in reality farthest advanced, he compared one of those stars whose light shines most brightly on this world when in reality it has long since ceased to exist. And who can say with assurance that the strong light still cast by the Kremlin on the dissatisfied peoples of the western world is not the powerful afterglow of a constellation which is in actuality on the wane? This cannot be proved. And it cannot be disproved. But the possibility remains (and in the opinion of this writer it is a strong one) that Soviet power, like the capitalist world of its conception, bears within it the seeds of its own decay, and that the sprouting of these seeds is well advanced.

PART IV

It is clear that the United States cannot expect in the foreseeable future to enjoy political intimacy with the Soviet regime. It must continue to regard the Soviet Union as a rival, not a partner, in the political arena. It must continue to expect that Soviet policies will reflect no abstract love of peace and stability, no real faith in the possibility of a permanent happy coexistence of the Socialist and capitalist worlds, but rather a cautious, persistent pressure toward the disruption and, weakening of all rival influence and rival power.

Balanced against this are the facts that Russia, as opposed to the western world in general, is still by far the weaker party, that Soviet policy is highly flexible, and that Soviet society may well contain deficiencies which will eventually weaken its own total potential. This would of itself warrant the United States entering with reasonable confidence upon a policy of firm containment, designed to confront the Russians with unalterable counter-force at every point where they show signs of encroaching upon the interests of a peaceful and stable world.

But in actuality the possibilities for American policy are by no means limited to holding the line and hoping for the best. It is entirely possible for the United States to influence by its actions the internal developments, both within Russia and throughout the international Communist movement, by which Russian policy is largely determined. This is not only a question of the modest measure of informational activity which this government can conduct in the Soviet Union and elsewhere, although that, too, is important. It is rather a question of the degree to which the United States can create among the peoples of the world generally the impression of a country which knows what it wants, which is coping successfully with the problem of its internal life and with the responsibilities of a World Power, and which has a spiritual vitality capable of holding its own among the major ideological currents of the time. To the extent that such an impression can be created and maintained, the aims of Russian Communism must appear sterile and quixotic, the hopes and enthusiasm of Moscow's supporters must wane, and added strain must be imposed on the Kremlin's foreign policies. For the palsied decrepitude of the capitalist world is the keystone of Communist philosophy. Even the failure of the United States to experience the early economic depression which the ravens of the Red Square have been predicting with such complacent confidence since hostilities ceased would have deep and important repercussions throughout the Communist world.

By the same token, exhibitions of indecision, disunity and internal disintegration within this country have an exhilarating effect on the whole Communist movement. At each evidence of these tendencies, a thrill of hope and excitement goes through the Communist world; a new jauntiness can be noted in the Moscow tread; new groups of foreign supporters climb on to what they can only view as the band wagon of international politics; and Russian pressure increases all along the line in international affairs.

It would be an exaggeration to say that American behavior unassisted and alone could exercise a power of life and death over the Communist movement and bring about the early fall of Soviet power in Russia. But the United States has it in its power to increase enormously the strains under which Soviet policy must operate, to force upon the Kremlin a far greater degree of moderation and circumspection than it has had to observe in recent years, and in this way to promote tendencies which must eventually find their outlet in either the breakup or the gradual mellowing of Soviet power. For no mystical, Messianic movement – and particularly not that of the Kremlin – can face frustration indefinitely without eventually adjusting itself in one way or another to the logic of that state of affairs.

Thus the decision will really fall in large measure in this country itself. The issue of Soviet-American relations is in essence a test of the overall worth of the United States as a nation among nations. To avoid destruction the United States need only measure up to its own best traditions and prove itself worthy of preservation as a great nation.

Surely, there was never a fairer test of national quality than this. In the light of these circumstances, the thoughtful observer of Russian–American relations will find no cause for complaint in the Kremlin's challenge to American society. He will rather experience a certain gratitude to a Providence which, by providing the American people with this implacable challenge, has made their entire security as a nation dependent on their pulling themselves together and accepting the responsibilities of moral and political leadership that history plainly intended them to bear.

Document Questions

1. Which does Kennan think is the more important influence on Soviet conduct: ideology or circumstances?

> Marxist–Leninist ideology is basic, but it is continually modified to operate with existing circumstances. Because the ideology promises inevitable triumph in the future, Soviet leaders can justify any retreat as a tactical necessity. They are patient, and so the United States can be patient in dealing with them.

2. Is real peace or friendship possible between the capitalist world and the Soviet Union?

> No; the innate antagonism between capitalism and Socialism is one of their basic assumptions. Moreover, the threat of external enemies justifies the continuing repression of any and all potential internal rivals. The Soviets must see their society as besieged to justify themselves.

3. What are the implications of this assumption of antagonism?

> "Basically, the antagonism remains. It is postulated. And from it flow many of the phenomena which we find disturbing in the Kremlin's conduct of foreign policy: the secretiveness, the lack of frankness, the duplicity, the wary suspiciousness, and the basic unfriendliness of purpose. These phenomena are there to stay, for the foreseeable future."

4. What should the U.S. policy be toward the Soviets?

> "The main element of any United States policy toward the Soviet Union must be that of long-term, patient but firm and vigilant containment of Russian expansive tendencies. It is important to note, however, that such a policy has nothing to do with outward histrionics: with threats or blustering or superfluous gestures of outward 'toughness.'
>
> "The Soviet pressure against the free institutions of the western world is something that can be contained by the adroit and vigilant application of counter-force at a series of constantly shifting geographical and political points, corresponding to the shifts and maneuvers of Soviet policy, but which cannot be charmed or talked out of existence. The Russians look forward to a duel of infinite duration, and they see that already they have scored great successes."

5. What weaknesses may a policy of containment exacerbate within the Soviet system?

> Changes of power will be difficult. The Communist Party has a few very old men in power and possibly impatient younger men rising. The Russian people are physically and spiritually tired, disillusioned, and skeptical. Parts of their economy are very weak; they still have no significant highway system, for example. And their ideology has its greatest appeal outside Russia, where it has not been implemented.

6. What does Kennan hope for the future?

> "The United States has it in its power to increase enormously the strains under which Soviet policy must operate, to force upon the Kremlin a far greater degree of moderation and circumspection than it has had to observe in recent years, and in this way to promote tendencies which must eventually find their outlet in either the breakup or the gradual mellowing of Soviet power."

> To avoid destruction, the United States need only measure up to its own best traditions and prove itself worthy of preservation as a great nation. In the light of these circumstances, the thoughtful observer of Russian–American relations will find no cause for complaint in the Kremlin's challenge to American society. He will rather experience a certain gratitude to a Providence which, by providing the American people with this implacable challenge, has made their entire security as a nation dependent on their pulling themselves together and accepting the responsibilities of moral and political leadership that history plainly intended them to bear.

CHAPTER TWENTY

OUT OF BALANCE

The Turbulent Sixties

Summary

THIS CHAPTER OPENS with a discussion of President Eisenhower's Farewell Address to the Nation. The address sets the tone for the chapter and raises profound questions for Americans, even today. The aftermath of World War II had created unprecedented conditions in the United States – a large standing military force and a vast array of manufacturers and technocrats to support a growing military presence and ever-expanding federal government. This was a far cry from the American republic as founded. Could we Americans continue to adhere to our original principles and yet meet the requirements of our changed circumstances? For Eisenhower, the answer was to keep things in balance. By the end of the decade, however, much in America seemed out of balance.

The presidencies of John F. Kennedy and Lyndon Baines Johnson are discussed in this chapter, as well as the significant movement for civil rights for African Americans, led especially by Dr. Martin Luther King Jr., culminating in the Civil Rights Bill (1964) and Voting Rights Act (1965). The chapter includes helpful biographical sketches of these men.

The presidency of John F. Kennedy was shockingly and tragically cut short by an assassin. Young, vibrant, full of promise, and with a progressive outlook, he left a mixed legacy in both domestic and foreign affairs. His economic policies were highly successful in promoting economic growth, and he energetically promoted America's space program. Many of his domestic policies had not come to fruition by the time of his death. In foreign policy, he pursued an anti-Communist policy of containment. He was responsible for a major failure in the Bay of Pigs invasion yet managed to win in a showdown with Russia over the Cuban Missile Crisis. His successor, Lyndon Baines Johnson, pushed through a transformational series of domestic welfare and civil rights policies. Many of the programs he championed remain a part of our political landscape. Johnson also vastly escalated the American involvement in Vietnam and instituted a military draft of young men for military service.

As the decade wore on, there were many signs of a culture unraveling, sometimes in violent ways. The peaceful and dignified civil rights movement lost its former unity as a series of terrible race riots broke out in major American cities. Opposition to the Vietnam War grew, particularly on college campuses, and while most demonstrations were peaceful, serious violent fringe elements were present in various protest movements. Worst of all, the year 1968 saw the assassinations of both King and Robert F. Kennedy.

Johnson faced so much opposition in 1968 that he decided against running for reelection. The 1968 Democratic Convention was itself a scene of violent conflict as antiwar protesters fought with Chicago police officers. All of this played out on the television sets of Americans at home.

It seemed a long way from the days of President Eisenhower. It would be his former vice president, Richard Nixon, who would win the election of 1968, in one of the most stunning career comebacks in modern American history.

Questions and Answers

1. Could Eisenhower have won a third term? Why couldn't he run? (p. 365)

> Yes, he was still popular, but the Twenty-Second Amendment (aimed by Republicans at the possibility of another FDR) prevented it.

2. Of what did Eisenhower warn in his Farewell Address to the Nation? (p. 366)

> He warned of the rising debt and the temptations of prosperity, as well as the "military–industrial complex" and a too-powerful government.

3. Yet Eisenhower had presided over the consolidation of the "**warfare welfare**" state, in which the demands of expensive New Deal programs and constant military readiness dictated a sprawling federal government. (p. 367)

4. The great need was for **balance,** a word Eisenhower used ten times in his fare-well speech. (p. 367)

> The teacher might also point out that Americans have historically been willing to see an expansion of government power and a curtailment of rights during an emergency – this happened repeatedly during the nineteenth-century wars and under Wilson during World War I – but they expect things to be restored to normal once the emergency is over. However, the Depression plus World War II, a fifteen-year emergency, now were followed by the Cold War. Is an "emergency" that goes on and on really an emergency any longer? Or is it the new normal?

5. Why was the 1960 campaign noteworthy? (pp. 367–68)

> Both candidates were young, and it was the first time debates were televised. Kennedy won them because Nixon seemed awkward on television by comparison to Kennedy. (Polls afterward showed that voters who listened to the debates on the radio thought Nixon had won.) The voters were ready for a change, toward youth, and though Nixon was only slightly older than Kennedy, he was identified with Eisenhower, now seventy and in fragile health. Kennedy had glamor that Nixon lacked. Also, the pattern has been that the same political party rarely wins the presidency three times in a row; FDR likely managed to do so only because of the outbreak of World War II.

6. What tone did JFK's inaugural address set? (p. 369)

> This is the "New Frontier"; "the torch has been passed" to a younger generation; "pay any price, bear any burden" to assure the survival of liberty; "ask not what your country can do for you – ask what you can do for your country."

7. Who did JFK recruit to run his administration? (pp. 369–70)

> He recruited top academics plus top businessmen, such as Robert S. McNamara from Ford Motor Company. "There was more than a whiff of Progressivism in it all," that is, rule by the "experts."

8. How effective was JFK in getting his programs enacted by Congress? (p. 370)

> Not very, though he did get the Alliance for Progress for Latin America and the Peace Corps. Plus his tax cut stimulated the economy.

9. What was the effect of slashing income tax rates? (p. 370)

    Over the next six years, personal savings and business investment rose sharply; GNP increased by 40 percent in two years; job growth doubled; and unemployment was reduced by a third.

10. Why was JFK so committed to the exploration of space? (pp. 370–71)

    The "New Frontier" idea suggested it, plus competition with Soviets; the goal of putting a man on the moon was clear and specific and inspired a national effort.

11. How effective was JFK's Cuban policy? (p. 371)

    It was disastrous in his supporting the CIA-organized invasion by Cuban exiles at the Bay of Pigs.

    Teachers may add that the invasion had been planned under Eisenhower. Kennedy should either have called it off or committed American military support to ensuring its success; instead, he allowed the invasion force (Cuban exiles) to be defeated and captured. "All or nothing" is often a good rule; halfway measures often are not.

12. What happened when JFK met Soviet leader Khrushchev two months later? (p. 371)

    "He savaged me"; then he built the Berlin Wall. JFK gave a great speech at the wall, but the United States did not challenge the wall for twenty-five years (until Reagan).

13. Who won the Cuban Missile Crisis? (p. 372)

    The Soviets withdrew their missiles but remained in control of Cuba. A "hotline" was established to help in future crises.

    Teachers may point out that it looked like Kennedy had won, as the Soviets backed down and withdrew the missiles. However, the outcome was to continue the status quo, which was a Soviet client state continuing to exist ninety miles from Florida.

14. What other foreign policy headache did JFK inherit? (p. 372)

    He inherited the war in Southeast Asia, especially Vietnam. JFK signaled approval of removing (and killing) Diem, which was a disastrous strategic error, as it made the war ours rather than theirs with us helping. Future Saigon governments were seen, more or less correctly, as American puppets. JFK also increased U.S. troop strength in Vietnam, which had been only a few hundred advisors under Eisenhower, to sixteen thousand.

15.   What was the effect of Kennedy's assassination? (pp. 372–73)

It was as profound a shock as the Japanese attack on Pearl Harbor; everything was unsettled afterward.

16.   What progress did the civil rights movement make after World War II? (pp. 373–75)

The first big breakthrough was the *Brown* decision by a unanimous Supreme Court that segregation is unconstitutional. Resistance in the South continued, producing the rise of nonviolent protest under Martin Luther King Jr. with "freedom riders" and "sit-ins." An important moment was the August 1963 March on Washington and MLK's "I Have a Dream" speech – done in part to keep pressure on Kennedy to see a civil rights bill passed.

Teachers may also point out that Kennedy was less effective at getting legislation passed than his successor, Lyndon Johnson, who had been a very effective leader in the Senate and was good at "arm-twisting" – and who was also a southerner. LBJ got the key Civil Rights Act of 1964 passed, where JFK had failed, as well as the Voting Rights Act of 1965.

17.   LBJ was described as **ruthless, conniving, deceitful, unscrupulous** – yet he had a heart for the underprivileged. This led to his **Great Society** programs, which went far beyond what the New Deal had created. (pp. 376–77)

18.   How did the Republican Party split in 1964? (p. 377)

Barry Goldwater's mostly Sunbelt conservatives seized control of the party from more moderate, mostly northeastern Republicans. Goldwater lost the election badly, but conservatives remained in control of the Republican Party thereafter.

19.   What were the two consoling features of Goldwater's loss for conservatives? (p. 378)

The new conservative movement took Ronald Reagan as their rising star, and the Republicans made large inroads into the previously solidly Democratic Deep South.

20. What were the main elements of Johnson's Great Society? (pp. 378–79)

They were Medicare and Medicaid, food stamps, National Endowments for the Humanities and the Arts, and more. There were major increases in federal spending on welfare.

21. How successful was the Great Society? (p. 379)

The jury is still out. There was some progress in reducing poverty, but at very high costs, and with increased dependency on cash supports rather than moving people into employment. Aid to Families with Dependent Children weakened family structures by disincentivizing marriage.

22. How did the emerging Black Power movement coexist with King's emphasis on nonviolence? (pp. 379–80)

There were many riots in 1965 and after, as well as a push to create a form of racial separation.

Teachers may also note that King succeeded in part because he drew on, or created, a lot of goodwill from within the white majority. The Black Power/black separatist movement of Malcolm X tended to frighten whites and reduced their sympathy.

23. What was the Gulf of Tonkin Resolution? (p. 386)

Congress gave LBJ a blank check in waging war in Vietnam, leading to a vast expansion (five hundred thousand troops) of the U.S. war effort.

Teachers may note that the army was mostly drafted from among young men who did not attend college. Also, LBJ was fighting his "War on Poverty" at the same time he was fighting a war in Vietnam.

24. To what extent was the U.S. involvement in Vietnam a product of the doctrine of containment? What were the difficulties of this? (pp. 380–81)

The justification was the idea of a domino effect that the fall of one nation to Communism would endanger others. But that assumed all Communism was one, whereas Chinese and Vietnamese Communism seemed different; China and Russia were rivals, even enemies. Also, Vietnam seemed a war designed not to yield any sort of victory. The United States wanted to apply the least amount of force necessary to prevent the enemy from winning.

Teachers may mention the *loss of strength gradient*, a principle in international relations that the farther from "home" and key interests a nation is fighting, the less its will to continue to fight will be. Winning the war was the *only* thing for North Vietnam; it was one of many goals for LBJ and the United States.

25. Why did popular support for the war drop? (p. 381)

See Questions 23 and 24, plus the war was on television every night. There was widespread and growing general disaffection from the American status quo, particularly among college and university students – whose poorer high school classmates were fighting and dying in Vietnam.

26. "Although often speaking a **communitarian** language, members of the counterculture tended to behave as **radical individualists**." (p. 382)

On the other hand, teachers may point out, perhaps with irony, that most individuals tend to conform to the people in their immediate circle, their friends. The "hippies" were possibly as conformist as their parents but modeled themselves on one another rather than on a previous generation.

27. When and what was the Fourth Great Awakening? (pp. 382–83)

It was a 1960s religious revival stressing reevaluation of the American focus on wealth and increased concern for the natural environment.

28. Why did LBJ not run again? (pp. 383–84)

He was challenged by Eugene McCarthy and made a poor showing in the New Hampshire primary; the Tet Offensive (misreported) turned opinion decisively against the war; and Robert Kennedy had been announced as a candidate.

29. Why did America seem to be falling apart in 1968? (p. 384)

There were the assassinations of MLK and Robert Kennedy; destructive riots in sixty cities; and chaos in Chicago at the Democratic Convention.

30. Who was the third candidate in 1968? How did the election come out? (pp. 384–85)

The election was George Wallace of Alabama versus Nixon and Humphrey. Nixon won a narrow popular vote victory but won 301–191 in the Electoral College, with Wallace getting 46 Electoral College votes. (Wallace had hoped to prevent a winner in the Electoral College, positioning himself to bargain in the House of Representatives, which resolves an election if no one wins the Electoral College.)

31. What did Nixon's victory (and Wallace's showing) indicate? (pp. 384–85)

> The majority of Americans were ready for a pullback from the frenzied pace of change under LBJ. Their hope was to regain with Nixon some of the balance that had been Eisenhower's trademark. This was an understandable wish – but would it be realized?

Objective Questions

Answers are in parentheses.

Put in order:

_____	Cuban Missile Crisis	(1)
_____	George Wallace gets forty-two electoral votes	(3)
_____	Gulf of Tonkin Resolution	(2)

Put in order:

_____	assassinations of MLK and Robert Kennedy	(3)
_____	Great Society	(2)
_____	Peace Corps established	(1)

Document

REV. MARTIN LUTHER KING JR., "I HAVE A DREAM," AUGUST 28, 1963

I am happy to join with you today in what will go down in history as the greatest demonstration for freedom in the history of our nation.

Five score years ago, a great American, in whose symbolic shadow we stand today, signed the Emancipation Proclamation. This momentous decree came as a great beacon light of hope to millions of Negro slaves who had been seared in the flames of withering injustice. It came as a joyous daybreak to end the long night of their captivity.

But one hundred years later, the Negro still is not free. One hundred years later, the life of the Negro is still sadly crippled by the manacles of segregation and the chains of discrimination. One hundred years later, the Negro lives on a lonely island of poverty in the midst of a vast ocean of material prosperity.

One hundred years later, the Negro is still languished in the corners of American society and finds himself an exile in his own land. And so we've come here today to dramatize a shameful condition.

In a sense we've come to our nation's capital to cash a check. When the architects of our republic wrote the magnificent words of the Constitution and the Declaration of Independence, they were signing a promissory note to which every American was to fall heir. This note was a promise that all men, yes, black men as well as white men, would be guaranteed the "unalienable Rights" of "Life, Liberty and the pursuit of Happiness." It is obvious today that America has defaulted on this promissory note, insofar as her citizens of color are concerned. Instead of honoring this sacred obligation, America has given the Negro people a bad check, a check which has come back marked "insufficient funds."

But we refuse to believe that the bank of justice is bankrupt. We refuse to believe that there are insufficient funds in the great vaults of opportunity of this nation. And so, we've come to cash this check, a check that will give us upon demand the riches of freedom and the security of justice.

We have also come to this hallowed spot to remind America of the fierce urgency of Now. This is no time to engage in the luxury of cooling off or to take the tranquilizing drug of gradualism. Now is the time to make real the promises of democracy. Now is the time to rise from the dark and desolate valley of segregation to the sunlit path of racial justice. Now is the time to lift our nation from the quicksands of racial injustice to the solid rock of brotherhood. Now is the time to make justice a reality for all of God's children.

It would be fatal for the nation to overlook the urgency of the moment. This sweltering summer of the Negro's legitimate discontent will not pass until there is an invigorating autumn of freedom and equality. Nineteen sixty-three is not an end, but a beginning. And those who hope that the Negro needed to blow off steam and will now be content will have a rude awakening if the nation returns to business as usual. And there will be neither rest nor tranquility in America until the Negro is granted his citizenship rights. The whirlwinds of revolt will continue to shake the foundations of our nation until the bright day of justice emerges.

But there is something that I must say to my people, who stand on the warm threshold which leads into the palace of justice: In the process of gaining our rightful place, we must not be guilty of wrongful deeds. Let us not seek to satisfy our thirst for freedom by drinking from the cup of bitterness and hatred. We must forever conduct our struggle on the high plane of dignity and discipline. We must not allow our creative protest to degenerate into physical violence. Again and again, we must rise to the majestic heights of meeting physical force with soul force.

The marvelous new militancy which has engulfed the Negro community must not lead us to a distrust of all white people, for many of our white brothers, as evidenced by their presence here today, have come to realize that their destiny is tied up with our destiny. And they have come to realize that their freedom is inextricably bound to our freedom.

We cannot walk alone.

And as we walk, we must make the pledge that we shall always march ahead.

We cannot turn back.

There are those who are asking the devotees of civil rights, "When will you be satisfied?" We can never be satisfied as long as the Negro is the victim of the unspeakable horrors of police brutality. We can never be satisfied as long as our bodies, heavy with the fatigue of travel, cannot gain lodging in the motels of the highways and the hotels of the cities. We cannot be satisfied as long as the Negro's basic mobility is from a smaller ghetto to a larger one. We can never be satisfied as long as our children are stripped of their self-hood and robbed of their dignity by signs stating: "For Whites Only." We cannot be satisfied as long as a Negro in Mississippi cannot vote and a Negro in New York believes he has nothing for which to vote. No, no, we are not satisfied, and we will not be satisfied until "justice rolls down like waters, and righteousness like a mighty stream."

I am not unmindful that some of you have come here out of great trials and tribulations. Some of you have come fresh from narrow jail cells. And some of you have come from areas where your quest – quest for freedom left you battered by the storms of persecution and staggered by the winds of police brutality. You have been the veterans of creative suffering. Continue to work with the faith that unearned suffering is redemptive. Go back to Mississippi, go back to Alabama, go back to South Carolina, go back to Georgia, go back to Louisiana, go back to the slums and ghettos of our northern cities, knowing that somehow this situation can and will be changed.

Let us not wallow in the valley of despair, I say to you today, my friends.

And so even though we face the difficulties of today and tomorrow, I still have a dream. It is a dream deeply rooted in the American dream.

I have a dream that one day this nation will rise up and live out the true meaning of its creed: "We hold these truths to be self-evident, that all men are created equal."

I have a dream that one day on the red hills of Georgia, the sons of former slaves and the sons of former slave owners will be able to sit down together at the table of brotherhood.

I have a dream that one day even the state of Mississippi, a state sweltering with the heat of injustice, sweltering with the heat of oppression, will be transformed into an oasis of freedom and justice.

I have a dream that my four little children will one day live in a nation where they will not be judged by the color of their skin but by the content of their character.

I have a *dream* today!

I have a dream that one day, down in Alabama, with its vicious racists, with its governor having his lips dripping with the words of "interposition" and "nullification" – one day right there in Alabama little black boys and black girls will be able to join hands with little white boys and white girls as sisters and brothers.

I have a *dream* today!

I have a dream that one day every valley shall be exalted, and every hill and mountain shall be made low, the rough places will be made plain, and the crooked places will be made straight; "and the glory of the Lord shall be revealed and all flesh shall see it together."

This is our hope, and this is the faith that I go back to the South with.

With this faith, we will be able to hew out of the mountain of despair a stone of hope. With this faith, we will be able to transform the jangling discords of our nation into a beautiful symphony of brotherhood. With this faith, we will be able to work together, to pray together, to struggle together, to go to jail together, to stand up for freedom together, knowing that we will be free one day.

And this will be the day – this will be the day when all of God's children will be able to sing with new meaning:

My country 'tis of thee, sweet land of liberty, of thee I sing. Land where my fathers died, land of the Pilgrim's pride, From every mountainside, let freedom ring!

And if America is to be a great nation, this must become true.

And so let freedom ring from the prodigious hilltops of New Hampshire.

Let freedom ring from the mighty mountains of New York.

Let freedom ring from the heightening Alleghenies of Pennsylvania.

Let freedom ring from the snow-capped Rockies of Colorado.

Let freedom ring from the curvaceous slopes of California.

But not only that:

Let freedom ring from Stone Mountain of Georgia.

Let freedom ring from Lookout Mountain of Tennessee.

Let freedom ring from every hill and molehill of Mississippi.

From every mountainside, let freedom ring.

And when this happens, and when we allow freedom ring, when we let it ring from every village and every hamlet, from every state and every city, we will be able to speed up that day when *all* of God's children, black men and white men, Jews and Gentiles, Protestants and Catholics, will be able to join hands and sing in the words of the old Negro spiritual:

Free at last! Free at last!
Thank God Almighty, we are free at last!

Document Questions

1. Why do you think King begins his speech with an invocation of Abraham Lincoln and the Emancipation Proclamation?

> He did it partly because he delivered the speech at the Lincoln Memorial. But on a deeper level, it was a way of signaling from the start that the movement he was leading was meant to be a fulfillment of American history and not a negation of it. He does the same thing by his repeated invocations of the Declaration and, brilliantly, by his use of the lyrics from the patriotic song "My Country 'Tis of Thee" as his speech rises toward its climax.

2. What is the importance of his use of the image of "cashing a check"?

> Again, it is a way of saying that the people in the protest movement he was leading were only asking for what was rightly owed them, ultimately through the "promissory notes" of the "magnificent" Declaration and Constitution. America had "defaulted" on the notes and had "given the Negro a bad check," which had been returned marked "insufficient funds." This was a brilliantly homespun and conservative way, grounded in the texture of ordinary, everyday life, to bring the point home.

3. What does King mean by "the fierce urgency of Now"?

> He is trying to emphasize, with a particular view to prodding President Kennedy to act on the Civil Rights Bill then before Congress, that the situation is ripe for action and that inaction may be "fatal for the nation." There is a subtle hint of the possibility of violence, too, in his plea to his followers to disdain the "cup of bitterness and hatred" and his praise for the majestic alternative of dignity, discipline, and "soul power."

4. What does King mean in saying "we cannot walk alone"?

> He means that there must be reconciliation of the races, an acceptance that the destiny of all races, and the freedom of all, are bound together in a common fate.

5. How strong a role does King's religious faith play in this speech? Where does one see it emerge?

> It's important to remember that King was a Baptist minister, and his faith plays a powerful role throughout this speech, both in the speech's sermon-like style and in its easy invocation of biblical phrases and concepts. Not only was he motivated by faith but he knew his audience would respond favorably to these aspects of his speech. When he breaks into the words of "the old Negro spiritual" at the conclusion of the speech – "Free at last!" – he brings into the speech something immediately and intimately familiar to his listeners.

CHAPTER TWENTY-ONE

FALL AND RESTORATION

Summary

THE FOCUS OF THIS CHAPTER is on the presidencies of Richard Nixon, Gerald Ford, Jimmy Carter, and Ronald Reagan. The office of the president suffered a tremendous decline in prestige and authority in the wake of Richard Nixon's resignation in 1974. It was not until Ronald Reagan became president in 1980 that the office once again enjoyed a renewal of the power and potential of an energetic and "transformational" president. The idea of a "transformational" president is explored in this chapter as it applies to Reagan. The chapter includes biographical vignettes of these men.

In foreign affairs, President Nixon's great successes were in improving our relations with China and Russia. He also brought the Vietnam War to an end, although in the end, Congress refused to offer any assistance to the South Vietnamese once U.S. troops had withdrawn, and South Vietnam quickly fell to the Communists. Carter's presidency was overshadowed by the takeover of the U.S. embassy in Iran by Iranian militants, who held Americans hostage for 444 days.

Domestically, the Watergate scandal and resignation of Richard Nixon brought both the country and the presidency to a low point. Yet even before these events, the U.S. economy was hobbled by inflation and high unemployment. Nixon, Ford, and Carter tried various policies, but the economy remained sluggish.

In the wake of Watergate and Vietnam, questions emerged about the nature of the presidency and whether it had strayed too far from the proper constitutional role of that office; had the office evolved into a kind of "imperial presidency"? And should we return to older forms? Or perhaps what we needed were greater leaders of vision – transformational presidents who could inspire and lift up the nation.

The election of Ronald Reagan in 1980 seemed to usher in just such a transformational leader. Domestically, his economic policies restored the economy. In foreign affairs, his great achievement was to restore America's standing in the world and to set the world on a path to ending the Cold War.

Questions and Answers

1. How was Nixon like Truman? (p. 396)

> Both were controversial and widely reviled in their times, and both left office with rock-bottom approval ratings. But the passage of time and the lessening of passions have led to significant reappraisals.

2. Nixon is a good example of why "it becomes more and more difficult to write about history with **perspective** and **balance** the more closely one's subject matter approaches **the present day.**" (p. 386)

3. Nixon was a **hardball** politician but also had a talent for **compromise** and **coalition** building. (p. 389)

4. "Balancing an assertive and consistently **anti-Communist national-security** policy with largely **moderate social and economic policies,** Nixon was always able to put together effective electoral combinations and eventually brought his formerly embattled party within hailing distance of majority status." (pp. 387–88)

> Teachers may remind students that under Goldwater, the Republican Party had become quite conservative. Nixon was *not* a conservative, but he was at least minimally acceptable to them, because he was such a strong anti-Communist, and that overriding priority was thought to outweigh his less conservative domestic policies.

5. What was Nixon's biggest piece of unfinished business upon coming into the White House? How did he deal with it? (p. 388)

> Advised by Henry Kissinger, Nixon implemented a strategy of "Vietnamization," withdrawing American troops as Kissinger negotiated an armistice, the Paris Peace Accords of 1973. Unfortunately, the agreement did not require the withdrawal of the North Vietnamese army from the South – ultimately a fatal mistake.

6. How did Nixon revise China policy?

He recognized Red China, opening diplomatic relations with it, thereby putting pressure on the Soviet Union, which feared a United States–China alliance. This was a practice of realism in foreign affairs. The United States would continue to support allies, but American national interest would be paramount.

7. Why could only Nixon have opened diplomacy with China? (p. 389)

Because he had impeccable credentials as an anti-Communist, he was immune to the accusation of being "soft on Communism."

8. Nixon's domestic policy was far less successful. Why? (pp. 390–91)

"The efforts of the Johnson administration to have both '**guns and butter**' – to expend vast sums of money both on the war in Vietnam and on large and lavish social programs, without imposing commiserate tax increases – had led to **large deficits and soaring inflation**." A recession followed, created partly by Nixon's clumsy efforts to raise interest rates. Democrats controlled Congress and were not cooperative. Nixon ended the convertibility of dollars into gold – Nixon's shock – which helped in the short run but created problems later.

9. What is *stagflation*? (pp. 390–91)

Keynesian economics held that a nation could either have a stable currency and less growth and higher unemployment or stimulate growth and full employment through government spending at the cost of inflation. But Nixon confronted a **stagnant economy plus runaway inflation**. He abandoned conservative orthodoxy to impose wage and price controls, treating the symptoms rather than the underlying disease.

Teachers may point out that postwar depressions are a common phenomenon in history, and Nixon was dealing with two "postwars": the military war in Vietnam and the still-continuing War on Poverty.

10. What was Nixon's New Federalism? (p. 391)

Nixon used "revenue sharing" to move power back to state and local levels, decreasing the centralization of government in Washington. It was not the original federalism of the Founders, but it was a move in a conservative direction, and the Democrats were willing to go along, an example of politics as "the art of the possible."

11. Nixon was reelected easily. But why was George McGovern in a sense the Democrats' Goldwater? (p. 391)

> He was a decent man but far too ideologically liberal (as Goldwater had been too conservative) to win a national election.
>
> Teachers may also point out that just as Goldwater conservatives seized permanent control of the Republican Party (by rewriting its rules), McGovern's liberal followers seized permanent control of the Democratic Party. Previously, both parties had been "big tent" coalitions across the ideological spectrum; there had been plenty of liberal Republicans (like Nelson Rockefeller) and also plenty of conservative Democrats. That is no longer the case; the range of beliefs within the Republican Party is now conservative to moderate, and the range for Democrats is liberal to moderate. The United States has had, since Goldwater and McGovern, two increasingly ideological parties.

12. What was "Watergate"? (pp. 392–93)

> Watergate was the name of an office complex used by the Democrats. "Burglars" working for Nixon's reelection campaign broke into it to plant listening devices and were arrested. Nixon's penchant for hardball politics got the better of him, and he allowed or indulged in "dirty tricks" that were eventually discovered after the "cover-up" failed. After a year of investigative journalism and congressional hearings, Nixon resigned rather than face near-certain impeachment.

13. What was Schlesinger's argument in *The Imperial Presidency*? (pp. 393–94)

> He argued that the presidency was out of control, expanding its power, and particularly leading to "indiscriminate global intervention."
>
> Teachers may point out the irony that Schlesinger made his reputation early on as a historian of Andrew Jackson (a very strong and active executive) and also served as advisor and speechwriter for John F. Kennedy, whose presidency was often likened to "Camelot" (King Arthur). Perhaps Schlesinger, like most of us, is OK with overly powerful leaders, as long as they are "our guys."

14. Who were the main victims of Nixon's downfall? (p. 395)

> The Democrats gained forty-nine seats in Congress and were sure to win the presidency in 1976 after President Ford (wisely and courageously) pardoned Nixon. But the main victims were the peoples of Southeast Asia. Congress refused to fund aid to South Vietnam, to uphold the peace

agreement Nixon and Kissinger had brokered, and the North quickly conquered the South. Even worse was the takeover of Cambodia by the Khmer Rouge, who massacred more than a million of their own people to eliminate "Western influences."

15. What event was most noteworthy of a generally very successful Bicentennial celebration? (pp. 396–97)

Most noteworthy was the Parade of Ships, tall ships from all over the world. (See the photo on the next-to-last page of the gallery.)

16. How did the election of 1976 turn out? (pp. 397–98)

Jimmy Carter started with a huge advantage and was a fresh face, but Ford fought hard, and Carter's inexperience showed in the first debate. But Ford and his running mate, Bob Dole, made injudicious comments in following debates, and Carter won a narrow victory in a low-turn-out election. Ronald Reagan challenged Ford for the nomination, unsuccessfully, but was clearly the next man in line for the Republicans in 1980.

17. How did Carter signal his rejection of the "imperial presidency"? (p. 398)

He walked to his inauguration, often dressed informally, and so on.

18. Why was Carter ineffective in dealing with energy policy and inflation?

He failed to include key political and industrial leaders in his deliberations and was generally impatient with the wheeling-and-dealing involved in practical politics. Inflation reached 14.76 percent in March 1980.

Teachers may wish to point out the realities of inflation in their effect on long-term borrowing like home mortgages. If a homeowner is paying 5 percent interest on her loan but inflation is 6 percent, the borrower is essentially getting "free" money, using less valuable money to pay back the more valuable money of the original loan. If a lender wants to earn 5 percent interest and inflation is 6 percent, the lender needs to charge 11 percent (5 percent plus 6 percent). But lenders have to guess what future inflation will be if they are lending money for twenty or thirty years, as is typical for home purchases. By 1980, many banks simply would not make home loans, which means people could neither buy nor sell their houses.

19. What was Carter's great foreign policy triumph? (p. 399)

He brokered a treaty between Egypt and Israel, the Camp David Accords. Success was only partial, and Egyptian president Sadat was assassinated by Islamic extremists, but it did mean Egyptian recognition of Israel.

20. What was Carter's great foreign policy disaster? (p. 399)

Iran – after Carter allowed the deposed shah to come to America for cancer treatment, Iranian militants stormed the U.S. embassy in Tehran and held more than fifty Americans hostage for 444 days. A rescue mission had to be aborted. The hostages were not released until Reagan was about to take office.

21. How did Carter respond to the Soviet invasion of Afghanistan? (p. 400)

We cancelled American participation in the Moscow Summer Olympics.

22. What are "transactional" and "transformative" leaders? (p. 400)

The first (e.g., Carter) operates within existing boundaries, rules, and limitations. The second (FDR historically, and Reagan) develops fresh political possibilities. (Politics can be defined, remember, as "the art of the possible.")

23. What were the groups composing the rising conservative movement that chose Reagan as its standard-bearer? What were the basics of conservative ideology? (pp. 400–401)

Social conservatives clashed with libertarians on issues like drug law. Some conservatives favored an American withdrawal from world leadership, while others thought U.S. leadership was vital. But there was a rough consensus on smaller government with lower taxes, an economy relatively free of government regulation, and anti-Communism.

24. How did Reagan's early life and career shape him? (p. 401)

He had been a liberal Democrat and retained the example of FDR as "a purveyor of hope and a prophet of possibility." He had the good looks and speaking skills of a Hollywood actor and (teachers may note) had been president of the Screen Actors Guild and engaged in hard-nosed negotiations with studio chiefs.

25. Reagan was thoroughly conservative and skilled at coalition building, joining the **evangelicals** in the so-called Religious Right with **blue-collar urban Catholics,** and both sets of social conservatives with **libertarian businessmen and free-market enthusiasts.** (pp. 401–2)

26. What was the outcome of the 1980 election? (p. 402)

Reagan carried forty-four states and 489 electoral votes, and the Republicans carried the Senate.

27. What was Reagan's tax policy? What was the result? (pp. 403–4)

He slashed personal income taxes 25 percent, reduced the top rate to 28 percent, and created tax-deferred individual retirement accounts (IRAs). Reagan also chopped business taxes and cut the budgets of many government programs.

In the short term, there was a recession, as the Federal Reserve imposed tight monetary policies to bring inflation under control. But by 1983, inflation was down to 2.5 percent, and the economy was growing steadily. Twenty million new jobs were created, and even with the tax cuts, government revenues doubled from $517 billion in 1980 to more than $1 trillion in 1990.

Teachers should explain that lower tax rates still produce increased revenue if the economy is growing.

28. What was Reagan's chief regret and failure? (p. 404)

Reagan did not reduce the size or cost of government as he had hoped to do. The national debt grew sharply, and government spending (especially on entitlements) rose by 102 percent.

29. What was Reagan's strategy for the Cold War? (p. 404)

"We win, they lose." The details changed, but the objective remained. This represented the abandonment of the containment strategy of the past thirty plus years.

30. How did Reagan win? (pp. 404–5)

He labeled the Soviet Union an "evil empire" and "the focus of evil in the modern world." He armed the Afghans resisting the Soviet invasion. He built up the U.S. military. He supported, with the help of Polish pope John Paul II, the anti-Communist labor movement in Poland, Solidarity, which eventually brought down the Communist regime there. He challenged the Soviets to an arms race – an anti-missile defense system, Star Wars – an immensely expensive competition that the Soviets could not refuse and could not win; the result, combined with U.S. and Saudi action to keep oil prices low, brought the Soviets to the brink of bankruptcy. He committed troops to prevent a Soviet base on Grenada. He supported Contra guerillas against the Soviet-supported regime in Nicaragua.

31. How did Reagan handle the "Euromissile crisis"? (p. 406)

> He first built up U.S. missiles in Europe, in the face of heated opposition. He refused to negotiate unless the new Soviet leader, Mikael Gorbachev, demonstrated a willingness to change. Eventually, an agreement was reached to abolish intermediate-range ballistic missiles, an actual reduction in both sides' nuclear arsenals.

32. Was Reagan or Gorbachev more responsible for the collapse of the Soviet Union? Did Soviet Communism fall? Or was it pushed? (pp. 406–7)

> Someone like Gorbachev was needed, but he was responding to Reagan's pressure. Reagan saw that Soviet Communisn was tottering and then pushed.

Objective Questions

Answers are in parentheses.

Put in order:

_____ Camp David Accords	(2)
_____ "evil empire" speech	(3)
_____ opening of diplomatic relations with China	(1)

Put in order:

_____ Ford presidency	(3)
_____ New Federalism	(1)
_____ Watergate	(2)

Document

RONALD REAGAN, REMARKS AT THE BRANDENBURG GATE, WEST BERLIN, JUNE 12, 1987

Chancellor Kohl, Governing Mayor Diepgen, ladies and gentlemen: Twenty-four years ago, President John F. Kennedy visited Berlin, and speaking to the people of this city and the world at the city hall. Well since then two other presidents have come, each in his turn to Berlin. And today, I, myself, make my second visit to your city.

We come to Berlin, we American Presidents, because it's our duty to speak in this place of freedom. But I must confess, we're drawn here by other things as well; by the feeling of history in this city – more than 500 years older than our own nation; by the beauty of the Grunewald and the Tiergarten; most of all, by your courage and determination. Perhaps the composer, Paul Linke, understood something about American Presidents. You see, like so many Presidents before me, I come here today because wherever I go, whatever I do: *Ich hab noch einen Koffer in Berlin* [I still have a suitcase in Berlin].

Our gathering today is being broadcast throughout Western Europe and North America. I understand that it is being seen and heard as well in the East. To those listening throughout Eastern Europe, I extend my warmest greetings and the good will of the American people. To those listening in East Berlin, a special word: Although I cannot be with you, I address my remarks to you just as surely as to those standing here before me. For I join you, as I join your fellow countrymen in the West, in this firm, this unalterable belief: *Es gibt nur ein Berlin* [There is only one Berlin].

Behind me stands a wall that encircles the free sectors of this city, part of a vast system of barriers that divides the entire continent of Europe. From the Baltic South, those barriers cut across Germany in a gash of barbed wire, concrete, dog runs, and guard towers. Farther south, there may be no visible, no obvious wall. But there remain armed guards and checkpoints all the same – still a restriction on the right to travel, still an instrument to impose upon ordinary men and women the will of a totalitarian state.

Yet, it is here in Berlin where the wall emerges most clearly; here, cutting across your city, where the news photo and the television screen have imprinted this brutal division of a continent upon the mind of the world.

Standing before the Brandenburg Gate, every man is a German separated from his fellow men.

Every man is a Berliner, forced to look upon a scar.

President Von Weizsäcker has said, "The German question is open as long as the Brandenburg Gate is closed." Well today – today I say: As long as this gate is closed, as long as this scar of a wall is permitted to stand, it is not the German question alone that remains open, but the question of freedom for all mankind.

Yet, I do not come here to lament. For I find in Berlin a message of hope, even in the shadow of this wall, a message of triumph.

In this season of spring in 1945, the people of Berlin emerged from their air-raid shelters to find devastation. Thousands of miles away, the people of the United States reached out to help. And in 1947 Secretary of State – as you've been told – George Marshall announced the creation of what would become known as the Marshall Plan. Speaking precisely 40 years ago this month, he said: "Our policy is directed not against any country or doctrine, but against hunger, poverty, desperation, and chaos."

In the Reichstag a few moments ago, I saw a display commemorating this 40th anniversary of the Marshall Plan. I was struck by a sign – the sign on a burnt-out, gutted structure that was being rebuilt. I understand that Berliners of my own generation can remember seeing signs like it dotted throughout the western sectors of the city. The sign read simply: "The Marshall Plan is helping here to strengthen the free world." A strong, free world in the West – that dream became real. Japan rose from ruin to become an economic giant. Italy, France, Belgium – virtually every nation in Western Europe saw political and economic rebirth; the European Community was founded.

In West Germany and here in Berlin, there took place an economic miracle, the *Wirtschaftswunder* [Miracle on the Rhine]. Adenauer, Erhard, Reuter, and other leaders understood the practical importance of liberty – that just as truth can flourish only when the journalist is given freedom of speech, so prosperity can come about only when the farmer and businessman enjoy economic freedom. The German leaders – the German leaders reduced tariffs, expanded free trade, lowered taxes. From 1950 to 1960 alone, the standard of living in West Germany and Berlin doubled.

Where four decades ago there was rubble, today in West Berlin there is the greatest industrial output of any city in Germany: busy office blocks, fine homes and apartments, proud avenues, and the spreading lawns of parkland. Where a city's culture seemed to have been destroyed, today there are two great universities, orchestras and an opera, countless theaters, and museums. Where there was want, today there's abundance – food, clothing, automobiles – the wonderful goods of the Kudamm. From devastation, from utter ruin, you Berliners have, in freedom, rebuilt a city that once again ranks as one of the greatest on earth. Now the Soviets may have had other plans. But my friends, there were a few things the Soviets didn't count on: *Berliner Herz, Berliner Humor, ja, und Berliner Schnauze* [Berliner heart, Berliner humor, yes, and a Berliner Schnauze].

In the 1950s – In the 1950s Khrushchev predicted: "We will bury you."

But in the West today, we see a free world that has achieved a level of prosperity and well-being unprecedented in all human history. In the Communist world, we see failure, technological backwardness, declining standards of health, even want of the most basic kind – too little food. Even today, the Soviet Union still cannot feed itself. After these four decades, then, there stands before the entire world one great and inescapable conclusion: Freedom leads to prosperity. Freedom replaces the ancient hatreds among nations with comity and peace. Freedom is the victor.

And now – Now the Soviets themselves may, in a limited way, be coming to understand the importance of freedom. We hear much from Moscow about a new policy of reform and openness. Some political prisoners have been released. Certain foreign news broadcasts are no longer being jammed. Some economic enterprises have been permitted to operate with greater freedom from state control.

Are these the beginnings of profound changes in the Soviet state? Or are they token gestures intended to raise false hopes in the West, or to strengthen the Soviet system without changing it? We welcome change and openness; for we believe that freedom and security go together, that the advance of human liberty – the advance of human liberty can only strengthen the cause of world peace.

There is one sign the Soviets can make that would be unmistakable, that would advance dramatically the cause of freedom and peace.

General Secretary Gorbachev, if you seek peace, if you seek prosperity for the Soviet Union and Eastern Europe, if you seek liberalization: Come here to this gate.

Mr. Gorbachev, open this gate.

Mr. Gorbachev – Mr. Gorbachev, tear down this wall!

I understand the fear of war and the pain of division that afflict this continent, and I pledge to you my country's efforts to help overcome these burdens. To be sure, we in the West must resist Soviet expansion. So, we must maintain defenses of unassailable strength. Yet we seek peace; so we must strive to reduce arms on both sides.

Beginning 10 years ago, the Soviets challenged the Western alliance with a grave new threat, hundreds of new and more deadly SS-20 nuclear missiles capable of striking every capital in Europe. The Western alliance responded by committing itself to a counter-deployment (unless the Soviets agreed to negotiate a better solution) – namely, the elimination of such weapons on both sides. For many months, the Soviets refused to bargain in earnestness. As the alliance, in turn, prepared to go forward with its counter-deployment, there were difficult days, days of protests like those during my 1982 visit to this city; and the Soviets later walked away from the table.

But through it all, the alliance held firm. And I invite those who protested then – I invite those who protest today – to mark this fact: Because we remained strong, the Soviets came back to the table. Because we remained strong, today we have within reach the possibility, not merely of limiting the growth of arms, but of eliminating, for the first time, an entire class of nuclear weapons from the face of the earth.

As I speak, NATO ministers are meeting in Iceland to review the progress of our proposals for eliminating these weapons. At the talks in Geneva, we have also proposed deep cuts in strategic offensive weapons. And the Western allies have likewise made far-reaching proposals to reduce the danger of conventional war and to place a total ban on chemical weapons.

While we pursue these arms reductions, I pledge to you that we will maintain the capacity to deter Soviet aggression at any level at which it might occur. And in cooperation with many of our allies, the United States is pursuing the Strategic Defense Initiative – research to base deterrence not on the threat of offensive retaliation, but on defenses that truly defend; on systems, in short, that will not target populations, but shield them. By these means we seek to increase the safety of Europe and all the world. But we must remember a crucial fact: East and West do not mistrust each other because we are armed; we are armed because we mistrust each other. And our differences are not about weapons but about liberty. When President Kennedy spoke at the City Hall those 24 years ago, freedom was encircled; Berlin was under siege. And today, despite all the pressures upon this city, Berlin stands secure in its liberty. And freedom itself is transforming the globe.

In the Philippines, in South and Central America, democracy has been given a rebirth. Throughout the Pacific, free markets are working miracle after miracle of economic growth. In the industrialized nations, a technological revolution is taking place, a revolution marked by rapid, dramatic advances in computers and telecommunications.

In Europe, only one nation and those it controls refuse to join the community of freedom. Yet in this age of redoubled economic growth, of information and innovation, the Soviet Union faces a choice: It must make fundamental changes, or it will become obsolete.

Today, thus, represents a moment of hope. We in the West stand ready to cooperate with the East to promote true openness, to break down barriers that separate people, to create a safer, freer world. And surely there is no better place than Berlin, the meeting place of East and West, to make a start.

Free people of Berlin: Today, as in the past, the United States stands for the strict observance and full implementation of all parts of the Four Power Agreement of 1971. Let us use this occasion, the 750th anniversary of this city, to usher in a new era, to seek a still fuller, richer life for the Berlin of the future. Together, let us maintain and develop the ties between the Federal Republic and the Western sectors of Berlin, which is permitted by the 1971 agreement.

And I invite Mr. Gorbachev: Let us work to bring the Eastern and Western parts of the city closer together, so that all the inhabitants of all Berlin can enjoy the benefits that come with life in one of the great cities of the world.

To open Berlin still further to all Europe, East and West, let us expand the vital air access to this city, finding ways of making commercial air service to Berlin more convenient, more comfortable, and more economical. We look to the day when West Berlin can become one of the chief aviation hubs in all central Europe.

With – With our French – With our French and British partners, the United States is prepared to help bring international meetings to Berlin. It would be only fitting for Berlin to serve as the site of United Nations meetings, or world conferences on human rights and arms control, or other issues that call for international cooperation.

There is no better way to establish hope for the future than to enlighten young minds, and we would be honored to sponsor summer youth exchanges, cultural events, and other programs for young Berliners from the East. Our French and British friends, I'm certain, will do the same. And it's my hope that an authority can be found in East Berlin to sponsor visits from young people of the Western sectors.

One final proposal, one close to my heart: Sport represents a source of enjoyment and ennoblement, and you may have noted that the Republic of Korea – South Korea – has offered to permit certain events of the 1988 Olympics to take place in the North. International sports competitions of all kinds could take place in both parts of this city. And what better way to demonstrate to the world the openness of this city than to offer in some future year to hold the Olympic games here in Berlin, East and West.

In these four decades, as I have said, you Berliners have built a great city. You've done so in spite of threats – the Soviet attempts to impose the East-mark, the blockade. Today the city thrives in spite of the challenges implicit in the very presence of this wall. What keeps you here? Certainly there's a great deal to be said for your fortitude, for your defiant courage.

But I believe there's something deeper, something that involves Berlin's whole look and feel and way of life – not mere sentiment. No one could live long in Berlin without being completely disabused of illusions. Something, instead, that has seen the difficulties of life in Berlin but chose to accept them, that continues to build this good and proud city in contrast to a surrounding totalitarian presence, that refuses to release human energies or aspirations, something that speaks with a powerful voice of affirmation, that says "yes" to this city, yes to the future, yes to freedom. In a word, I would submit that what keeps you in Berlin – is "love."

Love both profound and abiding.

Perhaps this gets to the root of the matter, to the most fundamental distinction of all between East and West. The totalitarian world produces backwardness because it does such violence to the spirit, thwarting the human impulse to create, to enjoy, to worship. The totalitarian world finds even symbols of love and of worship an affront.

Years ago, before the East Germans began rebuilding their churches, they erected a secular structure: the television tower at Alexander Platz. Virtually ever since, the authorities have been working to correct what they view as the tower's one major flaw: treating the glass sphere at the top with paints and chemicals of every kind. Yet even today when the sun strikes that sphere, that sphere that towers over all Berlin, the light makes the sign of the cross. There in Berlin, like the city itself, symbols of love, symbols of worship, cannot be suppressed.

As I looked out a moment ago from the Reichstag, that embodiment of German unity, I noticed words crudely spray-painted upon the wall, perhaps by a young Berliner (quote):

"This wall will fall. Beliefs become reality."

Yes, across Europe, this wall will fall, for it cannot withstand faith; it cannot withstand truth. The wall cannot withstand freedom.

And I would like, before I close, to say one word. I have read, and I have been questioned since I've been here about certain demonstrations against my coming. And I would like to say just one thing, and to those who demonstrate so. I wonder if they have ever asked themselves that if they should have the kind of government they apparently seek, no one would ever be able to do what they're doing again.

Thank you and God bless you all. Thank you.

1. Why does Reagan call Berlin "this place of freedom"?

    He is recalling the central role played by West Berlin in the Cold War, its strategic importance in containing Soviet efforts to extend their control to the whole of Germany, and particularly its location, as an island of freedom in the middle of Communist (and Soviet-dominated) East Germany. It is in Berlin, too, that "the Wall" separating the free parts of Europe from the Communist-dominated ones is most painfully evident, since it runs across the city itself.

2. The most famous lines of the speech are directed at Soviet general secretary Mikhail Gorbachev. What are they?

    "Mr. Gorbachev, open this gate. Mr. Gorbachev – Mr. Gorbachev, tear down this wall!"

3. What are some of the places in which Reagan is seeing a new birth of freedom?

    He is seeing it in the Philippines and in South and Central America.

4. What is Reagan's advice for the Soviet Union?

    It must make fundamental changes or become obsolete.

5. What was the crisis over the SS-20s, and why was it so important?

    "Beginning 10 years ago, the Soviets challenged the Western alliance with a grave new threat, hundreds of new and more deadly SS-20 nuclear missiles capable of striking every capital in Europe. The Western alliance responded by committing itself to a counter-deployment (unless the Soviets agreed to negotiate a better solution) – namely, the elimination of such weapons on both sides. For many months, the Soviets refused to bargain in earnestness. As the alliance, in turn, prepared to go forward with its counter-deployment, there were difficult days, days of protests like those during my 1982 visit to this city; and the Soviets later walked away from the table. But through it all, the alliance held firm."

6. How does Reagan turn the tables against the protesters against his visit?

    He does so by pointing out that, if they were to get the kind of government they wanted, they would no longer be able to mount protests.

CHAPTER TWENTY-TWO

THE WORLD SINCE THE COLD WAR

Summary

THIS CHAPTER OPENS with an observation on the nature of history and that the closer we get to the present, the more difficult it is to arrive at historical assessments. And so this chapter considers the era since the end of the Cold War in more general terms, with less detailed emphasis on a political narrative and greater focus on larger themes and questions facing Americans in the days to come.

In general, the end of the Cold War gave rise to many questions that have yet to be answered, both about our role in the world and about our ability to address serious problems facing the country. Domestically, the presidencies of George H. W. Bush, Bill Clinton, George W. Bush, Barack Obama, and Donald Trump have been characterized by increasing partisanship and increasing mistrust in America's institutions. Through an increasingly partisan divide, Congress has been unwilling to solve serious problems facing the country; the example given in this chapter is our national debt.

Internationally, the end of the Cold War raised many questions about the new international order and our role in that order. President H. W. Bush "presided" over the end of the Cold War and led an international coalition in Operation Desert Storm to protect an emerging new world order that would be lawful, democratic, peaceful. Each of his successors contended with violent, aggressive threats to the peaceful world order hoped for by George H. W. Bush. Most prominent, of course was the attack on the United States on September 11, 2001, by radical Islamic terrorists. But every president since GHW Bush has faced challenges from Islamic terrorists.

Questions and Answers

1. "Part of the discipline of thinking historically is developing the ability to be **skeptical** of what we think we see plainly before our eyes and of what 'everyone is saying' in the present moment." (p. 408)

> Teachers may invite students to name professions whose skill is making things seem like something they are not. Advertisers and politicians come immediately to mind.

2. "If history teaches us anything, it is that we only rarely have the power to grasp the **meaning of events** as they are occurring. Live long enough, and you will find out how true that is." (p. 408)

3. Most of the rest of this chapter comprises summaries, in turn, of the presidencies of George H. W. Bush, Bill Clinton, George W. Bush, Barak Obama, and Donald Trump (in progress). How aware does each seem to have been of the new range of "characteristic problems and issues that have emerged" since the end of the Cold War, and how effective does each seem to have been in dealing with them? What are those problems and issues? (pp. 408–9)

4. George H. W. Bush presided over the collapse of the Soviet Union, but did so with sober and cautious restraint. He "could sense that with the end of the Cold War, there were profound changes coming, many of which would be hard to predict." (pp. 410–11) Was Bush's presidency a success? In what respects? Why or why not? Be prepared to defend your position in class or in writing.

5. The Cold War had provided "**an ordering principle** to American foreign policy and much of American domestic life, even the nation's **self-understanding,** for half a century." (p. 411)

6. What is going to take the place of the Cold War as an ordering principle? (p. 411)

> Would the vast national-security state continue to be necessary? How would the post–Cold War world reorder itself? Would it be American led? Would it be a harmonious association of diverse, peace-loving nations? Would the new world order be a cosmopolitan one, with a global economy superseding all national ones? Would capital and people move freely across national boundaries? And would those boundaries all but disappear, and the primacy of national cultures and national identities disappear along with them? Or would the world revert to

something like the old balance-of-power national politics that had ordered Europe during the nineteenth century?

Teachers may wish to provide students with a few useful terms for understanding "world order." These assume that nation-states are the basic "building blocks" of international relations:

A unilateral system, usually called a *hegemony*, has a single superpower dominating every other nation or alliance of nations. The British Empire, thanks to its navy, had a worldwide hegemony between 1815 and the threat of a German naval buildup before World War I.

A *multilateral* system is one in which many nations are broadly equal in power. Preserving the balance of power may require many small wars but prevent a large one. Europe during the period 1648 to the late 1800s was this type of system. Attempts to establish a French hegemony under Louis XIV and then under Napoleon led to coalitions of nations surrounding France joining to maintain a multilateral European system.

A *bilateral* system has every nation in one of two camps. Europe became bilateral before 1914 with the formation of the Triple Alliance and Triple Entente. Most of the world was like this during the Cold War. Bilateral systems have fewer wars, but any war that does come may be the big one, the Great War.

It is possible, and perhaps likely if there is no single superpower, that particular regions may develop their own systems. For example, the establishment of Israel created a bilateral system in the Middle East, with Israel (backed by the United States) on one side and surrounding Islamic nations on the other. That system began to break apart following the Camp David Accords and, with Iranian and Russian involvement, is now (in 2020) multilateral.

A bilateral world order is very frightening, particularly when each side has a nuclear arsenal. But a multilateral world order is far harder to predict or control, and may well be even more frightening, especially when many nations, or perhaps even nonnations, have nuclear or other weapons of mass destruction.

The rise of "nonstate actors" such as al-Qaeda (especially considering the risk of new weapons of mass destruction) has given a pretty clear answer to the question of whether the vast security apparatus is still needed. But how much, and at what cost to liberty?

7. How did Desert Storm reflect a world picture that corresponded to the writing of Francis Fukuyama? What did he mean that we had reached "the end of history"? (p. 412)

Fukuyama meant that "all the possible alternatives to Western-style liberal-democratic capitalism had been exhausted." A U.S.-led coalition liberated Kuwait from Saddam Hussein but did not destroy his regime. This reflected the old containment doctrine of the Cold War. Hussein had blatantly violated the rules of the emerging new world order, and the "coalition of the willing" had enforced the rules and restored the order.

Teachers may suggest that students contrast the treatment accorded to Saddam Hussein by George H. W. Bush ("Bush 1") after Desert Storm in 1991, and then again by George W. Bush ("Bush 2") in 2003, when the Iraqi regime was overthrown and its leader executed. Bush 1 was criticized for allowing the Iraqi army to escape from Kuwait and for not overthrowing Saddam, whose regime was one of the most brutal in the world. Bush 2 corrected that mistake – if mistake it was. For Bush 2's attempt at "nation building" in Iraq failed, and the destruction of Iraq as a regional power contributed to the rise of Iran (which had been fighting a long, bloody, and indecisive war with Iraq) into a far greater threat to American interests than Iraq had ever been. Bush 2's efforts to turn Iraq into a democracy were also consistent with the "end of history" idea.

8. What was Samuel Huntington's theory in *The Clash of Civilizations* about the new world "order"? (p. 413)

He argued that the end of the Cold War between the United States and the Soviet Union, an ideological conflict, would likely be followed by conflicts, not between ideas or countries, but between civilizations. "The most important distinctions among peoples are no longer ideological, political, or economic; they are cultural." The chief conflicts of the future are likely to be between Western civilization, the Muslim world, and China.

Teachers may point out that some used to argue that there would never be a war between two Communist nations, because the workers of the world would never go to war against themselves. Yet we have now had sustained conflicts between Communist countries. Wars between and among Islamic nations are frequent, despite a common culture. Huntington's theory has some obvious validity and utility, but it seems premature to abandon emphasis on the nation-state just yet.

9. Historian Daniel T. Rodgers says we are living in an "**age of fracture**" in which all shared narratives are called into question. (p. 414)

> Teachers may illustrate this, perhaps, by asking what common cultural knowledge their students share – what things they all already knew before starting the course. Do they all know the old Mother Goose nursery rhymes, for example? Probably not, though they are more likely all to be familiar with Disney characters. They almost certainly do not all know the stories from the Hebrew and Christian Bible. Perhaps they all know of Paul Revere or Betsy Ross – but likely not.

10. Was Bill Clinton's presidency a success? In what respects? Why and why not? Be prepared to defend your answer in class or in writing. (pp. 415–16)

11. *For Thought:* The nation rallied behind Bush 2 after the 9/11 attacks, but this harmony did not last long. Are the occasions for national unity fewer and further between? And shorter lived? And are any other events besides an attack from outside likely to produce such unity? Be prepared to defend your position in class or in writing.

12. What were the political effects of the Great Recession of 2007–8? (p. 417)

> It wrecked Bush 2's presidency and led to the election of Barack Obama. But more broadly, "many Americans felt that those who were most responsible did not suffer any of the consequences.... It would further a growing disaffection with both parties, and distrust of government itself, and of the elite classes whose interest the government seemed to serve."

13. Barack Obama's election was epochal, but was his presidency a success? In what respects? Why or why not? Be prepared to defend your answer in class or in writing. (p. 418)

14. "It is far too early at this juncture to make any judgments or predictions about Donald Trump's success or failure. But two things can be said with relative confidence. First, while Trump seems unlikely to be the architect of a fresh national consensus, he has brought to the fore certain ideas, notably the emphasis on **a strong sense of nationalism,** that appear to be on the rise in much of the world, as in Great Britain and Italy.... And second, his election itself and the brutal, nonstop political combat that has ensued since it are symptomatic of the **growing distrust of established American political and governmental institutions** felt by a significant portion of the American public." (p. 419)

15. What is the great unresolved and bipartisan problem illustrating the dysfunction of our political system? (p. 420)

> It is the national debt, and the consequent imperilment of the nation's public credit. The debt is above $22 trillion, and our gross domestic product about $20 trillion, meaning our debt is now larger than our economy.
>
> It is a problem all can see and agree needs to be remedied. What is lacking is political will, which ultimately must come from We the People and not from politicians.

16. Review the opening passage from John Dos Passos. It is just when old institutions are caving in and being replaced by new ones that we most need to look **backward as well as forward.** (p. 422)

Objective Question

Answers are in parentheses.

Put in order:

_____	9/11 attacks	(2)
_____	Desert Storm	(1)
_____	execution of Saddam Hussein	(3)

Document

GEORGE W. BUSH, REMARKS AT THE NATIONAL DAY OF PRAYER AND REMEMBRANCE SERVICE, WASHINGTON NATIONAL CATHEDRAL, SEPTEMBER 14, 2001

We are here in the middle hour of our grief. So many have suffered so great a loss, and today we express our nation's sorrow. We come before God to pray for the missing and the dead, and for those who loved them. On Tuesday, our country was attacked with deliberate and massive cruelty. We have seen the images of fire and ashes and bent steel.

Now come the names, the list of casualties we are only beginning to read:

They are the names of men and women who began their day at a desk or in an airport, busy with life.

They are the names of people who faced death and in their last moments called home to say, be brave and I love you.

They are the names of passengers who defied their murderers and prevented the murder of others on the ground.

They are the names of men and women who wore the uniform of the United States and died at their posts.

They are the names of rescuers – the ones whom death found running up the stairs and into the fires to help others.

We will read all these names. We will linger over them and learn their stories, and many Americans will weep.

To the children and parents and spouses and families and friends of the lost, we offer the deepest sympathy of the nation. And I assure you, you are not alone. Just three days removed from these events, Americans do not yet have the distance of history, but our responsibility to history is already clear: to answer these attacks and rid the world of evil.

War has been waged against us by stealth and deceit and murder. This nation is peaceful, but fierce when stirred to anger. This conflict was begun on the timing and terms of others; it will end in a way and at an hour of our choosing. Our purpose as a nation is firm, yet our wounds as a people are recent and unhealed and lead us to pray. In many of our prayers this week, there's a searching and an honesty. At St. Patrick's Cathedral in New York, on Tuesday, a woman said, "I pray to God to give us a sign that He's still here."

Others have prayed for the same, searching hospital to hospital, carrying pictures of those still missing. God's signs are not always the ones we look for. We learn in tragedy that His purposes are not always our own, yet the prayers of private suffering, whether in our homes or in this great cathedral are known and heard and understood. There are prayers that help us last through the day or endure the night. There are prayers of friends and strangers that give us strength for the journey, and there are prayers that yield our will to a Will greater than our own.

This world He created is of moral design. Grief and tragedy and hatred are only for a time. Goodness, remembrance and love have no end, and the Lord of life holds all who die and all who mourn.

It is said that adversity introduces us to ourselves. This is true of a nation as well. In this trial, we have been reminded and the world has seen that our fellow Americans are generous and kind, resourceful and brave.

We see our national character in rescuers working past exhaustion, in long lines of blood donors, in thousands of citizens who have asked to work and serve in any way possible.

And we have seen our national character in eloquent acts of sacrifice:

Inside the World Trade Center, one man who could have saved himself stayed until the end and at the side of his quadriplegic friend.

A beloved priest died giving the last rites to a firefighter.

Two office workers, finding a disabled stranger, carried her down 68 floors to safety.

A group of men drove through the night from Dallas to Washington to bring skin grafts for burned victims.

In these acts and many others, Americans showed a deep commitment to one another and an abiding love for our country.

Today, we feel what Franklin Roosevelt called "the warm courage of national unity." This is a unity of every faith and every background. It has joined together political parties and both houses of Congress. It is evident in services of prayer and candlelight vigils and American flags, which are displayed in pride and waved in defiance. Our unity is a kinship of grief and a steadfast resolve to prevail against our enemies. And this unity against terror is now extending across the world.

America is a nation full of good fortune, with so much to be grateful for, but we are not spared from suffering. In every generation, the world has produced enemies of human freedom. They have attacked America because we are freedom's home and defender, and the commitment of our Fathers is now the calling of our time.

On this national day of prayer and remembrance, we ask Almighty God to watch over our nation and grant us patience and resolve in all that is to come. We pray that He will comfort and console those who now walk in sorrow. We thank Him for each life we now must mourn, and the promise of a life to come.

As we've been assured, neither death nor life nor angels nor principalities, nor powers nor things present nor things to come nor height nor depth can separate us from God's love. May He bless the souls of the departed. May He comfort our own. And may He always guide our country.

God bless America.

Document Questions

1. Bush's speech came three days after the 9/11 attacks on New York, Washington, D.C., and Pennsylvania by Islamist terrorists and was delivered at the National Cathedral in Washington. How does the speech reflect those things?

> It concentrates, at least at the outset, on mourning the loss of those who died. They are mentioned before any mention of the national purpose.

2. "Our responsibility to history is already clear: to answer these attacks and rid the world of evil." Was this an appropriate response?

> It was right for Bush to promise an "answer" to the attacks but wrong to promise to "rid the world of evil," something that no political leader can possibly do.

3. How does Bush answer those who fear that God might not "still be here"?

> He asks them to remember that God's signs are not necessarily the same things that we are looking for, but that is not a reason to doubt that the world has a "moral design."

4. What positive signs does Bush see coming out of these horrible events?

> He sees a willingness to sacrifice for others, a sign that the American national character is still strong, still capable of love and commitment to one another. "Our unity," he says, "is a kinship of grief and a steadfast resolve to prevail against our enemies."

5. How does Bush present the motives of the attackers?

> "They have attacked America because we are freedom's home and defender, and the commitment of our Fathers is now the calling of our time."

THE SHAPE OF
AMERICAN PATRIOTISM

Summary

AND OF HOPE IS OFFERED as a contribution to the making of American citizens. As such, it is a patriotic endeavor as well as a scholarly one, and it never loses sight of what there is to celebrate and cherish in the American achievement. That doesn't mean it is an uncritical celebration. The two things, celebration and criticism, are not necessarily enemies. Love is the foundation of the wisest criticism, and criticism is the basis of a judicious love. We live in a country whose flaws can always be openly discussed and where criticism and dissent are not betrayals or thought crimes but essential ingredients in the flourishing of our polity and our common life. We should not take these aspects of our country for granted. They have not been the condition of most human associations through most of human history, and they do not automatically perpetuate themselves. Hence they are among the very things we must be zealous to guard and protect rather than leaving them to chance.

So what do we mean by "patriotism"? If it means an unreflective love for what is one's own, then patriotism is something universal, shared by people everywhere. But American patriotism is not a simple thing and is not to be had in a visceral, unreflective way. There are at least two distinct aspects to American patriotism, and each one has its valid place.

Some argue that America is best understood not as a country in the usual sense but as an idea, or the embodiment of a set of ideas – a nation dedicated to, and held together by, a set of propositions, particularly those expressed in the preamble of the Declaration of Independence, propositions that apply universally. The defense of the United States, in this view, is not merely the protection of a particular society with a particular regime and a particular culture and history, inhabiting a particular piece of real estate, whose chief virtue is the fact that it is "ours"; it is something far greater and more inclusive than that.

This is a very powerful view, reflected in the fact that the United States has, for so much of its history, been so welcoming to immigrants. It sees that the particular mission of America is part of the universal quest of humanity.

But it is also balanced by the view that what binds Americans is not something universal but something unique: a shared story, a shared history. The American past is an essential part of American national identity, and it is something quite different from the "idea" of America. But it is every bit as powerful, if not more so. And it is a very *particular* force. Our nation's particular triumphs, sacrifices, and sufferings – and our memories of those things – draw and hold us together, precisely because they are the sacrifices and sufferings, not of all humanity, but of us alone. In this view, there is no more profoundly American place than Arlington National Cemetery or the Civil War battleground of Antietam or Gettysburg or Shiloh.

So there is a vital tension in the makeup of American patriotism, a tension between its universalizing ideals and its particularizing sentiments, with their emphasis on memory, history, tradition, culture, and the land. The genius of American patriotism permits both to coexist, and even to be harmonized to a considerable extent, therefore making them both available to be drawn upon in the rich, but mixed, phenomenon of American patriotism. It would be a mistake to insist on one while excluding the other. They both are always in conversation with one another, and they need to be.

That conversation, to be a real and honest one, must include the good, the bad, and the ugly, the ways we have failed and fallen short, not merely what is pleasing to our national self-esteem. But by the same token, the great story, the thread that we share, should not be lost in a blizzard of details or a hailstorm of rebukes. America is, and remains, a land of hope, a land to which much of the rest of the world longs to come.

Questions and Answers

1. What is the difference between being objective and being neutral? (p. 423)

    Being objective means listening to all sides, even when it involves confronting unpleasant and shameful things in our past. But neutrality implies indifference about the outcome.

    Teachers may suggest an analogy: if someone I love has a serious problem – perhaps he is an alcoholic – I would want to be objective in diagnosing and treating it. But I would hardly be neutral about the outcome!

2. "The two things, **celebration and criticism,** are not necessarily enemies. **Love** is the foundation of the wisest criticism, and criticism is the essential partner of an honest and enduring **love.**" (p. 423)

G. K. Chesterton states this powerfully (Pimlico was a horrible slum in London, and Chelsea was an upper-class neighborhood):

Let us suppose we are confronted with a desperate thing – say Pimlico. If we think what is really best for Pimlico we shall find the thread of thought leads to the throne or the mystic and the arbitrary. It is not enough for a man to disapprove of Pimlico: in that case he will merely cut his throat or move to Chelsea. Nor, certainly, is it enough for a man to approve of Pimlico: for then it will remain Pimlico, which would be awful. The only way out of it seems to be for somebody to love Pimlico: to love it with a transcendental tie and without any earthly reason. If there arose a man who loved Pimlico, then Pimlico would rise into ivory towers and golden pinnacles; Pimlico would attire herself as a woman does when she is loved. For decoration is not given to hide horrible things: but to decorate things already adorable. A mother does not give her child a blue bow because he is so ugly without it. A lover does not give a girl a necklace to hide her neck. If men loved Pimlico as mothers love children, arbitrarily, because it is theirs, Pimlico in a year or two might be fairer than Florence. Some readers will say that this is a mere fantasy. I answer that this is the actual history of mankind. This, as a fact, is how cities did grow great. Go back to the darkest roots of civilization and you will find them knotted round some sacred stone or encircling some sacred well. People first paid honour to a spot and afterwards gained glory for it. Men did not love Rome because she was great. She was great because they had loved her.

3. "We live in a country, let us hope, in which our flaws can always be openly discussed, and where criticism and dissent can be regarded not as **betrayals or thought crimes** but as essential ingredients in the flourishing of our polity and our common life." Yet we must not take this for granted; it is far from universal and does not perpetuate itself. (pp. 423–24)

4. Why is patriotism often treated as a dangerous sentiment, when it is such a natural thing? (p. 424)

> Breathes there the man with soul so dead,
> Who never to himself hath said,
> This is my own, my native land!
> Whose heart hath ne'er within him burn'd,
> As home his footsteps he hath turn'd
> From wandering on a foreign strand!
>   SIR WALTER SCOTT

"One of the deepest needs of the human soul is a sense of membership, of joy in what we have and hold in common with others."

Part of the answer is American individualism and the admiration we feel toward nonconformity. We also are suspicious of our government, and the greater the power, the greater the suspicion – and the reasons for suspicion. (p. 424)

5. Why is refining and elevating American patriotism not an easy task? (p. 424)

"Because American patriotism is not a simple thing. America can be hard to see because America itself is more than one thing."

6. What was the debate over the word "homeland" after 9/11? (p. 425)

It reminded some of the German concept of *Heimat*, a fatherland of blood and soil. But such an idea is alien to the pattern of American national identity.

7. What is the fundamental clash of perceptions about American national identity? (p. 425)

Is America something geographic or ethnic? Or is it a community built around widespread consent to a universal civic idea of "freedom"? A creed rather than a culture? Not shared descent but shared consent? Teachers will want to open this question for discussion.

8. As a nation of immigrants, Americans are made "**not so much by birth** as by a process of **agreeing to and consciously appropriating the ideas** that make America what it is." (p. 425)

9. Hamilton contended in *Federalist* 1 that America was to be a **test case** for all humankind, deciding whether it is possible for good governments to be constructed by "**reflection and choice**" rather than relying on "**accident and force**." (p. 425)

10. What is the other element, besides a strong sense of universalism, in American national self-consciousness and patriotism, if it is not "blood and soil"? (pp. 426–27)

> It is shared memories. "The nation, like the individual, is the culmination of a long past of endeavors, sacrifice, and devotion. To have common glories in the past and to have a common will in the present."
>
> "The ballast of the American past is an essential part of the American national identity, and it is something quite distinct from the 'idea' of America." (p. 426)

11. One finds this second element of national consciousness less **in academic settings** and more **in popular culture.** (p. 427)

12. "So there is a vital **tension** in the makeup of American patriotism, a **tension** between its universalizing ideals and its particularizing sentiments, with their emphasis upon memory, history, tradition, culture, and the land.... It would be a mistake to insist on one while excluding the other." (pp. 427–28)

13. Lincoln appealed to both in turn, with "the mystic chords of **memory,** stretching from every battle-field, and patriot grave, to every living heart and hearthstone," but also America as "the last best hope of earth." (p. 428)

> Teachers may, in class discussion or as written exercise, ask students to analyze particular expressions of American patriotism, stating whether each seems to reflect or appeal to a universal idea, or to a particular sentiment based on memory and shared experiences – or both. Here are a few (and of course there are many others):
>
> A. Walt Whitman, "I Hear American Singing," from *Leaves of Grass* (1860 edition)
>
> I hear America singing, the varied carols I hear,
> Those of mechanics, each one singing his as it should be blithe
>   and strong,
> The carpenter singing his as he measures his plank or beam,
> The mason singing his as he makes ready for work, or leaves off work,
> The boatman singing what belongs to him in his boat, the deckhand
>   singing on the steamboat deck,
> The shoemaker singing as he sits on his bench, the hatter singing
>   as he stands,
> The wood-cutter's song, the ploughboy's on his way in the morning,
>   or at noon intermission or at sundown,

The delicious singing of the mother, or of the young wife at work,
     or of the girl sewing or washing,
Each singing what belongs to him or her and to none else,
The day what belongs to the day – at night the party of young fellows,
     robust, friendly,
Singing with open mouths their strong melodious songs

B. Katharine Lee Bates, "America the Beautiful" (1911 version)

O beautiful for spacious skies,
For amber waves of grain,
For purple mountain majesties
Above the fruited plain!
America! America!
God shed His grace on thee
And crown thy good with brotherhood
From sea to shining sea!

O beautiful for pilgrim feet,
Whose stern, impassioned stress
A thoroughfare for freedom beat
Across the wilderness!
America! America!
God mend thine every flaw,
Confirm thy soul in self-control,
Thy liberty in law!

O beautiful for heroes proved
In liberating strife,
Who more than self their country loved
And mercy more than life!
America! America!
May God thy gold refine,
Till all success be nobleness,
And every gain divine!

O beautiful for patriot dream
That sees beyond the years
Thine alabaster cities gleam
Undimmed by human tears!

America! America!
God shed His grace on thee
And crown thy good with brotherhood
From sea to shining sea!

C. Lee Greenwood, "God Bless the USA" (1983)

If tomorrow all my things were gone,
I'd worked for all my life.
And I had to start again,
With just my children and my wife.

I'd thank my lucky stars,
To be livin' here today.
'Cause the flag still stands for freedom,
And they can't take that away.

And I'm proud to be an American,
Where at least I know I'm free.
And I won't forget the men who died,
Who gave that right to me.
And I gladly stand up,
Next to you and defend her still today.
'Cause there ain't no doubt I love this land,
God bless the USA.
From the lakes of Minnesota,
To the hills of Tennessee.
Across the plains of Texas,
From sea to shining sea.

From Detroit down to Houston,
And New York to L.A.
Well there's pride in every American heart,
And its time we stand and say

That I'm proud to be an American,
Where at least I know I'm free.
And I won't forget the men who died,
Who gave that right to me.
And I gladly stand up,

Next to you and defend her still today.
'Cause there ain't no doubt I love this land,
God bless the USA.

D. Langston Hughes, "Let America Be America Again" (1936)

Let America be America again.
Let it be the dream it used to be.
Let it be the pioneer on the plain
Seeking a home where he himself is free.

(America never was America to me.)

Let America be the dream the dreamers dreamed –
Let it be that great strong land of love
Where never kings connive nor tyrants scheme
That any man be crushed by one above.

(It never was America to me.)

O, let my land be a land where Liberty
Is crowned with no false patriotic wreath,
But opportunity is real, and life is free,
Equality is in the air we breathe.

(There's never been equality for me,
Nor freedom in this "homeland of the free.")

Say, who are you that mumbles in the dark?
And who are you that draws your veil across the stars?

I am the poor white, fooled and pushed apart,
I am the Negro bearing slavery's scars.
I am the red man driven from the land,
I am the immigrant clutching the hope I seek –
And finding only the same old stupid plan
Of dog eat dog, of mighty crush the weak.

I am the young man, full of strength and hope,
Tangled in that ancient endless chain

Of profit, power, gain, of grab the land!
Of grab the gold! Of grab the ways of satisfying need!
Of work the men! Of take the pay!
Of owning everything for one's own greed!

I am the farmer, bondsman to the soil.
I am the worker sold to the machine.
I am the Negro, servant to you all.
I am the people, humble, hungry, mean –
Hungry yet today despite the dream.
Beaten yet today – O, Pioneers!
I am the man who never got ahead,
The poorest worker bartered through the years.

Yet I'm the one who dreamt our basic dream
In the Old World while still a serf of kings,
Who dreamt a dream so strong, so brave, so true,
That even yet its mighty daring sings
In every brick and stone, in every furrow turned
That's made America the land it has become.
O, I'm the man who sailed those early seas
In search of what I meant to be my home –
For I'm the one who left dark Ireland's shore,
And Poland's plain, and England's grassy lea,
And torn from Black Africa's strand I came
To build a "homeland of the free."

The free?

Who said the free? Not me?
Surely not me? The millions on relief today?
The millions shot down when we strike?
The millions who have nothing for our pay?
For all the dreams we've dreamed
And all the songs we've sung
And all the hopes we've held
And all the flags we've hung,
The millions who have nothing for our pay –
Except the dream that's almost dead today.

O, let America be America again –
The land that never has been yet –
And yet must be – the land where every man is free.
The land that's mine – the poor man's, Indian's, Negro's, ME –
Who made America,
Whose sweat and blood, whose faith and pain,
Whose hand at the foundry, whose plow in the rain,
Must bring back our mighty dream again.

Sure, call me any ugly name you choose –
The steel of freedom does not stain.
From those who live like leeches on the people's lives,
We must take back our land again,
America!

O, yes,
I say it plain,
America never was America to me,
And yet I swear this oath –
America will be!

Out of the rack and ruin of our gangster death,
The rape and rot of graft, and stealth, and lies,
We, the people, must redeem
The land, the mines, the plants, the rivers.
The mountains and the endless plain –
All, all the stretch of these great green states –
And make America again!

Source: The Collected Poems of Langston Hughes, published by Alfred A. Knopf, Inc. Copyright 1994 the Estate of Langston Hughes. Used with permission. https://poets.org/poem/let-america-be-america-again

E. Wendell Berry, from *Jayber Crow* (2000)

It was a community always disappointed in itself, disappointing its members, always trying to contain its divisions and gentle its meanness, always failing and yet always preserving a sort of goodwill. I knew that, in the midst of all the ignorance and error, this was a membership; it was the membership of Port William; it was of no other place on earth. My vision gathered the community as it never has been and never will be gathered in this world of time, for the community must always be marred by members who are indifferent to it or against it, who are nonetheless its members and nonetheless essential to it. And yet I saw them all as somehow perfected, beyond time, by one another's love, compassion, and forgiveness, as it is said we may be perfected by grace. (p. 205)

F. Abraham Lincoln, Eulogy on Henry Clay, July 6, 1852

Mr. Clay's predominant sentiment, from first to last, was a deep devotion to the cause of human liberty – a strong sympathy with the oppressed everywhere, and an ardent wish for their elevation. With him, this was a primary and all controlling passion. Subsidiary to this was the conduct of his whole life. He loved his country partly because it was his own country, but mostly because it was a free country; and he burned with a zeal for its advancement, prosperity and glory, because he saw in such, the advancement, prosperity and glory, of human liberty, human right and human nature. He desired the prosperity of his countrymen partly because they were his countrymen, but chiefly to show to the world that freemen could be prosperous.

Source: http://www.abrahamlincolnonline.org/lincoln/speeches/clay.htm

A NOTE ON THE TYPE

A TEACHER'S GUIDE TO LAND OF HOPE has been set in Le Monde Livre. Designed in 1997 by Jean-François Porchez, Le Monde Livre adapts for book typography the award-winning 1994 type family Porchez created for France's Le Monde *newspaper, types now called Le Monde Journal. While the Journal types were specifically intended to be used at small sizes, the Livre family is suitable for larger, less dense settings planned for longer reading. The family was subsequently expanded with a more decorative variation (Le Monde Classic) and a sans-serif (Le Monde Sans). Graced with both style and readability, all of the Le Monde types display Porchez's considerable skill as a designer of typefaces and his deep knowledge of typographic history, particularly the rich heritage of French types from the sixteenth through nineteenth centuries. ❡ The display type is Hypatia Sans designed by Thomas W. Phinney for the Adobe Originals collection of types.*

DESIGN & COMPOSITION BY CARL W. SCARBROUGH